RE-EXAMINING PSYCHOLOGY

Typically, Western psychologists are reluctant to accept endemic racism within the discipline. Holdstock boldly challenges us to get our heads out of the sand and face the reality. He invites us, Western trained psychologists of all nations, to critically question our motives for neglecting folk or indigenous psychologies, especially sub-Saharan Africa. This book does more than that. It charges us with a duty to rectify this shortcoming in order to fulfil our mission to understand and serve humankind. In challenging us to acknowledge the right of people to differ individually as well as collectively, Holdstock renews the call for the development of indigenous psychologies or 'a global community psychology'. The author goes to great lengths to amass evidence from almost every branch of psychology and other disciplines to demonstrate the futility and danger of the wholesale acceptance and applications of Western methodologies, principles and practices in Africa.

Dr Kwame Owusu-Bempah, University of Leicester

Len Holdstock has studied and taught psychology in South Africa, the United States and The Netherlands. From 1989 until his retirement in 1999 he has held the chair in Clinical Psychology at the Vrije Universiteit in Amsterdam.

RE-EXAMINING PSYCHOLOGY

Critical perspectives and African insights

T. Len Holdstock

London and Philadelphia

First published 2000
by Routledge
11 New Fetter Lane, London EC4P 4EE

Simultaneously published in the USA and Canada
by Taylor & Francis Inc
325 Chestnut Street, Philadelphia, PA 19106

Routledge is an imprint of the Taylor & Francis Group

© 2000 T. Len Holdstock

Typeset in Goudy by Keystroke, Jacaranda Lodge, Wolverhampton
Printed and bound in Great Britain by Biddles Ltd, Guildford and King's Lynn

British Library Cataloguing in Publication Data
A catalogue record for this book is available from the British Library

Library of Congress Cataloging in Publication Data
Holdstock, T. Len.
Re-examining psychology : critical perspectives and African insights / T. Len Holdstock.
p.   cm.
Includes bibliographical references and index.
1. Psychology–Africa, Sub-Saharan. I. Title.
BF108.A3.H65 2000
155.8–dc21   99-044305

ISBN 0-415-18792-3

TO ALIDA, WHO, IN HER OWN INIMITABLE WAY,
HAS JOURNEYED WITH ME THROUGH
DEVELOPMENTAL TIME ZONES ACROSS
CULTURAL AND GEOGRAPHICAL LANDSCAPES

CONTENTS

CONTENTS

PREFACE

This book is an academic expression of the tendency we have to complete that which is incomplete. As pointed out by the early Gestalt psychologists we tend towards closure, to fill in the spaces where there are gaps. In the context of my involvement in psychology, the aspects that are in greatest need of attention relate to a critical evaluation of contemporary psychology and the neglect of the psychological dimensions indigenous to sub-Saharan Africa. Contemporary psychology assumes that it speaks for all people. Difficult as it may be for a discipline that has achieved a considerable measure of power and prestige to accept, this simply is not the case.

Moreover, the discipline can benefit greatly from indigenous perspectives other than its own. As has been indicated in sensory neurophysiology, contrast sharpens perceptual acuity. The same truth undoubtedly also holds with respect to juxtaposing African and Western approaches to human behaviour. The concern expressed by mainstream commentators about the orientation of the discipline and by others about the ideology of the culture to which psychology belongs, warrants serious reflection. It seems unlikely that psychological paradigms can be re-examined without the re-examination of broader features of contemporary Western culture. Such reflection is needed even more where psychology is applied in the context of the majority populations of the world.

It is imperative that we practise our discipline with full awareness of what is involved in order to fulfil psychology's potential to serve humankind. In its focus on the control and analysis of variables that can be concretised, the complexity of human existence is reduced to empirical expediency. Apart from the general disregard for the importance of the socio-economic-political context within which individual lives are contracted, the neglect of culture has been described as the Achilles heel of psychology. Knowledge of the cultural context is not only important in order to orchestrate the relevance of psychology for majority cultures, but also to facilitate the reorientation of contemporary psychology itself.

Several factors are in favour of such re-visioning. Not only are we entering a new millennium, which is of great symbolic significance for assessing our present position and where we want to go from here, but psychology is also showing an increasing maturity in its preparedness for self-examination. Since the discipline is rooted in Western culture, the self-examination necessarily reflects on aspects of this cultural base. In addition, the gaps in our knowledge of other cultural orientations, especially those belonging to sub-Saharan Africa, loom large. The psychological dimensions indigenous to this part of the world are different from but at the same time similar to approaches within the formal discipline. It shows the least kinship to the natural science approach to psychology and the greatest affinity with the human science approach. Somehow, this latter relationship is not surprising. Molecular genetics and palaeontology have established virtually without doubt that Africa is the cradle of humankind.

It is likely, therefore, that the common core between the folk psychology of Africa and the human science orientation of Western psychology may steer the discipline in a direction that will be of greater relevance and meaning to the human condition. Both approaches represent underdog positions with respect to the power wielded by the natural science orientation. A critical awareness of the ideological paradigms, upon which the power of the natural science approach to psychology rests, can be of great value in rectifying the present imbalance in the discipline and steer our young profession in exciting new directions. In this venture, the ancient wisdom buried in the psychological dimensions of sub-Saharan Africa can contribute useful guidelines.

The ideological perspective underlying this text can perhaps be summarised best by the words of Daniel Bell, the dean of American sociology, who said that in economics he was a socialist, in politics a liberal and in culture a conservative (Ignatius, 1999). In neurophysiological terms the text endeavours to fulfil a function similar to that of the corpus callosum in trying to integrate the different types of knowing and consciousness represented by the left and the right hemispheres of the brain. The difficulty in accomplishing this task can perhaps be ascribed to the lopsided, left hemisphere manner in which our educational system is structured.

The text reflects the influence of Carl Rogers on my career and I owe him a great deal. However, as I became immersed in the reality of psychology in Africa, I realised that the respect and empathy with which Rogers indwelled into the world of the individual client, needed to be extended towards the culture to which the individual belonged. My gratitude to the indigenous healers and ordinary African folk, whose teachings and way of being managed to remedy my half-brained education to some extent, is boundless. That they were not all that successful is certainly not their fault. They taught me so much about the psychology I knew nothing about after graduating from universities in South Africa and the United States. Being able to share their lives enriched my life immensely and in opening 'the doors of perception', they added immeasurably to my understanding of psychology. My thanks too, to Kwame Owusu-Bempah from the University of Leicester, for his valuable feedback and to Alida Holdstock for her comments on and proof-reading of this and all other material in the past.

ACKNOWLEDGEMENTS

I would like to thank the following for permission to reproduce quoted extracts: Excerpt from 'A Poet's Advice to Students', copyright © 1955, 1965 by the Trustees for the E. E. Cummings Trust. Copyright © 1958, 1965 by George J. Firmage, from A MISCELLANY REVISED by E. E. Cummings, edited by George J. Firmage. Reprinted by permission of Liveright Publishing Corporation.

I would also like to thank Dr Wally Serote for his kind permission to quote from a poem in *Yakhal'inkomo*.

Every effort has been made to trace copyright holders and obtain permssion to reproduce quoted material. Any omissions brought to our attention will be remedied in future editions.

Part I

A CRITICAL APPRAISAL OF CONTEMPORARY PSYCHOLOGY

1

AN INTROSPECTIVE
APPROACH TO PSYCHOLOGY

DOUBTS ABOUT PSYCHOLOGY'S ABILITY TO DELIVER THE GOODS

The basic motivation for this book derives from a lifetime of experiencing the paradoxes and the shortcomings of psychology as a human and a natural science. It also reflects an attempt to come to grips with my own role in perpetuating the psychological status quo. The text is not only to be read as an indication of some of the pitfalls and dead-ends into which contemporary psychology has led the society it serves, but it is also to be regarded as a passionate statement of my own search for meaning within the discipline.

Just as political systems need to be challenged, contemporary psychology needs to be challenged. Gergen and his colleagues (1996) advocated that instead of being the scrutinising subject, psychology be made the object of our investigations. In fact, nothing more than a revolution in our psychological awareness will suffice as we pass into a new millennium (Comas-Días, Lykes, and Alarcón, 1998; Mack, 1992). Fortunately, the discipline seems to have achieved the necessary maturity to allow for such a critical examination of its theories and practices. This newly found confidence heralds in the dawn of an exciting new adventure for those who have the courage to embark on it. Undoubtedly, it also poses an extraordinary challenge for the prevailing status quo of contemporary psychology. For instance, Bulhan (1985), the Somali psychologist, has stated that

> in spite of numerous studies, Euro-American psychology is far from unravelling the mysteries of the human psyche . . . Even staunch supporters of this psychological tradition concede that the discipline has fallen short of its stated aims and promises. They admit that the amount of time, money, and energy devoted to a plethora of studies are hardly commensurate with the limited and uneven advances of psychology as a discipline. (p. 64)

We've had a hundred years of psychotherapy and the world's getting worse, was the title of a book in which Hillman and Ventura (1993), expressed their concern

3

about the present state of affairs in clinical psychology. Others have been equally or even more critical (e.g., Cushman, 1990, 1991; Hall, 1997; Hall *et al.*, 1997; Marsella, 1998; Prilleltensky, 1989; Sampson, 1981, 1985, 1988, 1989a, 1989b, 1993, 1994). In short, these psychologists point out that psychology curtails and undermines its potential helpfulness when it wraps itself in the ideology of the status quo. By 'adhering to the practices of an objective technology and the ideology of self-contained individualism and the bounded self . . . it perpetuates the social problems that caused the patient's wounds in the first place' (Cushman, 1990, p. 607). According to Masson (1989) every therapy,

> (with the exception of radical and feminist therapies, which are beset with other problems), displays a lack of interest in social injustice . . . Each shows an implicit acceptance of the political status quo. In brief, almost every therapy shows a certain lack of interest in the world. (p. 240)

> psychotherapy cannot be reformed in its parts, because the activity, by its nature is harmful. Recognizing the lies, the flaws, the harm, the potential for harm, the imbalance in power, the arrogance, the condescension, the pretensions may be the first step in the eventual abolition of psychotherapy that I believe is, one day in the future, inevitable and desirable. (p. 254)

Not everyone is as despondent about the service rendered by psychology, though. During his term of office as President of the American Psychological Association (APA), Seligman (1998a) stated that psychology has made huge strides in the understanding of and therapy for mental illness. Claiming that 'millions of people have had their troubles relieved by psychologists' (p. 2), he, nevertheless, reminded his fellow professionals that 'Psychology is not just the study of weakness and damage, it is also the study of strength and virtue. Treatment is not just fixing what is broken, it is nurturing what is best within ourselves' (p. 2).

Seligman (1998b) reiterated the theme of psychology's preoccupation with the negative mental effects resulting from life's vicissitudes in his presidential column in the *APA Monitor*, a few months later. On this occasion he wrote that modern psychology, in its relentless focus on the negative, has become preoccupied with healing. 'It has, by and large, understood functioning within a disease model, and its main mode of intervention has been the repair of damage . . . while plumbing the depths of what is worst in life, psychology lost its connection to the positive side of life – the knowledge about what makes human life most worth living, most fulfilling, most enjoyable and most productive' (p. 2). Seligman's vision is that psychology will come to 'see beyond the remedial and escape from the muck-raking that has claimed it, that social science will become a positive force for understanding and promoting the highest qualities of civic and personal life' (p. 2). His aspirations for the actualisation of the full human potential echo those

4

of his immediate predecessors in the field of humanistic psychology. Throughout their careers, people like Carl Rogers, Rollo May, Abraham Maslow, and others, endeavoured to provide psychology with an alternative to the medical and positivistic models which were even more dominant a generation ago.

This book strives for the recognition that truth is a variable with multiple dimensions. It recognises that what is considered to be essential at any one point in time, or in any cultural context, can change over time or vary from one situation to another. During the past century the interest in psychology has shifted dramatically from one topic to another. In the clinical field, the shift has been from independent schools of psychotherapy, such as psycho-analysis, behaviour modification, existential and person-centred therapy, cognitive behaviour therapy, and a host of new and alternative therapies, to an eclectic approach, both in theory and practice (e.g., Barlow, 1996). In social psychology, 'classifications of social needs displaced classifications of instincts, which in turn were displaced by classifications of homeostatic states, which are now giving way to classification of cognitive modes of processing information' (Kipnis, 1997, p. 207).

Even the so-called cognitive revolution of the past three decades has not stood up to the test of time (e.g., Holdstock, 1994a; Sampson, 1994; Shweder, 1994). The cognitive revolution served a useful purpose in bringing the concept of mind back into psychology. Yet, its continued adherence to a model of the person as a self-contained and independent unit of the social system, perpetuates the idea that psyche and consciousness are to be located within the envelope of the individual. However, the individual is inextricably intertwined and constantly interacting with the socio-cultural environment. The one constitutes the other. Psyche is not independent of culture, they make each other up. According to Cushman (1991), culture comes to the infant, 'literally and figuratively, with mother's milk' (p. 215).

Although it may sound strange to those steeped in the assumptions under-lying mainstream psychology, the fundamentals of mental life are not 'by nature fixed, universal, abstract, and interior' (Shweder, 1994, p. 97). Shweder talks of 'subject-dependent objects (intentional worlds) and object-dependent subjects (intentional persons) interpenetrating each other's identities or setting the conditions for each other's existence and development, while jointly undergoing change through social interaction' (p. 100). In view of such an interactive and holistic perspective, it is clear that what is considered to constitute the essential nature of psyche and consciousness, will not only change over time, but will also depend on where, in which socio-economic-political, and geographic region of the world, one finds oneself. Having lived and worked on the African, the American, and the European continents, each for extended periods of time, has impressed upon me how contextually bound our values, beliefs, and behaviour patterns are.

Based on the totality of these experiences, I cannot help but be amazed by the effect of the psychological imprinting that we are continually subjected to and by our unawareness of the effects of such conditioning. It required the continued juxta-positioning of the different cultural contexts to help me appreciate the relative merits and shortcomings of each. However, the greatest effect has undoubtedly been the development of an appreciation for the unheralded psychological dimensions and practices of the African subcontinent, combined with a critical appraisal of contemporary psychology. The two aspects go hand in hand. The purpose of this text is, therefore, to provide an assessment of contemporary psychology in order to pave the way for a greater appreciation of what the informal psychological paradigms and practices of sub-Saharan Africa have to offer.

PSYCHOLOGY LACKS AWARENESS OF ITS UNDERLYING IDEOLOGY

An unawareness of the extent to which psychology is imbedded in the ideology of the Western world, is one of the many paradoxes that bedevil the discipline. Markus and Kitayama (1994) attribute the poor generalisability of basic social psychological findings across cultural groups to the fact that, 'When studies of social behavior are conducted within a single culture, the ways in which psychological functioning and theories about psychological functioning are culture specific and are conditioned by particular models of the self and the world is typically not obvious' (p. 118). Landrine (1992) echoes the words of Markus and Kitayama. According to her,

> Of the many definitions and meanings cultures take for granted, those regarding the self are the most basic, the 'deepest,' the furthest from awareness, and are thus rarely ever made explicit. Simultaneously, while assumptions about what a self is are furthest from our conscious aware-ness, they also are the most powerful and significant assumptions behind and beneath our behavior. (p. 402)

Even the influence of culturally constituted understandings on psychiatric concepts in Western societies, often goes unrecognised (White and Marsella, 1989).

The lack of appreciation of the importance of culture is complemented by unawareness, generally, of the ideology underlying psychology. Joan Robinson, a well-known Cambridge economist, stated that ideology is like your own breath, you cannot smell it. 'One of the distinguishing features of any culture is what people take for granted about the nature, the causes and the expectable results of human activity' (Bruner in Gilbert, van Vlaanderen, and Nkwinti, 1995, p. 229). According to Triandis (1996), 'all humans are ethnocentric . . . and suffer from *naive realism* that limits the full appreciation of "the subjective status of their own construals, and, as such, they do not make sufficient allowances for the uncertainties of construal when called on to make behavioral attributions and predictions about others'" (p. 407). In similar vein, Rogoff and Chavajay (1995) stated that 'people are notably unaware of the institutions in which they themselves act' (p. 872). Mack (1992) speaks of 'the forces that limit our thinking and inhibit our initiatives or creativity, consciously and unconsciously, within our specialities and organizations, the fears and rewards that keep us swimming in the mainstream' (p. 410), as manifestations of 'institutional resistance'. University departments and professional organisations are good examples of such resistance to examining and questioning established policies and values,

> For they are among our strongest centers of power and tradition, and do not usually reward with promotion and funding intellectual endeavours that challenge the basic assumptions of their disciplines. Yet the pressures of the global crises, and their intrusion into each of our lives, may force even the most conservative academic institutions to re-examine their academic priorities and investigative methods.
>
> (Mack, 1992, p. 410)

Writing from the perspective of the world religions, Smart (1983, 1989), similarly, points out that people are trapped within their own culture and belief system and are either reluctant, or do not have the opportunity, to explore the belief structures of other people. More often, worldviews different from those with which one is familiar are not considered worthy of exploration since they are regarded as primitive and uncivilised. Due to increasing globalisation, and in order to reassess one's own view of reality, however, it is imperative to take up room in another's point of view, even if it is, as the poet says, to know one's own position for the first time. For this purpose, Smart recommends a worldview analysis that focuses on description and not evaluation.

Apart from the lack of insight into the extent to which psychology is a product of the culture which gave it birth and provided the framework for its development, the lack of awareness in the discipline is especially noticeable with respect to the values it claims to be free of, but nevertheless, subscribes to.

> All psychological research and theorizing of course entail some basic assumptions about the world and human nature. Basic assumptions are implicit and often elusive. In their global assertions, basic assumptions are categorical and hardly permit exceptions. Basic assumptions are neither empirically derived nor open to scientific inquiry, but they nevertheless pervade our perceptions of the world and how we theorize about it. It so happens that the basic assumption of the dominant psychology is rarely examined or admitted. This avoidance in part derives from fears of undermining psychology's tenuous claims of its status as a science. To delve into the basic assumptions of a discipline

that overidentifies with the natural sciences is to open Pandora's Box of untestable cultural ethos, values, and beliefs.

(Bulhan, 1985, p. 65)

Upon the launching of the decade of behaviour by the APA, Lee (1998), therefore, called on psychologists to study their own behaviour, 'including ideologies and presumptions that shape our professional activity' (p. 3). Since, 'many behavior-based problems, at their core, may ultimately be value-driven' (p. 3), he suggested that psychologists consider their values system very carefully.

Also apparent in the behaviour of the psychological community is an unawareness of the political and the power implications of the ideological base underlying the discipline. 'Psychology's uncritical embrace of a value-assumption extolling control and prediction has fostered a willing complicity in social control and oppression. Moreover, this value-assumption keeps Eurocentric psychologists from understanding the psychology of the non-white, non-middle-class majority in the world' (Bulhan, 1985, p. 66). In many respects the discipline resembles a person who seems to function quite adequately without having any real insight into him or herself. In logical positivistic terms, variables that are of crucial importance in the psychological equation are left out of the formula for calculating what constitutes adequate behaviour.

Fox (1986), in keeping with Spence (1985), recommends that psychologists need to 'consider more closely the intertwined complexity of their politics, their theories and methods, and their professional and personal lives' (p. 232). Politics as used in this context convey much more than party politics. It refers, in the first instance, to all situations where some element of power determines the nature of the relationship between people. Thus, the structures associated with economic supremacy, technological skill, scientific knowledge, and religious belief, need to be considered in terms of their political implications. The same applies to the institutionalisation of the discipline and sub-disciplines of psychology. In fact, all psychology is a political act (Kelly and Llewelyn, in Bodibe, 1994).

According to Foucault's analysis of the political organisation of the human sciences, power and knowledge directly imply one another, there is not any power relation without the correlative constitution of some field of knowledge, nor any knowledge that does not presuppose and constitute at the same time power relations. Foucault rejects the Marxist idea of suppression by the ruling class. Instead, he suggests that suppression occurs through social structures, which come about rather arbitrarily between people. Thus, in terms of discourse analysis, 'some groups can be organized into politics while others are organized out' (van der Heijden, 1990, p. 39). It is imperative, therefore, that psychologists become aware of the metatheoretical assumptions underlying their theory and practice in order to be able to assess the relevance for and effect upon society (Retief, 1989). Craig (1990), similarly, urges the periodic examination of the relationship between the activities of psychologists and the analyses of philosophers of social science in order to inform our practices.

According to Farber (1990) 'the praxis of Institutional Mental Health is based on a model that is not oriented toward generating change, but toward maintaining social control' (p. 285). 'The main social function of public psychiatry is to provide a mechanism for covert, extra-legal social control without violating the principle of Rule of Law. This is accomplished by redefining deviant and undesirable conduct as mental illness' (Leifer, 1990, p. 249). In expressing his concern about the 'language of deficit' which has spiralled across the century of psychology, Gergen (1990) expresses the fear that 'all remaining patterns of action stand vulnerable to deficit translation' (p. 353). By 'constructing a reality of mental deficit the professions contribute to hierarchies of privilege, reduce natural interdependencies within the culture, and lend themselves to self-enfeeblement' (p. 353). The language of deficit and the social control which it exercises, is especially relevant with respect to the traditional tolerance in Africa of the 'mentally ill' and the involvement of the community in their treatment (Harding, 1975).

PSYCHOLOGY IS AN INDIGENOUS EURO-AMERICAN DISCIPLINE

According to the archetypal psychologist, James Hillman (1975), psychology

> emerged from the Protestantism of northern and western Europe and its extension westward into North America. To read psychology, to find psychologists, to do psychological research has meant coming to this piece of geographical soil as if the Japanese, the Russians, the Arabs, the Africans, and the Latins had no psychology. Moreover the soil has mainly been Germanic. Psychology has been mainly a creation of the German language out of the German soul. (p. 219)

According to Bulhan (1985),

> psychology as an organized discipline – psychology in the form today taught and practised – is undoubtedly Euro-American in origin and substance. In concepts as in assumptions, in instruments as in outlook, this psychology is Eurocentric through and through. It is nonetheless this psychology that is now fast proliferating in education, health, industry, and social policy. Even the non-European, non-Western majority of the world is gradually adopting this Eurocentric psychology. Yet in a world of cultural and racial heterogeneity, this Eurocentric psychology and its proliferation pose one fundamental concern: the fact of imperialism in psychology. (p. 64)

Representing the East, Sinha (in Gilbert, 1989), 'has argued that psychology is a product of the Western World and has an orientation which Jahoda (1973) calls

9

"Euramerican"' (p. 92). Others have narrowed the influence on psychology down even more. According to Hall and Barongan (1997), 'psychology has primarily been a reflection of the European American male domination and entitlement' (p. 12). While neither Sinha nor Jahoda deny 'that there may be universals in human behaviour and "Euramerican" psychology may have applicability to the Third World, they both argue that the type of issue that psychology examines may not be relevant to the Third World' (Gilbert, 1989, p. 92). In fact, a growing body of literature has been critical of the inadequacy of psychology to address issues which fall outside its 'Westrocentric' framework (e.g., Marsella, 1998; Sinha, 1994a,b). 'Mapping reality through Western constructs has offered a pseudounderstanding of the people of alien cultures and has had debilitating effects in terms of miscontruing the special realities of other people and exoticising or disregarding psychologies that are non-Western' (Gergen, Gulerce, Lock, and Misra, 1996, p. 497).

The two English psychologists, Howitt and Owusu-Bempah (1994), have expressed grave concern about the 'continuing European hegemony in psychology' (p. 117) and about 'the "colonisation" of black psychologists by Eurocentric thought' (p. 117). They argue that the lack of attention to alternatives to mainstream knowledge not only leaves the discipline impoverished, but 'The dominance of Eurocentric psychology helps legitimise world-wide inequality' (p. 117).

The ethnocentric blindspot of contemporary psychology manifests all too clearly in the ignorance regarding the psychological wisdom embodied in the ancient religious practices, the philosophical treatises (oral and written), the epics, the folklores, and the ritual ceremonies, derived from African, American Indian, Aztec, Buddhist, Confucian, Incan, Laotzian, and Mayan traditions. Wilpert (1995), the German organisational psychologist, speaks of 'The notorious neglect by traditional Western Psychology of the century old accumulation of psychological insight and wisdom by indigenous psychological traditions in non-Western societies' (p. 1). In place of the ancient psychological insights, psychology has come to rely on rational consciousness, what Hillman (1983) describes as 'ego-knowing'. Consequently, the contemporary discipline has come to suffer from the disease of literalism to such an extent that it has become demonic in the war it wages against images and the imaginative.

According to Hillman (1983), psychology's emphasis on ego knowing dates back to the time before Freud. As the present cognitive revolution indicates, the departure point of the discipline remains steadfastly anchored in the belief in the power of ego-consciousness. One of Freud's great contributions has been that he extended knowing oneself to mean knowing one's past personal life. After Jung, to know oneself has come to mean 'an archetypal knowing, a daimonic knowing. It means familiarity with a host of psychic figures from geographical, historical, and cultural contexts, a hundred channels beyond my personal identity. After Jung, I can not pretend to know myself unless I know the archetypes' (Hillman, 1983, pp. 62–63). It is a knowing with which Africa has great familiarity. The archetypes present themselves as images in consciousness and in the imagination. Fantasy is the clearest expression of the specific activity of the imagination. This lack of recognition in psychology of the importance of daimonic (as distinguished from demonic) knowing can not only bedevil our understanding of the human psyche in general, but also our understanding of the African psyche specifically.

Westrocentric psychology has even severed connectedness with its own past. Scientific psychology is considered to have started in 1879 with the opening of the first Laboratory of Psychology in Leipzig by Wundt. Yet, as the letter of invitation to the IV European Congress of Psychology in Athens in 1995 pointed out, Greece has had a tradition of searching for an understanding of the nature of the human psyche that dates back more than 2,000 years. Besides, contemporary psychology does not recognise that Wundt realised the limitations of the experimental method, which he is credited to have initiated. While he considered the experimental method appropriate for studying basic sensory processes, he regarded it as inappropriate for investigating psychological phenomena that are shaped by language, custom, and myth. These areas Wundt considered being the concern of *Volkerpsychologie* (folk, cultural or indigenous psychology). In fact, Wundt considered psychology to be part of the cultural and not the natural science tradition and he devoted the latter part of his life to investigate the socio-cultural influences on behaviour (Kim, 1990).

On the occasion of receiving the 1979 Distinguished Contribution to the Teaching of Psychology Award at the meeting of the APA in New York, Candland (1980) asked whether it was wise to believe that there was no Arab or Indian psychology merely because there were no such courses in the college catalogue? He went on to query how the future would judge 'our tacit definition of psychology as the study of the English-speaking, white male, preferably during infancy or as a college sophomore?' (p. 196), and cautions that 'We must take more seriously the contributions to psychology of those who live and think beyond our own experience' (p.196).

Guthrie (1970) highlighted psychology's ethnocentrism by pointing out that even the most widely used laboratory animal, the rat, was white. With respect to South African psychology I have, on several occasions, pointed out its lily whiteness (Holdstock, 1981b, 1982; 1985, 1987a,b). According to transpersonal psychologist, Tart (1975a), Westerners have 'little appreciation for the fact that there are many other psychologies. Zen Buddhism has a psychology, so do Yoga, Christianity, and Sufism' (p. 5). Cultural psychologist, Richard Shweder (1994), argues that 'consciousness is a complex contingent mechanism whose dynamic functioning is mediated by the system of meaning within which it is embedded' (p. 20). Thus, 'there are different psychological generalizations or "nomological networks" – a Hindu psychology, a Protestant psychology – appropriate for the different semiotic regions of the world' (p. 20). Within the South African context, Manganyi (1991) asks: 'What is South African psychology? What are its roots and ideological consequences as reflected in past and current theory and practice?' (p. 2).

These indigenous psychologies . . . are both similar and different from contemporary psychology. Contemporary psychology is best conceived as a Western indigenous psychology that is a special case of the universal psychology we, as contemporary psychologists would like to develop. When the indigenous psychologies are incorporated into a universal framework, we will have a universal psychology.

(Triandis, 1996, p. 407)

Wilpert (1995) and Cushman (1991) also refer to contemporary psychology as an indigenous manifestation of Western culture. 'There is no one cultural paradigm that is universally accurate about human nature. In fact, the single-minded pursuit of the universal laws of a transhistorical human nature is itself an artefact of a particular indigenous psychology' (Cushman, 1991, p. 207). In keeping with other social constructionists, Cushman, therefore, suggests that psychologists 'should embrace the inevitable and study local, historical, and particular phenomena and the indigenous psychologies of the multitude of cultures on earth' (p. 208).

In the mental health field, various workers have pointed out the necessity for Western trained professionals to take up position in the perspectives of another culture if therapy with individuals from that culture has any hope of being effective (e.g., Marsella and White, 1989). 'The priority that clinical training (historically) has given to individual psychotherapy reflects the primacy that Western culture has offered the individual; in this sense, clinical training like clinical concepts, is a product of Western-European culture, and so it needs to be culturally diversified' (Landrine, 1992, p. 409).

Even within the Western context, social psychologists have pointed out that their discipline, due to its origin in American cultural assumptions, cannot simply be applied to a European context (Parker, 1989). Since language structures specific ways of understanding the world, disciplines cannot be objective beyond the cultures in which they reside because the cultural crises are structurally incorporated into the disciplines themselves. Traditionally, social psychology, in keeping with its parent discipline, fails to explore appropriately the cultural and the political context of its research. Thus, it is dismissive of its own role in the reproduction of ideology and power. Far from offering solutions to the present crisis, contemporary social psychology is part of the very problem it studies. What is true of social psychology also holds for the parent discipline.

In an incisive review of the epistemology and aetiology of Western thought within the context of mainstream academic anthropology, Sahlins (1996) provides an analysis that can be of great value in enhancing the awareness within psychology of the ideological assumptions underlying the discipline. In his analysis Sahlins highlights the extent to which mainstream social science discourse reflects Judeo-Christian cosmology.

The deep influence of Christianity not only in creating social institutions which have dominated historical life in the West but, even

12

more significant, in creating cosmological conceptions including images of the self, a model of the relationship between self and nature, and a theory of the inevitability of miscommunication in human interactions and of the nonperfectability of human institutions has profoundly influenced the Western psyche.

(Clammer in Sahlins, 1996, p. 418)

Themes such as 'The pleasure-pain principle of human action, the idea of an irresistible and egotistical human nature underlying social behavior, the sense of a society as an order of power or coercion, and a confidence in the greater providential value of human suffering' (p. 395), continue to 'bedevil our understandings of other peoples' (p. 395).

Writing from an Africentric perspective, White (1984) points out how, 'In the Protestant ethic the feeling processes were considered the bad, destructive element in the human condition, an element that needed to be controlled by the mind. Feelings were sinful, evil, destructive, animalistic, and a reflection of the evil that must be resolved before humans could achieve salvation and develop an advanced civilization' (p. 11). As the invited commentators on Sahlins article indicate, Christianity, Judaism, and Islam, share a cosmology to a great extent, but Buddhism and Shinto present radically different worldviews. Attention needs to be directed to the worldview, which the people of sub-Saharan Africa have in common and which sets them apart from other geographical locations. Differences need to be respected and celebrated without infringing on the rights of others to do the same. That this has not been possible in the past does not mean that it cannot be done. I cling to the hope that the human race can learn from its past mistakes. Perhaps our greatest error has been in not acknowledging the right of people to differ individually and collectively. Our failure to facilitate differences, individually and collectively, can probably be attributed to the belief that such an approach will enhance rather than diminish competition for available resources. Since the intolerance and eradication of differences by force have been the cause of the greatest misery in the world, it seems imperative to introduce an alternative set of assumptions upon which we can base our behaviour. For too long have we assumed that the exercise of power over and assimilation of people are the only means by which diversity at national and international level can be handled.

In the political past of South Africa group differences have, quite para-doxically, been acknowledged. Unfortunately, the purpose of this recognition was not to provide a firm and equal footing for the different groups to interact on behalf of the greater good of all. Rather, the purpose was to divide and control in order to exploit on behalf of those with political and military might. In reaction to the imposed racial discrimination of the past, the danger exists that the developing democracy in the present South Africa will not have the inclination or the know-how to accommodate the aspirations of those who wish a group identity in order to benefit the community as a whole.

The political dilemma of coping in a democratic way with the need that some people have for a group identity is also apparent in psychology. For instance, even liberal and politically aware South African psychologists negate the possibility that respect for cultural differences can present a viable point of departure for the development of a psychology that can accommodate the aspirations of all the people in the country. The same is undoubtedly true of many psychologists elsewhere. Under the guise of searching for the universals in behaviour, the psychological community continues to further the ends of the ethnocentric perspective within which the discipline developed.

As Chapter 3 indicates, psychology has become increasingly fragmented and it will require all our skills to accommodate each of the sub-disciplines for the greater good of the discipline and the profession of psychology. In addition to accommodating the needs and the wishes of the various sub-disciplines within psychology, there is the additional problem of those perspectives that fall outside the scope of the empirical and the political status quo.

AWAKENING TO PSYCHOLOGY'S ETHNOCENTRISM

Fortunately, prompted by the increasing globalisation, the winds of change are blowing in psychology. On the one hand, there has been a call from within American psychology for a broader international base for the discipline. This call has been especially noticeable in the *American Psychologist*, the mouthpiece of the APA (Candland, 1980; Gergen *et al.*, 1996; Hall, 1997; Hall *et al.*, 1997; see Holdstock, 1990a, for additional references; Marsella, 1998; Mays, Rubin, Sabourin, and Walker, 1996; Moghaddam, 1987; Resolutions Approved, 1987; Segall, Lonner, and Berry, 1998).

The other development, which has stimulated development towards a broader cultural base for the discipline, resides in the fact that psychologists from the majority world have, over the past few decades, themselves begun to function as bridges in transmitting the wealth of knowledge of their ancient psychological traditions to the West (Adair, 1996; Atal, 1981; Azuma, 1984a,b; Bauserman, 1997; Hayashi, 1992; Jing, 1994; Kagitçibasi, 1996b; Kim, 1990; Leung, 1995; Misumi and Peterson, 1990; Sinha, 1990, 1994a,b, 1997; Wang, 1993; Yu, 1994). In the overall picture of the psychological discipline and profession, the output of these two developmental streams has been relatively slight. Yet, it has been sufficient to raise questions regarding the monocultural and ethnocentric nature of the paradigms underlying contemporary psychology. It has also highlighted the gap in our knowledge with respect to the psychological insights of the majority world.

A universal psychology, if it comes about, will be characterised by unravelling what the various indigenous psychologies have in common and what sets them apart. Thus, besides investigating the nature of the general laws that underlie the behaviour of people, it will also concentrate on the idiosyncratic laws that constitute the psychological uniqueness of each culture. The emphasis will be on 'Different but equal' (Shweder and Bourne, 1991, p.114).

'Although psychology as a Western science and profession is responding admirably to the challenges of our changing times, this has not resolved the growing concerns of many Western, non-Western, and ethnic-minority psychologists' (Marsella, 1998, p. 1285). Marsella therefore, strives to develop 'a new psychology that is responsive to our emerging global life contexts, conditions, and consequences – a global-community psychology' (p. 1284). 'Global-community psychology acknowledges the ethnocentricity of all psychologies and resists the hegemonic imposition or privileged positioning of any national or cultural psychology' (p. 1284). Care has to be taken to avoid the mistakes of the past that assumed that monocultural Western values are universally representative.

Bruner calls on psychology to understand the ordinary ways of being, to use 'folk psychology' as a guide to represent and comprehend the social world. These everyday ways of being are embodied in the local knowledge people use in their daily lives. He 'argues that every culture has a body of ideas and knowledge on which people draw in assigning meaning to the world' (in Gilbert *et al.*, 1995, p. 229). Fritz Heider (1958), whom I have had the privilege to have as a teacher, stated 'that scientific psychology has a good deal to learn from common-sense psychology. In interpersonal relations, perhaps more than in any other field of knowledge, fruitful concepts and hunches for hypotheses lie dormant and unformulated in what we know intuitively' (p. 5–6). Heider also talked of common sense or folk psychology as naïve psychology. Recently, Fletcher (1995) has spoken of the scientific credibility of folk psychology.

To a significant extent the move towards the recognition of indigenous psychologies has focused on, and attempted the integration of, the philosophies and mental health practices common to the East and the West (Boorstein, 1997; Brazier, 1996; Brown, Engler, and Wilber, 1986; de Wit, 1991, 1995; Epstein, 1995; Farthing, 1992; Goleman, 1972; Kwee, 1990; Kwee and Holdstock, 1996; Naranjo and Ornstein, 1971; Ornstein, 1972; Rao, 1997; Walsh, 1977, 1978, 1988; Walsh and Vaughan, 1993; West, 1987; Wilber, 1986, 1995, 1997). The initiatives to integrate the wisdom of the East with that of the West, is a task which has just begun and a great deal more needs doing in order to improve the existing bridges and to build new ones (Abi-Hashem, 1997). Apart from the impact of Eastern philosophies and healing practices, one of the most widely researched variables in psychology has been a comparison of the collectivism of Eastern societies with the individualism of Western societies (McCrae and Costa, 1997). Considerable attention has especially been devoted to the way the self is affected by the nature of society.

AFRICAN FOLK PSYCHOLOGY DESERVES MORE ATTENTION

Despite the calls for the development of psychology as an international discipline, the amount of attention devoted to African psychology has been minimal though. Even in publications highlighting indigenous psychological perspectives, Africa remains underrepresented (e.g., Heelas and Lock, 1981; Kim and Berry, 1993; Roland, 1992; Rosenberger, 1992). In formal psychological terms, Africa, north and south of the Sahara, continues to be the dark and forgotten continent.

Indeed, 'Psychology as an organised discipline, as taught and practised, ascribes little value to the experiences of black people' (Howitt and Owusu-Bempah, 1994, p. 127). Even more unfortunate is the fact that 'The history of universalistic or Eurocentric psychology is not a happy one for black people ... it traditionally acts more as an instrument of domination than a liberating discipline' (pp. 126–127). To the extent that the dialectic between Eurocentric psychology and black people has taken place, black people have been 'forced to see themselves in white people without the latter's reciprocating' (p. 127). Thus, when Africa is not neglected it is demeaned.

Yet, Africa is the mother continent, figuratively as well as literally. The oldest hominid remains have been found in East and South Africa. Rather synchronistically, at the very moment of writing this paragraph (8 November 1998), the BBC evening news bulletin reported on the discovery of 3.5 million year old hominid remains at the Sterkfontein caves near Johannesburg. In addition, the developing science of molecular genetics has revealed, virtually beyond a doubt, that humankind emerged from Africa (Cavalli-Sforza, 1998; Chu et al., 1998). Surely, we owe it to ourselves to regard the cradle of humankind with more respect. As a few psychologists and anthropologists have been brave enough to suggest, it is possible that Africa may contain the key to unlock some of the mysteries regarding the mental health problems with which the people of today are being faced (Comas-Díaz et al., 1998; Katz, 1983/84).

According to Mphahlele (1962) whites refused to be taught anything by the African who was continually forced to take, but prevented from giving to white culture. Mphahlele questioned whether whites would ever go farther than just an appreciation of, or an academic interest in, black cultures. Will they 'ever make an attempt to adopt certain Negro ways of life?' (p. 93). 'For a long time the white man in Africa has taken up various positions in his attitude towards the black man, all aimed at propping up "white supremacy"' (p. 63). At a conference on *Black Culture and Business*, which a colleague and I had organised in 1987, Mphahlele reiterated this theme by expressing his doubts about the teachability of Europe with respect to things African. He attributed the failure of Europeans to truly see the African people they were dealing with, as well as their inability to recognise the quality of being in Africa, to being blinded by the moral rectitude and the aggressive Western culture to which they belonged. Several African

American, British (e.g., Howitt and Owusu-Bempah, 1994), and South African authors (e.g., Seedat, 1997, 1998), have pointed out that 'the contributions of the descendants of Africa to many aspects of the social, economic, artistic, and spiritual evolution of the West has been sorely neglected in the textbooks and instructional manuals of every western nation on earth' (Penn and Kiesel, 1994, p. 401).

The late Sir Laurens van der Post (1975) wrote that 'We deny Africa its own uniqueness' (p. 20). The denial can be attributed to centuries of reliance on reason alone by people in the West that prevented them from appreciating any other manifestation of the self. In their blind trust in this single dimension of being, Westerners became divorced from their intuitive and affective selves. van der Post has been greatly influenced by Jung, as is evident in the following extract from his writing:

> A long period of pure reason which had begun with the Reformation and been stimulated by the French Revolution was deep at work in his spirit, setting him at variance with his intuitions and instinct. The materialism of the industrial revolution already dominated his values and motives. His mastery of the physical means of life and his increasing annihilation of distance together with the conquest of what he understood to be time, had already brought man far down the broad way to exceeding his humanity and setting himself up as a god and controller of destiny. Walking into Africa in that mood he was, by and large, quite incapable of understanding Africa, let alone of appreciating the raw material of mind and spirit with which this granary of fate, this ancient treasure house of lost original way of life, was so richly filled . . . European man arrived in Africa already despising Africa and African beings. He arrived there, not for Africa's sake, but for what he could get out of Africa on his own behalf. He arrived as a superior person ready to impose himself and his way of living on Africa, not doubting for a second that his was the better way and that it was all for Africa's good.
>
> (van der Post, 1975, pp. 41–42)

White (1984), an African American psychologist, echoes the sentiments of van der Post:

> The concept of manifest destiny has been very prominent in the thinking, behavior, and cultural attitudes of Euro-Americans. Anglo-Saxons, northern Europeans, the Nordic stocks, and their American descendants have marched across the globe operating under the belief that they were ordered by God Himself to take over the universe; first the earth, then the moon, the stars, and even life itself through the manipulation of genetic codes. Their interactions with other peoples have been governed by power, dominance, and control. An attitude of

cultural superiority has persisted to the present day. Differences between people, whether by race, geography, life style, or even sex were not seen as opportunities for mutual enrichment through creative synthesis, but as opportunity to take over, oppress, and impose their leadership on other people.

(White, 1984, p. 13)

Not only is Africa denied its own uniqueness, but as Kote Omotoso (1994), a Nigerian author now residing in South Africa, points out, the influence of African on European culture has also been neglected. 'European intellectuals need to accept without any reservations the validity of the African extension of the European experience' (p. 9). As an example he mentions how Louis Armstrong extended the possibilities of the trumpet. 'The imperial power was prepared to dump its cultural goods on the African market, but it was not interested in purposefully importing African culture back into Europe' (Mazrui, 1990, p. 6). With respect to psychology the ultimate question is whether the imperialistic attitude can be turned around.

Despite the moral rectitude and the aggressive attempt of Western civilisation to hijack African history and culture, it is unlikely that the uniqueness of Africa's cultural manifestations will ever be obliterated. Neither is the increasing globalisation likely to alter the essential nature of African culture. Adaptation to the changing economic realities will undoubtedly occur, but the underlying philosophy of life will persist. To the extent that it is possible, Africa will avail itself of the technological advances occurring elsewhere, and this will certainly bring about dramatic changes in the way of life on the continent. No doubt, some aspects of globalisation can pose problems of an inordinate difficulty. The nations of Africa will have to learn to cope with these. I am thinking, especially, of the weapons trade with the United States, Britain, and other European countries. Hopefully, Africa's blossoming love affair with Western weaponry, as a means of resolving conflicts, will not prevail to the extent that it has done in the West.

Recent developments give reason for hope. In Rwanda plans are afoot to judge the 125,000 Hutus, still in jail and charged in the massacre of and other crimes against the Tutsis, by a modified version of the traditional way in which village elders mediated the disputes of rural life (Fisher, 1999). The most dramatic example is embodied in the behaviour of President Nelson Mandela of South Africa. After 27 years as a political prisoner, he had every reason to be intensely bitter and full of hatred. Yet, he was able to build the new South Africa on the cornerstone of forgiveness and reconciliation. In so doing, he exemplified the essence of African philosophy, *ubuntu*, humanness in short, in the most concrete way possible. Contrary to the eye-for-an-eye approach to justice that prevails in the Judeo-Christian-Islamic world, forgiveness constitutes the basis of the Truth and Reconciliation Commission (TRC). The TRC was instituted by the Interim Constitution of the new South Africa to account for the atrocities committed by political rivals during the apartheid era (Saley, 1996). The principles upon which the TRC are based undoubtedly date back to the earliest times in Africa, as has been documented by the first missionaries (Setiloane, 1989).

Perhaps I am incredibly naïve, but I have experienced the basic humanism and spiritual dimension inherent in the African way of life too consistently in too many contexts during the height of the apartheid era, and have attended too many ceremonies and rituals, even in the heart of urban areas like Soweto, to believe differently. Mphahlele (1962, 1984, 1987) is of the same opinion. In 1962 he wrote that even in Africans, 'who have lost all tribal affiliations in terms of chieftancy, and their old moral codes . . . there remains something solidly African in them that has a distinct reference to the past. It has to do with the manner of self-expression through music, dance, song and patterns of behaviour' (p. 90). Omotoso (1994) stresses the importance of preserving indigenous African cultural aspects while keeping pace with the increasing globalisation occurring on the continent.

At the conference on Black Culture and Business, mentioned earlier, Mphahlele (1987) expressed his belief in the enduring quality of African culture even more strongly. He pointed out that although African culture in South Africa was a 'fugitive culture', which had been subjected to constant onslaught, it has not been destroyed. People have been forced from their ancestral ground, disinherited, dispossessed, and severely traumatised, and yet, even in the turbulent urban areas at the height of the apartheid era, African culture survived at the deeper spiritual levels. Even in the, at times, macabre burial ceremonies taking place in Soweto, Mphahlele (1984) detects a deeper meaning. In *Afrika My Music*, he wrote:

> So much violence is with us, so much death. To ritualise it, however grotesquely, may be a way of conquering the fear of death, of coaxing it, containing it. I begin to wonder if Soweto, as a paradigm of black South African life, is not striving in its own burlesque fashion to define something of communal experience that the collective memory still cherishes; the disinherited personality trying to salvage something from the collective memory and to give it definition so that people may survive the cruelty of the time. A survival culture, a fugitive culture.
>
> (1984, p. 256)

Harland (1996), a former diplomat from New Zealand, likewise, stated that Asian cultures are likely to discover the uniqueness they have in common with each other as American pressures on them grow. According to Harland, Asian countries are resisting Western individualism and asserting the validity of their own values. Ever since the Portuguese sailed past the Cape of Storms into Asian waters 500 years ago, Westerners have been accustomed to telling Asia and Africa what to do. That period has now come to an end. African and Asian countries will develop in their own ways, at their own speeds and Westerners need to accept their right to do so.

The same is true as far as the Arabic world is concerned. In *The Wretched of the Earth*, Fanon (1976) remarked how national feeling has been preserved in the Arab world, even under colonial domination. Could the alarming rise in Islamic fundamentalism, at present, not perhaps be described as an overbalancing of the attempt to restore the respect for the principles and the practices which the adherents of the faith consider to be warranted? Whatever the case may be, it is evident that 'Globalization from above and indigenization from below have resulted in a clash of cultures unparalleled in history' (Marsella, 1998, p. 1284). The greatest challenge of the new millennium will undoubtedly be to provide alternative ways of conflict resolution other than through violent and military confrontation.

In expressing their concern about the 'perilous problems of cultural dichotomies,' Hermans and Kempen (1998) suggested that psychology focused its attention on the contact zones of cultures. Necessary as such a focus certainly is, it is not without its own problems. Interaction between cultures at peripheral level invariably involves a decentralised minority interacting with a majority culture ensconced in an established socio-economic-political power base that encompasses mainstream psychology. The call for a focus on the contact zones of cultures, furthermore, applies primarily to those instances where the techno-logical advances that make globalisation possible, are experienced. As minority representatives have frequently pointed out, power is an important variable in the human equation that is all too often neglected in psychology. Concentration of psychology at the peripheral level of cultural interaction is likely to perpetuate the exclusivity that has inhibited the international development of psychology. Despite globalisation the majority of the world's population still does not encounter the technological advances that make globalisation possible at first hand (Holdstock, 1999).

IS THERE A PSYCHOLOGICAL IDENTITY COMMON TO SUB-SAHARAN AFRICA?

Since the focus of this book will be on the geographical region south of the Sahara, whenever Africa is mentioned in the text, it is this region that is intended. The Arab states to the north are organically linked more with societies which are Mediterranean in their culture than African (Fanon, 1976). Talking about Africa in a collective sense does not imply that the people of sub-Saharan Africa constitute a homogeneous whole. Indeed, the multiplicity of cultures is vast, as is the case in Asia, Europe, or the Western world, as representative entities. 'African is the Yorubu craftsman and the Tutsi lord, the Nairobi mechanic and the Ibadan professor, the Fulani nomad and the Congolese villager, the hunter of the great forest and the warrior of the high plateau, the woman trader of Dakar and the factory girl of Bonake, the Benin sculptor and the Luburabashi painter' (Maquet, 1972, p. 3).

However, despite existing diversity, sub-Saharan Africa does manifest systems of belief and behaviour which sets it apart from other parts of the world. The common elements are to be discerned in religious outlook, kinship patterns, language families, oral traditions, belief systems, worldviews, sculpture, art, music, dance, writing, drama, and healing practices. For instance, de Maret (1994) and Janzen (1994) have explored common religious elements for the whole of Central and southern Africa, while de Heusch (1994) pointed out the similarity between the codes embedded in Central and West African myths. Others have elucidated the corporeality of African culture, its anthropocentrism, where wealth was and still is counted in terms of people (van Beek and Blakely, 1994).

Gyekye (1987) and Maquet (1972) speak of a 'cultural unity'. According to Maquet, 'the African's existential experience is everywhere the same' (p. 21). Doob (1972) is another who acknowledges the similarities to be found amidst the great diversity in Africa. Wilson (1969) concluded that there 'has long been a very complex interaction of cultural traditions and of people of Africa' (p. 130). According to Asante (1992), there is 'one African Cultural System manifested in diversities ... All African people participate in the African Cultural System although it is modified according to specific histories and nations' (p. 2). Within the South African context, Manganyi (1980) writes that blacks are a homogeneous group with respect to their cultural heritage and experiences in a race supremacist society. Yet, within this 'socio-cultural stratification' (p. 53), heterogeneity, which has not yet been exploited to the full, exits. Despite the diversities, the countries of sub-Saharan Africa, nevertheless, display considerable commonalties in the evolution of psychology as a professional discipline (Nsamenang, 1993).

J.L. Stonier (1996) distinguishes between 'deterministic' and 'essentialistic' factors, which could have contributed to the presence of Africanness. Basically, the search for the factors responsible for the uniqueness of Africa boils down to nature and nurture issues. We know enough to realise that it is not a question of one or the other. Rutter (1997) has recently called 'for an explicit research focus on the forms of interplay between genes and environment' (p. 390). The harshness of the physical aspects of the African continent deserves special consideration though, as a force shaping the lives and the belief systems of the people on the continent.

This text has no intention of unravelling the nature of sub-Saharan Africa's distinctiveness, and the differences that exist within the region, in terms of the empirical tradition of mainstream psychology. Exploring the uniqueness of, and the regional differences in the African psyche by means of mainstream methodologies, to the extent that that is possible, will undoubtedly have to be the task for future generations of scholars. At present, not much more can be done than to highlight the need to investigate ways in which psychologists in Africa can 'incorporate the best of Western psychology without betraying their cultural values and identities' (Holtzman, 1997, p. 381).

Methodologies, principles, and practices, belonging to mainstream psychology have already been implemented in sub-Sahara Africa. However, since these applications have consistently had as their point of departure the paradigms of a psychology that originated on foreign soil, an unqualified acceptance of these applications has to be considered very carefully. 'Bulhan uses the term auto-colonialism to refer to the ways in which black professionals actively participate in the oppression and subjugation of black people' (Howitt and Owusu-Bempah, 1994, p. 139).

As Kim (1995) and others have pointed out, major differences exist between Euro-American cultural values and those of the societies of the majority world. Yet, within mainstream psychology the universality of its paradigms has been assumed rather blindly. In a very real sense, the assumption of universality can be compared to the practices of the missionaries of old who prophesied the Christian concept of God as the only true god. The missionaries simply gave overt expression to the implicit penetration of Judeo-Christian cosmology that has occurred in the social sciences. The possibility that the people of Africa may have their own concept of the divine was never considered. African beliefs in the divinity were denigrated as superstition, whereas Christian beliefs were regarded as scientific (Biko, 1975).

Even worse, as Mudimbe (1988) has pointed out, the missionary discourse was not only 'a language of derision, insofar as it fundamentally ridicules the pagan's Gods' (p. 51), but also 'a language of refutation or systematic reduction: all pagan religions constitute the black side of a white transcendental Christianity, and this metaphoric opposition of colors means the opposition of evil and good, Satan and God' (p. 51). In terms of Western criteria, the African concept of God can, at best, be regarded as the equivalent of a 'wise man', as I once heard the politically liberal white chairperson of a theological conference in South Africa state. Likewise, mainstream psychologists have neglected the possibility that Africa may have psychological dimensions, which are singularly unique and valid, requiring relevant methodologies to unravel. I have the uncomfortable conviction that the ethnocentrism that earmarked the missionary movement in the early and middle phases of this century is paralleled by contemporary psychology.

As has happened in the debate on what constitutes an African philosophy (Hountondji, 1983), many Africans and others who have been educated according to Western criteria will undoubtedly dispute the existence and the validity of indigenous psychological perspectives in Africa – the existence of an African ethnopsychology. However, the same criticism that has been directed at the philosophers, can be levelled at the disputing psychologists. Mudimbe (1988), for one, pointed out that philosophers like Hountondji, constitute a self-proclaimed elite who 'find in all discussions prior to their own, nothing but mythologies' (p.160). Besides, within contemporary psychology, appreciation has grown for a more inclusive holism, and if the ethnopsychology of Africa has an identifying characteristic, it is its holistic orientation. In addition, as already pointed out, in its quest for a broader international base, contemporary psychology is increasingly recognising the validity of indigenous psychologies. The prefix, ethno, no longer contains the negative connotations with which it has been associated in the discussions with respect to African philosophy.

Mudimbe (1988) points out that 'one might conceive the intellectual signs of otherness not as a project for the foundation of a new science, but rather as a mode of re-examining the journeys of human knowledge in a world of competing propositions and choices' (p. 79). He quotes Horton in stating that 'The kind of comparative conceptual analysis that the "philosopher of" traditional thought could offer would do much to help the contemporary intellectual in his struggle to think through the relationship between his two supercompartments (that is, tradition and modernity)' (p. 79). Horton pointed out that traditional thought was a many-stranded thing, whose various strands must be disentangled and their appropriate relations to modernity considered one by one.

2

ETHNOCENTRISM AND RACISM
IN PSYCHOLOGY

Ever since the Portuguese explorer Bartholomew Diaz reached the southern tip of Africa in 1488 in search of a trade route from Europe to Asia, the identity of the continent has been defined in European terms. Both the outer limits of the continent and the inner boundaries of many countries have been drawn by Europeans with a vested interest. Until Algeria's independence in 1962, the outer limits of the continent were considered to be the southern portion of France. Madagascar, 800 km across the Mozambique channel from the continent, and Mauritius, 1600 km away, were similarly considered to be politically part of the continent, whereas Greater Yemen, which is a short distance across the Red Sea, was not. With the opening of the Suez Canal in 1869, which was built to make it easier for Europe to trade with the rest of the world, north-east Africa and Arabia became part of two continents despite the similarity in geology, language, and culture (Mazrui, 1986). Partition of Africa by the imperial colonial powers led to the establishment of 48 new states, 'most of them with clearly defined boundaries in place of the existing innumerable lineage and clan groups, city-states, kingdoms, and empires without fixed boundaries' (Boahen, 1987, p. 95).

Furthermore, European cartographers grossly distorted the physical size of the African continent and decreed that the geographical location of Africa be below that of Europe on the global map. Satellite pictures, however, show that Africa is much bigger in relation to northern continents than has previously been depicted. And why should Africa be depicted as south and below Europe, rather than north and above? Interesting too, is the fact that western Europe was used as the geographic reference point for dividing East from West, and Greenwich 'mean time', the standard for the whole world! On the map of the world Europe was placed in the centre. Since 'people's perceptions of themselves can be deeply influenced by which continent or region they associate themselves with' (Mazrui, 1986, p. 37), Africa's physical dimensions need to be restored, if for no other reason than to be factually correct.

The political domination of the continent by the colonial powers has relatively recently come to an end, and we have to guard against substituting the political for the psychological. The dismantling of the 'legally' imposed systems

24

of inequality does not guarantee that the structures of consciousness, which gave rise to and nurtured systems of colonialism and discrimination, have also changed (Schutte, 1995). This is the conclusion of others as well (Howitt and Owusu-Bempah, 1994). With respect to South Africa, Stevens and Lockhat (1997) state that 'whilst apartheid-capitalism no longer exists, "racial" capitalism is still firmly entrenched' (p. 253).

Besides the economic, military, and political domination of colonial imperialism, Bulhan (1980) contended that the psychological domination of Africa has been perpetuated through Western education, which created a class of neo-intelligentsia. It is not surprising, therefore, that Agyakwa (1976) expressed disappointment that Ghana had no educational system that derived from and was based on Ghanaian cultural values. I have, on several occasions, expressed the same sentiments with respect to South African education and psychology (Holdstock, 1981b, 1982, 1985, 1987a,b). Indeed, cultural colonialism represents a most invidious form of colonialism. Even the recommendations of the National Commission on Higher Education, a body appointed by the South African parliament of reconciliation, have been challenged for their failure to provide a coherent philosophy of education based on the need for Africanisation (Pearce, 1996).

By using a systemic approach to investigate unconscious elements in the old and the new South Africa, Visser (1996) stated 'that the changes which took place in South Africa on the symptom level, have not been dealt with on the unconscious level' (p. 32). By not admitting moral guilt before the TRC for the apartheid misdeeds of the National Party, F.W. de Klerk, the leader of the party and former South African president, showed that he was still committed to the old South Africa. Described as a party of clever minds, dirty hands, and unrepentant hearts, the Nationalists were considered to have disqualified themselves from effective participation in the process of reconciliation and nation building.

COLONIALISM IS DEAD, LONG LIVE ETHNOCENTRISM

A classical double-bind situation exists in the United States and elsewhere in the Western world with respect to espousing the value of cultural pluralism, but condoning institutional structures that impose assimilation (Myers, 1993). Hall et al. (1997), pointed out that 'the natural and inalienable rights of individuals valued by European and European American societies generally appear to have actually been intended for European Americans only' (p. 654). I have experienced a similar double bind while teaching at the University of the Witwatersrand in South Africa. The university prided itself in its liberal tradition in being open to students of all races, yet it failed to make the minimum of concessions to the reality of being situated in the heart of the sub-continent.

It remained solidly entrenched in traditional Western paradigms with respect to the content and the methodology of all its courses. Students had the right to attend the university, but what was not made explicit was the fact that the terms for doing so were prescribed by the educational doctrines of a system based on a colonial past (Holdstock, 1987a,b).

It is especially in the social sciences and in psychology specifically, that the ethnocentrism of the liberal institution was most apparent. Many examples can indeed be cited. However, I will restrict myself to the introduction of African indigenous healers in the School of Psychology at the university. For this purpose I had redecorated a large room that had previously been part of my brain research laboratory to serve as a consulting room for the indigenous healers. My purpose for establishing an indigenous healing consulting room was basically twofold. First of all, I wanted it to serve as a means of introducing psychology students to indigenous healers and aspects of their practice. Secondly, I wanted to provide a general community service, especially for white people who did not have ready access to the indigenous healers. Apart from a small number of students, who complained that they had to pay for the consultations they were expected to have with the indigenous practitioners as part of the course requirement, the venture proved to be a success. Yet, during a period when I was on sabbatical leave in the United States, the consulting room was changed into offices. The reason given was that office space was of a higher priority than a 'witchdoctor' room.

The ethnocentrism of Western education is universal. In the School of Music at the university, where my son was a student, no attention whatsoever was paid to any aspect of African music. Although The Netherlands is becoming increasingly multi-cultural, and Amsterdam, where my present university is situated, has as many young children from parents born outside as inside Holland, the psychological curriculum continues to follow mainstream outlines. According to Biko (in Stubbs, 1979) 'it's all right with the liberals as long as you remain caught by *their* trap' (p. 25). Mazrui (1990), too, has pointed out that the provision of teachers and educational resources by foreign powers to the African continent constituted a disguised form of cultural aid. He regards 'African universities as subsidiaries of multinational cultural corporations of the Western world' (p. 200).

Aimé Césaire (1969), the famous French poet from Martinique, stated that the West has used such sophisticated weapons as efficient techniques of economic exploitation, pseudo-psychology, pseudo-anthropology, uprootment of large populations, and cultural indoctrination to distort the perceptions of native people they have colonised. To this list can be added religious, educational, and psychological indoctrination. Indo-China and Algeria have emerged from French domination; Indonesia from Dutch; Burma, India, Kenya, Zambia, and Zimbabwe from British; Angola and Mozambique from Portuguese; and Zaire from Belgian domination. In Australia, and South and North America, the indigenous peoples never had a chance against the European invasion. With 'the penetration of Western culture deeper and deeper in much of the Third

World ... Cultural authenticity among non-Westerners has never been in greater danger' (Mazrui, 1990, p. 40),

Recent events in Europe confirm the prejudice still existing in the part of the world which gave birth to psychology. Neo-Nazism is emerging again. A bloody and prolonged ethnic war raged in Bosnia. Kosovo has been cleansed of Albanians. In Germany and The Netherlands, the houses of immigrants from the Middle East are set on fire during the night and the families burnt to death (Albert, 1996). Nail bombs are aimed at minorities in London. The widespread incidence of white prejudice is demonstrated by the apology of the governor-general of Australia, Sir William Deane, in May 1997 to the Australian Aborigines for the injustice done to them in the past. The Aborigines only obtained Australian citizenship 30 years ago. Until that time they were dealt with under legislation pertaining to flora and fauna! Between 1880 and 1960 approximately 100,000 Aboriginal children were forcibly removed from their parents in terms of the assimilation policy of the Australian government.

Despite acknowledgement of such institutionalised injustices, the Aborigines nevertheless experience their living conditions as deteriorating significantly. The likelihood that things will change under the present conservative government is also very slight. The Australian Prime Minister, John Howard, has submitted a ten-point plan to water down the Aboriginal land ownership claims and has reduced government spending on Aboriginal affairs. While the Prime Minister added his personal apologies for the injustices of the past to those of the governor-general, he failed to do so in his official capacity. His statement, that the present generation of Australians cannot be held accountable for past events over which they had no control, is reminiscent of de Klerk's failure to accept responsibility for the crimes committed during the apartheid era ('Australia', 1997; 'Excuses', 1997).

Volumes can indeed be written about the variety of ways in which the prejudice of Western ethnocentrism continues to rear its ugly head. In his book, *Mixture of Massacre: The Genocide of a People*, Abdias do Nascimento documents the false sense of integration effected by the Portuguese in Brazil whereby African people were denied their Africanness (in Asante, 1992). Indeed, 'White cultural hegemony threatens the survival not only of Africans but of the human race as a whole' (Phillips, Penn, and Gaines, 1993, p. 352). Before discussing the documentation of racism in psychology and in the culture underlying the discipline by the English psychologists, Howitt and Owusu-Bempah (1994), a few more instances of the subtle ways in which the ethnocentrism, some would say racism, of the cultural bedrock of psychology manifests itself, need to be pointed out.

Although the power and vitality of African art is increasingly being acknowledged, the art of this region has in the past been, and is at present still being described as 'primitive' (Rubin, 1984a). In discussing the colonising of marginality, Mudimbe (1988) presents a summary of the many ethnocentric descriptions of African art as barbaric and primitive. In acknowledging the strong influence of African art on the great Western artists of the modern era, Rubin admits to the paradox of using the term primitive in describing African art by placing it within inverted commas. Almost a century ago, Kandinsky (1914/1977), at times at least, wrote 'Primitives' (p. 1) with a capital P in his acknowledgement that Western 'art is looking for help from the primitives' (p. 13).

However, no amount of inverted commas or capitalisation can eliminate the negative connotation associated with the word primitive. Rubin could, instead, have used African art as his point of departure and entitled the extraordinary exhibition of African and Western art in the Museum of Modern Art in New York in 1984, and the resulting publications, appropriately. In order to denote the direct influence of African art on that of the Western masters, or to put it more bluntly, the copying of African art, a more appropriate title than *'Primitivism' in 20th Century Art* (Rubin, 1984b) would, for instance, have been, *Plagiarism in Modern Art*. Alternately, in recognition of the commonality between African and Western art pieces that could not be attributed to any copying of African works, a more appropriate title could have been *Archetypes in Modern Art*. Or a combination of *Plagiarism and Archetypes in Modern Art* would perhaps have been the best description. How common the depiction of African art as primitive is, became apparent on a recent visit to the Musée d'Art Moderne de la Ville de Paris. Likewise, an exhibition of African art in the Royal Academy in London was reviewed a few years ago in *de Volkskrant*, a respectable Dutch newspaper, with the caption that there were a thousand African languages, but not a single word for art (Schipper, 1998).

Altizer (1962) even speaks of the 'primitive myths' of 'primitive cultures' in contrast to the 'refined mythologies of the higher religions' and civilisations (p. 96)! 'Higher civilisations' are equated with rational thinking and the valuing of empirical experiences! Even the term, 'developing societies', which is in vogue in psychology at present, smacks of ethnocentrism. The same can be said about the use of terms such as 'pre-modern' (Nsamenang and Dawes, 1998) or 'modernising' (Dawes, 1996). While it may be appropriate in an industrial and technological sense, it is inappropriate in many other respects. Myers (1993) discusses three definitions of development and mentions that more exhaustive accounts exist elsewhere. Why should development only be defined in economic terms and degree of industrialisation? What if communalism or humanism, rather than technological know-how and material well-being were to be the criteria for assessing development? Euro-American societies would in all likelihood then be depicted as developing, or even as underdeveloped. In his discussion of the world of tomorrow and the person of the future, Carl Rogers (1980) expressed a 'postmodern' view that resembles the 'developing' rather than the 'developed' societies.

Similarly, why should Caucasian features be the standard for describing that of Africans, as was done by the early anthropologists? Using African criteria, whites would be described as having undeveloped lips, pointed noses, limp hair, and pale skins. Is it surprising that Asante (1992) describes anthropology, which was originally responsible for the creation of such racial classifications as *Negroid*, *Mongoloid*, and *Caucasoid*, as the most political and ethnocentric of disciplines? 'In its inception and later in its conspiracies with sociology, it attempted to define the rest of the world in relationship to the European world' (p. 95).

On my first ride in a tram in Amsterdam I was struck by the sign, 'Zwart rijden is verboden' (Riding black on the tram is illegal, i.e., without paying). Associating an illegal activity with the colour black, while in keeping with the generally negative connotations associated with black, in a country renowned for its liberalism, is just another indication of how thoroughly prejudice is ingrained in the fabric of society. The Dutch are also coming in for severe criticism by immigrants from Surinam, a previous colony of the Netherlands, for perpetuating the personage of *Zwarte Piet* (Black Peter) during the Christmas season. *Zwarte Piet* is the servant of St Nicholas and goes about distributing candy to the children. In order to circumvent the critique and maintain the tradition of *Zwarte Piet*, modern versions attribute his blackness to the fact that he has to descend down the chimney.

> The word *Black* in the Euro-American world view connotes a meaning of sinister, evil, foreboding, dirty, unclean, death, and impending doom, while terms such as blackball, blacklist, black market, black sheep, and blackmail indicate behavior or situations that are unacceptable. The devil is black, the angels are white, whiteness as the psychological opposite of blackness is the essence of purity, cleanliness, goodliness and beauty.
>
> (White, 1984, pp. 15–16)

According to van der Post, white people started with an unfair advantage when they went to Africa in the image of whiteness, for Howitt and Owusu-Bempah (1994) found 55 negative connotations of the word black compared to only 21 for the word white. Conversely, they found 9 and 19 positive connotations of black and white respectively.

Psychology's prevailing ethnocentrism is, furthermore, all too transparent with respect to the opinions regarding the healers and the healing systems of the majority world cultures. Invariably, the healers are scathingly described as 'witchdoctors' and the healing systems as witchcraft (e.g., McManus, 1993). According to Torrey (1972) use of the term witchdoctor represents 'a vestige of imperialism and ethnocentrism – the reflection seen by those who would look out upon the world through their own umbilical cord' (pp. 69–70).

Several South African psychologists refer to an interest by white psychologists in the healing systems indigenous to the African population as an esoteric exercise. Due to the fact that for many years I have been closely associated with the African healers, I have been singled out for criticism. Behind my back I was called the 'witchdoctor professor' and it was said that I used to be such 'a good researcher'. My call, and that of a few other psychologists, for considering the African context within which mainstream psychology is practised in South Africa has been described as conservative and ideologically naïve (e.g., Dawes, 1985). In fact, we have been accused of tacitly supporting the ideological basis of separate development, thereby aligning us with the apartheid system of the Nationalist government of the time. Calling for the Africanisation of South African psychology was considered to render the discipline needlessly impotent (Nell, 1990; Seedat, Butchart, and Nell, 1991; Seedat and Nell, 1990).

In terms of his universalist orientation, Nell (1990) is especially critical of an Africentric approach. He considers an Africentric orientation to constitute 'a fundamental misunderstanding of psychology and of human nature itself' (p. 132), as a quest for 'mystical and unanswerable questions' (p. 137), as 'malignant forms of relevance and psychological fragmentation' (p. 134), and as a 'self-indulgent search for the exotic' (p. 138), which he regards as a remnant of the quest in nineteenth-century anthropology for the exotic. The 'anthropologizing of psychology' (p. 138), Nell argues, can be 'actively harmful' (p. 131) in disempowering psychology in fulfilment of its obligations to society. He is convinced that psychology's 'relevance can be quantified without reference to cultural variables' (p. 131). In fact, some of his South African colleagues have described culture as a euphemism (Dawes and Davids, 1983). The interpretation of African cosmology as holistic has, similarly, been labelled as idealistic (e.g., Swartz, 1986, 1987, 1991; Swartz and Foster, 1984).

Perhaps the most dramatic demonstration, as far as I am concerned, of how endemic Western ethnocentrism is, relates to the use of the term primitive by two generations of psychologists. In 1982 I had organised a visit to South Africa by Carl Rogers with whom I had studied in Wisconsin in the early 1960s and worked with in California during the middle 1970s. In arranging the visit I wanted to give Rogers something back for what he has meant to me during my formative years as a psychologist. I thought no gift could be greater than introducing him to the richness of the African way of life and being that so drastically altered the course of my career in neurophysiological and clinical psychology.

After a meeting in Soweto with a most gifted individual, Rogers summarised the visit by saying that the person exemplified the 'primitive wise man'. However, the 'primitive wise man' in question speaks at least six languages, sculpts, paints, authored several books in English, writes beautiful poetry but is too humble to think that it is worth publishing, is a custodian of the traditions of his ethnic group, and an orator in the best African tradition! Admittedly, he only has grade/elementary school education and his extensive use of metaphor and emphasis on the importance of imagery in Africa must have sounded very strange to Rogers, gifted as his ability to enter the world of another person undoubtedly has been. Sometimes, the cultural divide is simply too big, even for someone with the empathic ability of a Carl Rogers, to transcend. Differences do then take on evaluative connotations, for built into the Western psyche is the unerring trust in setting itself up as the standard according to which all things are to be judged (Albert, 1996).

Another aspect of the visit with the African sage impressed itself indelibly upon my mind. The discussion between the two persons who loomed large in my life started with the sage asking Rogers what he would like to discuss. Rogers replied by asking, 'What can I do for the country?' The reply was instantaneous: 'Nothing Dr Rogers, nothing'. In retrospect, I marvelled at the interpersonal dynamics that occurred during this brief opening interchange. Rogers was clearly taken aback by being invited to state what he wanted to know from the sage, instead of being addressed with a question acknowledging his stature as one of the world's leading psychologists. In his opening question about what he could do for the country, Rogers unwittingly portrayed the omnipotence so typical of Westerners with respect to African issues. The subtlety, with which the sage, who was familiar with the work of Rogers, established the power base of the meeting, also struck me as noteworthy.

An even more disturbing example relates to the reference made by a 'politically aware' South African psychologist to the call for the consideration of an indigenous African framework to healing, as a tendency 'to glorify the primitive' (Freeman, 1991, p. 145). The implicit racism implied in such a statement by a young, community psychologist who, at the dawn of the new South Africa, is challenging 'everyone in mental health ... to assist in achieving a society more conducive to mental health and promoting equity in mental health care' (p. 141), presents an alarming demonstration of how deeply rooted Western ethnocentrism really is.

Racism in psychology

In an editorial to the 22nd volume of *Psychology in Society*, Hayes (1997) stated that despite the good intentions of creating democratic, non-racial, and non-sexist institutions, the divisiveness of the apartheid past still lurked in South African psychology and in the country. In his account of the perpetuation of racism by South African psychologists, Foster (1993a,b) cites several American and British authors who are of the opinion that the apparent decline of racism in the Western world is only one of appearances.

Howitt and Owusu-Bempah have documented that this is indeed the case. In several publications they highlight the elusive quality of racism in psychology (Howitt and Owusu-Bempah, 1990, 1994; Owusu-Bempah and Howitt, 1994, 1995). Starting with an account of overt expressions of racism in psychology's theories and practices, their scholarly book continues with coverage of the various ways in which racism manifests itself covertly in psychology (Howitt and Owusu-Bempah, 1994). 'There are remarkable continuities in the racism of psychology which span much of the discipline's history and practice' (p. 1). In association with many African scholars and African American psychologists whose work will be discussed in later chapters, the English psychologists point out that psychology's racism merely reflects the cultural context in which the discipline is embedded. In fact, 'Psychology breathes in the air of racism' (p. 3). 'The history of modern Western psychology . . . shows its emergence in the context of European conquest, exploitation and domination' (p. 2). 'Modern psychology's origins in a climate of slavery, of domination and exploitation of black people, notably Africans, ensured that the burgeoning profession was imbued with racism' (p. 16).

> Psychology, like medicine, is a social institution mirroring societal values, including racism. Besides, the professionalisation of psychology was largely a phenomenon of the late nineteenth and early twentieth centuries, a period of unmitigated racism, empire building and white dominance. Institutions in this racist epoch inevitably served white society's interests – they were created to do no other, and the blueprint remains.
>
> (Howitt and Owusu-Bempah, 1994, p. 143)

Apart from biological racism, which expresses itself in terms of the notion of a defective genetic structure of blacks, white racism also manifests in the degradation of and assault on black culture (Owusu-Bempah and Howitt, 1995). Even those who are not biologically racist target black culture. So, for instance, has black family culture been demeaned as the focus of allegations of deficit and pathology. The black family has indeed become the primary focus of social pathology. The 'new racism' manifests in many disguised forms. In the 'symbolic racism' of the 1970s, basic American values, such as individualism, were used to express sentiments antagonistic to black people. More recently, the concepts of metaracism, aversive racism, and regressive racism have been employed to describe the covert racism of many so-called liberals. Metaracists are those who are not overly prejudiced but nevertheless acquiesce in the larger culture that continues the work of racism. Aversive racism is evident in the negative affect towards blacks that motivates avoidance rather than intentionally destructive behaviours on the part of racists, while regressive racism manifests under conditions of emotional arousal.

The writings and the work of historical figures, such as David Hume (1711–1776), Thomas Malthus (1766–1834), Herbert Spencer (1820–1903), and Sir Francis Galton (1822–1911), have set the tone for psychological racism (Howitt and Owusu-Bempah, 1994). Social Darwinism is held to be equally accountable. The denial of African culture can even be traced to Aristotle, who conspired to obscure the influence of ancient Egyptian scholarship and philosophy on his thinking. Closer to the present time, Howitt and Owusu-Bempah highlight the racism evident in the work of such luminaries in psychology as Thorndike, William McDougall, Terman, Konrad Lorenz, Karl Pearson, and the now infamous fraudster, Cyril Burt, as well as the recently deceased, Hans Eysenck. Of the present generation of psychologists, Arthur Jensen has heralded the inferior genes theory of blacks most prominently. Unfortunately, Jensen is not alone in this thinking.

Howitt and Owusu-Bempah (1994) present some of the twisted arguments that have been used in psychology by biologically based racist theorists. For instance, the reaction time of Muhammad Ali, who could float like a butterfly and sting like a bee during his prime, has been described as not more than average. Reaction time is considered to provide an index of the brain's ability to process information. The speed with which electrical impulses are transmitted along nerve fibres and across synapses relates to the 'neural efficiency model of intelligence' (Rijsdijk, 1997). Yet, in an earlier study cited by Howitt and Owusu-Bempah, the reaction time of whites, which was found to be slower than that of African American and American Indians, was considered to be a reflection of higher levels of mental functioning. In this instance the delayed reaction time of whites was attributed to their reflective ability, which supposedly indicated a higher form of intelligence.

According to Howitt and Owusu-Bempah (1994), even social identity theory, the feminist movement, and the discourse analysis of racism can be seen to covertly propagate psychological racism. They indicated that although Tajfel, who was closely associated with social identity theory, never intended to justify racism, his work, nevertheless, fuelled the ideology that regarded intergroup hostility as inevitable. This came about because his cognitive approach 'led him to see the process of categorisation as a basic characteristic of human thought' (p. 48). According to Tajfel's theory of 'minimal group participation', people tend to categorise themselves as belonging to a group on the basis of the most trivial things they have in common, and this tendency, inevitably, enhances intergroup hostility.

As far as the feminist movement is concerned, Howitt and Owusu-Bempah (1994) state that the movement neglects the needs and the cause of black women. In fact, the movement has 'overridden the perspective of black women' (p. 56). The problem with the discourse analysis of racism is that it inevitably assumes 'its detectability through language, its reproduction intergenerationally through language and, most significantly, that discourse analysts have a theory of racism. All of these assumptions are questionable and fundamentally misleading premises which reproduce the trap of marginalising racism to the statements of readily recognisable racists' (p. 57).

Howitt and Owusu-Bempah (1994) also expose the racism in psychology's textbooks, organisations, and institutions. They state that 'the political agenda of psychology textbooks has been largely ignored' (p. 69) and that 'much of the racism of psychological textbooks is a broad assault on the nature of black cultures' (p. 71). In recent times, American textbooks have become 'politically correct' in their portrayal of multi-cultural American society. However, they nevertheless remain 'parochially racist when dealing with cultures outside America' (p. 75). A white norm is consistently set as the standard by which others are judged. The two English psychologists trace the racism in psychology's clinical practices back to Freud and Jung, and point out its unabated continuation in the diagnostic and treatment practices of the present generation. In support of their conclusion, Louw (1997) has, for instance, pointed out the vital role that psychological testing has played in the professionalisation of psychology in South Africa. In becoming 'recognised as a source of authority on social controversies' (p. 235), psychological testing provided Christian Nationalism with the basis upon which it legitimised its educational and other policies, 'where race played a significant mediating role' (p. 235).

Earlier, Howitt and Owusu-Bempah (1990) demonstrated how the 'new racism' continued to be manifested through research writings in *The British Journal of Social and Clinical Psychology*. The apolitical orientation of articles in the *South African Journal of Psychology* has also been interpreted as the racist orientation that characterises the discipline in the country (Duncan *et al.*, 1997; Durrheim and Mokeki, 1997; Seedat, 1997, 1998). However, in contrast to the English authors who based their accusation of racism on articles dealing with racism specifically, the South African psychologists did so irrespective of whether the research was of a social or a neuropsychological nature. Labelling the mere omission of a political perspective in the published papers as racist does, however, raise the point to what extent room is left for individual interests to be expressed?

Howitt and Owusu-Bempah (1990) attributed the existence of racism in British psychology to the professional socialisation of psychologists in a psychological rather than a socio-psychological domain. Related to the psychological socialisation of psychologists is the fact that the 'ideological origins of much of social psychology' (p. 399) are founded in work on individual differences. Other reasons which they mention relate to the emphasis on measurement techniques in psychology rather than on the detail of what is being measured, the lack of a non-Western perspective, and 'Psychologist's inability to challenge their own assumptions (and societal assumptions) about Third World people' (p. 399). Lastly, 'The lack of opportunities for black psychologists in the academic world' (p. 399) is held accountable.

Howitt and Owusu-Bempah (1990, 1994) repeatedly indicate that racism is a societal problem. 'For some 500 years racism has been central to the activities of the European world' (p. 161). As a creation of that world, psychology has been hijacked to serve the ends of racism. Even the endeavours of psychologists like Allport, Rokeach, and Adorno, intended to highlight the issue of racism, indirectly served to propagate the problem. By equating racism with extremism on the part of certain individuals, the work of these doyens of psychology only served to marginalise racism. Thus, 'While much of psychological theory on racism has been either anodyne or, more obviously palliative' (p. 97), in individualising the concept of racism, the discipline merely obscured its own inherent racist nature. Due to the 'elusive quality of much of racism, psychologists ought to be constantly aware that traditional methods of assessing racism through direct questioning are unable to predict the subtlety of the expression of racism in action.

Our beliefs are no guide to our actions on such an ideologically complex matter as racism' (p. 102).

While Britain has been described as 'a nation with a shameful tradition of racism and racial exploitation' (Howitt and Owusu-Bempah, 1994, p. 142), the situation in the United States is not much better. Simone (1993) states that what 'remains is a social reality which may be just as pernicious and disempowering, but much more murky – where it is harder to get a grip on just what factors and forces constitute the nature of oppression' (p. 81). African Americans have consistently decried their country's failure to rise above race (Raspberry, 1997) and 'American psychology continues to struggle to have relevance for its own minority groups' (Gasquoine, 1997, p. 570). Not only does psychology lack relevance for minority groups, but, as discussed later in the book, various African American psychologists also consider the discipline to play an 'indirect oppressive function ' (e.g., Akbar, 1984a, p. 412). Others are of the same opinion. 'Social scientists, in the guise of a well-meaning liberalism, can serve black people a poisoned chalice' (Howitt and Owusu-Bempah, 1994, p. 44).

The Basic Behavioral Science Task Force of the National Advisory Mental Health Council (NIMH, 1995) pointed out that the extent of cultural bias needed to be a major consideration in psychology, for overt and covert discrimination was still a reality in the United States (Hall et al., 1997). 'For example, incidences of racial harassment have increased as much as 400% since 1985' (Penn, Gaines, and Phillip, 1993, p. 318). In the words of Kambon and Hopkins (1993), 'American culture is, in fact, white supremacy culture' (p. 344). Racism has been endemic in the United States since the founding of the nation (Fairchild, 1993a; Fairchild and Fairchild, 1993), and white supremacy will remain a part of the future until its existence is acknowledged and its elimination consciously programmed (Fairchild, 1993b).

Apart from the psychologists mentioned above, numerous other social scientists have expressed their disappointment at psychology's attempts to knit the uniqueness of the black American experience into the patchwork quilt of American multiculturalism (Akbar, 1984a,b; Anderson, 1993; Asante, 1983, 1992; Azibo, 1994; Baldwin, 1986, 1989; Boateng, 1983; Bulhan, 1985, 1993a, 1993b; Fairchild, 1994; Hayes, 1991; Jackson, 1982; Jones, 1991; Myers, 1991, 1993; Nobles, 1972; Semmes, 1981; Smith and Yates, 1980; White, 1984). Apart from the failure of American textbooks to acknowledge alternate cultural realities, it has been pointed out on numerous occasions that most of the results in psychology are based on white middle-class American college students (e.g., Lee, 1994; Reid, 1994). 'In spite of the percentage of African Americans among minority groups in the United States, their African heritage is perhaps the most marginalized of all cultures' (Michael, 1997, p. 241). Similar criticisms have been raised with respect to South African psychology (Seedat, 1997, 1998).

What ails psychology can be attributed to what the political scientist and cultural historian, Mazrui (1990), described as the 'dialogue of the deaf'. He wrote that 'Because Americans can communicate effectively, humanity is becoming

Americanized to some extent. Conversely, because Americans are bad listeners, their external relations are refusing to be humanized. In other words, the world is becoming Americanized culturally, but America is refusing to be humanized morally' (p. 116). Mazrui also tells the story of Mahatma Gandhi being asked what he thought of Western civilisation, whereupon Ghandi replied that he did not know the West had any. Gandhi did not dispute that the West had a culture. He was raising the question about the moral worth of the West's contribution to the human condition. Has it contributed to the human condition or not? As will be seen in the following chapters, considerable concern has been expressed about the disregard of values and the moral dimension in contemporary psychology.

PSYCHOLOGY'S SACRED RESPONSIBILITY

To close our eyes to the fact that psychology originated and flourished in the same cultural context as that which generated colonialism and still breeds overt and covert manifestations of racial prejudice, is to deny our collective responsibility for the negative aspects of the culture to which we as psychologists belong. The discipline of psychology behaves too much like the proverbial ostrich which puts its head in the sand rather than face reality (Holdstock, 1982). Nothing but the fundamental examination of the paradigms and the ideology underlying psychology and the culture to which it belongs can prevent the perpetuation of the ethnocentric orientation of the discipline as it expands internationally. Whether psychology can free itself from the inherent constraints of the culture within which it functions remains to be seen. Admittedly, there are glimmers of hope as indicated in the psychological literature.

As a product of the technologically advanced Western world, mainstream psychology wields enormous power and we have to be fully cognisant of the responsibility ensuing from such power. According to Moghaddam (1987), who proposed a division of psychology in terms of global power groups, the first power block consists of the United States, the second of all the other industrially developed nations and the third of the technologically undeveloped nations. Psychology in the United States is regarded as the first power block because of the large number of psychologists, extensive research infrastructure, and voluminous publications. Its influence in dictating the direction and the pace of the development of the discipline is enormous, and becomes even greater when it is fused with that of the second power block. Virtually the entire global psychological community is represented by these two major groupings. It is, therefore, imperative that the ideological shortcomings of the first two power blocks be highlighted in order to prevent its uncritical adoption and continued dominance of the formal and informal psychology of the third and upcoming fourth power blocks in psychology. The concept of the fourth world has recently been used to depict the native inhabitants of countries who have been dispossessed of their land (Gasquoine, 1997). Although these people do not constitute a psychological force as yet, it is not improbable that they will do so in future.

I often wonder how different the orientation and subject matter of psychology would have been if the discipline had originated in a cultural context other than that of the dominant psychological power blocks. Imagine the English, the Dutch, the Germans, or the Americans being studied in terms of the criteria indigenous to African, Arabic, or Asian psychologies! Such a proposition is unthinkable, though, for it is unlikely that the majority cultures would have attributed themselves the right to do so. In fact, in reviewing articles published in *The British Journal of Social and Clinical Psychology*, Howitt and Owusu-Bempah (1990) found 'an absence of studies which tried to understand the Western personality in terms of ideas developed through research in the "Third World"' (p. 399). Neither did they find any 'studies which attempted to explore, for example, the Ghanaian or Chinese personality structures in their own terms rather than through Western eyes' (p. 399).

In view of the fundamental question posed by Sahlins (1996) and others concerning the cosmology underlying the social sciences, a model employed in economics presents a means for understanding the relationship between sub-Saharan Africa and the West somewhat better. This model relates to the differentiation between the Southern and the Northern hemispheres in economic terms. Albert (1996) pointed out that the European North, in the name of reason, destroyed the religions and cultures of communities throughout the South, thereby creating the conditions for making rationality and objectivity the prerequisites for development and modernity. A world order was created in which the southern countries became incorporated into the worldwide structures of economic processes. The rational logic of Eurocentrism, seen by Albert as a productive force for the development of humankind, left little room for the intuitive wisdom implicit in the African way of being, however.

As one of the most prominent representatives of the sub-Saharan Africa, Leopold Senghor, the retired poet-president of Senegal, has often been criticised as being disturbingly naïve for confronting Hellenistic reason with Negro emotion; by facing European analytical thinking through utilisation with intuitive Negro reasoning through participation; and for celebrating 'the Negro-African, person of rhythm and sensitivity, assimilated to the Other through sympathy, who can say "I am the other . . . therefore I am"' (Mudimbe, 1988, p. 94). Senghor certainly did not deny the existence and validity of Eurocentric logic, but simply pointed out that there were additional dimensions of being which needed to be considered to complement the human experience in all its fullness. In this he has not been alone.

Many of the greats in psychology, starting with William James more than 100 years ago, until the recently deceased Sigmund Koch (Leary, Kessel, and Bevan, 1998), and many others in the humanistic and transpersonal fields, have endeavoured to imbue psychology with that type of understanding for which Senghor has been criticised. In envisaging the decade of behaviour which has been launched at the beginning of 1998, Lee (1998) suggested that 'we need to join psychological research with contributions from other sources of wisdom, such as religious teachings, literature and ethics' (p. 3). In fact, in a recent article entitled, 'Toward a science of the heart: Romanticism and the revival of psychology', Schneider (1998), documents the long and distinguished, though neglected, lineage of romantic ways of knowing in psychology. It is significant that this call for the return of romanticism was allowed space in the pages of the *American Psychologist*, the house journal of the APA. In his plea, Schneider points out that romanticism departed from a childlike openness to the lived world: 'romanticism emphasized three elements in its revolt against Enlightenment rationality: the interrelated wholeness of experience; access to such wholeness by means of tacit processes – affect, intuition, kinesthesia, and imagination; and qualitative or descriptive accounts of such processes' (p. 278). In the call of these contemporary psychologists and some of their predecessors for full openness to the complete range of one's experiencing is to be found the same 'childlike innocence' which Senghor considered to be an important contribution of Africa to a universal civilisation, and for which he has so often been criticised.

In fact the North–South differentiation can be elaborated even further by associating north and south with the peaks and the vales of experiencing. The fourteenth Dalai Lama of Tibet called the high and the light aspects of his being, *spirit*, and the dark and heavy aspects, *soul* (Hillman, 1979). Perhaps the placing of Europe above Africa on the global map by the early cartographers has not simply been an act of arrogance, but a manifestation of the archetypes of spirit and soul at work. Compared to the clarity and the blue lightness of spirit, soul is dark and murky. Spirit is associated with the coldness of the high altitudes, while soul is associated with the warmth of the savannah. Hillman situates soul in nature and community, in sleep and dreams, in personal and ancestral history, aspects of being closely associated with Africa. Out of this base grows the abstract, unified, and concentrated spiritual. Spirit is humble and humourless. Soul, on the other hand, is a wondrous quality of life, adding the humour so absent in the spiritual dimension.

Interestingly, the distinction between the Northern and the Southern hemisphere in terms of spirit and soul, also pertains with respect to more localised geographical regions, for instance, between northern and southern Europe. Even in small countries like Holland, a distinction in terms of spirit and soul can be made between the north and the south. In philosophy, Kimmerle (1995a) has called for a North–South dialogue. It would seem that the time is ripe to follow in the footsteps of the parent discipline.

3

CAN THE CENTRE HOLD?

Disunity and fragmentation in psychology

Although psychology is invariably defined as the scientific study of behaviour (Lindzey, Hall, and Thompson, 1975), in its very essence it represents the quest for meaning into the mystery of life. However, it is debatable whether the way in which psychology has become organised as the scientific study of behaviour is likely to provide the key to understanding 'life's secrets and hidden things' (Gibran, 1954, p. 1). The discipline fails in a number of essential respects in offering humankind the necessary guidelines to address the tremendous problems in living we are faced with. So many of these problems are totally of our own making and the issue is not only how to cope with these problems, but also of how to prevent them from becoming the insurmountable issues that lead to personal disintegration and international warfare.

Some argue that psychology not only fails with respect to prevention and cure but that it actually contributes to the creation of the problems it is supposed to alleviate (e.g., Hall, 1997; Hillman and Ventura, 1993; Tart, 1975a,b). Despite concerted efforts by many individuals to take stock of and to change the direction in which the discipline is heading, mainstream psychology continues inexorably on its chosen path. Since the investment in psychology is not to be turned back, and is likely to become increasingly more apparent outside the Western world as well, our only hope of bringing about a change in the discipline is to work towards an enhanced awareness of the extent to which it falls short of its potential to serve humankind (e.g., Bevan and Kessel, 1994; Gergen, 1994). In referring to psychology, Kimble (1994) suggested that before we bestow a gift on someone, the responsible thing to do would be to take it back and fix it.

In lighter vein, an adapted version of a story that is to be found in many traditions, and whose Western origins can be traced back to Poincaré (van der Hooft, 1979), serves to convey both the potential and the shortcomings of psychology. According to legend there once lived in a country far to the north a number of psychologists who were all blind in their own peculiar ways. None of them had ever seen an elephant and when it happened that the circus came to their capital city they all flocked to study the elephant which performed in one of the acts. The first to arrive was a Freudian who went immediately to the rear of the elephant and began his inspection of the animal from this chosen view

(Samples, Charles, and Barnhart, 1977). The behaviourist fed the elephant an M&M every time it blinked. When asked what she was doing she said that she wanted to know whether the eyelids of elephants conditioned as rapidly as those of rabbits. The cognitive psychologist began to coax the elephant into doing a newly designed test for the mapping of the mental strategies of elephants. The humanistic psychologist felt its ears and tried to convince the elephant that it could fly. The Rogerian observed the animal closely and tried to imagine what it must be like to be an elephant in captivity.

Since it was the decade of the brain, the biopsychologists received sponsorship for their visit to the elephant and arrived in great numbers. One tried to obtain a galvanic skin response from the footpads of the animal. Another observed its eye movements in order to determine whether elephants experienced REM sleep, and if perchance they dreamt. One of the neuropsychologists set out to determine the hemispheric asymmetry of elephants by examining its trunk and penis laterality. Another arrived with an arsenal of computer equipment to determine the latency of the P300 component of the event-evoked response in the parietal region of the elephant's brain. Since it was the decade of the brain, a whole team of electronics experts accompanied her. Some rushed around to set up the equipment while others applied the electrodes to the scalp of the elephant.

The cross-cultural psychologist shared an interest in the ears of the animal with the humanistic psychologist. By counting the number of times the animal flapped its ears he hoped to determine whether Asian and African elephants differed in this pattern of behaviour. The Africentric psychologist did not arrive and some said that (s)he considered the investigation of a single animal in captivity as not that meaningful since elephants were herd animals and could be conceptualised and appreciated best in their natural environment and in relation to each other.

MAINSTREAM CONCERNS ABOUT DISUNITY

Growing concern has been expressed about the disunity in psychology and a lively debate has ensued in discussing the issue and the consequences for the discipline (Abi-Hashem, 1997; Gergen *et al.*, 1996; see Holdstock, 1996a, for additional references; Rice, 1997; Shweder, 1994; Slife and Williams, 1997; Watts, 1992). The literature on the issue of disunity is so vast that reference will only be made to some of the more recently expressed concerns. 'The knowledge of psychology is an array of bits and pieces without an organizing theme' (Kimble, 1994, p. 510). Recently, Kimble (1998) reiterated his concern about the 'splin-tered' nature of the discipline. 'In recent years new technologies have produced new specialities, with subject matters and vocabularies so diverse that psychology has no unifying theme' (p. 3).

Speaking 'from the heart', Farley (1996), in his presidential address to the APA, expressed his concern about the neglect of spiritual values and the role of meaning, due primarily to the fact that 'psychology compartmentalizes things so much. We specialize in bits and pieces of the puzzle, but we rarely seek the whole picture' (p. 776). He said that psychology stands 'very close to being a discipline concerned with relatively superficial problems' (p. 775). Gergen (1995) warned that in becoming fragmented into small, self-protective enclaves, psychology would end up as a discipline speaking to itself. Schneider (1996), similarly, accuses psychology of being 'characterized by thousands of unrelated findings, to which more are added each day, raising questions about whether it is or can be a cumulating science' (p. 715).

Not only does Schneider (1996) call for the removal of the walls within psychology but he also pleads for the abolition of barriers between disciplines. Of the barriers within psychology, that between cognition and affect (*cognitive science* and *affective science*) is, according to him, in most urgent need of being lifted. Of the barriers between disciplines, the bottom–up approach to the study of the relation between biology and psychology and the 'top–down effects of a reciprocal emergent determinism' (p. 716) needs more attention, as does the interface between psychological and other macro levels of sociocultural analysis. That such integration will be no easy task is certain, for fragmentation is equally rampant in disciplines other than psychology. For instance, according to Shweder (1994), the parochialism of the 'two hegemonic intellectual regimes . . . made it difficult even to conceive of a meaningful collaboration between anthropologists and psychologists' (p. 94). Similarly, the structural barriers between psychology and sociology rule out the possibility of a merger between the two disciplines (Stephan, Stephan, and Pettigrew, 1991). 'The more psychology conceived of the person or the psyche as fixed, interior, abstract, universal, and lawful, the more anthropology chose to interpret sociocultural environments as exterior, historically variable, culture specific, and arbitrary and to renounce any interest in psyches or persons, or in the general causes of anything' (Shweder, 1994, pp. 95–96).

Abi-Hashem (1997), in criticising the tunnel vision approach to science and life in the West, points out how much more interconnected with other disciplines psychology is in technologically developing countries. In most Dutch and many European universities, students in psychology only study courses related to psychology from their first year at university. It is argued that their high school education provides them with sufficient background in the various other disciplines. The insularity of such an approach and the resultant alienation from the humanities, social, and natural sciences, do not bode well for the future integration of psychology in the affairs of humankind.

Some, like Sigmund Koch (1981) and Thomas Natsoulas (1990), argue that a unified science of psychology is an impossibility. Even if it were possible, the unification of psychology would, according to Natsoulas (1990), be undesirable. 'Imagine (with horror) a unified science of psychology!' he wrote (p. 175). Others, among whom Staats is the foremost proponent, recognise the present disunity and strive for unification. Differences of opinion exist, however, as to how the unification can be achieved (Green, 1992; Kukla, 1992). According to Kimble (1994), for instance, 'the incoherent discipline of psychology' can be brought together by the development of general principles adhering to 'the status of psychology as the science of behavior' (p. 510).

In contrast to the concern that disunity will lead to the demise of psychology, is the opinion that it indicates 'vitality rather than centrifugal disintegration' (McNally, 1992, p. 1054). Although there are those, like Matarazzo (1987), who believe that psychology is integrated rather than an ensemble of subspecialties, there is no denying the strong centrifugal tendencies that are leading towards the fragmentation and possible disintegration of psychology. It is of interest that Toffler (1980) describes a global process of 'social de-massification' (p. 249), which is very much in keeping with what is happening in psychology. Quite possibly the increasing specialisation within the discipline reflects a search for identity that is similar to that occurring in terms of ethnicity.

Whatever the case may be, the focus on specialisation has become so pronounced that Bevan (1991) considers psychology to have evolved into a balkanised discipline. He argues that specialisation has given rise to a regressive fragmentation which 'fosters a mind-set characterized by separateness, by competitiveness that is excessive, and by alienation from larger intellectual and human concerns' (Bevan and Kessel, 1994, p. 505). Fowers and Richardson (1997) refer to the 'unintentional but increasing balkanization of psychology' (p. 660). Staats (1981), in similar vein, described psychology as being constructed of 'small islands of knowledge . . . organised in ways that make no connection with the many other existing islands of knowledge' (p. 239). Scott (1991) stated that it was only as an administrative unit that psychology continued to exist. And even as an administrative unity the future of psychology is being threatened. With the forming of new alliances between subspecialties of psychology and those of other disciplines, alternative administrative structures are likely to come about in the next century. In the Netherlands this new structure has already been put into effect in an attempt to upgrade the quality of the research and enhance the competitiveness of the research units for the limited funds available (Holdstock, 1992–1993, 1994b). Wesner (1996), among others, has also pointed out the political ramifications of disunity for journal review processes and for funding collaborative research.

To a certain extent, forming new alliances between the subspecialties of various disciplines answers to the call made by Schneider (1996) for breaking down the walls between disciplines. However, in the process of establishing interdisciplinary specialities, new and perhaps firmer barriers than those, which existed before in psychology, are being erected. It is especially the divide between the applied and the fundamental research orientation of psychology which threatens to become more acute (Holdstock, 1994b).

As things are at present the diversity and fragmentation of contemporary psychology is evident in the dozens of highly specialized, and largely noninteracting sub-disciplines; the different conceptions of what constitutes the proper subject matter of psychology, different methodological approaches; different theories with regard to the same phenomenon; differences in underlying philosophical assumptions; the many (and increasing) divisions within psychological organizations; the disagreements with regard to appropriate training and educational models; and in the practitioner–scientist (professional–academic/applied–pure) schism.

(Wissing, 1990, p. 5)

Staats (1991) contends that psychology is suffering 'from a crisis of disunity' (p. 899). According to him the discipline 'is already drowning in diversity' (p. 904). He expresses concern that there is 'so much mutual discreditation, inconsistency, redundancy, and controversy that abstracting general meaning is a great problem' (p. 899) in psychology. 'In our modern disunified science the typical approach is to take one side of the schism, attempt to enhance it, and discredit the other side – the discreditation then being taken as further support' (p. 906). In agreement with others (Berkowitz and Devine, 1989), Staats 'criticizes the current state in which researchers are driven to produce novelty, and not look for commonality. This helps show the relationship of disunity to the fadishness that is endemic in psychology' (pp. 901–902).

There is much support for the persistent concern expressed by Staats (1981, 1983, 1991). Maher (1985) describes the present state in psychology as 'one of fragmentation and chaotic diversity' (p. 17), a position which MacIntyre (1988) regards as an indication of the pre-scientific stage of development of the discipline. By describing psychology as a nineteenth-century enterprise, Bevan (1991) is in obvious agreement with the evaluation of MacIntyre.

Concern about the disunity in psychology transcends purely methodological issues. At the heart of the concern seems to be the irreconcilable separation between matter and spirit that has ensued in the development of psychology, culminating in the estrangement from our bodies, each other, the science we practise, and the world we live in. It is this tendency towards fragmentation that poses such a threat for the development of a psychology in keeping with the holism that forms such an integral part of the African worldview.

Something happened in the historical development of psychology that brought about the adoption of Fechner's measuring approach, for which he has duly been remembered as the father of psychophysics, and Wundt's experimental psychology, without acknowledging the additional aspects of their respective contributions. For Fechner, mind and matter were inseparable, matter was imbued with spirit. He 'refused to accept the new dogma that man has a consciousness, spirit, or subjectivity separated from the material world' (Kruger, 1988, p. 2). Fechner distinguished between the objective and the subjective view of reality in terms of the metaphor of the night and the day (van den Berg, 1980). Similarly,

Wundt's nine-volume *Volkerpsychologie*, in which he used anthropological, linguistic, and other qualitative data, has been left out of the equation of his contribution to psychology (Kruger, 1988). The factors responsible for adopting some and negating other aspects of the work of the founding fathers of psychology pose an interesting question for the historians of psychology.

DISUNITY WITHIN THE SUB-DISCIPLINES

Not only is psychology breaking up into a myriad of sub-disciplines, but the sub-disciplines are becoming fragmented themselves. Even theoretical psychology has been criticised as 'fragmented, because it addresses increasingly isolated subspecialties and because it fails to take into account the theoretical themes and problems that motivate the enterprise of psychology as a whole' (Slife and Williams, 1997, p. 118). Magnusson and Torstar (1993) caution that 'The fragmentation of personality research into sub-areas is one of the greatest impediments to scientific progress' (p. 432). According to Urie Bronfenbrenner and his colleagues, developmental psychology is 'looking more and more at less and less' (Bronfenbrenner, Kessel, Kessen, and White, 1986, p. 1219). They illustrate their point with a different version of the story of the elephant and the psychologists. Their rendering is of the Russian tale of a man who visited the zoo and saw all manner of creatures, such as flies and beetles, ladybirds, butterflies, and insects with heads no bigger than pins; however, he missed seeing the elephant. Bronfenbrenner, therefore, 'urged psychologists to incorporate expanded views of the context in which development occurs' (Scarr, 1985, p. 501).

Fragmentation and individuocentrism within social psychology

Social psychology is one of the sub-disciplines where expanded views of the context can be expected. However, the critique of the reductionistic and fragmented nature of social psychology has been as strong, if not stronger and more applicable, than in the other areas of psychology (e.g., Adamopoulus, 1988; Armistead, 1974; Billig, 1991; Gergen, 1985; Harré, 1993; 1998; Jacoby, 1977; Jahoda, 1988; Jones, 1986; Resler and Walton, 1974). Billig challenged his colleagues to move beyond individualistic models of social action, while Harré called for a reappraisal of social psychology. Harré (1993) considered the 'rigidity of thought and conservatism of method' (p. 27), not only to have 'bedevilled' the subdiscipline, but the methodology to be 'wildly inappropriate to the subject matter of the research' (p. 25).

In a recent text on *The Future of Social Psychology*, Stephan, Stephan, and Pettigrew (1991) point out that there tends to be an inverse relationship between the degree of statistical sophistication used by psychologists and the meaningfulness of much of their research. Psychology is advised to learn from sociology the need to take into account larger social contexts when building theories, planning research, and explaining findings.

The criticism of social psychology's fragmentation and insularity gathered force in the 1970s with Gergen, Moscovici, and Pepitone being credited with initiating the critical perspective (Gabrenya, 1988). According to Gergen and Gergen (1988), 'the emphasis on stable mechanisms or processes "within the heads" of single individuals (e.g., attitudes, stereotypes, schemas, traits) has inhibited the growth of theory that takes social interdependency to be its major focus' (p. 53). 'Pepitone (1981) notes how the values of psychology as a whole – empiricism, objectivism, behaviorism, operationalism, reductionism, materialism, mechanism, universalism, and individualism – have in turn shaped social psychology, particularly its individuocentric treatment of group dynamics' (Gabrenya, 1988, p. 50). Due to these values social psychology, as well as the other sub-disciplines of psychology, have become increasingly more insular and isolated from the social sciences.

> Western cultural views tend to emphasize the separation and independence of the self from the environment . . . Conceived as existing in a hypothetical state free of society, the 'true' self tends to be identified with that which is unique to the agent, relatively enduring, and independent of social role.
>
> (Miller, 1988, p. 273)

> In its attempt to develop a rigorous, universalistic social psychology, the social cognitive group has brought to social psychology an even lower unit of analyis deep inside the organism, and has promoted cultural and disciplinary insularity to a greater extent than any other single development.
>
> (Sampson, 1981, p. 53)

Due to these values social psychology, as well as the other fields of psychology, have become culturally increasingly more insular and isolated from the social sciences (Adamopoulus, 1988). It is not surprising, therefore, that Jacoby (1977), in criticising 'the individualistic orientation of present-day social psychology' (p. 105), accused the discipline of suffering from social amnesia. Lee (1994) is another who states that the limitations of reductionism, ethnocentrism, and individuocentrism in American mainstream psychology are even more apparent in the subdiscipline of social psychology. Rather than the consideration of sociocultural and relationship variables, social psychology focuses on the behaviour, cognition, and information processing of individuals. When it does look at interpersonal relationships, it concerns itself with a micro-social analysis (Hayes, 1984).

According to Cushman (1991) the subdiscipline also disregards the political and the ideological context of people's behaviour. Armistead (1974) asked social psychology to look carefully at the social context of behaviour and experience and be involved in bringing about social change. According to Resler and Walton (1974), 'What is necessary for the reconstruction of social psychology is to analyse people's psychic development and responses within a historical perspective, which recognized that the limits on behavior are shaped by the relations between power, politics and people' (p. 290). On the basis of the social constructionist critique of the search for the foundational laws of a universal, transhistorical human nature by the dominant branch of modern psychology, Cushman (1991) decreed that psychology's decontextualised programme

> is both philosophically impossible and politically dangerous. Psychology's program is impossible because human being is constructed by the social practices of local communities. Any attempt to remove individuals from the history and culture in which they are embedded and to study them as isolated, decontextualized monads is, from a constructionist point of view, a neo-Enlightenment fantasy – it is simply not doable. (p. 206)

The political danger of psychology's decontextualised approach is especially to be found in the fact that an approach is proposed which is relative and political without appearing to be so, thus obscuring the ideologies embedded in the underlying theories and practices of the discipline.

Kipnis (1997) recently took the criticism of social psychology's fragmented nature and individuocentric orientation an interesting step further. According to him 'focusing on psychological states serves to inhibit the systematic study of societal changes (particularly changes in technology) that are affecting and shaping all aspects of human existence' (p. 205). Social psychology should focus on the study of interactions between technological events and changes in consciousness. Kipnis contends that 'modern technology is shifting social behavior in dramatic ways, including how people interact, communicate, and perceive themselves and others' (p. 208). Since the Internet is the latest, and considered by some potentially the most revolutionary technological development yet, its negative and positive effects are being weighed up. For instance, while it provides the opportunity for connecting people electronically, it can also affect their emotional well-being adversely. Apart from people becoming addicted to online living, the greater use of the Internet leads to shrinking social support and happiness, as well as enhanced depression and loneliness (Kraut et al., 1998).

Fragmentation within clinical psychology

It is not only at the conceptual, the experimental, and the methodological level that the fragmentation within psychology is rampant, but also at the applied level (Lemmes, de Ridder, and van Lieshout, 1991). Within the applied division the same fragmentation and tension is apparent as within psychology generally.

For instance, the relation between the science and the practice of clinical psychology has been described as 'a complex and often hostile relationship' (Beutler, Williams, Wakefield, and Entwhistle, 1995, p. 984). The gulf between psychotherapy practice and research is like the twain that shall never meet, and has been the topic of discussion on numerous occasions (e.g., Barlow, 1991; Brown, 1987; Jacobson and Christensen, 1996; Newman and Tejeda, 1996; Peterson, 1985; Seligman, 1996; Stricker, 1997; Stricker and Trierweiler, 1995).

Recently, pressure from managed health care and biological psychiatry to justify clinical practice empirically has heightened the urgency to bridge the gap between science and practice. However, the danger exists that these pressures may result in the adoption of a medical model of outcome research, bringing about the compartmentalisation of the client population, the symptom category, and the type of therapy. Goldfried and Wolfe (1996) have, therefore, called for the development of a new paradigm for outcome research in psychotherapy to combat the medical model. These authors also plead for orienting process research in psychotherapy away from the earlier focus on discrete and isolated transactions between therapist and client. Their suggestion is to shift attention to functional units that might conceivably reflect the process of change. Brown (1997), writing from a feminist perspective, accuses the burgeoning approach of managed mental health care of attempting 'to capture, enslave, and exile psychotherapy' (p. 454).

Clinical psychology's fragmentation manifests itself in divergent ways. For instance, Fox (1982) criticised the profession for offering specialised services to a select few, while ignoring other important tasks that are within its scope. 'We have devoted 90% of our efforts toward serving the needs of the 10%–15% of the population that suffers from diagnosable (and thus reimbursable) mental illnesses' (p. 1052). Fox advocates the reorientation of clinical psychological services towards transition services for people who have been hospitalised, better interfacing with the rest of the health care system, the establishment of comprehensive service centres, and a more deliberate focus on prevention, entailing the education of people regarding personal health habits and life-styles. For the South African psychologist, Eli Daniels (1986), 'Primary preventative intervention involves changing those social factors that undermine or in any way retard the development of the powerless, the poor and the oppressed people in our society' (p. 21). In order to be effective in this regard the professional psychologist is required to go 'beyond his quintessentially clinical/traditional role without necessarily abdicating it' (p. 21).

In 1959 Harper described 36 systems of psychoanalysis and psychotherapy. With the publication of *The New Psychotherapies* in 1975 he found the proliferation too extensive to tabulate numerically. Others have done so, however. According to one account the number of theories of psychotherapy has doubled during the past 10 years (see Staats, 1991). In 1980 more than a 100 were noted and a decade later the estimate has doubled once more. According to another report the 'schools' of psychotherapy have risen like 'a fevered white cell count', from an estimated 130 in 1976, to 250 in 1980, and 300 in 1986 (Kazdin, 1986). Other accounts place the number over 400 (Karasu, 1986) and even over 460 (Omer and London, 1988)! And we have the audacity to diagnose individuals as having multiple personalities. Even within each of the established therapeutic orientations divisiveness and conflict are the order of the day.

The fact that clinical psychology not only is one of the fastest growing professions of the century (Gergen, 1990), but also one of the most divisive, is furthermore evident in the diagnostic armament available today. According to Buros (1975) there were 2,467 standardised tests in print in 1974. Of these, 441 were personality tests. With an increase, estimated by Buros to be 3.2 per cent per year, the number of personality tests could be calculated to have grown to 826 by 1999. Besides the tests being marketed, there are certainly thousands of unvalidated/unpublished tests in use. The evaluation of the abilities, short-comings and characteristics of people has grown into a major industry.

It is especially with respect to the diagnosis and labelling of what is wrong with people that our expertise has achieved a particularly finely attuned level. 'You' messages in the form of labelling inappropriate behaviour and problems in living proliferate. Levy (1992), (somewhat tongue in the cheek, but nevertheless in all seriousness) suggested that our obsession with labelling represents a disorder in its own right, deserving of the label 'pervasive labelling disorder'. Bruno Bettelheim is reported to have said that we attach labels in order to cover up our ignorance. Gergen (1990) has expressed great concern about the 'diffusion of deficit' (p. 353), which has been 'expanding exponentially within the present century' (p. 360), as a result of the 'obsessive preoccupation with diagnosis' (Sarbin, 1990, p. 272). 'As the language of deficit has expanded, so have we increased the culture's hierarchies of discrimination, damaged the naturalized patterns of interdependence, and expanded the arena of self-deprecation. In effect, as the language of deficit has proliferated, so has the culture become progressively infirmed' (Gergen, 1990, p. 361).

With the ascendancy of the DSM-IV (American Psychiatric Association, 1994), there has been a narrowing of 'focus on symptoms and symptom reduction as the goal of psychotherapy, which has become closely coupled with issues of cost-effectiveness' (Strupp, 1996, p. 1021). The latest edition of the DSM-IV lists more than 300 separate disorders.

> To describe a person as 'mentally ill,' 'schizophrenic,' 'manic-depressive,' etc., means operationally that therapists hold low expectations for these individuals. We cannot help human beings to solve their developmental crises if we insist on defining these crises as symptoms of chronic mental illnesses. If we verbally encourage human beings to succeed while expecting them to fail, our encouragement is facile.
>
> (Farber, 1990, p. 298)

How may I fault thee? Let me count the ways . . .

Impulsive personality	*Low self-esteem*
Malingering	*Narcissism*
Reactive depression	*Bulimia*
Anorexia	*Neurasthenia*
Hysteria	*Hypochondriasis*
Mania	*Dependent personality*
Psychopathia	*Frigidity*
Peter Pan syndrome	*Voyeurism*
External control orientation	*Authoritarianism*
Anti-social personality	*Transvestism*
Exhibitionism	*Agoraphobia*
Seasonal affective disorder . . .	

(Gergen, 1990, p. 353)

The disease construction of mental illness is in keeping with the medical orientation to the discipline and 'originated during a period of rapid growth of biological science based on mechanistic principles' (Sarbin, 1990, p. 259). Besides the authors already cited, others have also pointed out that blind adherence to the medical model and the pretension of belonging to the hard sciences have impeded an understanding of 'mental illness' (e.g., Brown, 1987, 1990; Frank, 1990; Mirowsky, 1990; Mirowsky and Ross, 1989). In 1653, one B. Carcian stated that 'Many times is an evil made worse by the remedies used . . . The learned physician needs just as much wisdom in order not to prescribe, as to prescribe, and often the greater art lies in doing nothing . . . There is no better remedy for turmoil than to let it take its course, for so it comes to rest of itself' (in Wilmer, 1976). We desperately need to revision our language of deficit and develop

> alternative vocabularies within the mental health profession, vocabularies that (1) do not trace problematic behavior to psychological sources within single individuals and (2) ultimately erase the concept of 'problem behavior' itself. I am speaking here first of the development of a vocabulary of relatedness that would come to equal the rhetorical power of individualized language in making the social world intelligible.
> (Gergen, 1990, p. 365)

What Gouldner (in Louw, 1988) called the 'culture of critical discourse' also serves to create a gulf between clinical psychologists and their clients. While the technical terms provide a means for the psychotherapists to communicate among themselves, it serves to set them apart from the lay public. In itself the technical language becomes an expression of power.

> Mental patients do not hold dances; they have dance therapy. If they play volleyball, that is recreation therapy. If they engage in group

discussion, that is group therapy. Even reading is 'bibliotherapy' . . . To label a common activity as though it were a medical one is to establish superior and subordinate roles, to make it clear who gives orders and who takes them, and to justify in advance the inhibitions placed upon the subordinate class. It ordinarily does so without arousing resentment or resistance either in the subordinates or in outsiders sympathetic to them, for it superimposes a political relationship on a medical one while still depicting it as medical.

(Edelman in Louw, 1988, p. 77)

Louw maintains that 'the increased emphasis on application and profession-alization of psychology, often in an unholy alliance with powerful social institutions, are at odds with the contribution psychology can and should make to a healthier way of life' (p. 75). Besides we need to become aware of how the disease or defect model serves the interests of the bureaucratic networks at national and local level and how it legitimises the hypothetical nature of such diagnostic categories as schizophrenia (Farber, 1990; Gergen, 1990; Sarbin, 1990). Furthermore, abundant evidence exists which indicates the cultural relativity of what constitutes socially maladjusted behaviour (Holdstock, 1979; Marsella and White, 1989).

SPECIALISATION HAS BECOME FRAGMENTATION

Koch (1981), the respected scholar delegated by the APA and the National Science Foundation to assess the status of psychology as a science, concluded that 'much of psychology's history can be seen as a form of scientistic role playing which, however sophisticated, entails the trivialization and even evasion of significant problems' (p. 257). According to Koch, this state of affairs came about because psychology decided on its methods before it developed its questions. In similar vein, Schneider (1996) speaks for many when he expresses being 'disenchanted with method-bound and method-driven science, with operation-alism, with scientism masquerading as science' (p. 719). As an epitaph for our time he adopted 'a phrase of Anne Roe's that described the problem with terse eloquence: "better and better research design for matters of less and less importance"' (p. 719). Cattell (1993), another respected figure in psychology, remarked that during his lifetime he has 'seen periodic "retreats" from handling the real complexities of behaviour' (p. 22). According to Roger Walsh (1984) the distraction from the deeper, more important concerns can be attributed to our 'tranquillisation by the trivial' (p. xvi).

According to Bevan (1991), the intellectual character of psychology is flawed. In following the ideological tradition of the physical sciences of the nineteenth century, psychology adopted a 'stubbornly reductionistic and mechanistic approach' (p. 476), resulting in 'a fragmented collectivity of studies of varied cast . . . narrowly focused and compulsively insular . . . We persevere in looking at small questions instead of large ones and our view of the forest is forever obscured by the trees' (p. 475). Scarr (1985) expressed the same point of view from a somewhat different perspective. She pointed out that 'Psychologists have a distinct preference for proximal variables to explain behavior . . . most of our theoretical lenses had a very short focus that blurred or ignored distal events . . . Even though our horizons have expanded, most psychologists retain a preference for nearby causal explanations' (p. 501).

In its quest to be scientific, psychology tends to emphasise 'the individual as a biological unit' (Jahoda, 1988, p. 91). Internal or experiential phenomena, being considered as 'inherently unreliable and unreal, must be reduced to physiological or behavioral data to become reliable' (Tart, 1975a, pp. 24–25). Although I have never regarded experiential data as unreliable, during the early phase of my career I nevertheless regarded such data as not exact and challenging enough to constitute the basis for research of a 'scientific' nature. Although I am no longer active in brain research, the approach has, none the less, not lost its fascination for me. Thus, I would be the last person to devalue the merits of neuro-physiological or other biological research. Others, too, have cautioned against neglecting consideration of biological factors (e.g., Slife and Williams, 1997). Nevertheless, the limitations of an exclusive biological focus have to be realised. 'Nature and nuture do not operate independently of each other, and there needs to be an explicit focus on the interplay between them' (Rutter, 1997, p. 396).

Barlow (1991) argues that the growth of cognitive and behavioural sciences has, in part, been because people realised the inherent dangers of biological reductionism. 'Psychology has long been weary of our biological colleagues who would reduce behavior and cognition to electrical impulses in the brain or biochemical activity at a cell synapse' (p. 104). Peele (1981, 1990) is convinced that the promise of biochemical and neurological research to find explanations for basic aspects of human behaviour and mental disorder, will never be realised since it 'fails to incorporate individual personality and subjective needs or situational and cultural variables' (1981, p. 807). Peele attributes the appeal of reductionist thinking to 'its concreteness and its conciseness. It organizes behav-ior into exact, discrete categories; by drawing physical connections between behavior and the nervous system, it offers compact causal explanations; finally, and most important to its appeal, reductionist thought holds out the promise of clear-cut remedies to problems that otherwise seem painful beyond solution' (1981, p. 807). In commenting on the emphasis in the human movement sciences on anatomical and physiological detail, O'Brien (1989) describes the obsession with detail as the tyranny of the abstract. Although his comments are not directed at psychology, they are, nevertheless, applicable.

In general, Bevan (1991) is concerned about 'the dominance of the cult of the specialist' (p. 476). If we are not careful, specialisation can give rise to a regressive fragmentation, and 'fragmentation fosters a mind-set characterized by separateness, by competitiveness that is excessive, and by alienation from larger intellectual and human concerns' (Bevan and Kessel, 1994, p. 505). Specialisation has created an obsession with 'mindless and routine recitation of detail' (Bevan, 1991, p. 476), resulting in trivial papers. The quantity of publications has come to outweigh the quality of thought. Bevan is not alone in questioning the value of many journal articles. Jahoda (1988) even headed a section in one of his articles with the title, 'The journals: More and more about less and less' (p. 88). Jahoda's heading is reminiscent of a statement by a student in an examination several years ago. The student wrote that so little is known in psychology by so many about so few attributes. Jahoda describes much of psychological research as 'futile exercises', 'pedestrian', 'sometimes bizarre studies carried out with admirable methodological sophistication', which when 'stripped of their jargon' expose 'the poverty of the core' (p. 88).

Donald Lindsey (1977), doyen of physiological psychology, questioned how it was possible 'that so much triviality, illiteracy, and dullness is yearly entered into the scientific publication stream?' (p. 579). To Lindsey's question, Nisbett (1978) provides a possible answer. According to Nisbett the chance of getting an article published improved by avoiding creative or innovative experimental designs and by concentrating one's efforts on areas that are easy to test and are noncontroversial. Kupfersmid's (1988) explanation is in similar vein. According to him '(a) Many articles focus on irrelevant topics; (b) the use of statistical significance testing often results in meaningless or unusable findings; and (c) the decision-making process for manuscript acceptance/rejection may be biased' (p. 635).

In his summary of 374 reports of experiments designed to illuminate the concept of schizophrenia, Sarbin (1990) came to the same conclusion as the above authors. He stated that all the studies 'were constructed for the purpose of vigorously testing miniature hypotheses' (p. 265). Petrinovich (1979), too, questions the adequacy of traditional research designs to yield generalisations beyond the particular experimental paradigm. He queries whether it is possible to prevent the essence of human existence from getting lost in the manner in which psychologists approach their science.

Peterson (1985) cautions against quenching the concern of students 'for others in a cold objectivity that does not suit our discipline in the first place' (p. 450). For most of his career Carl Rogers expressed similar concerns. Throughout the time that I have known him as a teacher at the University of Wisconsin, he pleaded for a graduate education in psychology that respected the students as human beings and not just as information processing entities. Shortly before his death he once more wrote that the living, acting, whole human being was afforded very little place in psychology (Rogers, 1985). He again stressed the importance of searching for models of science that would be appropriate to human beings.

How widespread the concern is about the direction in which psychology is progressing is indicated by the well-known brain researcher, Paul MacLean

(1967), who stated that 'We are beginning to understand enough about the brain and behavior to realize – with a little chagrin – that we have outlived the time when it is fashionable to put an overriding emphasis on impersonalized basic research' (p. 382). Laura Brown (1997) uses the biblical metaphor of 'dry bones' to describe the practice of a psychology that is devoid of the value of social justice. Earlier I had written that it was debatable whether psychology's uninvolvement with feelings provided the appropriate platform upon which to build the discipline in Africa (Holdstock, 1981b, 1982). Deutsch (1993) advocated that schools should offer the values, attitudes, and knowledge that promote constructive relations and prepare children to live in a peaceful world, rather than encourage individualistic, competitive (and often destructive) values. Without saying, the same applies to the teaching of psychology.

According to Tseëlon (1991), we need to be fully aware of the fact that the method of no-frills empiricism represents an ideology that shapes outcome and produces meaning in a very definite way. She argues that all methods are 'ideological in that they are the codes through which facts are defined, and acquire meaning. The implications . . . are that a choice of method is neither a technical neutral move, nor a choice between more or less truthful accounts of reality; rather, it is commitment to a particular metaphor of human behaviour, and a particular picture of reality' (p. 300). 'Thus, by choosing a certain method we are opting for a particular picture of humans. It is not a question of accuracy, but a question of values' (p. 313). Method determines outcome and meaning and at the same time reflects the values of the dominant culture or ruling class. It is for these reasons that it is necessary that we are fully cognisant of the implications of our choice of method.

Dissatisfaction with the atomistic orientation of psychology is not something new, as has already been indicated by the balanced, though neglected perspectives of Fechner and Wundt. During the early part of this century, various other psychologists have expressed their concern about the manner in which psychology established itself as a scientific discipline. The ideologically divergent approaches to psychology were at that time already considered to represent a crisis or even chaos in psychology (Cahan and White, 1992). Among the concerned were John Dewey and William James (in Magnusson and Törestad, 1993). William James, in 1890, stressed the idea of the individual as a whole human being, while Dewey, in 1896, warned against the danger of an atomistic psychology. Among other early dissenters count such historical figures as James Baldwin and George Herbert Mead. According to Cahan and White these four eminent persons (Baldwin, Mead, Dewey, and James) considered 'the possibility and necessity of nonexperimental psychology' (1992, p. 229).

In a distant part of the world the renowned South African statesman and scientist, Jan Christian Smuts (1926), proposed a similar option. Smuts wrote that 'the procedure of psychology is largely and necessarily analytical and cannot therefore do justice to Personality in its unique wholeness' (p. 293). He, therefore, proposed the establishment of a new holistic science of 'Personology', which would not be a mere subdivision of psychology, but an independent science of synthesis. It is likely that the calls for a 'nonexperimental psychology' and for 'a new holistic science of "Personology"' of these early pioneers, as well as Rogers' dream of a psychology appropriate for human beings, may still become reality if the confidence of Farley (1996) is anything to go by. In his presidential address to the APA, he expressed the view that psychology will change significantly in the early twenty-first century since 'we are going through deep shifts in our conceptions of acceptable research methodologies' (p. 773). If there can be a greater awareness and appreciation of the psychological dimensions indigenous to sub-Saharan Africa, the development of psychology can be facilitated even more, and not just with respect to the way research is being conducted.

FACTION FIGHTING BETWEEN THE CULTURES OF PSYCHOLOGY

In fact, concern about the 'chaos of fragmentation and diversity' (Royce, 1970, p. 275) in psychology has reached such proportions that Anastasi (1990) describes the present movement towards unification as 'a significant event in the history of psychology' (p. 20). The emotive tone of the descriptions depicting the reductionism in and fragmentation of psychology which have been high-lighted, is a clear indication that the disunity of the discipline is an issue of major concern. In fact, we can rightly speak of an iatrogenically caused sickness in psychology. A student once remarked that it was rather paradoxical that psychology was so successful in creating a neurosis about itself. Although he did not have the disunity issue in mind, his words are nevertheless applicable in the present context.

Furthermore, I cannot help but see a similarity between the fragmented science of psychology and the condition of schizophrenia. According to a number of renowned psychologists and psychiatrists the major problem in schizophrenia is the lack of acceptance by the individual and others of the strange and unfamiliar images which the person labelled as schizophrenic is experiencing (Hillman, 1975; Laing, 1969, 1970; Perry, 1974; Szasz, 1961, 1987). Not only is there a lack of acceptance of the alternative aspects of the self in schizophrenia, but there is also an active rejection of, and open warfare between, the separate manifestations. The same is true between the various specialisations in psychology. In terms of the prevailing competitive model there simply is not enough room for all the specialities and sub-specialities to coexist independently. The psychological household has, therefore, become embroiled in a family feud (Kimble, 1984).

With a world-wide economic recession the battle for a share of the available resources often occurs to the detriment of the discipline itself. Paradigms clash and, as Kuhn (1962) has shown, bitter emotional antagonisms and a total rejection of the other results from such clashes. If anything, the internal squabbles have become even more divisive as of late. 'Psychologists live in quarrelsome cultures whose interactions are determined more by temperament than reason' (Kimble, 1994, p. 510). Fox (1996) considers current differences between schools of thought in psychology to be 'marked by more venom and personal animosity' (p. 779) than was the case earlier. As mentioned in the section on Disunity in Clinical Psychology, the relation between the science and the practice of clinical psychology has been described as often complex and hostile (Beutler et al., 1995, p. 984). The South African psychologist, du Preez (1991), pointed out that the rivalry between psychologists from different orientations has become more like gang warfare than harmonious family life. Competitors are ignored or mis-represented. Goalposts are shifted. Rivals are embarrassed by loftily advising them how they should have done what they did. With respect to South African psychology, he wryly observes that those writing about liberation are better at denouncing and unmasking one another than at building.

While major political changes have taken place in the communist bloc of countries and in South Africa, psychology shows little evidence of resolving its paradigm conflicts. Is it too much to hope for the de-emphasis of competitive individualism in order to think and act collaboratively across the sub-disciplines in psychology and the disciplines outside it, as Schneider (1996) proposed? Psychology might yet prove to be more intransigent than the most rigid and conservative political regimes.

In order to identify some of the issues involved in the battle within psychology, the metaphor of cultures within the discipline can perhaps be of value. Peterson (1985) described the ideological conflict in psychology as one between the *cultures of science and practice*. 'The vaunted linkage between science and practice in psychology training and practice . . . has been an area of continuing dispute' (Stricker, 1997, p. 442). More recently, Rice (1997) characterised the tension within psychology in terms of *theory versus practice* or as *science versus profession*. Earlier William James (1907) distinguished between *tough- and tender-minded* intellectual styles, a polarity conceptualised by Kimble (1984) as that between *scientist and humanist* values. Following James, Fodor distinguishes between *rational and naturalistic psychology* (in de Jong, 1992). Rational psychology adheres to the principle of methodological solipsism; that is, mental processes are studied as they exist in the mind, without regard to the environment. Naturalistic psychology, on the other hand, entails a relational concept of mind, focusing on the interaction between the organism and the environment. As previously stated, even before William James, Fechner and Wundt had already highlighted the necessity of an approach to psychology that can account for the psychological phenomena that do not lend themselves to investigation by means of the experimental method. Wundt called this approach *Volkerpsychologie* (indigenous, folk, or cultural psychology) (in Kim, 1990).

Spence (1987) speaks of the *hard-headed and the soft-hearted*, a distinction which is reminiscent of that which has been made between psychology as a *cognitive and an affective science* (Schneider, 1996). Staats (1991) described the historical tension as one between a *natural science psychology and a human science psychology*, which is reminiscent of the earlier description by Sigmund Koch of the *psychological science versus the science–humanism* antinomy (in Leary, Kessel, and Bevan, 1998). In their obituary in honour of Koch, Leary and his colleagues praise this doyen of the discipline for having had the courage to recognise the '"cognitive pathologies" . . . of so many scholars and scientists (including himself) to rule-driven methodological strictures and all-encompassing theoretical dogmas' (pp. 316–317). Manicas and Secord (1983) use the terms *objectivist and subjectivist* to identify the divergence in social theory.

The distinction between the two orientations to psychology can be embedded in the broader cultural context of preferred language use, as elucidated by Omotoso (1994). Writing within an African perspective, Omotoso differentiates between *mind-sets underlying the oral and the writing traditions*. Senghor distinguished between Africa's intuitive and Europe's discursive reasoning. Of all the cultural clashes, which earmark psychology, none has a longer history and is of greater importance than that between the orientation towards psychology as a natural and a human science, or whichever of the above distinctions one wishes to use. The 'values according to which status is ascribed in academic systems' require 'that faculty identify with the scientist role in order to avoid an experience of alienation and failure within the larger institution' (Trierweiler, 1987, p. 410). It is primarily for this reason that the natural science model has prevailed in psychology despite the chorus of voices being raised against it as the dominant paradigm. While the natural science orientation depicts the strength of Euro-American psychology it is also, according to De Groot, a doyen of Dutch psychology, to be held responsible for impoverishing European psychology and deforming psychology around the world (van Strien and Hofstee, 1995).

In a special issue of *The Journal of Mind and Behavior* (Summer/Autumn 1990), devoted to Challenging the Therapeutic State, Farber (1990) stated

> that psychology must choose between two different modes of being in the world. By continuing to pursue the ideal of the objective scientist who can stand outside of history and subject humanity to methodological control, psychology is only succeeding in tightening the 'mind-forged manacles' that prevent human beings from realizing their innate potential. This idolatry of scientific method represents the most tragic kind of epistemological hubris. Its claim to validity is belied by the findings of experimenter bias . . . We are not machines in a mechanical universe but artists in a wonder-land where God (i.e., meaning) is continually assuming unexpected guises, startling us with unpredictable revelations and opportunities. (p. 297)

4

REVISIONING PSYCHOLOGY'S UNDERLYING ASSUMPTIONS

THE ISSUE OF VALUES

Of the many voices which have critically examined the scientific nature of psychology, mentioned in the previous two chapters, several have focused their attention on psychology's attempt to be objective and free of values (eg., Flanagan and Sommers, 1986; Houts and Krasner, 1983; Howard, 1985; Leary, 1983; Manicas and Secord, 1983; Scarr, 1985). According to these concerned authors, psychologists are not neutral truth seekers who follow a value free pursuit of knowledge. Like Shep (in Bronfenbrenner *et al.*, 1986), they believe that psychology is a moral science (Jones, 1994). Even Watson and Skinner who were devout materialists, devoted considerable attention to the topics of values and morality (Hergenhahn, 1994). In fact, not even physics is free of values (Capra, 1982).

Referring to the prospering of psychology in Nazi Germany, Howitt and Owusu-Bempah (1994) regard it as an important lesson for psychology to realise 'that a "neutral science" can be hijacked to serve causes that most psychologists abhor. The ethical basis of the discipline is not grounded in psychological knowledge as such, but in the actions of practitioners. In other words the moral debate that must surround psychology is as vital as its knowledge base and simply cannot be left to take care of itself' (pp. 18–19).

Like some of their colleagues in psychology, Gill and Levidov (1987) maintain that the teaching of science from a value-free/objective/neutral perspective is not possible and that the distinction between science and politics is false. Political priorities guide and eventually determine what is regarded as science and what is researched. Supposedly value-neutral science can, in fact, serve a racist society in many subtle ways and engages the teacher and the pupil in maintaining structural racism.

The flourishing of psychology in South Africa during the apartheid era is an equally telling example of how a scientific discipline can come to serve the political ends of those in power. It also calls for a close examination of the values underlying the practice of mainstream psychology. Louw (1997), an historian of South African psychology, identifies psychological testing as playing an important role both in mediating the professionalisation of psychology in South Africa, and in providing Christian-Nationalism with the basis upon which it legitimised its educational and other policies 'where race played a significant mediating role' (p. 235).

The implications of the political system of apartheid and of a discipline of psychology developed and practised in that system and its colonial predecessor can be likened to the effect of French colonialisation on the medical profession in Algeria. According to Fanon (1965) the 'French medical service in Algeria could not be separated from French colonialism' (p. 123), which was founded on 'military conquest and the police system' (p. 122). Neither can South African psychology be freed from the ideology on which it is based. Indeed, the South African situation illustrates in no uncertain fashion the dangers involved in a psychology that claims to be a science free of values and without acknowledgement of its ideological foundation.

How was it possible for psychology to flourish amidst such an unjust political system that kept power in the hands of the white minority and allowed the exploitation of the socio-economic conditions for the benefit of that minority, culminating in increasing estrangement between the various population groups in the country? Liberal and political aware white psychologists blamed the government but neglected to do any soul searching themselves. They never considered that in asserting the reality of their ethnocentric psychology, they might be part of the problem endemic in the country. In their assumption that psychology was a universal science, they basked in the safety of the premise that the rules of behaviour applicable to them also applied to people belonging to other cultures. The result was that they remained unaware of the existence of alternate realities, and therefore never experienced the need to adapt or change their approach. In their defence it must be said that the South African political structure made it very difficult for people to meet and get to know each other. Although the legacy of apartheid and colonialism continue to bedevil relationships between the people in the country, even after the advent of the new political dispensation, there is no longer any structural excuse for allowing the estrangement to continue. In essence, it is the not knowing of each other and the belief that *a psychological reality* exists that fosters a climate in which prejudice flourishes.

The parallels between contemporary psychology and the political system of apartheid are striking. Although there will certainly be those in psychology who object to such a comparison, an uncanny commonality nevertheless exists between the political system and the professional discipline. The scale of the political experiment was just grander than could ever be envisaged by even the most inclusive of research projects in psychology. In fact, the political experiment approached the ideal of eliminating sampling statistics by involving the total population. The entire country became a laboratory. It is not surprising, therefore, to find critical descriptions of psychology that fit the homelands policy of the Nationalist government like a glove.

As mentioned in Chapter 3, Staats (1981), in his ongoing concern about the fragmentation of psychology, described the discipline as being 'constructed of small islands of knowledge . . . organized in ways that make no connection with the many other existing islands of knowledge' (p. 239). Bevan (1982), similarly, considered psychology to have evolved into a balkanised discipline. Specialisation has given rise to a regressive fragmentation which 'fosters a mind-set characterized by separateness, by competitiveness that is excessive, and by alienation from larger intellectual and human concerns' (Bevan and Kessel, 1994, p. 505).

That the fragmentation and competitiveness characteristic of contemporary psychology also reflect the ideological context within which apartheid developed, is certainly no coincidence, for, as Fanon (1976) has stated, 'The colonial world is a world divided into compartments' (p. 29). Bodibe (in press), a South African psychologist, stressed that the 'Western paradigm gave us the apartheid system'. The same paradigm gave us psychology. It is significant that the father of apartheid was Hendrik Verwoerd, 'at one time the first Professor of Applied Psychology in South Africa, later Prime Minister of the country' (Louw, 1997, p. 251). In his grand political experiment ethnicity constituted the independent variable of interest according to which the country was divided into separate homelands. Unfortunately, the design of his political experiment was flawed in several respects.

Apart from the immorality of assuming total control over the majority population for the benefit of a minority, the independent variable, ethnicity was confounded with concepts of race, culture, language, and socio-economic conditions. South African whites constitute different ethnic, language, cultural and socio-economic groups; yet, in the political experiment ethnicity was not applied to them. The reason for this neglect was presumably due to the notion that ethnicity only related to people of non-Western origin. Even in the confounding of the variables of ethnicity and race, the apartheid experiment closely parallels psychology. Recent debates on ethnicity and race highlight the complexity of these two concepts and psychology's unsophisticated approach to them as variables of importance in determining behaviour (e.g., Helms and Talleyrand, 1997; Phinney, 1996; Rudin, 1997).

The relationship between apartheid politics and psychology can certainly be elaborated extensively. One last remark, relating to the issue of morality, will have to suffice, though. Contrary to psychology's claims to be independent of moral values, the grand designers of apartheid emphasised that they intended the greater good of the people of the country. Nobel Peace Laureate, de Klerk (1995), has stated that 'There was the idealistic objective of liberation by means of the creation of separate states for ethnic groups, that would co-exist within a confederal association' (p. 5). However, as history has indicated, the implementation of that idealistic objective went disastrously wrong in its application. It rapidly developed into a system that was blatantly without any moral consciousness. The change of heart that brought the system to such an astonishing end hopefully happened not just because it became economically unfeasible, but also because of the realisation that it was morally indefensible. Thus, while the implementation of apartheid was repugnant, the moral courage that was required for its termination contrasts sharply with the proclaimed neutrality of psychology. In fact, the reluctance of mainstream psychology to modify its assumptions and methodology in response to the steady stream of criticism levelled at it since its inception is evidence of a reluctance to accommodate alternative perspectives that exceeds even such an undemocratic regime as that of the Nationalist Party of South Africa.

As several feminist writers and others have indicated, the time has arrived to accept that moral values underlie the scientific enterprise (Brown, 1997; Gilligan, 1982; Haan, 1982a,b; Levy, 1984). In so doing we shape the nature of our discipline as surely as when we choose not to consider moral issues. In her acceptance of the Award for Distinguished Professional Contributions from the APA, Brown pointed out the harmful effects of the 'timeworn notion that psychologists can be objective observers, or "pure" scientists' (1997, p. 450). She continued to say, 'psychology may be unique in its attempts to maintain a collective professional mythology of pure empiricism and objectivity in which social constructions of reality are denied or minimized' (p. 450).

In his address on the occasion of receiving the Award for the International Advancement of Psychology at the 105th Annual Convention of the APA in Chicago, Marsella (1998) presented the viewpoint that

> A growing number of non-Western psychologists are noting that the worldwide acceptance and popularity of Western psychology, complete with its academic emphases on the individual, objectivity, quantification, narrow disciplinary specialization, and universal 'truths,' may be irrelevant and meaningless for non-Western people and their life contexts. They argue that international organizations, training programs, research activities, and publications remain rooted within Western psychology and thus cannot serve as the foundation for a psychology that is responsive to our present global context. (p. 1285)

Prilleltensky (1997), therefore, proposed a framework for examining the moral dimensions of psychological discourse and practice. His proposition of an emancipatory communitarian approach for psychology can fit well into an Africentric paradigm. The suggested communitarian approach 'promotes the emancipation of vulnerable individuals and . . . fosters a balance among the values of self-determination, caring and compassion, collaboration and democratic participation, human diversity, and distributive justice' (p. 517).

The plea for a scientific approach, which would be more appropriate to human beings, also finds expression in the juxtapositioning of metaphysical and materialistic values in the scientific process (Akbar, 1984a,b; Bevan, 1991; O'Donohue, 1989; Schwartz, 1990). Bevan is of the opinion that 'psychology's failure to confront fundamental metaphysical issues is what makes it a "would be discipline'" (p. 475). Schwartz contends that the scientific study of values will not progress unless we can accept the metaphysical components of our discipline. O'Donohue points out that 'the practice of science and psychotherapy involve metaphysics to such an extent that the clinical psychologist ought to be considered a metaphysician-scientist-practitioner.' (p. 1460).

Vandenberg (1991) argues that the omission of existential theory in the work of Piaget and other mainstream approaches to development, represents a serious shortcoming in developmental theory. 'Our lives are dominated by central existential concerns, and the recognition of the importance of these issues greatly expands and enriches our understanding of development' (p. 1284). From within the paradigm of transpersonal psychology, Tart (1975a) states that 'Orthodox, Western psychology has dealt very poorly with the spiritual side of human nature, choosing either to ignore its existence or to label it pathological. Yet, much of the agony of our times stems from a spiritual vacuum' (p. 5). James Hillman (1975) echoes the view of Tart and others. According to Hillman, 'this psychology, for which we erect great buildings to which the students flock, with its libraries, lectures and laboratories, journals and therapies, mental health clinics and mental health grants, has been and still is impotent. Nothing, nothing, nothing . . . Its pragmatism, whether in clinic or in laboratory, kills fantasy or subverts it into the service of practical goals' (p. 220). Hillman pleads passionately for the restoration of the psyche of psychology. And with him and the others, so do I. Without acknowledgement of the role of values in psychology and of the metaphysical dimensions of our discipline, there can be no hope of coming to an understanding and integration of the indigenous psychological perspectives of Africa.

UNIVERSAL LAWFULNESS AND OBJECTIVITY REPRESENT FAILED ASPIRATIONS

A great deal of psychology's investment has focused on establishing general rules that guide the behaviour of people everywhere (nomothetic lawfulness – Kimble, 1994). However, as extensive as the search for universal laws has been, it has not succeeded in eliminating the fact that however carefully people are classified in terms of some criteria, individual differences continue to be the rule rather than the exception. Individuals simply defy classification in general and overall terms (ideographic lawfulness). It is likely that the nomothetic orientation in psychology will turn out to be one of the discipline's most extensive and expensive wild-goose chases. Perhaps more progress towards the discovery of general principles governing behaviour could have been made if the focus of the discipline had been ideographic rather than nomothetic. Nomothetic science has been highly successful in dealing with the set of experiences we attribute to physical reality, and it has historically become associated with the philosophy of physicalism, the belief that physical reality exists independently of our perception of it, and is the ultimate reality. Thus the philosophy of physicalism says that a good explanation is an explanation which describes things in terms of physical matter and its properties and interactions.

(Tart, 1975a, p. 21)

Out of the philosophy of physicalism grew the idea of detached observation. The act of observing was supposed to have no effect on the phenomena observed. The falsity of this assumption has been pointed out, not only in psychology (Jourard, 1971; Rosenthal, 1966), but also in the physical sciences. In fact, the physical chemist, Polanyi (1960), speaks of the 'crippling mutilations imposed by an objectivist framework' (p. 381). He contends that once we have rid ourselves of these false assumptions 'many fresh minds will turn to the task of reinterpreting the world as it is' (p. 381). In *Personal Knowledge*, Polanyi argues with rigorous logic that the scientist's personal participation in his/her knowledge, in both its discovery and its validation, is an indispensable part of science itself. Even in the exact sciences, 'knowing' is an art, of which the skill of the knower, guided by a passionate sense of increasing contact with reality, is a logically necessary part. In the biological and social sciences the relation between the scientist and scientific information becomes even more apparent.

The experimenter, unwittingly, has a considerable effect in determining the results of his or her experiments. By acknowledging the dialogical nature of the experimental relationship and structuring the experimental procedure accordingly, we can, as Jourard (1971) has shown, obtain diametrically opposite effects than by the orthodox objective approach. Yet, the implicit trust in the physicalistic paradigm underlying the scientific study of psychology is so ingrained that it has prevented the discipline from listening to the facts obtained by its own methodology. I have even experienced the experimenter effect in research with rats in the laboratory. During the period when I was investigating the importance of the subcortical areas of the brain in behaviour, I was working with animals of which the septal region of the brain was lesioned, making previously docile animals highly reactive. Three of us tested the animals routinely on different days according to a standard procedure involving a specific behavioural task. All it really involved was taking the animals from their home cages and placing them in the test situation. However, we consistently obtained amazingly different results. It became clear that the explanation lay in the way we handled the animals.

Apart from obtaining false or, at best, biased results, another consequence of the belief in the notion of an objective observer has been the absence of courses in self-awareness in the training of psychologists. When such courses are included in the curriculum, orthodox psychology uses its considerable power to combat their legitimacy. For instance, external examiners have refused to evaluate essays or examination questions, which dealt with the experiential component of courses I have taught. My evaluation of such essays has also been criticised as being subjective. The fact is, however, that the degree of factual information relating to the bodily and emotional awareness of students during the writing of an examination can be evaluated as 'objectively' as any other information.

In keeping with the ideographic paradigm, it has been said that it would have been better to focus on the self in order to understand others, than to have studied others in an attempt to understand the self. However, even in instances where the focus has been ideographic, the self has been approached exclusively as an independent unit of the social system. As will be discussed in a later chapter, it is now realised that the self is by nature dialogical. As such it is continually interactive. Within the changing pattern of relationships within which it manifests, the construal of the self is continually adjusted and readjusted. Viewing the self as an ongoing process, an open system, evolving in the context of other open systems, it should be obvious that it is virtually impossible to concretise all the variables that constitute the individual as a dialogical entity existing in time. Yet, much of psychology continues to regard the person, in analogy to the old physics upon which it is modelled, as a closed entity that can be defined and described with and within certain universal parameters.

If the discipline persists in using the exact sciences as an example of how to be scientific, it will do better to choose as a model the 'new' physics of Bohr, Heisenberg, Prigogine, and others, and not the classical physics of Newton and his compatriots. In the early part of the twentieth century, the new physics, as it is today called, has already broken with the concept of the universe as a 'giant Newtonian billiard table' made up of a 'complex of distinct things and boundaries' (Wilber, 1981, p. 36). Physicists have come to view the structure of the outer universe of space, as well as the inner universe of the atom, as something akin to a spider's web, where in the words of the novelist, Thomas Hardy, every part quivers when one point is touched. Once having adopted its scientific model, psychology unfortunately has not kept pace with the advances in science. If physicists consider things and events, from the molar universe to the molecular atom to be mutually dependent and interactive, then psychologists can do well to think of persons who are the units of the discipline in the same light. We, too, are interconnected webs of relations whose parts are only defined through their connections to the whole. This is what indigenous African philosophy believes.

However, the recognition of the importance of the ideographic approach to the study of behaviour does not deny that there are undoubtedly basic principles that underlie the behaviour of people everywhere, even if the form in which these principles find expression will differ. After all, we all derive from a common African heritage. Progress in evolutionary psychology and behaviour genetics has provided the rationale for examining universals of human nature that transcend cultural differences (McCrae and Costa, 1997). Considerable progress has also been made in classifying intelligence, personality, attitudes and interests with the aid of psychometric procedures and factor analysis. For instance, assessing personality in terms of the five-factor model revealed a remarkably similar trait structure between men and women drawn from the United states, Israel, Germany, Portugal, Korea, Japan, and China (McCrae and Costa, 1997). Since the people in the samples spoke languages representative of five different language families that together include the native tongues of most of the earth's inhabitants (languages indigenous to sub-Saharan Africa were notable omissions), the experimenters concluded that a common human structure of personality seemed likely to exist. While the power of such statistical techniques as factor analysis, which was used in the study of McCrae and Costa, is evident, its limitations to build classifications in the social sciences must also be realised. Dimensions identified are not exclusive of each other and share common variance. Neither is it possible for all the variables to be identified as belonging to any of the classifications.

Only recently have psychologists begun to question the assumption of universality underlying the paradigms of their discipline. It is gradually being realised that the variation in the behaviour and beliefs of individuals are super-imposed upon variations in the behaviour and beliefs of the groups they belong to. The tendency towards universality, which has earmarked the development of psychology thus far, is steadily being replaced by the recognition that while there may be common elements underlying the behaviour of people everywhere, cognisance has to be taken of the interaction of such common elements with the multiplicity of belief systems within and between groups of people. The seeming paradox between the ideographic and the nomothetic approaches to psychology relates to the distinction between Africa and the West in terms of the approach to psychology as a quantitative, empirical, and natural science versus the approach as a qualitative, contextual, and human science.

BELIEF IN BELIEF

Another seeming paradox in psychology relates to the belief in factual data, but not in the primacy of belief itself. In its positivistic quest psychology rejects all unseen postulated forces or entities as nonsense. 'The first commandment of positivism is the prohibition on transcendent entities . . . and the first transcendent entity to go is the idea of a reality hidden behind appearances' (Shweder, 1994, p. 57). However, 'The things (humans have) created with (their minds) and worshipped in the spirit are as real to (them) as the material things (they have) made with (their) hands. The belief in the supernatural and in the immortality of the soul must be accepted as real facts that have led to action and results' (van Beek and Blakely, 1994, p. 19). The words of St Augustine of so many centuries ago are as true today as they were then. He wrote that 'I do not seek to know in order to believe, but I believe in order to know – for human wisdom will break itself on the rock of faith ere it breaks that rock.' In the *Center of the Cyclone*, John Lilly expressed the idea that, 'In the province of the mind, what is believed to be true is true or becomes true within certain limits, to be found experientially and experimentally. These limits are beliefs to be transcended. In the province of the mind there are no limits' (in Tart, 1975a, p. 62). 'Thoughts influence all living things' was the way Matthew Manning phrased this universal truth.

The placebo effect has long been known, although the role of belief in the effect has not received sufficient recognition. However, mental health workers are coming to respect the importance of belief in accounting for the power of the placebo effect. As long as patients believe they could be getting a 'real' drug, the administered agent can alleviate symptoms or even cure a disease. In analysing recent research, Enserink (1999) reports that the placebo effect is coming to be seen 'not as a problem but as a source of insight into mental health' (p. 238). The sheer size of the phenomenon 'suggests that it is an integral part of the effectiveness of almost all antidepressant drugs' (p. 239). Enserink cites the meta-analysis of 19 antidepressant trials done by Kirsch, a psychologist from the University of Connecticut, in which Kirsch attributed 75 per cent of the 'real' antidepressant drug effect to the placebo effect. Kirsch went even further. In arguing 'that even the 25% "real" drug effect might be little more than a disguised placebo effect' (p. 240), he challenged 'the scientific basis of much of the multibillion-dollar market for antidepressant drugs' (p. 238).

The reality of the intangible reality comes to expression through the use of a variety of terms. Invariably, mind, spirit, consciousness, belief, conviction, mental representation, dream, image, imagination, myth, and symbolism, have been invoked to convey the domain of the unverifiable reality. Each of these terms deserves to be discussed in full, not only because they represent the forgotten dimension of contemporary psychology, but also because they represent important dimensions of African psychology. Unfortunately, only brief reference to some of the terms can be made here. Neither will the differences between the concepts be discussed. After all, books have been written on each of them.

In his theory of knowledge, Whitehead (1927) advanced the thesis that symbolism in its widest sense was an important factor in the way human beings functioned. Symbolism is 'no mere idle fancy or corrupt degeneration, it is inherent in the very texture of human life; language itself is a symbol' (p. 62). Cassirer, similarly, argues that symbolism, which for him includes language and myth, is a proper source of human knowledge on par with the senses and mathematics (in Agyakwa, 1976).

That poets see beyond the appearance of things is not surprising. The literary critic and poet, C. Day Lewis (1965) said that there 'are such things as unverifiable truths' (p. 35). The poetic image is one such truth. According to Lewis, the power of the poetic image is to be found in its ability to reveal the unity underlying all phenomena as well as the discovery of new relationships. For Baudelaire, 'Great poetry is essentially stupid; it believes and that is what makes its glory and force.' 'Hell is a state of mind,' Goethe wrote, while Emerson stated that 'The foundations of man are not in matter, but in spirit.' According to James Allen (1959, p. 1):

> Mind is the Master power that moulds and makes,
> And Man is Mind, and evermore he takes.
> The tool of Thought, and, shaping what he wills,
> Bring forth a thousand joys, a thousand ills:
> He thinks in secret, and it comes to pass!
> Environment is but his looking-glass.

Gerard Manley Hopkins portrayed the imponderable depth of the mind by invoking the imagery of nature. Of the many instances where Hopkins utilised the outer landscape to portray, what he described as the 'inscape', he wrote that:

> mind has mountains; cliffs of fall
> Frightful, sheer, no-man-fathomed.
> (in Milward and Schoder,
> 1975, p. 83)

If psychology had more affinity for literature the discipline would perhaps not have strayed so far from acknowledging the potential of the human mind.

> . . . Not Chaos, not
> The darkest pit of lowest Erebus,
> Nor aught of blinder vacancy, scooped out
> By help of dreams, can breed such fear and awe
> As fall upon us when we look
> Into our Minds, into the Mind of Man,
> My haunt, and the main region of my song.
> (Wordsworth, in Lewis, 1965, p. 60)

According to neuropsychologist, Kenneth Pelletier (1978), 'consciousness is primary to matter'. In my pocket diaries of past years I have noted various authors proclaiming that the physical universe was spirit in form. Sir Laurens van der Post often stated that in the beginning there was a dream and that dream demanded that it should be lived. This dream was with God and indeed was God. Eastern philosophies believe as strongly, if not more strongly in the primacy of the mind and its 'inscapes'. Aurobindo stated that spirit was the subtlest form of matter and the densest form of spirit, while the Bhagavad Gita stresses that we are made by our belief. When the mind is able to turn inward upon itself, the realisation of Atman becomes possible (Prabhavananda and Isherwood, 1953). 'The mind is everything, what you think you become,' the Buddha is considered to have said.

Within formal religious practices, the power of convictions to shape one's understanding and interpretation of the world is undoubtedly better realised than in a psychology that is battling to make its peace with the fact that the mind is everything but empty. Nürnberger (1988) talks of the power of religiously held beliefs as 'convictions' and 'ultimate convictions'. However, convictions do not necessarily have to be rooted in one form of religion or another.

Recently, several psychologists have joined their colleagues from other disciplines in affirming the centrality of belief in the determination of behaviour. According to Scarr (1985), we 'cannot perceive or process knowledge without the constraints of belief' (p. 499). According to Tart (1975a), 'Every action we undertake and every thought we have rests on an assumption – and usually many assumptions' (p. 61). Brown (1997) wrote that particular standpoints create the lens through which understanding human behaviour is, or is not achieved. Kipnis (1997) stated that 'our mental representations of the world and the choices we make on the basis of these representations, govern our behavior' (p. 208), a view in keeping with the so-called cognitive revolution. Although present-day cognitive psychologists are still hesitant to call a spade a spade and embrace belief wholeheartedly as an important cognitive variable, their acknowledgement of the concept of mind nevertheless represents a giant step away from the logical positivism of the past decades (Holdstock, 1994a).

Hillman (1975) does not have any fears in invoking parameters of the mind to convey his archetypal concepts. In fact, he steps into the archaeology of the psyche by invoking the primacy of images. According to him, image is at the basis of every action and of each object. Soul's first freedom is 'the freedom to imagine' (p. 39). Discussing the appropriate framework required in anthropology for understanding the different ways in which alternate realities, markedly different from one's own, are manifested, Shweder (1994) uses language similar to that of Hillman. According to Shweder, 'the senses and logic alone cannot bridge the gap between existence and pure being. Left to their own devices, all that the senses and logic can see is a mindless nature, "fallen and dead." Transcendental things are beyond their scope. To make contact with the really real, the inspired (= divinelike) imagination of human beings must be projected out to reality; or, alternatively, the gods must descend to earth' (p. 9).

It is doubtful that the fundamental importance of images and of individual and collective belief systems we construe on the basis of these images in shaping the consciousness of Western, and especially African, people can be emphasised enough. To acknowledge the importance of images does not deny the influence of the evolving technologies on human behaviour. As Kipnis (1997) has pointed out, modern technology is shaping and reshaping human behaviour and consciousness in dramatic ways. Just think of the tremendous impact of advances in transport and communication systems, especially computer networking. However, all the technological developments were initially conceived as images in the minds of their inventors. Companies and organisations are known to conduct think-tanks, when practical issues need solving, where the name of the game is playing with images.

Belief is not only personal, but collective as well. Mainstream psychology has not only neglected the importance of personally held beliefs, but also failed to acknowledge the influence of culturally held beliefs on privately held ones (Holdstock, 1994a). The disregard of psychology for collective belief systems results most probably from its unawareness of its own ideological embeddedness, which goes hand in hand with the monocultural nature of the discipline. In its ethnocentrism psychology has assumed, naïvely or arrogantly, depending on ones point of view, that its belief system is universally valid. With others, Bevan pleads for a thorough examination of the ideological assumptions underlying psychology. He implores psychologists to become aware of how they perpetuate the mythologies underlying the institutional structures of their discipline and profession (Bevan, 1991; Bevan and Kessel, 1994; Fox, 1986; Rogoff and Chavajay, 1995).

Writing from an Africentric perspective, Myers (1993, p. 5) stated that the way we view the world was so

> important because it ultimately determines our experience, our history. All people view the world based upon a particular belief system which, at another level, is structured by a conceptual system, i.e., the philosophical assumptions and principles on which one's beliefs are based. Often, these assumptions are not part of our conscious awareness; yet, the assumptions shape our beliefs. The conceptual system through which we relate to reality determines the way we perceive, think, feel, and experience the world. In the West we seldom entertain the idea that there may be a way to perceive the world differently from the way in which we were socialized to perceive it. In the context of human history the intellectual hegemony of the West is short-lived, yet it has effected some devastating consequences never before witnessed in recorded history.

In her *Understanding an Afrocentric World View*, Myers (1993) refers to blind adherence to a belief system as a mental bondage, which Hilliard described as a form of invisible violence. She, therefore, stresses the importance of becoming aware of the embeddedness of one's thinking in the cognitive structure of the dominant culture. 'The importance of the subjective in cognitive processes must be stressed, but the psychogenesis of an individual's knowledge is the social context through which meanings have been ascribed' (p. 88) . . . 'the social context of the psychogenesis of knowledge must also be examined in reference to cultural world view and its particular conceptual system' (p. 89).

The scientific era requires a paradigm shift in its attitude towards what constitutes fact. Generally held beliefs are as real as any scientific fact. At times they are even more real, especially in their effects. Science forgets that it, too, is but the enactment of a mythological theme. It forgets that the primary motivating principles operative in our laboratories are really grounded in mythology, that our search for the first principles, the return to the origin, the yearning after the creation of things, are but an enactment of the mythology living in us. By manipulating variables that are observable and amenable to control in an 'objective' manner psychology believes that it will arrive at the essential truths underlying human nature and unravel the mysteries of human existence. It, furthermore, unquestioningly accepts that to achieve its goal, increasingly detailed and careful inspection and dissection of the parts that make up the whole will be necessary.

Not only have poets throughout the ages marvelled about the power of the human mind, but they have been equally ecstatic about the power of imagination. To Shelley, the imagination was God, and he himself its prophet: 'Imagination is the immortal God which should assume flesh for the redemption of mortal passion' (in Lewis, 1965, p. 65). However, Shelley's idea of imagination was also very down to earth and included empathy, which allowed him to speak of imagination as 'the great instrument of moral good' (in Lewis, 1965, p. 29). According to Keats, 'The imagination may be compared to Adam's dream – he awoke and found it true' (in Lewis, 1965, p. 27). This image of Keats says that imagination has miraculous qualities that need not rise to conscious awareness in order for substance and truth to be created from it. In keeping with Shelley, William Blake called Jesus the Imagination.

Unfortunately psychology has lost the ability to perceive with wonder, for wonders crowd so thick and fast around us that we have become totally desensitised to the magnificence of the natural and man-made world. And even if we still have a feeling for the spirit or essence of things, it is quite divorced from the sense of their material utility. At the conference of the International Transpersonal Association in Kyoto, Japan during the 1980s, the African sage, to whom I referred in Chapter 2 with respect to Carl Rogers, remarked how untranspersonal the transpersonal people were. For instance an astronaut who had walked in outer space delivered a paper totally devoid of any wonder about the experience, whereas stepping onto an 'ordinary' plane was sufficient inspiration for the African sage to be moved to express his experience in verse.

> Things were different when men felt their programme
> In the bones and pulse, not only in the brain,

MacNeice wrote in his *Autumn Journal* (in Lewis, 1965, p. 109). The image allows a drawing-back from the actual, the better to come to grips with it. Thus, every successful image is a sign of an encounter with the real meaning behind the appearance of things. The power of the image lies in its ability to express empathy and oneness with the natural world and the relationship between things and feelings, to claim kinship with everything that lives or has lived.

Images satisfy the human yearning for order and for completeness, they tie together intangible elements in the universe; they harmonise, as Housman said, 'the sadness of the world'; they persuade us through the power of their vitality, and our answering sense of revelation, that soul there must be – that there is beneath the appearance of things a life whose quality may not be apprehended in our everyday intercourse nor be gauged by the instruments of science. Thus, in order to reach towards 'That something still which prompts the eternal sigh,' we have to restore the imaginative in our lives and in our psychology. The restoration of the image does not mean literal reinstitution of the image in what we see but in the way we see it. It means bringing the imaginal perspective, bringing fantasy, to all that we encounter. And with that change of view we come to view ourselves differently. We see that we too are ultimately a composition of images. Without an appreciation of the power and the importance of the imaginative, African psychological dimensions cannot be comprehended.

THE IMPORTANCE OF MYTHOLOGY

Of the many aspects of the mind, which require recognition, none is in greater need of attention than the way it is collectively manifested in the mythology underlying the belief systems and practices of the various cultures. Mythology is the master software programme directing the affairs of even the most advanced technologies. As Bevan (1991) and other psychologists have remarked, we are quite unaware of the extent to which the essential mythological themes are manifested in mainstream psychology. The primary motivating principles operative in the carrying out of our daily affairs is really to be found in mythology, in the dream dreaming us, as the San of the Kalahari desert believe. Myths inevitably reveal that the world, and the life of humans in this world, has a supernatural origin and history and that this history is significant, precious, and exemplary. Myth is a resurrection of primeval reality. It is a vital ingredient of human civilisation, a statement of faith and moral wisdom of a more relevant reality, by which the existence and activities of humankind are determined (Campbell, 1973; Eliade, 1964, 1967; Malinowski, 1926).

In his monumental *Historical Atlas of World Mythology*, Joseph Campbell (1983), the internationally recognised authority on mythology, wrote that myths and mythic symbols, not only inspired and gave rise to civilisations, but also ensouled modern science. According to him the formulae of science remained dead unless they could be read as tokens, not only of practical information, but also of life's mystery.

Campbell (1983) attributes four functions to mythology, the first of which is the mystical. It is intended 'to waken and maintain in the individual a sense of wonder and participation in the mystery of this finally inscrutable universe' (p. 8). The second is 'cosmological – that of converting every feature of the locally envisioned order of nature into, as it were, an icon or figure revelatory of Yahweh, Tirawa, Shiva, Huracan, or the Tao' (p. 9). The third function 'is the sociological one of validating and maintaining whatever moral system and manner of life-customs may be peculiar to the local culture' (p. 9). 'A fourth, and final, essential function of mythologies, then, is the pedagogical one of conducting individuals in harmony through the passages of human life' (p. 9).

Despite its advances, modern science, with psychology in the forefront, unfortunately, negates or is ignorant of the mythology underlying its own frame of reference. The scientific community, in general, derides the mythological consciousness at the base of its own belief system and that of African cultures. Invariably the holistic worldview of African cultures is labelled with such negative connotations as animism, anthropomorphism, and personalism, or referred to as an innocent idealisation.

The power of 'mythical consciousness' has been recognised earlier in this century by some anthropologists, cultural historians, and psychologists, notably Carl Jung. According to Malinowski (in van der Hooft, 1979), 'Myth is ... live actuality, not dead past' (p. 40). Myth is knowing the unknown. According to Eliade (in van der Hooft, 1979), mythology represents the ultimate reality. It represents the essential means according to which order is established in the world in which we live. Without mythology life was not possible. With Mead, Levi-Strauss and others, Leenhardt, a missionary, in contrast to many of their predecessors in theology and the social sciences, came to recognise that the thinking of the non-Western peoples they came into contact with was indeed not illogical, but fittingly appropriate to the belief system they adhered to.

The dream dreaming Africentric psychology begins in mythology. It is a big dream, one that aspires towards godhood, towards realising the wonder and essence of all things. It endeavours to imbue life with meaning, sacrilising the animate as well as the inanimate world around us. In searching for its essential nature in the context of mythology, Africentric psychology hopes to come to an understanding of the origin and essential nature of things, of the purposive character of the universe. In a very real sense, African psychology dreams of redeeming, not only the discipline and profession of psychology, but of the entire human condition. It dreams of initiating a science that will enable us to understand the universal nature of our being, of establishing a relationship with the world around us. What Coleridge has said of poetry can be applied equally well to Africentric psychology, 'in ideal perfection', it 'brings the whole soul of man into activity'.

5

CULTURE
The Achilles heel of psychology

The political change which has occurred following the withdrawal of the colonial powers from Africa, and the momentous transfer of political control recently in South Africa, undoubtedly have far reaching implications for psychology and the other social sciences on the continent. Apart from coping with the problems in living which arise under ordinary circumstances, the violence, the turmoil, and the estrangement, created by Africa's colonial past, have bequeathed on the continent a socio-economic-political- and psychological legacy which has significant implications for mental health.

It is not only in a clinical sense that psychology in Africa faces a daunting task. Following the distinction that Cook (1985) made between a reactive and a pro-active approach to psychology, the discipline's greatest challenge is of a proactive nature. An equally thorough revisioning of the existing practices of psychology on the African continent is required as has occurred in politics, if the obligation, which DeLeon and others feel the discipline has to society, is to be fulfilled (DeLeon, Sammons, and Sexton, 1995). How can the common good best be served by psychology? In an article entitled, 'Who must do the hard things?' Payton (1984) questioned psychology's responsibility with respect to social issues. Do we have a role as social change agents or are we basically restricted to doing research and conducting psychotherapy (Albee, 1982; Russell, 1984; Sarason, 1981)? Kagitçibasi (1995), the Turkish developmental psychologist, points out that although 'there are some psychologists who are keenly aware of social issues and who have been involved in pioneering service-oriented research in such areas as public health, family planning, education, rehabilitation in war and conflict . . . the relative number of psychologists so involved is quite small' (p. 293). She would like to see the concept of human development extended to be more in keeping with how it is defined by the United Nations. The agencies of the organisation conceive of human development in such macro terms as 'life expectancy at birth, access to health services, access to safe water, access to sanitation, daily calorie supply (percentage of requirements), adult literacy, combined primary and secondary school enrolment rates, daily newspaper circulation' (p. 293), etc.

Moghaddam (1990), similarly, points out that psychologists in all three psychological worlds, discussed in Chapter 2, tend to be modulative in orientation. They react to, rather than instigate societal change. What is needed is a 'generative psychology' that attempts to initiate and influence macrolevel change. Such a 'generative psychology' will have important and widespread implications. It entails 'despecialisation' in focusing on the relationship between psychology and power structures, the role of psychological factors in national development, and the relationship between the speed of change in psychological, economic, and other spheres.

Closer to the traditional ways in which psychology's relevance is conceptualised, one of the most crucial questions facing the discipline in Africa is whether it can help those who have been colonised to reinvent themselves amidst the turmoil bequeathed by the colonial era. What role can psychology play to imbue the people of Africa with a trust in the uniqueness of their African heritage in order to aid them in the preparation for the task ahead? Perhaps it is unrealistic to expect psychology to be able to facilitate the undoing of some of the effects of colonialisation, seeing that it is a brainchild of the same mind that has been responsible for such widespread exploitation of and domination on the African continent. Before that can happen, perhaps the discipline will first have to reinvent itself.

Apart from avoiding the pitfalls into which mainstream psychology has fallen, the proactive or generative challenge awaiting the discipline in Africa consists primarily in the considered withholding of itself in its traditional role. To do, in accordance with the Zen principle of *wu-wei*, by not doing (Watts, 1957). It means thinking of psychology along the lines suggested by Kagitçibasi and Moghaddam. It also means not setting up psychology as the domain of experts, but referring to the community as the experts. As psychologists the best we can do is to facilitate the community, which may consist of materially poor and oppressed majorities, to develop both a critical awareness of their condition and an appreciation of their strengths.

However, before we can facilitate a critical awareness in large cultural groups, we have to work on how we regard our own role as psychologists, to place the discipline under scrutiny, as Gergen and his colleagues (1996) recommended. At the present stage of development, merely an awareness of the dangers inherent in an uncritical adoption of mainstream paradigms can go a long way towards preventing the perpetuation of psychology as a colonial enterprise. In conjunction with a critical attitude towards the status quo in psychology, the proactive challenge also requires openness to the indigenous psychological principles and practices that are of relevance to self and cultural empowerment in Africa.

As is evident from the previous chapters, the assumptions underlying mainstream psychology have come under meticulous scrutiny by some of the doyens of the discipline and the profession. In his Presidential address to the American Psychological Association in 1982, Bevan, for example, wanted to know who psychologists really were. If the professional identity of American psychologists is an issue in need of clarification, the same is undoubtedly true of their African counterparts. Most African psychologists have been trained according to mainstream principles, with little or no acknowledgement of indigenous African psychological realities. Because such training is considered to constitute *real* education, the institutionalisation of structure and accreditation ensures that the graduates will be unlikely to sacrifice their hard-earned professional status, even if its relevance is of questionable validity. As far as American psychology is concerned, Green (1980) acknowledged that it would be difficult for them to break free from the mainstream mould in which they have been trained, but warned that such training offered 'a far too narrow human constituency' (p. 343) to serve as a viable base for the discipline of psychology. It will behove psychologists in Africa to heed the warning issued in the American context.

MULTICULTURALISM IN PSYCHOLOGY

The growing realisation in psychology of the importance of culture in determining the way we feel and think and behave (Betancourt and López, 1993; Bevan and Kessel, 1994; Bhavnani and Phoenix, 1994; Fowers and Richardson, 1996; Fowler, 1996; Gergen *et al.*, 1996; Hall, 1997; Hall *et al.*, 1997; Landrine, 1992; Lee, 1994; Levine, 1970; Locke, 1992; Matsumoto, Kudoh, and Takeuchi, 1996; McGovern, Furumoto, Halpern, Kimble, and McKeachie, 1991; Miles, 1996; Minoura, 1996; Myers, 1993; Phinney, 1996; Phinney and Devich-Navarro, in press; Reid, 1994; Rogoff and Chavajay, 1995; Rosenzweig, 1984; Shweder, 1994; Shweder and Sullivan, 1993; Staub, 1996; Tomasello, 1996; Toomela, 1996a,b; van der Veer, 1996; Voestermans, 1992a,b), is of special significance to African psychology. Culture has been defined in a multitude of ways. According to many authors (see Bodibe, 1993; Patel, 1997) there is no best definition of culture. Jahoda (1984) regards it as an elusive and Triandis (1996) as a controversial term. Draguns (1982) describes culture as 'a global and complex variable of high order of abstraction' (p. 54).

However difficult it may be to find a satisfactory operational definition of culture, it is certain that 'Each person is embedded within a variety of socio-cultural contexts or cultures (e.g., country or region of origin, ethnicity, religion, gender, family, birth cohort, profession). Each of these cultural contexts makes some claim on the person and is associated with a set of ideas and practices (i.e., a cultural framework or schema)' (Markus and Kitayama, 1994, pp. 91–92). The ideas represent the cultural 'software' and the practices the cultural 'hardware'. In the context of this book, the framework referred to when culture is spoken of incorporates both. Staub (1996) referred to cultural 'software' as 'the perspectives and meanings shared by members of a group: their views of the world and of themselves; their beliefs, values, and norms of conduct; their myths and conceptions of God and the spiritual' (p. 117; also Al-Issa, 1982). In his description of culture as a system of meanings, Geertz (1971) describes human beings as animals suspended in webs of significance they have spun themselves. According to social constructionism, all cultural enterprises are 'constituted by shared understandings, the values and mores of everyday life, and the everyday practices that express and construct those values' (Cushman, 1991, p. 207).

Culture not only incorporates and expresses the societal and physical embodiment of these conceptual frameworks and practices, but is also determined by them, as it is by the geographical situatedness of the group. In the context of African societies, it means that there are commonalties as well as differences between the people on the continent. And within each of the principal groups are subdivisions based on such factors as language, gender, religion, and socio-economic status.

Even within the approach to science different cultural orientations can be depicted (e.g., Snow, 1963). The same holds for organisations (e.g., den Hartog 1997) and for psychology, as the faction fighting between the sub-disciplines indicates. An intricate relationship exists between the more and the less encompassing group determinants of culture. One or more of the lesser determinants can be more influential in determining the experience of culturally belonging than some of the more molar determinants.

Furthermore, as anthropologists have indicated, the concept of culture does not imply a static, but a dynamic concept. However, in the process of evolving, the existing cultural belief systems, practices (e.g., schools, legal system, religion, police, the family), and behaviour patterns are not eliminated, but incrementally adjusted, with the core remaining relatively unaltered. It is especially in the interaction of people who have different belief systems in a situation of cultural change that new meanings as well as new opportunities are created (van Beek and Blakely, 1994).

Voestermans (1992b) described the failure to consider the extent to which 'the form of mental processes may be affected by culture' (p. 339) as the Achilles heel of much of psychological research. According to Smedslund (1984), culture constitutes the invisible obvious in psychology. Betancourt and López (1993) pointed out that, 'The main limitation of mainstream theories is that they ignore culture and therefore lack universality' (p. 634). Shweder (1994) describes psychology as the 'nonsocial social science', indifferent 'to the "extrinsic" stuff of culture, society, meaning and context' (p. 95). As Trimble (1988) has pointed out, less than 1 per cent of the pages of 14 prominent social psychology texts gives the concept of culture attention in any form. In South African psychology culture is not simply neglected, but actively rejected as a major factor in shaping behaviour and belief (e.g., Dawes and Davids, 1983; Nell, 1990). However, as Sampson (1994) states, it is necessary to realise that 'differential forms of consciousness' result 'as a function of persons' historical and socio-cultural locations' (p. 818). In the words of Sapir, 'the worlds in which different societies live are distinct worlds, not merely the same world with different labels attached' (in Shweder, 1994, p. 97). 'In many areas of the world, psychologists are working to establish local varieties of psychology that are compatible with and appropriate to the local culture' (Rosenzweig, 1984, p. 880). According to Triandis (1996) 'each culture may have, at least to some extent, its own psychology' (p. 407). 'Respect for differences – up to a point and if they are without malevolent effect – is part of all respectable moral systems' (Haan, 1982b). Just 'as our biogenetic diversity is life enhancing, so also can be our sociocultural diversity' (Penn and Kiesel, 1994, p. 399).

Equally many voices have admonished therapists to be culturally sensitive (Brent and Callwood, 1993; Durie and Hermansson, 1990; Jackson and Sears, 1992; López et al., 1989; Rogler, Malgady, Constantino, and Blumenthal, 1987; Sue and Zane, 1987). Special journal issues have been devoted to cultural factors in understanding and assessing psychopathology (Butcher, 1987), although the necessary caution of overemphasising the influence of culture has also been voiced (Jovanovski, 1995). Hermans and Kempen (1998) warned against an overemphasis on cultural dichotomies, which they considered to constitute a 'perilous problem'. However, the neglect or avoidance of cultural realities poses as serious a problem for psychology. In failing to credit cultural identity with a central role in international and national politics, as well as in the everyday lives of people, we are burying our heads in the sand like the proverbial ostrich. The increasing fragmentation of the world order, in terms of groups adhering to some cultural identity or another, is an equally if not an even more astounding phenomenon than globalisation (Holdstock, 1999).

Valid as the call for a focus on the contact zones of cultures certainly is, it applies primarily to those instances where the technological advances that make globalisation possible are experienced. Concentration of psychology at this level is likely to perpetuate the exclusivity that has inhibited the international development of the discipline and the profession. Despite globalisation, the majority of the world's population does not experience its effects at first hand. These are the people about and from whom psychology has to learn more by indwelling in their frames of reference with an approach that is in keeping with the worldview of the cultures about which we would like to know more.

Multicultural courses have been introduced in psychology programmes. The APA and other psychology groups are hosting a variety of conferences on multicultural issues. Books with *indigenous psychology* in the title or with an emphasis on indigenous psychology are increasingly being published (e.g., Burlew, Banks, McAdoo, and Azibo, 1992; Heelas and Lock, 1981; Kim, 1990; Kim and Berry, 1993; Roland, 1992; Rosenberger, 1992). New journals with a cultural emphasis have emerged, e.g., *Ethnic and Cultural Studies, Ethnic and Racial Studies, Journal of Multilingual and Multicultural Development*, and the *European Journal of Intercultural Studies*. Existing journals devote increasing space to ethnic-minority research and clinical issues (Sleek, 1998). After 20 years of publication, the *International Journal of Intercultural Relations* has increased its size by 100 pages in order to accommodate the influx of new material in this subject area. However, caution has also been expressed about regarding the burgeoning of research in ethnic and cultural psychology as an indication 'that the field is responding to the pressure of indigenous peoples and people of colour that psychology be more responsive to and reflexive about their realities' (Comas-Díaz et al., 1998, p. 780). These authors claim that a *psychology of liberation* that draws on and responds to the realities of a broader swath of humanity still has to be realised. The quality of multicultural education, similarly, needs to be improved (Sleek, 1998).

However, an additional benefit of the new consciousness about culture is not just cognisance of other cultural frameworks, but the realisation of the value and the limitations of the culture to which one belongs: 'For psychologists and other behavioral scientists concerned with socially relevant phenomena, efforts to understand the world views, value orientations, and belief systems of their own society may help them to rise above their preconceptions and to open their research and theories to other possibilities' (Spence, 1985, p. 1286).

The worldview of sub-Saharan Africa differs to such an extent from that of the West that one wonders to what degree a psychology originating in northern Europe and elaborated in the United States can be applied on the African continent? Is there room for a monocultural Western psychology in sub-Sahara Africa (Holdstock, 1981a)? Can psychology in Africa claim to be a responsible profession if it neglects to move toward the Africanisation of the discipline? And yet, how viable is such a transition in those African countries that have inherited a colonial past?

Almost three decades ago, Levine (1970) had already stated that 'The social sciences in Africa need psychology, but the psychologists and psychiatrists have been generally incapable of providing it in terms that make sense in Africa' (p. 107). He pointed out that 'Psychologists in Africa have often taken a high-mindedly nomothetic stance' (p. 107) without any acknowledgement of the importance of the environmental contexts in which the behaviour occurs and develops. According to Segall (1970) the functional inadequacy of psychology in Africa can be attributed to the reliance on its empirical approach, which is its strength, but can also be its weakness. The methodological sophistication of psychology requires that a study be designed and planned well in advance of being carried out. The hypothesis to be tested and the means by which it is to be done are stipulated without any cognisance being taken of the more inclusive socio-cultural context. Armed with a hypothesis, a research design, and techniques to analyse the data, the research project is usually launched from the perspective of the researchers and not from the people being investigated.

In Central and West Africa where the discipline is less firmly entrenched than in South Africa, the problem of breaking free from the exclusive adherence to mainstream paradigms is perhaps of a lesser degree, yet nevertheless of essentially the same nature (see Peltzer and Bless, 1989). A similar question can, in fact, be raised with respect to psychology in the United States and countries in Europe where the ethnic diversification of the populations continues to grow unabated. As has already been intimated by the discussion on ethnocentrism in earlier chapters, great concern exists about the relevance of psychology for minorities in the United States and for the African majority in South Africa. One of the greatest challenges facing psychology, as we embark on the twenty-first century, is undoubtedly how to cope with multiculturalism within and between the borders of the various countries.

THE CHALLENGE OF ETHNOPOLITICAL CONFLICT

Cultural diversification is a growing phenomenon throughout the world. At present there are four times more nations in existence than when the United Nations was formed. It is estimated that by 2050 we could have between 1,000 and 2,000 nations, many of which are likely to come into existence fairly bloodily (McGuire, 1998b). Since the publication of Toffler's *The Third Wave* in 1980, his prediction of escalating ethnic identity conflicts has been uncannily verified in various parts of the world. Fortunately, we have also seen the peaceful acceptance by people of each other's cultural differences. Unfortunately, these instances have been alarmingly few. It would seem that the fragmentation of psychology follows this global pattern of the break-up of nation states.

On one hand, ethnic 'groups are rightfully concerned about the preservation of their autonomy and cultural identity; on the other, a well-functioning, multiethnic, global society requires that we overcome the inherent limitations associated with tribalism, racialism, and nationalism' (Penn and Kiesel, 1994, p. 398). In his extensive work on the cultural-societal roots of genocidal violence, Staub (1996) stresses that pluralism has tremendous value but that it is difficult to create and maintain. The more pluralistic a culture is, the more minorities (i.e., their values and characteristics, including their differentness from the majority) are accepted. When that does not happen, genocide and mass killing result, as in the Germany of the first half of the twentieth century, where a limited set of values and beliefs, such as efficiency, order, obedience, and loyalty to the group, were dominant.

> In the former Yugoslavia, differences among ethnic-religious groups were negated. The communist government attempted to create a cohesive society by prohibiting not only expressions of hostility, but even the discussion of differences among groups . . . However, acknowledging deep-seated historical hostility is part of the work of overcoming it . . . Together with other instances, the events in the former Yugoslavia show that time alone does not heal deep historical wounds, nor does it eliminate ideologies of antagonism. Active steps are required, including dialogue and engagement between members of antagonistic groups and the identification or creation of shared goals.
>
> (Staub, 1996, p. 120)

Apart from the ethnic cleansing in the former Yugoslavia, with the latest violence being directed at the Albanians in the Kosovo province of Serbia, ethnic and religious conflict continues unabated in various parts of the world, and also in Africa. 'Psychology, therefore, will have to address, henceforth more than ever before, the promises and dangers implied by diversity. Diversity is variety and richness. It offers the opportunity to enlarge our appreciation of many different life styles with their potential for mutual cross-fertilisation. On the other hand, diversity may generate cleavages, conflict and prejudice' (Wilpert, 1995, p.11). According to the historian Samuel Huntington, 'Western, Arabic, and Eastern civilizations are headed for a momentous confrontation because of different worldviews and values' (in Marsella, 1998, p. 1282). Within the APA, concern about the role psychology can play in preventing ethnopolitical conflict is becoming evident (e.g., the *American Psychologist* of July 1998 and the *APA Monitor* of August 1998). At a meeting in Northern Ireland a 'new discipline' that will encourage psychologists to focus their endeavours on ethnopolitical conflicts, was envisaged (McGuire, 1998a).

The guest editors of the special issue in the *American Psychologist* (July 1998) reiterated the aspirations of the Northern Ireland conference. They stated that their goal was 'to challenge the discipline to examine the adequacy of psychology's current theories, tools, and intervention strategies for ameliorating ethnic conflicts internationally as well as in the United States' (Mays, Bullock, Rosenzweig, and Wessells, 1998, p. 739). They stated that an estimated 100 national and minority groups participated in armed conflict between 1945 and 1990. This decade alone has counted two dozen internecine wars 'that have claimed 30 million lives across the world and made refugees of another 45 million' (McGuire, 1998b, p. 1). The psychologically and physically maimed fatalities are undoubtedly even higher. In the special issue, ethnopolitical conflict and warfare in such geographically diverse regions of the world as the Middle (Rouhana and Bar-Tal, 1998) and Far East (Rogers, Spencer, and Uyangoda, 1998), Northern Ireland (Cairns and Darby, 1998), Central Africa (Smith, 1998), and Central and South America (Comas-Díaz et al., 1998) featured.

Despite the incidence of racial hate crimes and civil disturbances in the United States, the country is considered to have been relatively successful in uniting the members of the different subgroups, which constitute the nation, through the common ethos of patriotism and nationalism (Staub, 1996). Since patriotism and nationalism have destructive potential, the countries of Africa need to establish superordinate identities, which can unite their people through alternative means to nationalism. A guide to the nature of such a transcending ethos can be found if the people can rediscover the value of some of the core principles which have been held dear on the African continent. That such a statement is not just an expression of naïve romanticism is exemplified by the reconciliation which came about in South Africa and the behaviour of Nelson Mandela, whose greatness is surely to be attributed to his embodiment of some of the arcane wisdom of the continent. On the other hand, this wisdom has yet to be realised in countries like Rwanda, Angola, and Mozambique. What the variables are that differentiate the peaceful resolution of ethnopolitical conflict in Africa from the violent need to be investigated by the envisaged 'new discipline'. That such an investigation will have to entail the collaborative effort of people from various professions and various layers of the population goes without saying.

Even in the absence of violent ethnopolitical conflict, the imposition of ethnocentric principles of one group on another can be debilitating. In this respect psychology has some housecleaning to do, for imposing mainstream psychological practices on people from the majority world has deleterious consequences for their mental health. The iatrogenic causation of illness, which Illich (1977) pointed out with respect to the practice of medicine, is equally applicable in the profession of psychology. With respect to the mental health of the Canadian Innu, Gantous (1994) claimed that the interventionist strategies based on 'the traditional scientific paradigm serve to contribute more to the problem than to illuminate paths to solutions' (p. 3). In New Zealand the practice of psychology was not only deemed irrelevant to the Maori and considered to be a tool of suppression, but, clinical psychology was considered to have contributed to the abnormalisation of the Maori (Gergen et al., 1996). As will be seen in a later chapter, many African American psychologists view psychology as part of the mental health problem that it tries to combat. Akbar (1984a) argues that the ethnocentric preoccupation with deviancy and excessive involvement with victim analysis have become conceptually incarcerated in the approach to non-Western people.

Can 'American psychological imperialism' (Gasquoine, 1997, p. 570) be sufficiently modified to be of relevance to African, Arabic, Asian, Latin, and other collectives, if the application on its home base is as seriously questioned as it has been by the work reviewed? The title of an article by Hall (1997), 'Cultural malpractice: the growing obsolescence of psychology with the changing U.S. population', conveys the intensity of her concern. In it she implores the psychological profession to stop talking about cultural diversification and to take action in revisioning its curriculum, training, research, and practice in order to be more relevant to the growing diversification of the United States population. Hall's concern about the lack of praxis in psychology at national level in the United States is, as has been pointed out, been echoed at international level (Comas-Díaz et al., 1998). I have expressed myself along similar lines with respect to South African psychology (Holdstock, 1981b, 1987a).

The time has arrived, Peavy (1996) argues, for a New Look in counselling by conceptualising it as a cultural practice rather than a scientific undertaking. Defined as a culture of healing, mental health services need to be 'constructed more from (1) "folk wisdom," (2) culturally sensible ways of communicating, (3) local, rather than decontextualised knowledge, and (4) bits and pieces of knowledge developed through research, both scientific and humanistic' (p. 147).

The lure for African psychologists to adopt mainstream psychology as a model for developing a formal discipline in their respective countries is not at all surprising. The power of Euro-American psychology and its associated technology and marketing structure, which have, invariably, been described as psychological imperialism (Gasquoine, 1997) and intellectual imperialism (Myers, 1993), present a most formidable force. Whereas several authors (e.g., Gaubatz, 1997; Teo and Febbraro, 1997) have pointed out that insufficient attention has thus far been devoted to the analysis of the link between psychological thinking and structural domination and power, even less attention has been paid to the global implications of this relationship. The majority of people in Africa, South America, and many other parts of the world, live on or outside the margins of power and present a formidable challenge to the professional practice of psychology. The challenge awaiting African psychology is to trust and employ an inward frame of reference as its point of departure while maintaining contact with developments in contemporary psychology. To trust inwardly undoubtedly presents African psychology with a most daunting challenge. The words which e.e. cummings, the renowned American poet, used to address the battle to remain true to oneself, are equally applicable in the case of the development of an Africentric psychology. According to cummings (in Firmage, 1965): 'To be nobody-but-yourself – in a world which is doing its best, night and day, to make you everybody else – means to fight the hardest battle which any human being can fight; and never stop fighting' (p. 333). However, contrary to the individualistic context of Western culture within which the words of cummings must be interpreted, the Africentric self can only be discovered in the context of Africa's cultural and historical past. Culture, history, and geographical context are inextricably intertwined in shaping behaviour and in determining the collective and the individual identity. Writing about the quest of Puerto Ricans in search of their identity, Comas-Díaz and her colleagues (1998) wrote, 'Delving into the indigenous psychological arcanum can once more prove beneficial. As art sometimes unveils the future, rescuing and affirming traditional resources may suggest a path' (p. 789).

If African psychology can be true to the ways of life and spiritual dimension unique to the continent, it is my belief that it can contribute a great deal to world psychology. In stressing the importance of culture, a pluralistic approach seems to offer the best option, as discussed earlier (also Asante, 1992; Myers, 1993), for there are many cultures, each with its own birthright. In a later chapter the ongoing debate amongst African American psychologists about own-group preference, will be outlined (e.g., Baldwin, 1989, Penn et al., 1993; Penn and Kiesel, 1994; Phillips et al., 1993; Kambon and Hopkins, 1993).

TOWARDS A SOUTH–NORTH DIALOGUE

It is likely that we cannot do more at present than initiate a dialogue between the ideological perspectives underlying psychology in Africa and the West along the lines suggested by the cultural philosopher Kimmerle (1995a,b,c). The intercultural philosophy of Kimmerle is heavily dependent on the principles of hermeneutic philosophy, although it rejects the universalist assumption of the hermeneutic approach that the other is in principle always understandable, irrespective of context or culture. Intercultural philosophy strives for establishing a dialogue between people maintaining different cultural perspectives, even accepting the impossibility of overcoming cultural differences. My own experience, as is perhaps apparent from the tenure of the text, is very much in keeping with that of Kimmerle, not just with respect to differences between Africa and the West, but also with respect to the different orientations within psychology and even within some of the subdivisions.

In essence, intercultural philosophy resembles the fourth model of Shweder and Bourne (1989, 1991), which they rather jocularly (one presumes), referred to as confusion(ism). Confusion(ism) expresses the honest confession that one often fails to comprehend the framework of another culture. In their respect for cultural differences, social constructionists acknowledge that 'These differences may mean that certain actions are difficult or even impossible to interpret from the point of view of another cultural understanding' (Cushman, 1991, p. 207). Foucault is another who stresses that 'discourse in general and scientific discourse in particular, is so complex a reality that we not only can but should approach it at different levels and with different methods' (in Mudimbe, 1988, p. xi).

Kimmerle (1995a,b,c) highlights the difficulties imposed by the structure of language in trying to build bridges between African and European worldviews, and vice-versa. According to him, it would be much more fruitful to accept that the mutual understanding of certain cultural frameworks is so difficult to achieve that the best that can be done under such conditions is to adopt a strategy of mutual listening. 'Dialogue can only occur when two parties engage in periods of silence and listening, allowing the other party an opportunity to speak' (Hall *et al.*, 1997).

Since twentieth-century philosophers, from Wittgenstein to Derrida, have pointed out the inability of language to describe the underlying reality (in Gaubatz, 1997), the problem certainly becomes even more critical when realities belonging to one language family have to be translated into that of a totally different family. Nevertheless, as the South African poet, Wally Serote (1978), while living in exile in Botswana, emphasised, a dire need for communication exists:

> White people are white people,
> They are burning the world.
> Black people are black people,

They are the fuel.
White people are white people,
They must learn to listen.
Black people are black people,
They must learn to talk.
(pp. 50–51)

Others are in agreement. 'The issue in nation-building is not language but communication, not a particular language but the ability to communicate with one another' (Alexander and Smolicz, 1993, p. 5). These two authors nevertheless stress the importance of linguistic, as well as cultural pluralism, in societies with different language groups.

Although Kimmerle (personal communication) is unfamiliar with the therapeutic approach of Carl Rogers, the 'methodology of listening' which is emphasised throughout his work is remarkably similar to Rogers' (1951, 1980) therapeutic approach. The parallel views of Kimmerle and Rogers, like Derrida's (1984) deconstructionism, try to do away with those aspects within Western tradition which are aimed at domination. Kimmerle warns against the 'noble intentions towards power'. Intercultural philosophy has no other motive than to facilitate dialogue between people maintaining divergent orientations.

The philosophical and psychological viewpoints of Kimmerle and Rogers are complemented by ideas expressed within an anthropological and a religious context (see van der Hooft, 1979; Smart, 1983, 1989). Half-a-century ago the anthropologist, Herskovits (in van der Hooft, 1979) already stated that 'one seeks to understand the sanctions of behavior in terms of the established relationships within the culture itself, and refrains from making interpretations that arise from a preconceived frame of reference' (p. 38). An equally long time ago, Leenhardt already emphasised the need for continued communication with the people of New Caledonia, an island in the south-west Pacific, on the grounds that their 'mythical' thinking represented a valid system of knowledge (in van der Hooft, 1979). According to Leenhardt, the analytical consciousness predominant in the West could not afford to do without 'mythical' consciousness, for the latter provided validation for the authenticity of existence.

Smart's (1983, 1989) emphasis on description rather than judgement in his 'worldview analysis' of religion, shows commonality with the 'methodology of listening' of Kimmerle and the necessary and sufficient conditions for therapy elucidated by Rogers. In fact, Smart (1983) refers to his approach of crossing the frontiers of one's own culture 'into the minds and hearts of another tradition' (p. 18) as 'structured empathy'. Structured empathy requires, similar to Rogers' therapeutic approach, that one suspends one's own beliefs in an effort to understand the world of the other. Smart points out that one does not 'start from the assumptions of baseball in trying to understand cricket' (p. 18). Structured empathy does not imply rejection of one's own belief system. It is rather a temporary suspension of one's own assumptions in order to understand the worldview of the other better. Implicit in structured empathy is also the Rogerian attitude of respect or positive regard for the reality of the other.

In addition to learning about other traditions through personal contact with people from those traditions, Smart suggests worldview analysis through fictional and pictorial form. By studying the literature, the arts, the crafts, and the music of foreign cultures, as well as by studying the symbols operative in another culture, one can attempt to gain an understanding of that culture. These symbols can be artefacts, buildings, places, ceremonies, and rituals in either a religious or secular context.

In view of the long-standing tradition of respect for alternate realities amongst scholars in some of the social sciences, the current debate on multiculturalism in psychology in the United States is to be welcomed. However, the debate reflects just how entrenched psychology is in its universalist attitude. The entrenchment is so severe that doubt has been expressed whether the attempts of those who strive towards multiculturalism will ever be successful (Hall and Barongan, 1997). Trying to understand someone from another culture in terms of his or her perspective is bound to be considered as posing the threat of extreme relativism, opening 'the discipline to irrationality, in which there is no single underlying logic to psychological investigation' (Yanchar and Slife, 1997, p. 659). In their hermeneutic approach, Yanchar and Slife find it difficult to be at ease with a situation 'where there can be no foundation or common ground on which to evaluate rival theories, methods, and knowledge claims' (p. 658–659).

In association with Fowers and Richardson (1996), Yanchar and Slife (1997) contend that the lack of a basis for comparison and evaluation can only lead to relativistic nihilism. It is on the basis of establishing a 'universal foundation for evaluating claims of knowledge or cultural correctness' (p. 659), that Yanchar and Slife hope to bring about a pluralistic psychology 'that promotes equality and tolerance and a conceptual diversity that fosters human dignity, worth, and freedom' (Yanchar and Slife, 1997, p. 658).

The universalist aspiration of philosophical hermeneutics (e.g., Fowers and Richardson, 1996; Yanchar and Slife, 1997) seems antithetical to the attainment of the aims of a multicultural or pluralistic psychology. Can respect for alternate perspectives be possible in a theoretical approach so heavily dependent on evaluation, where there is such a desperate need to assess 'rival' theories, methods, and knowledge claims, and where the lack of an evaluative base is considered to lead to chaos (Yanchar and Slife, 1997)? Is the search for a uniform or universal reality not a wild-goose chase? As discussed a while back, anthropologists have, for a considerable time already, realised that if their observations and the interpretations of these observations were to have any validity, then the reality they encountered in their contact with other cultures, had to be respected. 'To recognize that right, and justice, and beauty may have as many manifestations as there are cultures is to express tolerance, not nihilism' (Herskovits, in van der Hooft, 1979, p. 38). In response to the accusation that social constructionism advocates a radical relativism in which there is no objective reality or transcendent moral code, implying that it is an amoral orientation, Cushman (1991) has pointed out that 'social constructionism is rooted in the moral. But it is not a moral code that receives its authority because it is removed from, transcends, and is superior to the particulars of every day living. The everyday is real and moral, it is just not transcendently real and moral' (Cushman, 1991, p. 207).

Kagitçibasi (1995) raises an interesting and valid point with respect to the moral implications of relativism. She warns that relativism harbours the dangers of maintenance of double standards by accepting existing inequalities between people as the status quo. All societies undergo change and not to allow for, or work towards change, especially with respect to the improvement of environmental conditions that can enrich the cognitive development and the lives of the underprivileged, is an abuse of the concept of relativism. 'It is important to make sure that tolerance of diversity and relativism do not impede efforts to improve the environments of socioeconomically disadvantaged children' (p. 299).

In a major work on the subject of African religion, the contributors chartered a course of 'relative relativism', between the Scylla of universal categorisation, which van Beek and Blakely (1994) regarded as ethnocentrism in disguise, and the Charibdis of extreme relativism. 'In the first case cultures have no fundamental differences; in the latter one they share neither rhyme nor reason' (p. 3). Similar to Shweder, van Beek and Blakely argue that

> Cultural expressions can be understood, but never fully, and can be communicated transculturally, but not without loss of meaning and the creation of new meaning. Our observations are interpretations, first of all, rendered understandable by both a shared humanity with all people and by a shared academic culture that . . . is both a major means and an important obstacle for understanding other cultures.
>
> (1994, pp. 3–4)

Not even at a physical level does a reality exist, neither at the molar nor the molecular level (e.g., Cohen, 1977; Rogers, 1980). The earth is a constantly expanding and contracting mass and, in the realm of subatomic physics, the entire universe appears '"as a dynamic web of inseparable energy patterns" that always includes the observer in an essential way' (Campbell, 1983, p. 8). A '"judicious vacillation" between "a world of waves and a world of particles as suits one's purposes"', has been suggested as a policy for modern physics (Shweder, 1994, p. 67). Physics is not considered a lesser science, though, because mutually incompatible theories, for instance, of light as a wave and a particle function, are entertained.

Earlier in the text the concern about the disunity in psychology, resulting from the divergent theories and methodologies, has been discussed. Perhaps it would be more meaningful to regard the divergence, not as evidence of disunity, but as an indication of the existence of alternate realities. Just as we are more likely to find common ground between ourselves by respecting each other's uniqueness, we are likely to find the common ground between the divergent theoretical and methodological orientations by respecting the unique contribution which each can make. What is needed is 'a form of Jamesian pluralism . . . where multiple, independent epistemological perspectives (or different frames of reference) are recommended' (Howard, 1991, p. 188). The same applies to cultural differences. For instance, during an encounter group between black and white South Africans that Carl Rogers facilitated in Johannesburg in 1982, a politically conscious African woman expressed greater trust in a conservative white male than in liberal white male and female members of the group.

From totally different perspectives, Hillman (1975) and Shweder (1994) have described a post-Nietzschean world, in which God is not dead, only positivism and monotheism are dead. Polytheism is alive and well. Instead of a uniform reality, these eminent scholars celebrate the relativistic idea of multiple objective worlds. The challenge for the development of psychology as an international discipline is to transcend the partial views of any single approach, tradition or culture. Why the concept of relativism should be demeaned by equating it with nihilism and chaos as Yanchar and Slife (1997) do, is difficult to understand.

One wonders how the belief in psychic unity as the only valid reality came about, living as we do amidst such incredibly rich diversity in the world. Furthermore, history indicates that it has been adherence to a monotheistic, and not a polytheistic perspective that has created so much turmoil in the world, and continues to do so. In light of the infinite diversity with which we are surrounded, it seems so much simpler to believe in and accept multiple realities than to do battle to uphold one uniform reality. Perhaps this is too naïve a statement, for humankind's individuocentrism, will to power, and need to control others is likely to stand in the way of implementing such a vision.

In order to steer psychology towards a new paradigm that does not adhere to the outdated search for the person, the mind or the psyche, in terms of a central processing mechanism, which is assumed to be abstract, interior, universal, fixed, and content free, the emerging discipline of cultural psychology developed (Shweder, 1994). According to Shweder,

> Cultural psychology is the study of the way cultural traditions and social practices regulate, express, and transform the human psyche, resulting less in psychic unity for humankind than in ethnic divergences in mind, self, and emotion. Cultural psychology is the study of the ways subject and object, self and other, psyche and culture, person and context . . . live together, require each other, and dynamically, dialectically, and jointly make each other up. (p. 73) . . . Cultural psychology assumes that intentional persons change and are changed by the concrete particulars of their own mentally constituted forms of life. (p. 97) . . . Every person is stimulus bound, and every stimulus is person bound. That is what it means for culture and psyche to make each other up

(p. 99) . . . Psyche refers to the intentional person. Culture refers to the intentional world. Intentional persons and intentional worlds are interdependent things that get dialectically constituted and reconstituted through the intentional activities and practices that are their products, yet make them up. (p. 101)

A multicultural perspective does not only provide hope in bridging cultural differences between nations or ethnic groups, but also in bringing the estranged sub-disciplines in psychology to a better working relationship. As stated earlier in the text, faction fighting between adherents of various paradigms in psychology is rife. In addition, the therapeutic value of a polytheistic orientation to the understanding and the acceptance of our fragmented selves must not be forgotten. Cultural psychology can be regarded as the polytheistic integration of the various indigenous psychologies. Towards the end of 1997, the first ever African Congress of Psychotherapy was held in Uganda, initiating the integration of indigenous African and Western psychotherapies.

Similar calls for the adoption of a multicultural perspective have gone out in theology (Oduyoye, 1996) and education (e.g., CERI/OECD, 1987; Grugeon and Woods, 1990; Holdstock, 1987a; Leicester, 1989; J.L. Stonier, 1996). The recently started *European Journal of Intercultural Studies* provides a forum for analysis of intercultural educational issues. Religious education seems to be considerably advanced in acknowledging the many faces of the deity and of paying homage to the diversity in religious practices (Chidester, Mitchell, Omar, and Phiri, 1994; Mitchell, Mndende, Phiri, and Stonier, 1993; J.E.T. Stonier, 1996; Stonier and Derrick, 1997; Weisse, 1995). Even science education is being considered from a cultural perspective (Patel, 1997; Wachtel, 1996). 'Technology and transportation are fast changing the world and the concept of a global village has never been more real. The "New World Order" as proclaimed by George Bush and Mikhail Gorbachev, has proclivity to disorder unless new multicultural understanding is embraced' (Michael, 1997, p. 231).

6

REVISIONING THE CONCEPT OF THE SELF

In addition to the challenges about its 'empiricism, objectivism, behaviorism, operationalism, reductionism, materialism, mechanism, universalism' (Gabrenya, 1988, p. 50), as well as its ethnocentrism, racism, scientism, and sexism, psychology has recently come in for criticism regarding its individuocentrism. It is the independent and self-sufficient individual that is regarded as the unit of the social system. Considering psychology's adherence to the approach of scientific analysis, which is of necessity reductionistic, it is perhaps not all that surprising that the individual as a self-sufficient entity has become the focus of the discipline. Concern about psychology's individuocentrism has been widespread. Unfortunately, space limitations prevent a full discussion of all the areas from which concern has emanated.

MAINSTREAM CONCERN ABOUT PSYCHOLOGY'S INDIVIDUALISTIC FOCUS

The debate about psychology's individualistic focus has been especially evident in the pages of the *American Psychologist*, the official mouthpiece of the American Psychological Association (see Holdstock, 1996c, for references). This is not to imply that such concern is restricted to American psychology. On the contrary, consideration of psychology's individualistic orientation has been evident in other parts of the world as well, for example The Netherlands (de Lange, 1989; Jansz, 1991) and England (Harré, 1998). With a few exceptions, the majority of the articles in the *American Psychologist* concerning the individuocentric basis of psychology question that orientation. Among the exceptions are the voices of Perloff (1987), Spence (1985), and Waterman (1981). The latter, for instance, argues that the critics of individualism maintain 'an outmoded 17th-century conception of individualism . . . making a dialectical dichotomy between individual and social interests' (p. 766). He states that normative (ethical) individualism 'entails the pursuit of personal goals (self-interest) through self-chosen, pro-social interdependencies reflecting a sensitivity to the needs and values of others' (p. 764). Similarly, Ayn Rand, generally considered as an arch

88

individualist, maintained that *rational egoism* encompassed the values necessary for human survival (Locke, 1988).

While the pursuit of 'ethical' and 'rational' individualism cannot be faulted, its incidence is undoubtedly too limited for comfort. Donald Campbell (1975) would, otherwise, not have accused modern psychology of being hedonistic, 'explaining all human behavior in terms of individual pleasure and pain, individual positive and negative valence, individual needs and drives' (p. 1115). In his APA Presidential Address, he reminded us that,

> psychology and psychiatry, not only describe man as selfishly motivated, but implicitly or explicitly teach that he ought to be so. They tend to see repression, and inhibition of individual impulse as undesirable, and see all guilt as a dysfunctional neurotic blight created by cruel child rearing and a needlessly repressive society. They further recommend that we accept our biological and psychological impulses as good and seek pleasure rather than enchain ourselves with duty.
>
> (Cambell, 1975, p. 1104)

In tracing the history of the Western self over the course of the last 2,500 years, Cushman (1991) argues that the 'self changes over time not because of some essential inner nature or metaphysical evolution' (p. 208), but in order to accommodate and comply with the political and economic requirements of specific eras. The predominant form of the masterful, bounded Western self, which Cushman describes as 'the communally isolated, empty, consumer self, hungry for food, consumer items, and charismatic leaders' (p. 208), is therefore attributed to the historical context of the post-World War II era. Cushman warns that 'To consider this self to be the single, universal self is to overlook its particular, local nature and thus to excuse its characteristic illnesses, mystify its political and economic constituents, and obscure its ideological functions' (p. 208). Sampson (1989b), similarly, warns that the self as a 'distinctive universe is said to reflect the sham and the illusion that is the bourgeois individual, not its reality' (p. 3).

Sampson (1988) calls on Bateson and Lewin to point out that although Western culture locates the origin of control inside the person, the actual determination lies within a larger system or field. He also argues that the work of Foucault and Weber demonstrates that the historical process of individualisation reflects a change in societal control rather than a freeing of the individual from social authority. Collective and communal loyalties and responsibilities are replaced by bureaucratisation of aspects of social life governed by highly abstract, impersonal rules and principles. The loss of the communal self necessitates the institution of laws to govern the behaviour of people. Although the illusion of being freer is created, people have less freedom. Failure to adhere to the dictates laid down by bureaucratic institutions is met by more severe sanction than that experienced under a system of communal obligation. Moving to Holland has made the reality of the bureaucratic type of control abundantly clear to me.

In an influential article, Markus and Kitayama (1991) discussed the psycho-logical merits of 'attending to the self, the appreciation of one's difference from others, and the importance of asserting the self' (p. 224). They stated that there 'is a faith in the inherent separateness of distinct persons. The normative imperative . . . is to become independent from others and to discover and express one's unique attributes . . . behavior is organized and made meaningful primarily by reference to one's own internal repertoire of thoughts, feelings, and action, rather than by reference to the thoughts, feelings, and actions of others' (p. 226).

A multitude of descriptions depicting the orientation to the self, as described above by Markus and Kitayama (1991), has emerged in the psychological literature during the past two decades (Holdstock, 1996b). The disillusionment with the approach to the self as an independent entity is portrayed by the nature of the various labels that have been used to describe it. To start with, the monocultural self indicates that the emphasis on the individual as a self-sufficient entity reflects primarily the dynamics and values pertaining to the Western world. Apart from the primacy of personal goals, personal interests, and personal fate over in-group goals, interests, and fate, personal achievement, emotional detachment, and independence from one's in-group are valued. Competition and confrontation within in-groups are accepted.

Terms related to monocultural, which have been used, are monotheistic, monadic, and ethnocentric. Other frequently employed concepts refer to the monocultural self as egocentric and egotistical, egocentric-contractual, individualistic, idiocentric, separate, autonomous, individuocentric, singular, selfish, self-contained, bounded, boundaried or limited, closed, linear, self-reliant, independent, a centralised equilibrium structure, rationalistic, bourgeois, empty, minimal, abstract, private and entrepreneurial, saturated, referential, and terminal (see Holdstock, 1996b, for references).

To this list of descriptions belongs the concept of the unchecked self, which Levenson (1992) used to describe the psychopathic personality. Psychopathy is construed as a mode of consciousness exemplified by the trivialisation of the other that is shared by respectable as well as disreputable persons. Of special interest is Levenson's extension of the concept of the unchecked self to include psychopathic tendencies evident in societies as a whole and in organisations within societies.

In contrast, the self that is proposed as an alternative has been described as 'seeing oneself as part of an encompassing social relationship and recognizing that one's behaviour is determined, contingent on, and, to a large extent organized by what the actor perceives to be the thoughts, feelings, and actions of *others* in the relationship' (Markus and Kitayama, 1991, p. 227). The alternative self strives towards harmony, interdependence, and co-operation with others. Emotional closeness is valued. Conflict is avoided. Group, rather than individual goals, interests, and achievement , is prized (Rhee, Uleman, and Lee, 1996).

The fundamental connectedness of human beings to each other determines the overt expression of such inner attributes as abilities, opinions, judgements and personality characteristics. Voluntary 'control of the inner attributes constitutes the core of the cultural ideal of becoming mature. The understanding of one's autonomy as secondary to, and constrained by, the primary task of interdependence distinguishes interdependent selves from independent selves, for whom autonomy and its expression is often afforded primary significance' (Markus and Kitayama, 1991, p. 227). Various terms have been suggested to conceptualise this interdependent view of the self. Among the proposals are the following: open, embedded, embodied and dialogical, socio-centric-organic, allocentric, a decentralised non-equilibrium structure, a vital force in participation, oscillating, indexical, bipolar, extended, ecological and interpersonal (see Holdstock, 1996b, for references). Other adjectives which have been used to describe the interdependent self are communal, ensembled, collective, contextual, connected, constitutive, polytheistic, pluralistic, holistic, personalised, allocentric, and relational. The concept of the absorbed self, used by Benson (1993) to describe the tendency of people to become something other than themselves when they view a painting or listen to poetry or music, indicates the same sense of unity of the self with the context.

The conceptual distinction between primary and secondary control alludes to the same distinction as described in the previous paragraphs (Weisz, Rothbaum, and Blackburn, 1984a,b). Primary control is directed at changing the external world so that it fits the needs and interest of the individual, whereas secondary control targets the internal world of the individual in order to accommodate internal states or mental representations to fit in with the external world.

An issue that is closely related to primary and secondary control, as well as to the independent–interdependent construal of the self, refers to the internal or external locus of control (Rotter, 1990; Strickland, 1989). However, care has to be taken to avoid the tendency towards dichotomisation that has characterised psychology (Allik and Realo, 1996; Hall and Barongan, 1997; Hermans and Kempen, 1998; Schwartz, 1990). Independence and interdependence can, at best, be understood to represent superordinate constructs with many specific subordinate components.

Earlier Angyal (1965/1982) indicated that 'the life process as a whole, is always a resultant of two components, autonomy and heteronomy – self-government and government from outside' (p. 6), since the life 'process does not take place within the organism but between the organism and the environment' (p. 5). Besides considering autonomy purely in physiological-biological regulatory terms, Angyal also regards autonomy as being directed outwards, towards others and the inanimate world. 'The function of each organ is to maintain both itself and other organs in working condition . . . The function of each organ is defined in what it accomplishes for the rest of the organism' (p. 3). He proposed the term homonomy to convey the basic striving of the organism to be in harmony with that which is beyond the individual self to which it nevertheless belongs. Angyal described homonomy as 'neededness', the need 'to mean something to someone else' (p. 18). He equated homonomy, quite simply, with love.

The direction of the autonomous and homonomous trends is different, and they appear to be opposites, but in a well-integrated person the two orientations are complementary rather than conflicting. In fact they logically presuppose each other . . .

Far from being irreconcilable opposites, the autonomous and the homonomous trends can be viewed as part aspects of one trend or perhaps as one trend functioning in two directions.

(Angyal, 1965/1982, p. 29)

The concepts of autonomy and homonomy have resurfaced with the renewed interest in the way the self is construed. In keeping with the concern about dichotomising the self, Kim and her co-workers (1996) indicated that independence and interdependence are not to be regarded as polarities on a single dimension, but as two orthogonal (separate) dimensions along which each person can vary. If these two dimensions are independent, then it is possible for the different poles of each to coexist, producing four categories of people. A high independent self-construal can be associated with a high or a low interdependent self-construal, and a low independent self-construal can, similarly, be associated with a low or a high interdependent self-construal. Most people are likely to cluster to varying degrees on each of the two dimensions.

Kagitçibasi (1996a) prefers to consider the two dimensions of independence and interdependence in terms of the concepts of agency and interpersonal distance. The two poles of the agency dimension are, similar to Angyal, considered to be 'autonomy and heteronomy; those of the interpersonal dimension are separateness and relatedness' (p. 180). Her interpersonal distance dimension is Angyal's homonomy. Kagitçibasi's rephrasing of Angyal's original classification highlights the importance of these dimensions.

The extent to which the self is construed in terms of each of the dimensions is undoubtedly dependent on larger cultural and subcultural influences, as well as the individual's particular individual and social development. The gender, race, religion, and social class, to which the individual belongs, contribute significantly to the development of the self-construal. Thus, within any one culture, considerable variation is likely to exist in the way the concept of the self is construed. However, irrespective of the variation that exists between and within cultures, the way the self is construed on the independent and interdependent dimensions is important in the determination of what constitutes mental health and mental illness, as well as psychotherapy.

CLINICAL PSYCHOLOGY'S INDIVIDUOCENTRIC ORIENTATION

Clinical psychology has been criticised with respect to its predominant individuocentric focus (e.g., Albee, 1982, 1986; Ho, 1985; Holdstock, 1990a, 1991a,b,

1993, 1996c,e; Perloff, 1987). Sarason (1981) actually blames the asocial nature of social psychology for contributing to the psychiatric course which clinical psychology has been following. If social psychology had been more social it would have formed the basis for a clinical psychology which emphasised primary prevention and the social determinants of maladjustment. If this had been the case clinical psychologists would have been better able to work effectively within the political environment to formulate public policies to aid these efforts. Sarason describes the advent of clinical psychology during the post-World War II period as 'the beginning of a disaster' (p. 827) because it failed to prepare psychology for the public arena. For his steady critique of psychology's tendency to rivet on the individual organism at the expense of social context, the APA honoured Sarason with its Gold Medal Award for Life Contributions by a Psychologist in the Public Service. Others are in agreement with the views of Sarason (e.g., Albee, 1986, 1990; Ryan, 1971; Wineman, 1984).

Albee (1982) pleads for recognition of the 'role of poverty, meaningless work, unemployment, racism, and sexism in producing psychopathology' (p. 1043). 'Nowhere is the futility of psychotherapy as obvious as among the poor and powerless whose suffering, crowding, and despair will yield only to social and political solutions . . . one-to-one treatment, medical or psychological, does not, and cannot, affect incidence' (Albee, 1990, p. 369). Albee warns against an 'increasing medicalization of psychiatry, along with strong and growing opposition to efforts at social change aimed at alleviating the environmental stresses that are responsible for the higher rates of emotional disturbance among the poor, the powerless, the disenfranchised and the exploited' (Albee, 1982, p. 1043). Just as the promotion of physical health is primarily due to improved environmental conditions (Illich, 1977), the promotion of mental health is likely to be subject to improvement in the socio-economic and political conditions. But how do we break out of our reactive cocoon? As a first step it would seem necessary that we become aware of and question the validity of our prevailing paradigms (e.g., Nelson, 1985). Cook (1985) queries whether we are content to be merely reactive or should we at least try to be innovative and proactive in fulfilling our duty as clinical psychologists? How do we promote human welfare other than by just practising psychotherapy? (Levy, 1984).

During his term of office as APA President, Stanley Graham pointed out to a group of leaders convened to discuss postdoctoral professional education

> that current postdoctoral education tends to focus on dynamic, long-term psychotherapy and does little to prepare practitioners to meet the needs of a world confronted with vast social changes. For a large portion of the population, failing social networks have led to increased poverty, violence, and wasteful addictive diseases. Resources have fallen far short of the needs of children and the aged, and deinstitutionalization has filled U.S. cities with thousands of people who are unable to care for themselves. Graham contended that psychology has failed to establish

an effective system of community services to ameliorate these social ills and he called on those assembled to plan postdoctoral training programs that would produce practitioners with the vision and expertise to develop service delivery systems that were both cost efficient and productive of positive results.

(Graham and Fox, 1991, p. 1034)

Since its influence has been so pervasive, the Person-Centered approach of Carl Rogers has been singled out for criticism in failing to prepare psychology for the public arena. Sarason claims that while publication of Rogers' (1942) *Counseling and Psychotherapy* effectively initiated 'The age of psychotherapy . . . it defined . . . the problems of people in terms of an individual psychology: Problems were personal or narrowly interpersonal and for all practical purposes independent of the nature and structure of the social order' (Sarason, 1981, p. 830). Farson (1974) also criticises Rogers for paying too little attention to the importance of power, status, politics, culture, history, systems, and technology in human relationships.

Considerable debate exists as to whether Person-Centred therapy has an exclusively individual focus (e.g., Geller, 1982; Ho, 1985; Holdstock, 1990a, 1991a; Patterson, 1986; Rogers, 1979; Sarason, 1981). Rogers undoubtedly rejected narcissistic individualism. 'We seem as a culture to have made a fetish out of complete individual self-sufficiency, of not needing help, of being completely private except in a very few selected relationships' (Rogers, 1979, p. 12). Yet, his point of departure remained firmly embedded in empowering the individual person (Rogers, 1977). Since its inception the self-actualising and self-directing qualities of people have been core assumptions of the Person-Centred approach. Even in the social outreach of the theory, empowering the individual remained the focus through which societal change was thought to be brought about.

How can we ever hope to combat the mental health problem if we continue to focus on the individual while the context within which the individual is embedded is in need of attention? It is also necessary to realise that socio-economic and political, as well as cultural variables are not only inextricably intertwined with the subject matter of our discipline but with who we are as psychologists. In addition, we need to be aware that how we behave as psychologists not only reflects, but also shapes, the socio-economic-political-cultural status quo. It is in the context of the unawareness of our contextual relatedness that the damning critique from within as well as from outside the discipline, especially from African American and third world social scientists and scholars need to be considered.

The shift in awareness towards holistic perspectives has focused attention on a number of important issues. One, in particular, relates to the variety and the complexity of problems involved in cross-cultural counselling and mental health (see Cox, 1986; Hammond, 1988; LaFromboise, 1988; Sue, 1988; special issues of

94

the *Journal of Consulting and Clinical Psychology*, 1987, the *Counseling Psychologist*, 1985). Psychotherapists have been admonished to be culturally sensitive (Rogler *et al.*, 1987; Sue and Zane, 1987). However, even if therapists possess sufficient cultural sensitivity, the question remains whether cross-cultural psychotherapy is really a viable option to be pursued in the promotion of mental health. Since people in different cultures have strikingly different construals of the self, of others, and of the interdependence of the two, these 'construals can influence, and in many cases determine, the very nature of individual experience, including cognition, emotion, and motivation' (Markus and Kitayama, 1991, p. 224). Needless to say, conceptions of mental health and psychotherapy are also likely to be influenced by the different construals of the self.

With a few exceptions within the field of clinical psychology the focus of the profession remains centred on the individual as an independent and self-sufficient unit of the social system. It is inconceivable that we will be able to combat the mental health crisis effectively, even in cultural contexts where the concept of the independent self is applicable, by propagating a model of the self which is primarily responsible for a great deal of the problems we are faced with. Even in therapy the focus on the independent self bedevils the effectiveness of the treatment model. The importance of the therapeutic relationship is generally acknowledged, yet our therapy continues to be directed at facilitating the client to become totally self-sufficient.

The paradoxical approach to the self within clinical psychology finds intriguing expression in Gestalt therapy. Gestalt psychology, on which Perls based his therapy, has emphasised the inter-relatedness of the part with the whole, as its famous figure-ground principle demonstrates. 'The organism is not a closed system; it is part of a larger functional context' (Köhler, in Heider, 1958, p. 216). Yet, the Gestalt prayer of Perls fails to acknowledge the importance of the larger context or 'field' within which the individual exists.

Being related archetypally

Intriguingly, concern about psychology's individualistic orientation has also emanated from archetypal psychology. In *Insearch*, Hillman (1979) writes that: 'The ground of being in the depths is not just my own personal ground; it is the universal support of each, to which each finds access through an inner connection' (p. 37). Hillman (1972) is adamant that we cannot go it alone: 'The opus of the soul needs intimate connection, not only to individuate but simply to live. For this we need relationships of the profoundest kind through which we can realize ourselves, where self-revelation is possible, where interest in and love for soul is paramount, and where eros may move freely' (p. 92). It is only through an intimate relationship that it becomes possible to reveal oneself. Hillman stresses that it is 'reveal thyself' and not 'know thyself' which is of the greatest importance. For it is only when we experience being known and accepted as we really are, naked, without frills, with all our strengths and weaknesses, that we truly experience the divine power of what love can really be like. 'To meet you, I must risk myself as I am. The naked human is challenged. It would be safer reflecting alone than confronting you' (Hillman, 1972, p. 91).

Although Jung is often criticised for emphasising the importance of inner life at the expense of outer life, there can be no doubt about his awareness of the important role of relationships. He stressed that life lived very intensely with the world of inner images was met in the outer world with a very vivid, colourful connection with others. In fact, the inner life depends on relationships 'out there'. Jung's own life stands as a good example of his beliefs. He had an unusually large capacity for love of others, be they family, friends, patients, or the world at large, and at the same time he worked hard at his own individuation process. The depth of his inner world certainly begot depth in the outer. The transpersonal element of Jung's theory, in which the concept of the self is situated within the concept of the collective unconscious, is not to be forgotten either.

The self is undoubtedly reflected in the inner and outer world and at the very deepest levels these two worlds are one, as the above quotations indicate. There is reciprocity between them. Changes in one affect the other. What we do in our outer life affects the inner and vice-versa. The two are in rhythm, like breathing in and breathing out. Sometimes it is necessary to withdraw to relate to oneself in order to be able to relate better to the outer world. This separating and connecting are really two halves of a whole. We need both halves to be whole. The sense of relatedness is indeed at the very root of individuation.

There really could be no self if it were not in relationship. The self is related-ness. It does not exist without relationship. Jung is reported to have said that the goal of the self is to be in motion between individuals. Therefore, it is not simply what you are but what you do that is the self, for deeds always involve relatedness. Deeds are something you produce that is outside yourself, between yourself and your surroundings. It is under these conditions that the self is visible. The self is not something we discover and keep to ourselves. It finds expression in sharing and being shared.

Jung used the image of a game that was played with a golden ball in the early church to elucidate the dialogical aspect of the self. Members of the ancient church stood in a circle with one person in the middle, forming a mandala, with the centre moving from one person to another. The golden ball was passed from one to the other. The centre, the circle, the golden ball and the passing of the ball are imbued with symbolic meaning. The centre represents an image of the self, so does the ball, as well as the circle. Passing the ball indicates that the self is not identical with one particular individual. There is no individual who can boast to have a self, but there is only self that can boast of having many individuals, a whole circle. The notion of the self in motion with another also finds expression in the words of Walter Rinder (1973), a poet-essayist of the present era, who wrote that, 'My life is one of inner travel towards myself with others'.

DEVELOPMENTAL PSYCHOLOGY'S
INDIVIDUOCENTRIC FOCUS

The exclusive focus on the individual as the unit of the social system has also been described as a major stumbling block for developmental psychology (Furth, 1995). Cushman (1991) critiqued Stern's 'respected theory of infant development from a social-constructionist perspective in order to demonstrate how decontextualized psychology theories inadvertently perpetuate the political status quo' (p. 206). By 'mythologising the monadic self' Stern, in keeping with the indigenous Western approach, prescribes how the self is to be regarded, and 'Those who "own" the self control our world . . . the battle over the self – who knows it, who is responsible for it, who can heal it – is a central aspect of this era's struggle for power and hegemony' (Cushman, 1991, p. 218).

At a recent meeting of the Jean Piaget Society, Gergen (1991) expressed the opinion that the continued 'belief in the individual as the center of meaning' (p. 4) prevented Piaget and developmental psychology from determining how understanding could occur between children, and ultimately how meaning could be transmitted between people. According to Gergen, developmental psychology needs to shift its focus towards 'relational accounts of human development. That is, rather than viewing development either in terms of ontogenetic unfolding (heredity), or in terms of environmental impact (environment), analysis may profitably center on relational units and processes' (p. 24). He calls for the consideration of human development, not only in terms of family, friends and the community, but 'fully enmeshed in the economic, political, educational, technological and other practices of the culture' (p. 25).

In keeping with Gergen's (1991) criticism of Piaget, Vandenberg (1991) also claimed that our relationships with others, which is so crucial in moral development, is absent in Piaget's cognitive model of development. Vandenberg points out that the innate abilities of looking, hearing, sucking, and grasping of the infant are not only geared towards the development of cognitive functions, as Piaget assumed, but are structured patterns geared towards 'enhancing social interactions between infants and their caregivers' (p. 1281). Vandenberg further states that such additionally manifested social sensitivities of infants as empathic crying, and the remarkably selective tuning towards visual, auditory and olfactory features of caregivers, 'reveal a strongly developed sense of relationship with others that is present from birth. The infant is biologically anchored and oriented in the social world' (p. 1282). Vandenberg describes this anchoring as a primitive form of attunement with others. 'Infants have core selves that are in a relationship with the core selves of others, and this relationship forms a crucial axis of development' (p. 1282).

Indeed, individuals develop through their relationship with others (Fogel, 1993). Fogel argues that creativity, which is at the heart of all human development, arises out of a social dynamic process called co-regulation. He focuses on the act of communication – between adults, between parents and children, among animals, even among cells and genes – in his model of human development.

SOCIAL CONSTRUCTIONISM

The concern expressed about individualism in psychology in general and in the subspecialities of clinical and developmental psychology, is shared by other orientations in psychology, such as the humanistic (e.g., Greening, 1986), and social psychology (see Chapter 3). The overwhelming emphasis on the individual self in psychology at present is rather difficult to understand, for a social constructionist perspective of the self dates back to both the distant and the recent past. In the *Phenomenology of Spirit*, Hegel (1770–1831) constituted that 'the individual self was in no sense immediately given, but a socially created concept' (in van der Veer, 1985, p. 7). According to Hegel there was no individual self prior to the interaction with other people. The self is formed through the interaction with other people.

Van der Veer (1985) traces the influence of Hegel in the thinking of William James and through James, but also directly, in the work of Herbert Mead and Vygotsky. The influence of Hegel and James is not only to be found in the writings of the symbolic interactionists (Mead, 1968), and the early social constructionists (see Gordon and Gergen, 1968), but in the writings of the cognitive theorists (Kelly, 1955; Lewin, 1951; Rotter, 1954) as well. Especially the recent renaissance of Vygotskian theory testifies to the shift towards the social.

Social constructionism constitutes the self not only in interaction with others, but also socio-economically and politically, as well as historically and culturally. In view of Africa's oral tradition, Tiryakian's (1968) statement that 'I am what I say' (p. 80) is enlightening. 'The self's disclosure in language means that it is a giving – and perhaps the fundamental gift and giving as a human activity is words' (p. 81). Hillman (1975) agrees. Although he cannot be regarded as a social constructionist, Hillman calls for the rediscovery of the oral tradition. True to his archetypal orientation he argues that words 'burn and become flesh as we speak . . . We need to recall the angel aspect of the word, recognizing words as independent carriers of soul between people . . . Words, like angels, are powers which have invisible power over us' (p. 9). Translated in constructionist terms Hillman pleads for recognition of the dialogical nature of words. 'Words acquire communicative capacity by virtue of shared usage' (Gergen and Gergen, 1988).

Hermans and his co-workers (1992) consider the self to be a dialogical narrator, '(a) spatially organized and embodied and (b) social, with the other not outside but in the self-structure, resulting in a multiplicity of dialogically interacting selves. The embodied nature of the self contrasts with conceptions of a disembodied or "rationalistic" mind' (p. 3). More recently, even recognition of the narrative component of the physical body has been called for (see Holdstock, 1991c).

In several of his publications Gergen has reiterated the self as a narrative constructed within social life. Narratives 'of the self are not fundamentally possessions of the individual; rather they are products of social interchange' (Gergen and Gergen, 1988, p. 18). It 'is not the individual who preexists the relationship and initiates the process of signification, but patterns of relationship and their embedded meanings that preexist the individual' (Gergen, 1991, p. 12).

> Yet, to focus on the face-to-face relationship may ultimately be delimited. For we find that whether I make sense is not under my control, nor is it ultimately under the control of the dyad in which the potential for meaning initially struggles toward realization. Rather, meaningful communication in any given situation ultimately depends on a protracted array of relationships, not only 'right here, right now,' but how it is that you and I are related to a variety of other persons, and they to still others – and ultimately, one might say, to the relational conditions of society as a whole. We are all in this way interdependently interlinked – without the capacity to mean anything, to possess an 'I' – after all, a position within discourse – except for the fact of a potentially assenting world of relationships.
>
> (Gergen, 1991, p. 18)

FEMINIST STUDIES

Several feminist and post-feminist writers have proposed an alternative to the autonomous and non-relational model of the self (e.g., Gilligan, 1982). According to them the emphasis on the separation-individuation side of identity reflects the male perspective. The fixation on achieving a separate and individuated self is seen as a result of a male dominated psychology, which is a result of a male dominated culture. The female perspective refers to '"the other voice" with which many women seem to confront the world and in terms of which they frame their understanding. This is the voice of connections and relationships rather than the voice of boundaries and separations' (Sampson, 1988, p. 18).

'Women move along in the world through relational connections . . . The notion of a separate identity or a separate sense of self is not quite the same in women as in men' (Josselson, 1987, p. 169–170). Women grow up with a relational sense of self. Identity means 'being with'. Without others there is no sense of a fulfilled self. The more there is of others the more there is of self, and vice-versa. Identity seems to be a matter of defining the internal experience of the self through attachment to others. Unlike males, who are brought up in a culture stressing self-assertion, mastery, individual distinction, and separateness, what Bakan (1966) called agency, women are raised in a culture of communion, stressing contact, union, co-operation, and being together. For many women communion is more important than agency. To be related is itself an expression of agentic needs for assertion, mastery, and achievement. Skill and success in relatedness become keystones of identity. Women's sense of self is organised around the ability to make and maintain relationships.

Josselson (1990) discusses seven dimensions of relationship as foundations and expressions of identity. According to her, the needs for holding, attachment, and libidinal gratification are the most basic. The fourth dimension is that of being affirmed or negated by others. The fifth dimension of relatedness, idealisation and identification, like the fourth, affords one the opportunity to find oneself by being mirrored in another's validation. As her sixth dimension of identity she regards emdeddedness as being of vital importance. Identity emerges from the groups in which one is embedded. It is the soil in which identity grows. The self is part of the social world and the social world is part of the self. The *We* of *Me* conveys the intimate linkage of the self to the social world.

Finally, identity emerges from what one offers to others in the form of care. Tenderness and care are seldom talked about in terms of identity. It simply is not part of the developmental ethic, which we hold as important in raising our children. This is especially true in the socialisation of boys. Elsewhere I have written that 'Boys should be exposed to the same training that girls traditionally receive in our society, and should be encouraged to develop similar kinds of socially positive, tender, co-operative, nurturing, and sensitive qualities' (Holdstock, 1990c, p. 363). It is very unlikely that relatedness is central only to the identity of women. It is as central to the identity of males, even though that fact is not quite realised, geared as we are towards the language of power and assertion.

'Our developmental psychology, as well as our culture, has tended to equate maturity with independence and impenetrable personal boundaries, thus relegating the interpenetration of selves in relatedness to a less mature form of existence' (Josselson, 1987, p. 185). We should rather strive to make heroic the achievement of intimacy and care. However, we lack the terms of discourse to conceptualise the myriad of connections that people make with one another. The poverty of the language and its ability to capture the depth of feeling is especially important in light of the dialogical aspect of the self and the importance of searching for the soul in words, as Hillman (1975) has so eloquently elucidated.

Miller (1984) prefers to think of being-in-relationship rather than of being-within-relationship. In the new thinking the self cannot be regarded as a unit out-of-relation-with-others (Jordan, 1984, 1987). In fact, Surrey questions the idea of a self-structure and suggests that it be replaced with the concept of process (in Surrey, Kaplan, and Jordan, 1990). '"Self" is based on separation from others and self-other-differentiation, self-versus-other, which may then become self-over-other' (Bergman, 1991, p. 3). The moral of the feminist perspective shifts the accent from the emphasis on control, power, comparison, competition, aggression, logic and rationality to connectedness, caring, and nurturing. Power-over-others becomes power-with-others: relational power.

The moral of the feminist perspective is clear. Embeddedness and care need to be respected and valued more highly by society. Just as our developmental ethos needs to be changed with respect to the raising of boys, our psychological and scientific ethos also needs to change. Natural science oriented psychologists need to be trained in the same way as we need to, but not as we do, educate boys. We need to encourage the ability of psychologists to be intimate and to care. However, we also need human science oriented psychologists to be able to utilise cognitive information processing strategies in their professional endeavours. We need to realise that the functional hemispheric asymmetry of our split brain psychology prevents the achievement of our optimal potential.

BEING PART OF THE UNFOLDING OF AN ENFOLDED ORDER

Apart from the sources of critique of the independent self, mentioned above, critical voices have also emanated from many other areas. Among these should be noted, critical theory, the challenge to liberal individualism, deconstruction-ism, transcultural disciplines (e.g., cultural and psychological anthropology, transcultural psychiatry, cross-cultural and indigenous psychologies), human movement studies, philosophy, and various scientific disciplines (see Holdstock, 1996b, for references). Maffesoli (1995) presents a sociological theory of modern identity that questions the idea that individualism is a defining feature of modernity. While the old determinants of identity, such as class, have faded, there are new tribal determinants. Sexual, political, or professional identities are being replaced by identifications of a new order and flavour. Groupings of a musical, sporting, spiritual, or touristic nature have emerged in the midst of 'mass' society.

The diversity and the severity of the critique of psychology's individuo-centrism highlight the need for awareness that the self and the other constitute a fluctuating figure-ground relationship. The one without the other is not possible. Just as with any other aspect of one's experience, for example the state of the body, the other, even in his or her physical absence, is important in the construal of oneself. There needs to be a fluid alternation between the self and the other. If the other is never allowed to be part of the foreground of one's experience, the lack of awareness is likely to be as debilitating as the lack of awareness of one's physical being. Bringing the other into the foreground of awareness, however, means that the other is cathected with the necessary energy to care and respect for that part of oneself which is the other.

THE NON-WESTERN CONCEPT OF THE SELF

It is rather paradoxical that the postmodern concept of the self as an inter-dependent entity, is commensurate with the way the self is construed in those parts of the world described as 'third world', 'developing', and 'emerging'. Whereas all cultures recognise the individual as empirical agent, most cultures do not retain the individualistic conceptions of the person (Jahoda, 1988; Marsella, 1998; Miller, 1988). Indigenous psychologies 'often have very different and more socially orientated notions of what constitutes a person' (Jahoda, 1988, p. 91). The other and society are not only of importance in establishing a concept of the self, as the symbolic interactionists and social constructionists emphasise, or in providing the context within which social roles are to be enacted, but are also integrated components of the self. According to Geertz (1974), the

> Western concept of the person as a bounded, unique, more or less integrated motivational and cognitive universe, a dynamic center of awareness, emotion, judgement and action organized into a distinctive whole and set contrastively both against other such wholes and against its social and natural background, is however incorrigible it may seem to us, a rather peculiar idea within the context of the world's cultures. (p. 275)

Concomitant with the realisation that individuals in Western nations do not adequately represent human populations everywhere grew the awareness that cultures differ appreciably with respect to the way the self is construed. In contrast to the individuocentric model of the self, which prevails in the West, a concept of the self independent from others, is unthinkable in the majority world. Attending to and 'fitting in with others and the importance of harmonious interdependence with them' (Markus and Kitayama, 1991, p. 224) is what is of the greatest importance. The 'self is viewed as *inter*dependent with the surrounding context, and it is the "other" or the "self-in-relation-to-the other" that is focal in individual experience' (p. 225). Thus, it is not the inner self but the *relationships* of the person to other persons that is of the greatest importance.

A wealth of information has accumulated in cultural and psychological anthropology, transcultural psychiatry, as well as in cross-cultural and indigenous psychologies during the past few decades, indicating that the other and society are integral components of the self in non-Western cultures. Kohlberg (in Gibbs and Schnell, 1985) describes the basic unit of society in the majority world as a 'bi-polar self–other relationship . . . born out of the social or sharing process' (p. 1074). Baldwin (1968) speaks of the bipolar self in developmental terms. According to him 'the only thing that remains more or less stable, throughout the whole growth, is the fact that there is a growing sense of self which includes both terms, the ego and the alter. In short, *the real self is the bipolar self, the socius*' (p. 165). Shweder and Bourne (1989) describe the bipolar self as sociocentric-organic in contrast to the egocentric-contractual self of the West. 'Linked to each other in an interdependent system, members of organic cultures take an active interest in one another's affairs, and feel at ease regulating and being regulated . . . the concept of the autonomic individual, free to choose and mind his own business, must feel alien, a bizarre idea cutting the self off from the interdependent whole, dooming it to a life of isolation and loneliness' (p. 132).

Many non-Western cultures have thus far been documented as portraying 'the self as constituted by social context rather than by an individuated psychological core' (Miller, 1988, p. 273). These cultures, listed in alphabetical order, are: African, Balinese, Cheyene, Chewong of Malaysia, Chinese, Filipino, Gahuku-Gama of New Guinea, Indian, Inuit (Eskimo), Islamic, Japanese, Javanese, Lohorung of eastern Nepal, Maori, Moroccan, Ojibwa Indians of North America, and the Zapotec of Mexico (see Holdstock, 1993, for references).

The self in the majority world has been defined both in terms of the nature of the self–nonself boundary and in terms of the location of power and control (Heelas and Lock, 1981). Thus, concepts like field control and a decentralised non-equilibrium structure (Sampson, 1985) have been used to distinguish the attitude of the majority world towards the self. However, there are 'wide variations in what counts as the self' (Tedeschi, 1988, p. 19) among those cultures which hold a sociocentric conceptualisation of the self. Landrine (1992) distinguishes between sociocentric cultures where the interdependent self 'takes the form of social roles' (p. 407) and those where 'the self is understood as a mere vessel for immaterial forces and entities' (p. 410).

In addition, when considering the way the self is conceptualised, account must be taken of such variables as modernisation (Triandis, 1988), hierarchical group membership (e.g., caste and social class) (Gudykunst, 1988), and the dominance of the masculine aspect within the culture (Hofstede, 1980). The complexity of self and identity in a changing cultural context is becoming all too apparent as researchers attempt to unravel the mystery of the relation between the self and culture. Zwier (1998) recommends the use of a parametric approach to clarify the complexity of the independent–interdependent dichotomy in different domains, such as the family, peers, and society. For instance, she found students from an independently oriented culture, the Dutch, to score higher than students from Turkey, a collectively oriented culture, on family interdependence, but not on several other categories.

In many cultures, such as the African and the Maori, the fluidity of the self–other boundary does not only pertain between the individual, the family, and society, but also between the individual and the physical universe and metaphysical reality. In other societies, for example those of India, this fluidity acknowledges the world of other people, but focuses primarily on the relationship with the metaphysical. Whereas Hinduism accentuates the immutable self to the extent that the individual self is regarded as an illusion, Chinese Confucianism establishes the person, and hence the self, centrally within the community of others. Inuit culture shows a similarity to Hinduism in that the importance of the individual is curtailed. At the same time, it shows a similarity to Confucianism in its emphasis on the importance of the individual's role as part of a community (DeVos, Marsella, and Hsu, 1985; Shweder and Bourne, 1989). In the following section and chapters, the interdependent nature of the African self will be discussed.

THE AFRICAN CONCEPT OF THE SELF

While a fair amount of work has been done with respect to the way the self is constituted in Asian and Western cultures, hardly any attention has been focused on the concept of the self as it manifests in Africa. As mentioned previously, to speak of African culture in a collective sense is as absurd as to speak of Asian or Western culture in a collective sense. Yet, despite the multiplicity of and variation between cultures within sub-Saharan Africa, the same *relative* universality applies as in the case of the Arabic north or the regions of the world known as the East and the West (Idowu, 1975; Mbiti, 1975; Sawyer, 1970; Taylor, 1963).

An apparent paradox exists with respect to the various descriptions of the self in Africa (Holdstock, 1990b). On the one hand the Africentric self has been described as an 'illusionary being' (Akbar, 1984a, p. 400), a view which contrasts vividly with the Western concept of self as a bounded, masterful entity (Cushman, 1990). On the other hand the Africentric self has been described as the 'centre' of the world (Asante, 1983). Such a view of the self would seem more in accordance with Western notions and contrary to that amongst other cultures of the majority world, such as the Inuit (Eskimos), who place relatively little emphasis on the individual (Harré, 1981).

The description by anthropologists of the African worldview as personalised, provides an understanding of the apparently contradictory notions of the Africentric self as being both the centre of the world and an illusion. A personalised worldview implies that no sharp distinction is made between ego and the world. In fact, the self is but an unfolding of the enfolded order of the universe. The self can never unfold by itself, for it is inextricably intertwined with this total unfolding of the enfolded order. 'Individuality emerges and expresses itself communally' (Ogbonnaya, 1994, p. 79). Thus, it is as a self-contained entity that the African self is perceived as an illusion. Being the centre of the world implies the acceptance of the responsibility of being-in-relation. In contrast to the Western self-as-thinker (Cantor, 1990) it is the self-as-actor which is of primary importance in Africa. 'By your actions you are known.' Thus, in the African concept of the self, it is important how one behaves in general and towards others. In this regard African cosmology complements the ideas of the Scottish philosopher, John MacMurray (see Dokecki, 1990) and the contemporary postmodern developments in the social and natural sciences which entertain more sociocentric and holistic notions of the self.

The interactive holism of African cosmology also finds expression in the concept of the self. In the words of Ogbonnaya (1994), 'the African assumptions of the cosmos are borne out in terms of the concept of self' (p. 77). The self is not only in 'intimate relationship' with other people, but also with the animate and inanimate world of nature, as well as with the ancestor spirits. The one-ness with all things, living and non-living, which exists among the majority of African people, even among the urbanised population, represents a reality which Westerners, with their centuries-old tradition of compartmentalisation, find extremely difficult to comprehend. In fact, I am reminded of Shweder and Bourne's (1989, 1991) classification of interpretative models used by anthropologists to render intelligible the variety of human experiences. In addition to the three principally used models referred to as universalism, evolutionism and relativism, Shweder and Bourne proposed a fourth model, confusion(ism) to express the honest confession that one often fails to comprehend the framework of another culture. This lack of comprehension also applies to the holistic embodiment of the African concept of the self.

The concept of self as a vital force in participation with other vital forces

In the African worldview, the person is best conceptualised as a vital force in participation with other vital forces. While David Bohm considers the universe to be the unfolding of the enfolded order, African cosmology considers it to be the unfolding of a vital force (Tempels, 1959). The vital force 'is in all men and creatures and forms the bond between them' (Parrinder, 1969, p. 123).

The participative aspect of being a vital force once more emphasises the activity component in the African concept of the self. The self cannot be complete if it remains enclosed, but it has to seek out the other if it is to become actualised. Indeed, the interrelatedness of the African concept of the self cannot be stressed enough. A person can only be really human when other people are there to complete his or her humanness. The individual cannot be human alone. One's personhood is dependent upon one's relationships with others. The Cartesian dictum of 'I think therefore I am' becomes 'I belong therefore I am'. It is said, 'we are because I am and I am because we are'. The Zulu expression, *umuntu ngumuntu ngabantu*, which means that a person is a person through other persons, captures the essence of the African concept of the self well.

Individuals are conceived and born into the family of humankind. Therefore, no-one is a stranger. The earth is our common home, the property of us all. When we die we depart but do not leave this family. If I gain my humanity by being born into a relationship with other people, then it follows that my humanity comes to me as a gift. It is not something that I can acquire, or develop by my own isolated power. My humanity can only be fulfilled as long as I remain in touch with others, for it is in relationship with them that I am empowered. Mutuality and individuality go hand in hand. Real 'subjectivity is only possible within the context of inter-subjectivity' (Van Eercke, 1975, p. 245). Being in relationship with others is not just a sociological notion but a moral one. It provides a foundation for an ethics that is infinitely human. Not only do I have a duty to myself but to others as well. In facilitating the growth of others, I facilitate my own development, and vice-versa.

The belief in being part of a universal spiritual network of energies provides great sustenance for the African person. However, it also places great responsibility on the individual to discover and maintain the proper relationship with the multiple strands of the network of relationships. 'The person alone in his or her "isolated being" lacks power. It is only as part of the whole, that is, by being understood as representative in his or her being of the whole, that he or she gains force, takes on meaning, or becomes relevant' (Richards, 1981, p. 223): Clearly then, in Africa no person is considered to be an island.

Ubuntu

The nature of one's interaction with others is governed by a code of ethics which is best described by the concept of *ubuntu*, the supreme African virtue which will be further elaborated in the section on the interpersonal dimension in Chapter 9. Patrick Dooms (1989), at the time a student in psychology at the University of the Witwatersrand, has raised some interesting points about the notion of *ubuntu*. He argued against attempts to define *ubuntu* in purely theoretical terms. According to him African cosmology was too holistic to warrant the reduction of an attribute of such an undefinable quality as *ubuntu*, in concrete terms. He argued that rational understanding alone could never bring about an understanding of *ubuntu*. It was something that had to be experienced if one really wanted to know what it was about. Nevertheless, in the absence of an experiential knowing of *ubuntu*, perhaps the next best thing is to try and initiate at least a rational understanding of such an important mode of being.

Another criticism of Dooms about the prevailing view of *ubuntu* is less easily resolved. He argued against the exclusively positive interpretation of *ubuntu* as being humane almost to a fault. Dooms maintains that the portrayal of *ubuntu* as some sort of ultra humanness is too good to be true. Such a view does not take account of reality and harbours the danger of perpetuating a worldview that in the past has been responsible for the extent to which African people have been exploited and oppressed. Regarding anti-social behaviour as falling outside the domain of *ubuntu* places the concept outside the bounds of reality and equates it with the biblical Garden of Eden. If *ubuntu* has to have any significance in explaining the continuing conflict in the world, Dooms contends, then it has to account for the full range of human behaviour and attitudes, including the potential to be inhumane.

In essence, the question raised by Patrick Dooms highlights the absence of the concepts of evil and of hell in the African worldview as the opposites of the concepts of good and of heaven. What Dooms seems to be arguing for is the recognition, in Jungian terms, of the potential of the shadow side of the personality to create human misery. He certainly speaks from within his own experience, for growing up during the apartheid era as a young black male, he has encountered more than his share of the horrors that humankind is capable of.

Dooms is in good company in his concern whether *ubuntu* incorporates, besides its positive message, also negative components. Apart from being a constant topic of discussion throughout the centuries of Western civilisation, such greats in humanistic psychology as Carl Rogers and Rollo May have debated the issue and agreed to differ (May, 1982; Rogers, 1982). May stated that 'we must include a view of evil in our world and in ourselves no matter how much that evil offends our narcissism' (1982, p. 18–19). Rogers sees 'members of the human species, like members of other species, as *essentially* constructive in their fundamental nature, but damaged by their experience' (1982, p. 8). He writes:

> I do not find that this evil is inherent in human nature. In a psychological climate which is nurturant of growth and choice, I have never known an individual to choose the cruel or destructive path. Choice always seems to be in the direction of greater socialization, improved relationships with others. So my experience leads me to believe that it is cultural influences which are the major factor in our evil behaviors.
>
> (Rogers, 1982, p. 8)

Rollo May, however, points out that the 'evil in our culture is also the reflection of evil in ourselves, and vice versa . . . It takes culture to create self and self to create culture; they are the yin and yang of being human. There is no self except in interaction with culture, and no culture that is not made up of selves (1982, p. 12). African humanism seems to be on the side of Carl Rogers in emphasising the positive and the good, although it recognises that *ubuntu* can be lost completely. However, the lack of *ubuntu* is regarded as just that, and not as being bad or being evil. One faces the consequences of one's actions in the life that one is living and not in some afterlife of heaven or hell. Thus, instead of the notion that the individual becomes a pawn in collectivist African culture, each person faces immense responsibility in determining the nature of his or her relationship to others and to the community at large.

However, Patrick Dooms has raised a valid point. Too much havoc has been created in Africa, by Europeans and Africans alike, to ignore humankind's potential for inflicting the greatest cruelty on each other. The concern of Dooms is not just about the absence of *ubuntu*, but about the direct opposite of what it stands for, not just the lack of humanity, but actual inhumanity. Indeed, it is important that the potential of the shadow, in Jungian terms, to become destructive, be realised in conjunction with its potential for the greater good. According to Jung and, more recently, Rollo May (1982), the danger is in being unaware of the destructive potential of the daimonic within the psyche.

May regards 'the human being as an organized bundle of potentialities. These potentialities, driven by the daimonic urge, are the source *both* of our constructive and our destructive impulses' (p. 11). Without an awareness of the destructive potential within each individual, the chances are enhanced that the daimonic forces in the psyche can become demonic. If, on the other hand, the destructive potential is recognised, the possibility exists that the untapped potential of the daimonic can become integrated within the psyche and contribute meaningfully towards actualisation of the individual's unique potential.

According to the concept of congruence, which is one of the basic tenets of the Person-Centered theory of Rogers, it is important to be in touch with one's inner experiences without necessarily having to express those experiences. Relating the concept of congruence to the concern of Patrick Dooms about the absence of the shadow in opinions about *ubuntu*, means that it is important to become aware, not only of emotions, feelings, and actions that are experienced as acceptable, but also of those feelings and actions that are less acceptable or even experienced as unacceptable. Only by doing so can one become fully whole. Thus, it is important that we become aware of our anger, our hate, our frustration, and whatever other 'negative' emotions we may be experiencing.

Moreover, *ubuntu* differs from the theories of Rogers and other clinical and counselling psychologists in its focus on the need to become aware of the implications of our actions in relation to others, including the deceased. What *ubuntu*, on the other hand, can possibly incorporate from the greats in psychology is to direct more explicit attention to the importance of an awareness of the world of inner experiencing. If we are aware of our inner world, we can choose whether we want to express it and, if we want to, how we want to express it. The underlying rationale is that such awareness will prevent the daimonic from seeking expression in demonic ways. At the same time, it affords us the opportunity to look for acceptable ways in which to express the unacceptable, which is important, since *ubuntu* is primarily the dynamic manifestation of oneself in relation to others.

The necklace killings within the African community during the latter phase of the apartheid era can be regarded as the demonic expression of the unrecognised rage, anger, helplessness, frustration, and loss of hope, experienced by members of the community. The necklacing of people who are otherwise regarded as 'brothers' and 'sisters' possibly represents the outward manifestation or projection of inner experiences that are unacceptable and unrecognised. Where there has, conceivably, been greater awareness of inner experiencing, the same feelings were put to use constructively through political activity, and by writing poetry and plays, as well as by the creation of art and musical productions intended to raise awareness about political inequities. There is a very fine line indeed between the creative and the destructive potential of the psyche. Following the theory of the 'scapegoat mechanism' of ritual sacrifice of Girard, Chidester (1991) interprets necklacing, and similar incidents of killing of individuals by a social group, as a means whereby the potential uncontrolled violence in society is contained. In technological societies, the judicial system is regarded as fulfilling a similar function.

The proceedings of the Truth and Reconciliation Commission (TRC), which is an attempt to build a solid foundation for the new dispensation in South Africa, are of particular interest with respect to the issue whether *ubuntu* incorporates both good and evil. The principles, upon which the TRC is based, indirectly acknowledge humankind's capacity for inhuman deeds. These principles seem to be in accordance with the belief of Rogers that evil behaviour is a result of 'cultural influences', for it accepts that the political reality that prevailed at the time can serve as an extenuating circumstance in evaluating the crimes committed.

In allowing for the possibility of remorse and forgiveness, the TRC also calls upon humankind's potential for the greatest good. Those individuals who experience genuine remorse and who publicly acknowledge the atrocities they committed have a chance of being pardoned for their crimes. The individual comes face to face with the demonic in him or herself. In that awareness is the potential for integration and transcendence of the demonic aspect of the self. The persons who have been victimised, similarly, face their potential for both good and evil in their ability to forgive or not to forgive their torturers or the murderers of their loved ones. Thus, the TRC has, in its own way, come to address the concern raised by a concerned younger citizen of the country.

As one of the few processes in the world, where atrocities committed in situations of political conflict and war have been dealt with by means of reconciliation rather than exacting 'rightful justice', the TRC implicitly expressed a great deal about the nature of the concept of the self in southern Africa. In a pragmatic and holistic manner that is in keeping with the way of being in Africa, the TRC gives voice to the theoretical notions of some of the greatest psychologists of this century.

As will be evident from the discussion of African holism in the final chapters, the concept of the self in Africa not only incorporates other people, but also other refractions of the deity. Without such relatedness to the larger universe of animate beings and even inanimate nature, the existence of the individual is incomplete. Those of a higher order have the responsibility to respect those of a lower order, in short, to evidence *ubuntu*, in all aspects of their behaviour. Ogbonnaya (1994) conceptualises each individual as a community of selves, including 'a community of ancient selves, contemporary selves, and emergent selves in constant interplay' (p. 83).

The holistic interdependency of the African self does not imply a dependency on, but rather a respect for and responsibility towards the other. The same respect is bestowed on the self, which is never regarded as being of lesser importance than the context to which it belongs. Speaking from Senegal, Leopold Senghor wrote, 'the very being of being is to persevere in one's being' (Reed and Wake 1979, p. 97). Marquard, another Senegalese, has stated, 'Know thyself before they tell you who you are' (in Bodibe, 1993). Akbar (1984a,b), like Biko and others, similarly, writes that self-knowledge is empowering. He argues that the plight of his fellow African Americans is exacerbated in their ignorance of themselves and he encourages them to understand their roots, their history, their culture, and indeed themselves. Akbar maintained that such understanding would enhance their dignity as human beings.

Numerous examples are cited in Chapters 9 and 10 of the ways in which the interrelated nature of the person in African culture finds expression. Among these is the person-centred nature of the majority of contemporary African art, the purpose and the nature of the music, the importance of the oral tradition, the mythology of creation, as well as the daily interaction between people. The interdependent nature of the African concept of the self is also evident in the approach to sickness, health, and healing.

7

AFRICAN AMERICAN PERSPECTIVES ON THE IDEOLOGICAL BASE UNDERLYING PSYCHOLOGY

The ethnocentrism of mainstream psychology is even apparent in the publications regarding the appraisal of the discipline. The critical view from within the African American community has not found its way into the journals of the APA to an extent that is in keeping with the challenging nature of the comments. By failing to give voice to the full range of reservations expressed about psychology, the journal editors effectively protect the status quo, even though their publication of the critique by mainstream psychologists seems to indicate differently. Hall (1997) actually draws attention to 'insensitive and discriminatory behaviors' (p. 644) by some of those on the predominantly white body of male editors. Conceivably, editorial policy assumes that the minority viewpoint of the African American perspective does not warrant the same amount of journal space as majority viewpoints. 'The chauvinism of Western psychology is a deterrent to changing the profession. The need for change has not been a priority because the status quo fulfils the majority's needs' (Hall, 1997).

Whatever the case may be, the failure of APA journals to highlight the scope of the critical assessment by the ethnic minority of mainstream paradigms, is another indication of the ethnocentrism still inherent in psychology. Although African Americans may be in the minority in the United States, they represent vast numbers of people on the African continent and the African Diaspora outside the United States. Their opinions, therefore, need careful consideration. Besides, a psychology that is basically relevant to a particular majority can never hope to fulfil its aspirations as an international or even a national discipline.

I have encountered a similar schism in the acceptance of articles submitted for publication. Apart from the customary quibble about relatively insignificant detail, I have never experienced any difficulty in getting papers based on my brain and sleep research published. The same cannot be said about articles in which I have appraised mainstream paradigms from an African perspective. Based on the feedback I received it would seem that the Africentric viewpoint was experienced as too stringent in its evaluation of contemporary psychology and my representation of it too 'naïve' and 'esoteric'. Basically, however, Africentric

111

viewpoints and principles are just too different, too foreign, to be comprehended as meaningful for Euro-American psychology. Asante (1992), noted that 'It is the apparent antagonism of the African worldview that causes many academics to shudder. They are wary when an afrologist challenges the validity of their measures, or advises them on the proper and improper questions to be raised about social life' (p. 63). According to Myers (1993), 'The intellectual imperialism of Western patriarchy has proven to be viciously intolerant of any perspective that breaks the bonds of its conceptual incarceration' (p. 4).

TAKING A SECOND LOOK AT THE CULTURAL ETHOS WITHIN WHICH PSYCHOLOGY IS EMBEDDED

There is another likely reason for the difficulty others and I have experienced in getting our views on the ethnocentrism of psychology aired in some of the mainstream journals. Our papers do not simply critique the principles and the practices of psychology, but take a hard look at the cultural ideology within which the discipline is embedded. The critique of the cultural ethos underlying psychology by the present generation of African American scholars is in many respects analogous to perspectives which have, in the late 1960s, been considered to be politically revolutionary. The black revolutionaries of then saw 'White culture as decadent, lacking in humanistic concern for others, and they predicted the ultimate death of white civilization with the emergence of a new order of human values based on respect for human dignity' (White, 1984, p. 48).

Myers (1993) wonders about the mentality and mind set of Western cultures that

> have sought to such great extent to colonize the world; enslave a race of people through a uniquely dehumanizing form of slavery; steal the land of a people and nearly annihilate them in the process; promote two world wars, in one attempting to exterminate one race of people to ensure another's purity; totally disregard the ecological balance of nature, promoting environmental pollution and the depletion of natural resources; and create a society in which women feel they must totally reject their male counterparts. (p. 11)

A related puzzlement for Myers is why, 'over time the European-Americans would distort, deny, change, and repress their awareness of past behavior and the knowledge of the behaviors of their forbears to the extent that they would accept no responsibility for past actions and refuse to recognize any connection of the past to their current functioning' (p. 9). It is, therefore, no small wonder that Myers regards the worldview underlying Western thought and Euro-American culture to be inadequate to serve as a basis for an optimal psychology.

Its materialistic focus continues to spawn individualism, competitiveness, and dichotomous thinking, assumptions with negative consequences for a wide range of mental health and social issues facing contemporary society. In fact, Baldwin (1989) describes America, South Africa, and the whole European dominated world as a 'nightmare' (p. 76). The *vested interest of Western society itself is to oppress Black people* (p. 71). Others share Baldwin's view. For instance, Bulhan (1985) stated that 'Euro-America strove to *master* nature and *control* people' (p. 65).

The emphasis in the Western world on an external material reality constituted by separate entities generates research methodologies which, despite their claims of objectivity, lead to false knowledge of the self and construct barriers to the development of knowledge regarding black people (Myers, 1993). The time honoured psychometric tools of psychology 'are not only biased against black people but fall short of providing any useful data in predicting talents, capabilities, or skills for the majority of black youngsters' (Guthrie, 1991, p. 35). The fragmented, material, and externalised worldview underlying Western science and adopted by psychology is regarded by Guthrie to have caused the discipline to evolve 'into a sterile, pedestrian science' (p. 24), 'essentially useless as an instrument of human liberation' (Akbar, 1984a, p. 399).

> The Euro-American worldview spawned a reductionistic psychology concerned with categorization, mental measurement, and the estab-lishment of norms. The primary unit of study was the individual, and emphasis was Centred on the early years of child development. Differences and diversity from established norms were treated as deviant. Unacceptable thoughts, feelings, and impulses were regulated into the unconscious. Despite claims of scientific objectivity in the measurement of mental abilities, the outcome of these measurements has consistently supported the popular belief of Anglo intellectual superiority.
>
> (White, 1984, p. 14)

> The Afro-American perspective as the foundation for the psychology of Black folks was largely ignored in the first hundred years of formal psychology . . . In the pages of psychology textbooks, Afro-Americans were like Ralph Ellison's *Invisible Man* (1947) – unacknowledged and unseen. When there was a brief mention of Afro-Americans under the generic rubric of Negroes, the emphasis was on deviance, pathology, and abnormality, using descriptive terms such as impulse-ridden, passive-dependent, disorganized, emotionally immature, poor self-image, self-hatred, identity confusion, psycho-sexual conflicts, and cultural deprivation.
>
> (White, 1984, p. 15)

Green (1980), among many others, shares the view that 'traditional psychology has either ignored Black problems or described them inaccurately' (p. 337).

Similar to the situation in South Africa, Green laments the misuse of psychological tests and their disproportionate contribution 'to the justification of personal and institutionalized racism which characterizes America' (p. 337).

With respect to African Americans who must contend with negative stereotypes about their abilities in many scholastic domains, Steele (1997), in an interesting series of studies, has pointed out how the threat of being stereotyped negatively 'can affect the members of any group about whom a negative stereotype exists' (p. 614). Thus, stereotype threat, which 'is cued by the mere recognition that a negative group stereotype could apply to oneself in a given situation' (p. 617), 'may be a possible source of bias in standardized tests, a bias that arises not from item content but from group differences in the threat that societal stereotypes attach to test performance' (p. 622).

Traditionally, psychological diagnoses have ascribed the lower test performance of African American students to internal processes ranging from genes to the internalisation of negative stereotypes about their group. By bringing about situational changes that reduce the threat of being stereotyped, the schooling of stereotype-threatened groups can be improved. Steele (1997) mentions the importance of optimistic teacher–student relationships within which the expandability of intelligence is stressed. In the present context, it is especially his suggestion that the focus must be on challenging students, rather than on remediation, that is of the greatest interest, for 'remedial work reinforces in these students the possibility that they are being viewed stereotypically' (p. 625). Steele produced evidence of this being the case. Thus, despite the good intentions of minority remediation programmes, such programmes can backfire by institutionalising the racial stereotype which minority students are threatened by.

The deficit-deficiency model should make way for a concentration on the strengths Black folks have used to survive and actualise themselves under oppressive conditions in various parts of the world. It is no small wonder, therefore, that Blake (1981) suggested that the term 'method' be rethought Africentrically. In psychology the exclusive use of statistical criteria should be supplemented with consensual 'validation, oral history, intuitiveness, and the word of the people as witnesses of their own direct experience' (White, 1984, p. 19). For alternative theoretical perspectives and new approaches to conducting research relevant to the experience of African Americans, Part I of the text edited by Burlew and associates (1992) presents a rich pool of information.

It is time that the conclusion-oriented approach to psychological research, focused on developing psychology as a 'pure science', be replaced by decision-oriented research, with a problem-centred and applied base, in order to narrow the gap between knowledge and action (Green, 1980). The 'esoteric interests of the affluent' (p. 336) should make way for attending to crucial issues facing the poor and the oppressed. Green points out that what seems to be behavioural problems in urban environments are often normal reactions to abnormal environmental conditions, which cannot be solved by one-to-one therapy and a focus on individual responsibility.

Since the worldview upon which Western psychology is based, is 'anti-black/anti-African' (Baldwin, 1989, p. 73), it must be rejected as a framework within which to search for the philosophical assumptions and methodology to improve the lives of black people. 'It is very difficult, if not impossible, to understand the lifestyle of black people using traditional theories developed by white psychologists to explain white people' (White, 1991, p. 5). Akbar (1984a), is of the opinion that 'The oversimplification of Western social science, though impressively more manageable, is disastrously myopic in its exclusion of blatantly causal realities. Logical positivism and reductionism have tried to make men and women thoroughly rational and minute enough to fit a micro model of a unidimensional view of humanity' (p. 405). The critical perspective of the Somali psychologist, Bulhan (1985), fits in well with the opinion of his American colleagues. Bulhan pointed out that 'most psychological problems – and certainly all *relevant* human experiences – are inevitably complex, dynamic, and rarely amenable to neatly controlled experimentation or reducible to meaningful quantification' (p. 66). He is particularly scathing of 'psychology's fetish for quantification and . . . failure to appreciate not only the total context but also the qualitative peculiarity of the human psyche' (Bulhan 1993a, p. 13). According to Bulhan (1985), psychology's failure to live up to the expectations of the discipline, are, apart from its ethnocentric bias, due to what he describes as the discipline's methodological solipsism.

> The net consequence of this approach is that psychological reality is reduced to what can be codified, counted, and computed. In such a reduction, psychological reality is decontextualized, reified, and trivialized. The wish to attain scientific respectability forces a rigid adherence to count-measure rituals that compromise the salience of meaning and value in human experience . . . human experience is seen to exist only insofar as it permits the 'operational definitions' of Euro-American psychologists.
>
> (Bulhan, 1985, p. 68)

Asante (1992) criticises what he describes as the religion of Western science, for sacrificing a holistic perspective for the sake of a world of specific phenomena where nothing except humankind is sacred. In keeping with the mainstream psychologists who deplore the fragmentaion and the depreciation of values in psychology, Asante considers the scientific approach too shallow to fulfil the humanistic and spiritual dimensions of an Africentric psychology. The emphasis on methodology becomes a politics of manipulation, devoid of emotion, feeling, and soul.

Semmes (1981) challenges 'European ideas about progress and the Western world's faith in materialism and technology' (p. 16). He considers the growth and development of European societies to 'reflect a kind of cultural regression in terms of the evolution of mankind and human culture' (p. 16). Aspiring towards the control of nature, rather than living in harmony with nature, 'is counterproductive to the liberation and development of the human spirit' (p. 16).

Myers (1993) has even stronger criticisms of the Euro-American worldview underlying psychology. She regards it as 'suboptimal' for fostering psychological development. In fact, 'the sub-optimal worldview creates disorder' (p. 15). Myers even describes it as evil in so far as its segmented nature prevents the coming about of the greater good as exemplified in the holistic order of which it is part, and through which it becomes fully actualised. The only redeeming feature about the Western worldview, as far as Myers is concerned, is the fact that it can serve as an indication of what the nature of the optimal conceptual system ought to steer away from.

PSYCHOLOGY AS A TOOL OF OPPRESSION

Apart from Asante (1992), several African American psychologists are of the opinion that the assumptions underlying mainstream psychology do not only render the discipline ineffective with respect to the lives of black people, but that it actually perpetuates the system that oppresses them. According to Akbar (1984a) the exclusive reliance on 'individualism, rationalism and materialism . . . renders Western social science an effective instrument of human oppression and exploitation' and 'an ineffective instrument for human growth and liberation' (p. 403). Akbar also quotes Nobles as stating that 'Western Science, particularly social science, like the economic and political institutions has become an instrument designed to reflect the culture of the oppressor and to allow for the more efficient domination and oppression of African peoples' (p. 395). Akbar goes on to state that 'Consequently, the uncritical acceptance of the assumptions of Western science by African peoples is to participate in our own domination and oppression' (p. 395). In the 'garb of "science" the Western world has utilized a social and psychological paradigm that functions to legitimize the assertion of their racial and national superiority. What has been assumed to be a political, objective system is, in fact, the essence of Euro-American, Caucasian politics' (Akbar, 1984a, p. 400–401). Myers (1991) regards the assumptions underlying psychology as basic tools 'of oppression and intellectual imperialism' (p. 23). Like Akbar and Myers, Asante (1983), Baldwin (1986), Bulhan (1985, 1993a, 1993b), and Hayes (1991) also regard the adoption of the rules of science by psychology as the fostering of a complicity in social control and oppression. Under the guise of being scientific investigators of human behaviour, psychologists 'find expression for their cultural and racial biases' (Hayes, 1991, p. 65).

As a scholar of and inspired by the work of Frantz Fanon, Bulhan (1985) is especially devastating in his critique of psychology. He, too, places psychology firmly within the history of conquest and domination. According to Bulhan, psychology 'revealed itself more as a part of the problem of domination than as a discipline readily amenable to the resolution of oppression' (p. 5).

> Euro-American psychologists, with the narrow definition of their profession, tended to show little interest in oppression. Unlike other disciplines of the human sciences, they traditionally ignored the problems of underdevelopment in the Third World, the dynamics of domination, the reactions of the oppressed, and the patterns of social change. On the occasions they did study people of color . . . the result was historically disastrous. In the realm of theory, they universally adopted the legacy of victim blame. When they worked clinically with the human debris of Europe's historical assaults, they tended to be instruments of social control, extolling the aim of adjustment to the status quo, however intolerable and hostile to human needs. Even when they conducted 'cross-cultural research' without the ostensible racism of earlier researchers, their concern has been less in understanding or changing the plight of the oppressed and more in testing hypotheses to advance Euro-American psychology or to settle academic debates at home. This general disinterest, or 'mis-placed' priorities of Euro-American psychologists, has limited the diversity and general relevance of psychology.
>
> (Bulhan, 1985, p.8)

Arguing 'that psychology does not exist in a social vacuum and that psychologists are rooted in their society and time,' Bulhan (1985, p. 10) contends that psychology cannot be divorced from the cultural ethos which gave it birth, an ethos which Baldwin (1989) described 'as a "nightmare" for black men and women, boys and girls' (p. 76). According to Asante (1992), 'Five hundred years of constant propaganda, cultural exploitation, information distortion, and physical annihilation have left the African world shocked out of its own historical reality and purpose in the world . . . European aggression has been equated with intelligence and Africa reels from the effects of this aggression unable to shake the theoretical, political, economic, or cultural chains' (p. 104). Bulhan finds it remarkable that a discipline renowned for its commitment to unmasking the repressed has so persistently failed to address 'the historical avarice and violence' (1985, p. 58) unleashed by Europe on the world. Throughout the history of psychology a culture of silence has prevailed with respect to Europe's 'history of global rampage on people of color' (p. 63). 'Conveniently omitted also are the bigotry and complicity of major pioneers who defined the priorities, content, and methods of establishment psychology' (p. 58). Instead of confronting the amnesia with respect to the violence and the oppression 'psychologists have stood apart, or acted as neutral agents, in the history of oppression' (p. 38).

Even more serious is Bulhan's contention that psychology has not merely stood apart, but,

> The specialists whose profession it is to make sense out of madness and heal psychic wounds are themselves enmeshed in that historical rampage and violence. Euro-American psychology itself is now a veritable arsenal. Those who profess and practice it are waging wars within wars, even when the immediate victim is a child whose IQ is being tested. There is a culture of silence on Europe's violence and a convenient amnesia among established psychologists.
>
> (Bulhan, 1985, p. 58)

Thus, psychology remains enmeshed in 'a scandal of global dimensions' (p. 9), in a history of 'conquest and violence' (p. 37), characterised by 'the crimes of Europe and its descendants against people of color' (p. 13). The theories and tools of psychology merely perpetuate the colonial conquest and 'demonstrate the historical complicity of Euro-American psychology in global oppression . . . Thus as we find armies fulfilling aims of conquest for their society, so do we discover psychologists justifying domination and conquest' (p. 10).

> The ascendancy and globalization of Euro-American psychology indeed correlates with the ascendancy and globalization of Euro-American military, economic, and political might. Viewed from this perspective, the organized discipline of psychology reveals itself as yet another form of alien intrusion and cultural imposition for the nonwhite majority of the world. It is strange but true that the human psyche, even in a remote African village, is today defined, studied, and mystified according to the techniques and styles of Europe and its Diaspora. There is a remarkable irony here. The Europeans and their descendants who embarked on violent assaults on the rest of the world now dictate the theories and methods of comprehending the essential of human psychology.
>
> (Bulhan, 1985, p. 64)

The power of this intrusion is so pervasive that Bulhan regards its uncritical adoption by non-Western people as a manifestation of the imperialistic powers which psychology has achieved.

Akbar (1984b) attributed the colonial conquest by European countries to the conviction of the inhabitants of this part of the world that they were created in the image of God. Apart from endowing them with an unnatural perspective on themselves and others, this belief gives rise to an 'addiction to excess' (p. 45), which Akbar believes is likely to lead to the eventual destruction of the Western world, 'because it no longer has the capacity to correct itself' (p. 44).

THE IMPORTANCE OF REMAINING TRUE TO ONE'S ORIGINS

Baldwin (1989), Bulhan (1985), Akbar (1984b), and Asante (1992) take those of their African American colleagues to task who unwittingly adopt the dominant Western paradigm, and in so doing participate in the oppression and psychological destruction of black people. The same critique is directed towards professional organisations that do not have the African American experience as their primary objective. Kambon (aka Baldwin) and Hopkins (1993) fail to understand how African American scholars can overlook the impact of the persistent racism in America and the world community of Europeans over the past 400–500 years. Baldwin speaks of 'the psychological genocide of Black people by Black psychologists' (p. 67–68). He states that, 'Black psychologists, by and large, have functioned in the service of the continued oppression and/or enslavement of Black people rather than in the service of our liberation from Western oppression and positive Black mental health (unconscious on our part, no doubt, but the consequences are still the same)' (p. 67). 'Black psychologists must first remove the alien Eurocentric self-consciousness' (p. 75) from their own psyches before they can uncover the fundamental realities of their own African experience. Asante compares those who are 'looking whitely through a tunnel lit with the artificial beams of Europe' (p. 1), to ants battling against impossible odds. He also regards the adoption of Islamic cultural customs in America by African people as a serious and perhaps tragic mistake. 'Our problems come when we lose sight of ourselves, accept false doctrines, false gods, mistaken notions of what is truly in our history, and assume an individualistic, antihumanistic, and autocratic posture' (p. 6). He wrote 'that there are blacks who are so thoroughly educated in the American system of racism that they have become racist against themselves' (p. 91). The liberation of the minds of 'These anti-black blacks or the "unblack blacks" who cannot see from within but see other "blacks" as objects from without' (p. 91), 'will be a tougher battle than the eradication of settler regimes' (p. 105). According to Akbar (1984b), 'The real irony is the number of highly aware African-Americans who are literally locked-in intellectually to the authority and intellectual leadership of non-African people. The authority may be Marx, Freud, Skinner or Jesus, but the underlying basis for the authoritativeness of the figure is his similarity to the Caucasian image' (p. 54) of the divinity. It is no small wonder then 'that the only qualities that are civilized qualities are those that are associated with Caucasians' (p. 57). The false sense of self can lead to disorders which Akbar described as alien-self and anti-self disorders (in Myers, 1993). Through denial of their cultural/historical background, African Americans can become so estranged from whom they are that total rejection of the ancestral origins and the self occurs. In the anti-self disorder, the self becomes exclusively defined in terms of the external criteria of the dominant group. Such estrangement, or rather, endorsement of Anglocultural values, was found to be associated with a higher incidence of delinquency, aggression and

Machiavellianism – the manipulation of others for one's own purpose – among inner-city African American children (Jagers and Mock, 1993).

According to Baldwin (1989), 'the highest level of positive Black mental health is this vital psychological orientation that we refer to as African self-consciousness' (p. 74). Based on the evidence of a strong relationship between effective psychological functioning and conscious adherence to an Africentric worldview, Jackson and Sears (1992) proposed restructuring the worldview of African American women who experienced low levels of emotional well-being, as a means 'to counter the negative images that often result in stressful appraisals of an oppressive and hostile environment' (p. 184). Myers (1993) also proposed Belief Systems Analysis as a therapeutic approach based on cognitively restructuring the belief system of African Americans in terms of Africentric principles.

The link between ethnic preference behaviour and healthy identity and personality development has been called into question, however, (Penn, Gaines, and Phillips, 1993; Penn and Kiesel, 1994; Phillips, Penn, and Gaines, 1993). In accordance with the warnings about cultural dichotomisation mentioned earlier, Penn and his co-workers warn about the danger involved in own-group preference on the part of minorities living in societies, which are becoming increasingly multicultural. The assassination of Martin Luther King, Jr. in 1968, is seen as the turning point in the endeavour of African Americans to achieve interracial unity. With the resultant loss of hope that racial solidarity and justice can ever be achieved, those African Americans who have been socially active redirected their energy into racially segregated movements. However, Penn and his colleagues warn that no ethnic and cultural group constitutes an autonomous and self-sufficient unit. They accept that love and appreciation of one's race, culture, or ethnicity is necessary, but they do not consider it sufficient for healthy functioning in the multicultural and multiracial society of the United States today. Their concern is that own group preference, as a reaction to the prejudice experienced by minorities, can become as ethnocentric as the ethnocentrism it is a reaction against. They warn African Americans to be careful not 'to adopt the prejudices that have characterised Eurocentric thinking for so long' (Phillips et al., 1993, p. 355).

The transcendence of racial and cultural boundaries is, therefore, considered to be essential for functioning optimally in the world of today. The vision which Penn and his associates have for the future of humanity is the establishment of a global human consciousness in order to 'protect, promote, and celebrate the diverse and invaluable elements that comprise us' (Phillips et al., 1993, p. 353). They propose to achieve the ideal of a global human consciousness through articulating 'an organic (dialogic) metaphor for conceptualizing interethnic relations' (Penn and Kiesel, 1994, p. 398). Although the nature of the proposed 'organic dialogue' is not apparent in their writing, in principle these psychologists seem to subscribe to the dialogical perspective that is gaining increasing recognition in contemporary psychology.

However, it is clear from the comments on the ideas of Penn and his co-workers that the nature of the dialogue will depend greatly on the way in which the power structure in the dialogical relationship is perceived. Kambon and Hopkins (1993) maintain that the distribution of power is persistently so heavily in favour of the dominant Euro-American group that African Americans need to develop strategies to survive and develop their strength as a collective entity. A determined focus on the African nature of their identity seems to offer the best alternative in order to be able to enter into dialogue on a more equal footing.

Earlier, Asante (1983) had already pointed out that intercultural communication that is in any way meaningful cannot be achieved unless it is realised to what extent those who wield economic, political, and cultural power, define what is right, logical, and reasonable. Asante, therefore, stressed that 'effective intercultural communication must be based upon the equality of the interactants' (pp. 5–6). For the development of an African cultural base to hold its own against that of the West, the collective support of the whole community is needed and any deviation from this goal is perceived as a betrayal of the common purpose. Due to the skewed existing situation, it is felt that nothing but a concentrated focus on celebrating the African component of the African American experience will suffice. In addition, Kambon and Hopkins call upon their colleagues to be prepared

> to engage in serious intellectual battle if we are to ultimately liberate the African experience in the world from the incarceration of Eurocentric/White supremacy scholarship. The enemies of African cultural sovereignty are amassing just beyond the horizon. While they may not presently be in our full view, make no mistake about it – (with history as our witness) they are surely flexing their muscles, sharpening their weapons, and preparing themselves to launch their full-scale attack.
>
> (Kambon and Hopkins, 1983, p. 348)

Clearly, many African American psychologists and social scientists feel that dialogue is not possible unless the disparity with respect to the present distribution of power can be eliminated, and that can be done best, they argue, by strengthening their African identity, rather than by means of cultural accommodation or assimilation. As Asante (1986) stressed, 'All intercultural relations begin with the perception of self and then extend outward, but to be meaningful it must be knowledgeable' (p. 18).

In their critique of the uncritical adoption of mainstream psychological paradigms by their fellow African Americans, and in their call for the development of an Africentric identity, Akbar, Kambon, Myers, and others, are in keeping with the ideas of their colleagues in countries further south (e.g., Biko, in Stubbs, 1979; Bodibe, in press; Bulhan, 1985; Fanon, 1965, 1976; Freire, 1970). For instance, with respect to the development of self-awareness, Fanon (1976) wrote that 'The consciousness of self is not the closing of a door to communication. Philosophic thought teaches us, on the contrary, that it is its guarantee. National consciousness, which is not nationalism, is the only thing that will give us an international dimension . . . It is at the heart of national consciousness that international consciousness lives and grows' (p. 199).

DEVELOPING AN AFRICENTRIC PSYCHOLOGY

Social scientists in the United States have been criticised for responding to the challenge of desegregation in a reactive rather than an innovative fashion (Cook, 1985). It is for this reason that African American psychologists have embarked on a vigorous campaign to develop a proactive psychology (Asante, 1983, 1992; Baldwin, 1986, 1989; Jackson, 1982; Jones, 1991; Myers, 1993; Nobles, 1972; White, 1984). The movement towards an Africentric base is not restricted to psychology, but is also evident in education (e.g., Boateng, 1983), black studies (e.g., Smith and Yates, 1980) and the social sciences generally (Akbar, 1984a; Anderson, 1993; Semmes, 1981). 'Africentricity is the form of a new paradigm for the social sciences. It grows out of the increasing inadequacy of the Eurocentric model to address the escalating social problems of Western society adequately. Most importantly, the model seeks to correct the indirect oppressive function played by traditional Western science' (Akbar, 1984a, p. 412). 'The Africentric model is comfortable with global conceptions and metaphysical conceptions, and offers a macro model that actually exceeds the manipulation of the observing observer whose object of observation is ultimately himself or herself' (Akbar, 1984a, p. 405). Akbar also cautions that 'The Africentric model must be viewed as a perspective independent of the Eurocentric model; otherwise, it too will become merely reactive and therefore persistently dependent on the European model' (pp. 398–399). Baldwin (1989), Semmes (1981), and others are in agreement. Bulhan envisages Afrocentric psychology to set

> for itself the task of grasping not merely the quantifiable segments of behaviour but of the total experiences of Africans in the continent and the Diaspora. This scientific discipline does not, on the basis of idealism *invent* its own subject-matter but *discovers* creatively the true psychology of Africans from their lived activities, social relations, material conditions, as well as history. Indeed more than intellectually grasping the experiences of Africans, scientific African psychology embraces its revolutionary task of not only *interpreting* the African world but of *changing* it.
>
> (Bulhan, 1993a, p. 28)

The debate in the United States has already reached the stage where the appropriate title for the new movement is being discussed. Among the titles being considered are that of Black Psychology (Jackson, 1982; White, 1984), African Psychology or African-Black Psychology (Baldwin, 1986). Initially Black Psychology served as an appropriate title. Jackson traces its origins to 'the 1920s when Afro-American psychologists first published research studies to dispel the notion of Afro-American inferiority and sought to increase the psychological services rendered to the Afro-American community' (p. 342). Baldwin goes back much further in history, 'as long as African people have existed, so has African (Black) Psychology, whether Black people ever actually formally expressed it (in the Western sense) or not' (p. 237). White is in agreement. 'Black psychology is as old as African heritage . . . The job of Black psychologists was to articulate in psychological terms what was already present in the Black experience' (p. 18). The initial studies 'were stimulated primarily by a reaction to the existence of institutional racism' (Jackson, 1982, pp. 243–244). However, Black Psychology has developed a far broader base than being exclusively a reactive discipline. 'Black psychology is something more than the psychology of the so-called underprivileged peoples . . . African (Black) Psychology is rooted in the nature of Black culture which is based on particular (originally indigenous to Africa) philosophical assumptions . . . Briefly, it must examine the elements and dimensions of the experiential communalities of African peoples' (Nobles, 1972, pp. 18 and 31). Baldwin expressed similar sentiments. He wrote that

> African (Black) Psychology . . . derives naturally from the 'worldview' or philosophical premises underlying African culture itself (as does Western Psychology relative to the worldview of European culture) . . . the justification for African (Black) Psychology's existence as well as its independence from Western Psychology inheres in the fundamental distinctness between and independence of African and European Cosmologies.
>
> (Baldwin, 1986, p. 237)

According to White,

> Black psychology, the psychology of blackness, is the attempt to build a conceptual model to organize, explain, and understand the psychosocial behavior of Black Americans based on the primary dimensions of an Afro-American world view . . . At the root of the Afro-American frame of reference is an identifiable African cultural influence that has persisted despite the continuing exposure of the Black American psyche to the Euro-American culture during the past 350 and more years of geographical and temporal separation from Africa.
>
> (White, 1984, p. 3)

Indeed, most workers in the field agree that 'Africanity' is the focus and strength of the developing discipline (Akbar, 1984a,b; Asante, 1983, 1992; Baldwin, 1986, 1989; Jackson, 1982). Africentric (Baldwin, 1986) or Afrocentric (Asante, 1983, 1992; Semmes, 1981) psychology seems, therefore, to be the most appropriate title. Both terms are used interchangeably in this text. Recently, liberation psychology (Azibo, 1994) and optimal psychology (Myers, 1993) have been proposed as titles. In essence, Africentric psychology 'is a composite of reactive, inventive and innovative components and extends . . . "to the total behavior in all situations of Black people throughout the world"' (Jackson in Baldwin, 1986, p. 241). Similarly, Fairchild (1994) stated that 'Black psychology has had both reactive and proactive components . . . Both components, in fact, are necessary, because Euroamerican psychology continues virtually unabated in its attack on the essence of the African personality/community' (p. 370). In terms of its holistic nature, it is appropriate that Africentric psychology incorporates both reactive and proactive components.

The spiritual isolation that African Americans experience in a society which constantly bombards them 'with anti-Africa rhetoric and symbols' (Asante, 1992, p. x), is undoubtedly one of the factors which contributed to the pronounced 'Afrocentric assertion' or 'intellectual activism' (p. x), which has been portrayed in this chapter. In addition to the reactive component of Africentric psychology, Asante (1992) regards Afrocentricity as the centrepiece of human regeneration. 'It is purposeful, giving a true sense of destiny based upon the facts of history and experience' (p. 1). Afrocentricity is the basis underlying an Africentric psychology. It provides the framework by which all human enterprise is to be approached. The 'Afrocentric cultural project is a holistic plan to reconstruct and develop every dimension of the African world from the standpoint of Africa as subject rather than object' (Asante, 1992, p. 105). Asante speaks of Afrocentricity, 'as a transforming agent in which all things that were old become new and a transformation of attitudes, beliefs, values, and behavior results. It becomes everywhere sensed and is everywhere present. A new reality is invoked; a new vision is introduced. In fact, it is the first and only reality for African people; it is simply rediscovery. Our eyes become new or rather what we see becomes clearer' (p. 2). 'Afrocentricity is a liberating ideology' (p. 102), a 'revolutionary consciousness' (p. 101). It decolonises the mind, cleanses it of European interpretations and the misreading of history and historical events. 'The Afrocentric paradigm offers a method of structuring consciousness which . . . seeks to unify human finite consciousness with infinite God consciousness' (Myers, 1993, p. 35). 'Afrocentricity as a science and method seeks to change the way we refer to ourselves and our history . . . The search is not for a naive nationalism nor a superficial socialism but rather a deep, self-conscious, positive relationship with our own experiences' (p.105).

Afrocentrism has a rich history. The persons, places and events of importance in this history need to be honoured in the same manner that the other great cultural traditions of the world honour their past. 'Our cultural heritage and history have been negated, while the cultural heritage and history of sub-optimal thinkers have been elevated' (Myers, 1993, p. 16). Asante maintains that identity cannot be found unless there is recognition of rootedness in one's collective history. Acceptance 'of the past will be the beginning of our liberation' (1992, p. 29). 'You must always begin from where you are, that is, if you are Yoruba begin with Yoruba history and mythology; if you are Kikuyu, begin with Kikuyu history and mythology; if you are African-American, begin with African-American history and mythology' (Asante, 1992, p. 7).

Based on the historical contributions of such African Americans as Booker T. Washington, Marcus Garvey, Martin Luther King, Jr., Elijah Muhammad, W.E.B. Du Bois, Malcolm X, Maulana Karenga, and others, Asante (1992), therefore, formulated *Njia*, the Way towards the collective expression of an Afrocentric worldview in the United States. *Njia* represents an awareness and acceptance of a universal African consciousness and, in so doing, an acceptance of the African American centre as the core for determining everything one does. 'Njia establishes a link to our fundamental primordial truths' (p. 22). It is through the process of rediscovering the African heritage that Afrocentric psychology came to be formulated in the United States (Myers, 1993).

THE AFRICAN BASE OF THE AFRICAN AMERICAN WORLD VIEW

According to White (1984), the defining characteristics of the African American worldview, which has its roots in African cosmology and the American experience, are expressed by emotional vitality, realness, interrelatedness, resilience and revitalisation, as well as distrust and deception. To this list, spirituality, faith in a transcendental force, and belief in the concept of oneness or cosmological unity must certainly be added.

> Spirituality connotes a belief that all elements of reality contain a certain amount of life force. It entails believing and behaving as if nonobservable and nonmaterial life forces have governing powers in one's everyday affairs. Thus a continuous sensitivity to core spiritual qualities takes priority in one's life and indeed is vital to one's personal well being. Although often expressed in God concepts, this ongoing core spiritual sensitivity is not necessarily tied to formal church doctrine or participation. Indeed, it goes beyond church affiliation. Moreover, it connotes a belief in the transcendence of physical death and a sense of continuity with one's ancestors.
>
> (Jagers and Mock, 1993, p. 394)

Emotional vitality is reflected in spontaneity, in ease with physical contact and in touching, and openness to direct experience, to sensuality and feelings of sadness and joy. Realness is manifested in being down-to-earth, in genuineness and authenticity (White, 1984). Emotional vitality and realness can be integrated by the concept of affect, which Jagers and Mock (1993) used in their operationalisation of Afrocentric perspectives. In addition, it can also be summarised as an acceptance of self and of others (Penn and Kiesel, 1994). In addition to emotional expressiveness, the affective value of information and, in particular, sensitivity to the emotional cues given off by others, is implied. 'It connotes behaving toward others largely in light of the feelings or attitudes that others project and the "vibrations" they give off. It denotes placing a low priority on holding back emotional expression. It implies the integration of feelings with thoughts and actions such that it would be difficult to engage in an activity if one's feelings toward the activity run counter to such engagement' (Jagers and Mock, 1993, p. 394). The importance of interrelatedness in the Africentric perspective is evident in the many ways in which it is described – as interdependence, connectedness, cooperativeness, communalism, mutual support, collective sharing, respect for others, especially the elderly, the importance of the extended family, and the oral tradition. The 'Highest value is placed on positive interpersonal relationships' (Myers, 1993, p.13).

> One's orientation is social rather than being directed toward objects. There is overriding importance attached to social bonds and social relationships. One acts in accordance with the notion that duty to one's social group is more important than individual rights and privileges. Hence one's identity is tied to group membership rather than to individual status and possessions. Sharing is promoted because it confirms the importance of social interconnectedness. Self-centredness and individual greed are frowned upon.
>
> (Jagers and Mock, 1993, p. 394)

> These interdependent relationships and social networks are connected across time and space by the oral tradition, the power of the spoken word. The spoken word, the language of Afro-Americans, represents a shared participatory space in which both speaker and listener continuously affirm each other's presence within the context of a call-response dialogue. The goal in Black social interaction and language patterns is to be able to move harmoniously with the rhythm of what's happening, to be in time and in touch with the flow, pace, and tempo of events as opposed to being on time. Time is not a commodity rigidly controlled by a metric system, but a series of events that are experienced and shared with others throughout the course of the life cycle.
>
> (White, 1984, pp. 3–4)

The logical extension of the connectedness between humans is oneness with nature or cosmological unity. In elaborating the metaphysical significance of metallurgy in Africa, Richards (1981) hopes to inspire her fellow African Americans with the wonder and the wisdom of Africa's unitive cosmology.

Due to the hardships of life and of living in a racist society, black children acquire resilience at an early age in their development. On the basis of first-hand experience they learn that life is not easy. The confluence of African American and Euro-American values within which they grow up confront black American children with an inclusion–exclusion identity dilemma. It is through the network of family and peers in the immediate psychosocial environment that a workable balance can be found and a frame of reference established through which their impressions of the white world can be filtered without undue influence on their sense of self (White, 1984). The same has been true of blacks in South Africa. As they grow into adults, 'The openness to a balanced spectrum of human emotions in Black Consciousness unencumbered by guilt, shame, and self-debasement makes it easier to draw upon the revitalization powers of sensuousness, joy, and laughter' (White, 1984, p. 31).

> The willingness to laugh in the face of misfortune without denying the seriousness of adverse reality is part of the survival equipment of Afro-Americans. Humor grounded in reality is psychologically refreshing; it defines the situation in manageable terms and prevents the build-up of unbearable anxieties by not allowing people to take themselves too seriously. Soul is the ability to laugh while growing with hardships, paying dues, and transcending tragedies.
>
> (White, 1984, p. 33)

White's definition of soul parallels the distinction made in archetypal psychology between soul and spirit (Hillman, 1979).

According to White (1984), distrust and deception of the white community have also become part of the psychological perspective of African Americans. The distrust of white people has resulted in linguistic deception being developed into a fine art. Since the spoken word is such a pervasive force in the African American community, the extensive use of metaphor in Black speech, and the tonal rhymes with which it is expressed, make Black language and speech an ideal tool to hide and convey hidden meanings. 'Black metaphoric expressions generate multiple meanings' (White, 1984, p. 38). The meanings are dependent on the cultural connotation associated with the use of the metaphor in a specific situation. Thus, the use of culturally different semantics enables Blacks to conceal the real intent of their words from white folks while still maintaining a high level of clarity in their communications with brothers and sisters. Words, phrases, and statements that are taken to mean one thing when interpreted from a Euro-American frame of reference can mean something entirely different when translated through an Afro-American ethnotropic filter (White, 1984).

Because Africans have shown such a remarkable ability to humanise any language they have spoken, Asante (1992) has suggested that it was 'in the soul

127

of our people to seize and redirect language toward liberating ideas and thought'
(p. 32). Indeed, language is of great importance in the control of thought. Asante
wants the language of African Americans to be aggressive and innovative, to be
a new language of consciousness. He wants the creation of a new language to
counter the manipulation of the African reality that has, thus far, been effected
by means of language. He urges creativity, innovation, and the bombardment of
the communication channels with positive images to counteract racist repression
and to celebrate the African American experience in terms of its separateness
from, as well as its connectedness to, a Pan-African world.

As an example of what Asante (1992) has in mind is his use of the term *endarken*
to indicate *enlighten*. To him, the concept of continent is associated with Africa
and not with Europe, as is generally implied. Being a Judas, becomes a 'Vesey's
tattler' (Vesey was the pseudonym of Samual Allen, an African American poet).
'Masai' is substituted for Spartan. The word, minority, is abandoned because the
identity of the people intended has to be stipulated in African custom. Asante,
furthermore, advocates constant vigilance of the implications of such concepts
as urban jungle or the definition of excellence in one form or another, in terms
of European antecedents. He points out that imagination literally means to
image-a-nation!

With a concerted Africentric evaluation of language, the same awareness
of implicit racism can hopefully be achieved as occurred with respect to the
awareness of sexism in language. Asante's call to put language to use in furthering
Africentricity, thus, seems to build on a process that has been set in motion
during the time of the slaves. That this process is gathering force is evident in
developments regarding Ebonics. Towards the end of 1996, the Oakland,
California, school board passed a resolution to accept Ebonics or AAVE (African
American Vernacular English) as a language to be used as a bridge to teach
standard English (Williams, 1997). Recently, the *Journal of Black Psychology*, has
devoted a special section on the Ebonics controversy ('Ebonics', 1997).

Additional aspects of the oral tradition that need to be nurtured in Africentric
psychology relate to the educational value of fables, folktales, legends, myths, and
proverbs. These components of oral literature served an important function in
the past in bridging the gap between the generations and preparing the youth for
their responsibilities as adults in their communities without ever feeling that they
were bombarded with rules and regulations (Boateng, 1983).

In addition to language, Asante (1992) also stresses the necessity of translating
Afrocentricity into programmes of psychological and political action. Work in
one area will be of significance in the other. The psychological will facilitate the
political and vice-versa. A great deal of misunderstanding exists with respect to
all aspects of African American psychology. These misunderstandings relate
to the psychosocial dynamics of black family life, the psychological development
of black youth, their teaching, as well as the requirements for a mental health
delivery system to the African American community. White (1984), therefore,
highlights the Africentric perspective in these areas in order to delineate the

inadequacy of the models on which mainstream applications are based and to provide a relevant basis on which to proceed in future.

Asante (1992) points out the importance of such relatively simple deeds as the way one dresses or the choosing of an African name to renounce the use of white personal identity symbols. Besides rejecting slave names, the choice of an African name signifies an acceptance of one's African origins, a desire for an identity separate from that of whites. James Baldwin, for instance, changed his name to Kobi Kambon. Asante points out how unthinkable it is for whites or Asians to be known by African names. He also criticises the choice of names inspired by Islam as preventing full consciousness of one's Africentric core. The choice of an African name alters one's consciousness. The knowledge of belonging to the great African cultural tradition, dating back to the earliest times, enhances one's self-affirmation. It also determines how others perceive one. Since whites have never had to react to blacks in America as a people with a history apart from slave history, choosing an African name is a small, but significant step in altering the perception of others. During the era of white rule in South Africa, it was customary for an African child to be given at least one European first name. As the end of political domination drew to a close, the use of African first names became increasingly more popular, however.

The same attitude of vigilance with regard to respect for one's heritage pertains to the arts and the sciences. Asante (1992) maintains 'that there is no *classical* music to you other than that which comes out of your culture' (p. 46). 'Music sits astride our traditions, it will monitor our future' (p. 66). He differentiates between classical European concert music and the classical polyrhythms and syncopated eighths of Ellington, Coltrane, Gillespie, and others. The spirit of the ancestors can even be found in the blues of the jazz nightclubs. Asante does not negate the values, which other cultures hold dear, but is adamant that African Americans must start from a nationalistic and not a foreign base. He maintains that 'the true nationalist is never a racist' (p. 5). An Africentric psychology will, therefore, strive for the 'restitution of the collective conscious will of Africa' (p. 48), of developing an Afrocentric awareness, which is equated with liberation of the mind of African Americans. 'Afrocentricity is like rhythms; it dictates the beat of your life' (p. 49). Asante regards the aspiration towards Afrocentric cultural and spiritual awareness as the highest value for African Americans to strive towards, more important even than such socio-economic issues as housing and employment.

Indeed culture is the most revolutionary stage of awareness, that is, culture in the sense that Amilcar Cabral, Frantz Fanon, and Maulana Karenga have written about . . . 'Afrocentric awareness is the total commitment to African liberation anywhere and everywhere by a consistent determined effort to repair any psychic, economic, physical, or cultural damage done to Africans. It is further a pro-active statement of faith we hold in the future of African itself' (Asante, 1992, p. 50).

Apart from the self-conscious advancement of Africentricity in every sector of society, Asante (1992) proposes the term *Afrology* to indicate the formal study of concepts, issues, and behaviours of the Diaspora and the continental African world, by people in the West with a committed Africentric orientation. *Afrology* has a pan-Africanist focus, emphasising the relationship between black people from all parts of the world with respect to the full range of human endeavours. Indeed, Asante sees the move forward for Afrocentricity in the propagation of the cultural and intellectual interchange begun in the Négritude and the African Personality movements which occurred during the middle part of this century in West Africa. However, it is not just continental Africa that has much to offer, but the developing Africentricity in the Diaspora as well. In fact, the Diaspora is vast. For instance, even more New World Africans live in Brazil than in the United States. Due to increasing mobility, physical interchange between Africa and the Diaspora will become an ever more significant reality and will eventually ensure the development of Africentricity as a global movement.

Despite the fact that the church in America has adapted the religious needs and spiritual hunger of African Americans to Christian form, Asante (1992) and White (1984) maintain that the African essence, which has been maintained in the church services, harbours the greatest potential for creating 'economic, social and political programs to address the present and future needs of Africans in America' (Asante, 1992, p. 76). It is in the participatory nature of the church services, the music and the dance, as well as in the fellowship, that the African roots of the church are to be found. However, Asante would like to see the rhythmic catharsis produced by the polymeters of African music extended to optimise the power of the church to 'create economic, social and political programs to address the present and future needs of Africans in America' (p. 76).

Although many African American scholars acknowledge the spiritual essence of the Africentric worldview, no one stresses it more than Myers (1993). She emphasises the primacy of spirit 'as the basis of all that is' (p. 19); 'spirit is the essence of all things' (p. 22); 'everything is spirit (the vital force of life known in an extra-sensory fashion as energy, consciousness, god, quarks, solitons, and so on), appearing materially (known through the five senses)' (p. 19). In her view of humankind as 'a spiritual force not apart from infinite spirit, infinite energy, infinite consciousness, and/or God (supreme or ultimate reality)' (p. 8), Myers places Afrocentric psychology directly in line with developments in the new physics during the past few decades, where a probabilistic conception of reality has replaced a material one. The universe is regarded more like a dynamic web of inseparable energy patterns than a constellation of absolute physical substances.

In the optimal psychology of Myers (1993), the purpose is, therefore, to strive towards embodying the oneness, the indivisible unity of spirit and matter, which underlies reality at the molecular level of analysis, in both one's professional and personal capacity. No room is left for maintaining different criteria in the consulting room and at home. Those who are trained in the compartmentalised thinking of Western science are likely to argue that an Africentric celebration, such as the one outlined here, belongs to the area of African studies and not to Africentric psychology. However, in keeping with the views of Baldwin (1986) and Jackson (1982), the development of Africentric psychology is intertwined with African culture as it manifests on the African continent and in the Diaspora.

Furthermore, in the holistic Africentric perspective, psychology is not to be divorced from everyday life. An Africentric approach has to guard against the appropriation of life and its vicissitudes by a small band of people proclaiming to have acquired title and deed to the discipline and the profession of psychology. It is to be expected that the differentiation between everyday and professional behaviour on the part of psychologists is not as pronounced as in other disciplines. 'The truth of one's being had to be manifest' (Myers, 1993, p. 13). 'Let each person take his post in the vanguard of this collective consciousness of Afrocentrism! Teach it! Practice it! And victory will surely come as we carry out the Afrocentric mission to humanize the Universe' (Asante, 1992, p. 6). Africentric psychology is an attitude and an approach that find expression at work and at home. It is in this sense, as Baldwin (1986) has stated, that psychology has been an implicit aspect of the behaviour of African people since the earliest of times.

8

TOWARDS AN AFRICAN CONSCIOUSNESS

A HISTORICAL INTRODUCTION

Some leading Africans echo the reservations of African American psychologists about the adequacy of the Euro-American worldview to provide a basis upon which to build a psychology that can be universally representative. The most conspicuous among these are the poets, the writers, and the statesmen of various countries. Although these critics differ from each other and from Africans in the Diaspora with respect to the nature of the contact that they have had with Western culture, they have in common that their views are experientially based.

Mphahlele (1987) credits a missionary, called Edward Blyden, as being the forerunner in drawing attention to the outrageous behaviour on the part of the missionaries and other Westerners in Africa. Blyden who had come from the West Indies originally, had immigrated to Liberia in the nineteenth century after having lived in the United States. He became the first president of Monrovia University and the first person to speak of a distinctive African personality. As he travelled in Africa he became aware how his colleagues imposed Christianity on the African people without taking into account that they had a religion of their own. The Christians looked upon the Africans as heathens, godless, and as children of darkness. He also realised that the Europeans were not appreciative of indigenous poetry, philosophy, or history. He, furthermore, pointed out the alienation the African person had to cope with in being bombarded with messages negating their own and elevating European culture.

However, as Boahen (1987) has indicated, awareness of and reaction to colonial exploitation had already occurred within a few years after colonialism came into being. This was true of the traditional as well as the educated African elite. Meetings were organised in various capitals in Europe and in New York during the early part of the century by the intellectuals from different parts of the world to discuss the invasion of the African continent. Discussion of their common grievances, goals, and aspirations, 'not only internationalized the anticolonial movement but also inspired the nationalists in Africa and won them some converts' (p. 78). These meetings resulted in the formation of the

Pan-African Congress. Pan Africanism focused on the unity of African culture wherever black people found themselves in the world.

Mphahlele (1987) pointed out that Pan-Africanism contained a paradox in that it rejected racism, yet, without discrimination between the races, there existed no basis for Pan-Africanism. However, Pan-Africanism needs to be seen as a form of antiracist solidarity between Africans and those of African descent. It was based on the assumption that Africa had a history and a culture that was of great value to the world civilisation. Since it was evident that the answers to the issues, which faced African people in the various geographic regions of the world, were not going to come from the whites in political power, Pan-Africanism developed as a political ideology as well as a social theory. The history of Pan-Africanism and its psychological significance is undoubtedly far too extensive to cover in a few paragraphs (see Boahen, 1987; Chinweizu, 1987; Mudimbe, 1988; Omotoso, 1994). Only its inclusion as a fully-fledged division of the history of African psychology can do it justice.

In 1945 the Pan-African Congress met in London. Among those present were such young people as Nkrumah and Kenyatta, who hoped to be leaders of an independent Africa. They spearheaded the development of African nationalism, which was really an African consciousness, the precursor of Black Consciousness, as it later came to be known. Africans nurtured a growing awareness of who they were, and this awareness came about because of the violent way in which European 'civilisation' had invaded Africa. As a reaction to the spiritual rape, invasion, and attempt to annihilate their soul, Africans realised that they also needed to affirm their uniqueness as a people with a history, a culture, and a religion. Thus, the Organisation of African Unity was formed to counter the economic control of African affairs by neo-colonialists who had abdicated their political, but not their economic power.

Despite the broader goals of the Organisation of African Unity, Omotoso (1994) expressed disappointment that 'political power became the be-all and end-all of African leadership ambition, completely neglecting the vital areas of economics, culture, language and religion that affected each and every one of their people' (p. 6). He argued that Pan-Africanism before independence 'could not be carried over unaltered to a post-independence scenario. If one was to destroy the colonial structure, a new attitude would be needed to build an African structure in its stead' (p. 6). Care had to be taken that the traditional ways of the people were not neglected in the new order. Mazrui (1990) agrees that such neglect was one of the shortcomings of Pan-Africanism. Omotoso, for one, holds the neglect of traditional values responsible for the ambivalence in the minds of many Africans and for their feelings of marginality.

During the years of bouncing back from colonial exploitation, the contact between Africans from the continent and from the United States has not been without problems. For instance, although Langston Hughes yearned for an ancestral home and loved 'the surface of Africa and the rhythms of Africa' (Mphahlele, 1962, p. 45), he realised that he was not African. Richard Wright, another American author of the first half of the century, felt no kinship with his Ghanaian colleagues. James Baldwin, similarly, experienced difficulty in getting on with the Africans he met in Paris. He felt that the alienation, which had developed over three hundred years, presented too deep a chasm to be bridged. He confessed that Senghor frightened him 'because of his extraordinary way of being civilized and primitive at the same time' (Mphahlele, 1962, p. 48).

Fanon (1976) also pointed out how African Americans, in their discussions with Africans, came to realise that the problems confronting them were not the same as those confronting the Africans. In *Black Skin White Masks* (1970), he alludes to 'differences that separate the Negro of the Antilles from the Negro of Africa' (p. 12). What the people of African origin had in common was basically that they were all defined in relation to whites. Fanon was, therefore, prompted to write that 'There will never be such a thing as black culture' (p. 188). However, for other African American authors, like Samuel Allen, who wrote under the pseudonym of Paul Vesey, Africa remained the source of guidance as they searched for a new humanism, for new psychic ways, for the vital force to guide and inspire them in their artistic endeavours. As has been pointed out in the previous chapter, many African American psychologists are following the same route. I am as well. Although my more recent ancestors came from Europe, my genetic pool has indelibly been shaped by its exposure to the African geography and humanism of the far distant and the more recent ancestral and personal past.

Besides the early links between Africans from the continent and from North America, there was also the African-European connection, which was of great importance in the development of Black Consciousness. Within the African-European connection two parallel developments took place. The one focused on the English-speaking and the other on the French-speaking countries. The discussion on the African Personality in the English-speaking countries occurred especially in Ghana. In his presentation on the African Personality at the All-African People's Conference in Accra in 1958, Kwame Nkrumah expressed the longings and ambitions, the aches and torments, as well as the anger of the African (in Mphahlele, 1962). The concept of the African Personality expresses

> a burning desire for freedom, self-determination and the desire to reject the white man's 'civilizing mission' and to break away from his moral and cultural trusteeship. The 'African Personality' is evidence of a coming into consciousness of the black peoples and is a corporate reassertion of their dignity. This often means in essence the restoration of traditional values, ways of life, and eating and dressing habits.
>
> (Mphahlele, 1963, p. 133)

The 'coming into consciousness' of the 'African Personality' highlighted how African cultural values differed from those that were imposed upon them. Contrast is a law of nature. It is especially in the field of perception that its sharpening function is most apparent. However, its effects are equally important in other aspects of life. Thus, in addition to the bondage under which Africans had to live, the contrast of the foreign culture to that of their own enhanced the awareness of their own culture.

In the French-speaking countries the movement towards unravelling the uniqueness of the African Personality came to be embodied by the concept of Négritude. Aimé Césaire, the Caribbean nationalist writer, is credited with coining the term in a poem published in 1939 (in Reed and Wake, 1979). Together with other French-speaking intellectuals in the West Indies and Africa, Césaire developed the idea of Négritude. Prominent among the intellectuals were Senghor, the first president of Senegal, Leon Damas of Guyana, the Diops of Senegal, and Rabemananajara of Madagascar. As a slogan Négritude was intended to help Africans discover themselves. Living in Paris, they realised all too well that the city that took pride in its own cultural heritage, failed to grasp the essence of Africa's cultural dimension. Their purpose, therefore, was to describe the essence of African culture in French-speaking countries. They were convinced that without such awareness, French and world civilisation would lack the rhythm-section of its orchestra, the bass voice of its choir.

According to Mphahlele (1963), the realisation of how their complete assimilation into French culture had wrenched them from their African roots, gave rise to resentment against the pretensions of European civilisation. 'Négritude – the negro-ness of artistic expression – became thus an act of revulsion against things European' (p. 134). Alionne Diop, at one time secretary of the Paris-born Society of African Culture, and founder of the journal, Présence Africaine, gave as motivation for the existence of Négritude, the fact that 'the world has been taught there is no culture other than the West's, no universal values which are not hers. Négritude, then, is the complete ensemble of values of African culture, and the vindication of the dignity of the person of African descent' (in Mphahlele, 1962, p. 49). In elaborating Négritude, the French educated Africans used as a backdrop what they perceived to be the essential nature of the European personality. For instance, Senghor wrote that 'Classical European reason is analytical and makes use of the object. African reason is intuitive and participates in the object' (in Reed and Wake, 1979, p. 34). At times, descriptions of the 'European personality' can be quite chilling, as in Senghor's analysis of the European as

> an *objective intelligence*, a man of will, a warrior, a bird of prey, a steady gaze. He first distinguishes the object from himself. He keeps it at a distance. He freezes it out of time and, in a way, out of space. He fixes it, he kills it. With his precision instruments he dissects it in a pitiless factual analysis. As a scientist, yet at the same time prompted by practical consideration, the European makes use of the *Other* that he has killed in this way for his practical ends. He makes a *means* of it. With a centripetal movement he assimilates it. He destroys it by devouring it.

'White men are cannibals,' an old sage from my own country told me a few years ago. 'They have no respect for life'.

(in Reed and Wake, 1979, p. 29)

Such perceptions prompted Senghor to write:

Lord God, forgive white Europe.
It is true Lord, that for four enlightened centuries, she has scattered the baying and slaver of her mastiffs over my lands.

(in Reed and Wake, 1979, p. 134)

Yet, the remarkable thing is that Senghor was able to work with De Gaulle in persuading him that the African colonies could become independent within a French community of nations without things falling apart. It is, therefore, not surprising that Senghor is regarded to be essentially a theorist and a poet of synthesis, a synthesis derived not from 'imposing uniformity on disparate elements, but allowing the elements to develop diversely in order to serve the unity' (Reed and Wake, 1979, p. 13). Not only was he able to work with the French government but he succeeded in reconciling a modern political organisation with the preservation of traditional structures. For 20 years he was able, as a Christian, to lead the mainly Muslim country, being re-elected twice, before he voluntarily stepped down on 31 December 1980. Although his tremendous impact has undoubtedly been due to his role as politician and statesman, and not as poet, it is perhaps the integration within himself of the sensibilities of the poet and the practicality of the statesman, that contributed to his unique achievements and status as a figure of world renown. Holism is not a term that has been used in connection with Senghor, but it seems to be an apt description of the man and his policies.

BLACK CONSCIOUSNESS IN SOUTH AFRICA

In South Africa, the African National Congress built on the spirit of African nationalism, blending ethnic groups into one single movement. It expanded during the 1940s, culminating in the mass rallies and the defiance campaign of the turbulent 1950s. The laws of the country constantly reminded people that they were different, that they were black, and Black Consciousness was a natural outcome. As an interesting aside, although it was politically poles apart, the rise of Black Consciousness occurred simultaneously with the flourishing of the human potential movement in the United States and Europe after World War II. Following the banning of all Black Consciousness activities in South Africa, and especially the brutal murder of Biko, the movement lost its impetus and never became institutionalised. Yet, political tyranny can destroy the body, but not the mind (Mphahlele, 1987).

Although he was not a psychologist in a formal sense, the life and the work of Bantu Stephen Biko expressed most powerfully the aspiration of an African approach to psychology. It was through him that the Black Consciousness movement regained impetus in the late 1960s. It is timely that the psychological implication of Biko's endeavour, to raise the consciousness of his fellow Africans about the importance of being in touch with who they were and with the conditions under which they were forced to live, has recently received renewed recognition (Pityana, Ramphele, Mpulwana, and Wilson, 1991).

Just as 'conscientisation' in Brazil (Freire, 1970, 1971), as well as Négritude and Africanity in Central Africa, the Black Consciousness movement endeavoured to develop an awareness of self, a sense of dignity, both individually and as a race, among the voiceless majority of the country. Biko aspired towards a philosophy and a strategy for enhancing the consciousness of his fellow Africans.

> Black Consciousness directs itself to the black man and his situation, and the black man is subjected to two forces in the country. He is first of all oppressed by an external world through institutionalized machinery and through laws that restrict him from doing certain things, through heavy work conditions, through poor pay, through difficult living conditions, through poor education. These are all external to him. Secondly, and this we regard as the most important, the black man in himself has developed a certain state of alienation, he rejects himself precisely because he attaches the meaning white to all that is good, in other words he equates good with white.
>
> (Biko, in Woods, 1978, p. 175)

As a first vital step towards emancipating his fellow Africans, Biko wanted them to appreciate their innate goodness as people. Unlike Césaire, who, coming from Martinique with its history of black slavery, could not find pride in his ancestors, but only in himself, Biko, like Senghor, believed that the African's noble past only needed to be manifested again.

According to Biko (in Stubbs, 1979), several factors contributed to the poor self-image among South African blacks. Perhaps the most unfortunate was looking at themselves through the eyes of a Western culture, the material achievements of which could be persuasive. Because of its ability to solve many problems in the medical, agricultural, and technological fields, white culture tended to be regarded as superior culture. 'You tend to despise the *worker culture*, and this inculcates in the black man a sense of *self-hatred* which is an important determining factor in his dealings with himself and his life' (Biko, in Woods, 1978, p. 177). Almost everything the black child is exposed to during development reinforces a sense of inferiority. Schools, streets, houses, sporting facilities, and organisations are all different from those of whites. These differences create a sense of incompleteness '*in your humanity*, and that completeness goes with whiteness. This is carried through to adulthood' (Biko, in Woods, 1978, pp. 175–176).

Since black students do not have the same exposure to technology they are at a distinct disadvantage when competing with white students who grow up in a technologically advanced culture. Having to study through a language medium that is not the home language also handicaps black students. Reading and comprehension of prescribed material is more difficult, articulation less fluent, and black people, coming from a culture rich in the oral tradition, often have to say yes to whites articulating what they may be experiencing (Biko, in Stubbs, 1979).

In more ways than one the educational system has served a powerful function in depriving Africa of its own heritage. Syllabuses have been drawn up and methodologies determined by those steeped in the left hemisphere linearity of the Western educational system. Even the past has been looked at through white spectacles, the result being a distortion and disfiguration of black history. African culture became barbarism; religious practices and customs were referred to as superstition. The history of African societies was reduced to tribal battles and internecine wars. There was no conscious migration by people from one place to another. It was always flight from a tyrant (Biko, in Stubbs, 1979).

Black Consciousness stepped in to fill the vacuum. As a first step, Biko argued that black persons had to be made to take a critical look at themselves, their dormant potential had to be rejuvenated, they had to be infused with pride and dignity and reminded of the complicity in the crime of allowing themselves to be misused. An inward looking process had to be created. Although there was a great deal to be proud of which belonged to the past, the consciousness move-ment stressed being in the present. To BE is the essence of Black Consciousness. It cannot be identified in terms external to itself, be that Arabic, Western, or Asian culture. In order to BE it is essential that people become aware of all factors external and internal to themselves which are determining the nature of their existence. According to Biko, blacks have to develop an awareness of their situation, to be able to assess and analyse it and to provide answers for themselves that can improve their influence over themselves and their environment (in Woods, 1978; Stubbs, 1979).

Black Consciousness, like the conscientisation of Freire, desired to engage people in an emancipatory process, to free them from a situation of bondage. The real purpose was to provide some kind of hope, to set a new style of self-reliance and dignity for blacks as a psychological attitude leading to new initiatives (Biko, in Stubbs, 1979). The psychological importance of Biko's assertion of positive black identity and self-reliance runs like a continuous thread throughout the edited book by Pityana *et al.* (1991). After the killing of Biko in detention in 1977, Black Consciousness did not seem to be able to go any further. It was under siege. All Black Consciousness programmes had been banned and the leaders emerging from the ranks of the people were functionally or physically eliminated. Whereas earlier leaders in the black liberation struggle have been banned (Albert Luthuli and Robert Sobukwe), or detained for life (Nelson Mandela), Biko was the first national figure to die in the hands of the security police.

Even in the new South Africa there continues to be the need for Black Consciousness to express itself. This much was evident in the reaction to the report on tertiary education by the National Commission on Higher Education (NCHE), a body appointed by the South African parliament of reconciliation to find a new framework for higher education in the country. At the conference on *Black perspectives on tertiary institutional transformation*, the report of the NCHE was challenged for its failure to provide a coherent philosophy of education based on the need for Africanisation. Africanisation was considered a necessity, not a luxury. It was argued that a new body of knowledge and appropriate methodologies, 'based on the principle of liberation', needed to be developed. The underlying theme at the conference focused on the fact that political power might have transferred to the black majority, but cultural and educational resources continued to be dominated by what 'whites brought with them from Europe' (Pearce, 1996).

Upon his return to South Africa in 1977, Mphahlele (1984) wrote with pride on his African identity, which his extended stay in various countries outside South Africa, especially his sojourn in West Africa, helped him to rediscover. I have also discovered my African rootedness on foreign soil. As a Visiting Fellow at the Center for Studies of the Person (CSP), in La Jolla, California, the difference between the formalised Person-Centred approach of Carl Rogers, who was a Resident Fellow at CSP, and the person-centred way of being in Africa, became abundantly clear to me. In short, the Rogerian approach is basically a psychotherapeutic technique applied in clinical contexts. African person-centredness, on the other hand, is a way of life that finds expression in one's daily activities. Both Mphahlele and I have argued for an educational system at all levels in South Africa based on the concepts of African humanism, the essence of which is to be found in the principles of Black Consciousness (Stubbs, 1979; Woods, 1978) and 'concientising' education (Freire, 1970, 1971).

If higher education in the United States is considered to be 'out of synchrony with the needs of the times' (Altman, 1996, p. 371) and requires revisioning in terms of its curriculum and methodology, the same is undoubtedly true of higher education in South Africa and many African countries (Holdstock, 1987a,b). As the American society is striving towards achieving 'a viable balance of pluralism and unity' (Altman, 1996, p. 373) in its way of life, the same challenge awaits African societies. Whether psychology can model how such a balance is to be achieved in its theories, its training programmes, and its practices, is an open question. If psychology in sub-Saharan Africa is to follow in the footsteps of Biko, and those Africanists before him, it has, as a first step, to become aware of the extent of its encapsulation in the ideology of mainstream psychology, and of the implications of such embeddedness. In so doing, sub-Saharan psychology will not only stand a chance to develop in line with the ideals of the Black Consciousness movement, but will also be in step with those developments in contemporary psychology that endeavour to raise the consciousness of the discipline with respect to its future responsibilities. If the discipline can develop the perspectives and the skills necessary to utilise Africa's unique psychological culture as its point of departure, the potential exists to enrich the international status of psychological science considerably.

THE VOICE OF FRANTZ FANON

Two psychiatrists have been prominent in reflecting on the application of contemporary psychological principles in Africa. The Nigerian, Lambo, attributed the reluctance on the part of the West to accept and respect the framework of African culture to the moral arrogance of nineteenth- and twentieth-century Europe in setting up its civilisation as the standard by which all others should be measured (in Cheetham, 1975). Lambo (1971) stressed the inadequacy of applying mental health models, based on Western principles, to the people of Africa. Adaptation to the changing economic realities will undoubtedly occur, but the underlying philosophy of life will persist.

In order to understand Fanon, it is necessary to realise the impact Aimé Césaire, the revolutionary poet of Martinique, had on him during his formative years. On his return to Martinique, after winning a scholarship to go to France in 1931, Césaire became a teacher in Fort de France, and it was here that he taught Fanon during the latter's final year at high school. Césaire (1969) was merciless in his attack on Western civilisation in general and French culture in particular. According to Césaire a nation that colonises and a civilisation that condones colonisation, and therefore force, is a sick and morally diseased civilisation. Not only did he repudiate assimilation into the French culture, but he also asserted the inescapable essence of his African roots, of being black. For instance, in his epic poem *Return to my Native Land*, he wrote:

> Listen to the white world
> appallingly weary from its immense effort
> the crack of its joints rebelling under the hardness of the stars
> listen to the proclaimed victories which trumpet their defeats
> listen to their grandiose alibis (stumbling so lamely)
> Pity for our conquerors, all-knowing and naive!
>
> Heia for the reincarnation of tears and the worst pain brought back
>   again
> Those who never invented anything
> those who never tamed anything
>
> Heia for joy
> heia for love
>
> (Césaire, 1969, p. 76)

Clearly, Césaire is tongue in the cheek when he writes about the glorification of technology by the West. In accepting the white people's myths about Africans, he glorifies in them. The alternative would be to justify Africans by measuring them in terms of performance rather than in terms of whom they were. Against the Europe that, for centuries 'has stuffed us with lies' (p. 30), Césaire proposes a system of values that can teach the white man 'of the north' how to love, how to rediscover the essence of being human.

Fanon's identification with Césaire lasted until the latter, as Deputy to the French National Assembly for Martinique, supported the campaign for integration with France, instead of committing himself to independence for Martinique (Césaire, 1969; Bulhan, 1985). Césaire's failure to support independence for the colonised territories of France, including Algeria, convinced Fanon that Négritude was restricted to being a philosophical ideal that was necessary to be stated, but would never be sufficient to bring about the liberation of alienated blacks. In *The Wretched of the Earth* he wrote: 'It is around the peoples' struggles that African-Negro culture takes on substance, and not around songs, poems or folklore' (Fanon, 1976, p. 189). Earlier, in *Black Skin White Masks* he had, with Karl Jaspers' concept of metaphysical guilt in mind, written, 'Every one of my acts commits me as a man. Every one of my silences, every one of my cowardice reveals me as a man' (Fanon, 1970, p. 63).

Mphahlele's (1963) disenchantment with Négritude was even more pronounced than that of Fanon. Mphahlele described Négritude poetry as a 'romantic rhapsodizing of Africa – ancestors, naked feet, half-naked women and so on' (p. 136). Although Mphahlele gave credit to Négritude as the first attempt to define aspects of the African writing of certain regions, he stated that it did not provide the answer to what Africans, living in multi-racial communities and countries of British influence, expected of African writing. Thus, although Négritude and the 'African Personality' were complementary in the sense that both movements aspired towards the actualisation of the potential of black people, Négritude was of very little meaning to people who, like Mphahlele, had lived in multi-racial societies.

Fanon's great contribution has not only been his merciless dissection of colonialism, but the full extent to which he exposed its effects. He dealt with the psychology of the colonised peoples, both before and after decolonisation, as well as with the psychology of the colonial mentality. While mainstream psychology has devoted attention to racism and oppression, the focus has, in keeping with psychology's individualistic orientation, primarily been individualised. The context within which individual acts of racism and oppression occurred consistently escaped attention. It is to Fanon's merit that it did not escape his attention.

Since Fanon's contributions were made during the turbulent 1950s and early 1960s, when many colonised countries were in the throes of national liberation, his 'insights into the process of decolonization struck a responsive chord among the oppressed everywhere' (Bulhan, 1985, p.7). Fanon warned against imitating

Europe, for Europe has been incapable of bringing the vision of the person of tomorrow to fruition. 'Leave this Europe where they are never done talking of MAN, yet murder men everywhere they find them, at the corner of every one of their own streets, in all the corners of the globe. For centuries they have stifled almost the whole of humanity in the name of a so-called spiritual experience. Look at them today swaying between atomic and spiritual disintegration' (Fanon, 1976, p. 251). Fanon's key task was to understand the relationship between colonialism and the deformation of personality of the men and women who were rendered inferior by Europe's expansionist drive. After having experienced colonisation at home in Martinique and discrimination in Paris, he was, throughout his years of medical practice in Algeria, daily confronted with people who were subjugated to French rule. His exposure to these patients made him believe that they were the victims of colonial domination. Their sense of will and purpose in life had somehow been destroyed by the colonial system. This insight led him towards the theory of the colonial personality and the concept of the cultural sclerosis, which were to become the central themes of *The Wretched of the Earth*.

He rejected the ontogenetic focus of Freud on the Oedipus complex, and proposed instead a sociogenetic perspective, emphasising the importance of sociological and cultural factors on behaviour (Fanon, 1970). 'It will be seen that the black man's alienation is not an individual question. Beside phylogeny and ontogeny stands sociogeny' (p. 10). He also took issue with Jung's concept of the collective unconscious and argued that it was not a phylogenetic matter of inherited dispositions, 'But the collective unconscious, without our having to fall back on the genes, is purely and simply the sum of prejudices, myths, collective attitudes of a given group (Fanon, 1970, p. 133).

Fanon's sociogeny would suggest a closer affinity to Adler than to Freud and Jung. However, he could not fully embrace Adler either. Although Adler's psychology considers sociopathogenic factors in the development of mental health problems, his psychology remains focused on the dynamics of distinct egos within the family, without incorporating the family in a socio-historical and cultural context. According to Fanon (1970), 'It is not just this or that Antillean who embodies the neurotic formation, but all Antilleans. Antillean society is a neurotic society, a society of "comparison". Hence we are driven from the individual back to the social structure' (p. 151). While the governing principle in an Adlerian comparison is between two egos, that of the Antillean is 'not personal but social' (p. 153). The Antillean 'compares himself with his fellow against the pattern of the white man' (p. 153). Fanon's unwavering conviction was that the fundamental cause of mental health problems must be sought, first, in the debilitating consequences of the economic and cultural domination, and secondly, in the internalisation of societal inequity and violence.

This Fanonian perspective suggests the revisioning of the primary tasks of psychology and psychiatry. According to Fanon, the paramount objectives of these two disciplines are the unravelling of the relation between the psyche and the social structure, the rehabilitation of the alienated, and the transformation of the social structures that thwart human needs (Bulhan, 1985). Unfortunately it is unlikely that the present climate within which psychology is practised in Africa will be able to facilitate the objectives which Fanon envisaged. Apart from numerous other obstacles, the dominance of the natural science orientation to the discipline is too powerful for that to come about.

9

THE COLONISATION OF PSYCHOLOGY IN AFRICA

In contrast to the politicians, the poets and the writers of Africa, the voice of the psychological community on the ideological assumptions underlying their discipline, has been relatively muted. The most obvious reason relates to the fact that psychology has been imported as a ready-made product from the West. As Akin-Ogundeji (1991) states, 'The history of psychology in Africa is largely the history of colonialism' (p. 3). The lack of a critical perspective undoubtedly also relates to the fact that the discipline constitutes no more than a fledgling enterprise on the continent. It is only in South Africa that mainstream psychology is well established. Akin-Ogundeji (1991) estimated that there were about 150 psychologists in Zambia, Zimbabwe, and Nigeria. In other African countries, such as Botswana, Cameroon, Ethiopia, Gabon, Ivory Coast, Kenya, and Liberia, psychology is not yet an established field of study. In these countries 'Psychology is subordinated to long-established fields such as education, medicine, and psychiatry' (p. 3). Moreover, some of the critical African voices (e.g., Bulhan and Owusu-Bempah) are working in the West.

The debate on the role and the orientation of psychology in African societies that has taken place thus far has been conducted within the constraints of contemporary paradigms. Akin-Ogundeji (1991) laments the extent to which psychology in Nigeria 'is still largely a classroom-research enterprise' (p. 3), 'mainly concerned with the rigours of empirical work' (p. 3), which is of little practical relevance 'to the problems of living in contemporary Nigerian society' (p. 3). Research reports are 'too "artificial", "dry", "meaningless", or "irrelevant"' (p. 4) to be meaningful. He calls for the grounding of Nigerian psychology in the 'unique socio-cultural realities and human experiences in Africa' (p. 4). Like the parent discipline, Nigerian psychology is hampered by internal rivalries regarding the orientation of the discipline in the country and by the lack of openness regarding alternate perspectives.

Nsamenang (1993, 1995), a psychologist in Cameroon, similarly, is of the opinion that the Eurocentric nature of the developmental psychology that has been imported into Africa is of questionable relevance to the people of the continent. Conventional research methods are incapable of accessing and assessing Africa's developmental perspectives. In conjunction with Serpell in

144

Zambia, Dasen and Tape in the Ivory Coast, Nsamenang (1997) stresses the importance of culture in development and advocates a contextualist approach in order to gain an understanding of human development in Africa. Apart from indigenising theory, research methodology needs to be contextualised, and culture-sensitive assessment tools within an applied but collaborative and inter-disciplinary framework need to be developed (Nsamenang, 1996).

Similar arguments have been raised with respect to psychology in Malawi (Carr and MacLachlan, 1993; MacLachlan and Carr, 1997). Their work points out how difficult the application of mainstream paradigms in an African context can be, for their approach has been criticised quite severely as Eurocentric and as perpetuating 'psychology's historical abuse of Africans' (Owusu-Bempah and Howitt, 1995, p. 463). Ager (1993), who had previously worked in Malawi, also warned that the 'use of non-indigenous constructions of thought and behaviour' (p. 490), as employed by Carr and MacLachlan, can inadvertently serve to 'marginalise traditional discourse' (p. 490) and be perceived as 'neo-colonialist cultural hegemony' (p. 490).

APARTHEID HAS MANY FACES: PSYCHOLOGY IN SOUTH AFRICA

Divergent perspectives with respect to what constitutes a relevant psychology also pertain to the discipline in South African. In fact, Louw (1992), a historian of South African psychology, stated that the discipline is 'absorbed in intro-spective self-criticism and plagued by self-doubts about the progress it has made' (p. 353). Gerdes (1992) reiterated the same theme. She said that South African psychology is 'grappling with problems of identity which suggests that it has reached adolescence and is moving toward maturity' (p. 39). Needless to say, every aspect of South African psychology is, either by omission or commission, intertwined with the political situation in the country. According to Butchart and Seedat (1990), there is 'A pressing need to develop methods of social analysis by which to identify and eliminate oppressive influences. This requires that psychologists and all social scientists engage in critical self-reflection with a view to reclaiming their own power and agency, which at the least entails examining how the form and content of their ideas reproduce the discourse of domination' (pp. 1100–1110).

However, the opinions as to how 'the discourse of domination' is perpetuated in South African psychology and how the profession can exercise its agency differ sharply. The one camp uses the psychological status quo as its point of departure. This is by far the dominant group. The other calls for the revisioning of that status quo. Within and between the camps rather strange alliances are to be found. For instance, those who adhere to maintaining the status quo (the 'mainstream' group) can again be divided into two distinctly different factions. On the one hand are those who have called attention to the psychological effects of apartheid and advocated that attention be focused on the victims of apartheid (the 'reactive mainstream' group). Members of this group have also described themselves as 'progressive', 'liberatory', and 'political'. Then there are those, the majority, who have conducted psychology as is customary and who have seemingly been uncritical of the discipline's political inertia during the apartheid era (the 'conservative mainstream' group).

In comparison to the two mainstream groups is a third group of psychologists whose critique extends beyond the party political to incorporate the ideological bedrock of contemporary psychology (the 'proactive' group). According to this latter group, a monocultural psychology with serious shortcomings, if not flaws, in its ideological base is unlikely to provide an effective foundation for a discipline that is to serve all the people in the country. The proactive call, therefore, is to acknowledge the shortcomings of contemporary psychology. The intention is certainly not to throw the proverbial baby out with the bath water. The focus is on critically appraising to what extent psychology perpetuates not just apartheid, but colonial practices and attitudes. In addition, proactivists argue that cognisance and recognition of the indigenous psychological viewpoints in South Africa can go a long way towards revisioning the discipline nationally and, in so doing, contribute to psychology's development internationally. This group constitutes by far the smallest fraction of the psychological community. Not even the dramatic political change in South Africa has made any real dent in the ethnocentric bias dominating the practice of psychology in the country.

Despite the fact that political power in the professional body of psychology has passed into the hands of black psychologists, they still represent only 10 per cent of psychologists in the country. Moreover, the lives of the black population are virtually untouched by any positive benefits that may accrue from the practice of psychology as a science and a profession. The facilities of psychology remain unequally distributed (Kottler, 1988; Kriegler, 1993; Manganyi, 1980; Swartz, 1986,1987) and the relevance of existing curricula for the training of psychologists gives cause for concern (Kriegler, 1993).

Apart from the limitations of the parent discipline that have already been discussed, there are other shortcomings in which South African psychology shares.It continues to elaborate the sickness model and emphasises 'pathology at the expense of paying sufficient attention to the potential of the vast majority of people who function quite adequately' (Holdstock, 1981b, p. 123). The emphasis is on one-to-one therapy rather than on group and community approaches. More recently, Sharatt (1995) has reiterated the same concern. She stated that in the advent of the new South Africa, 'National finances will not permit the extension of therapeutic services as they are presently conceptualised and practised to the whole of the South African population, and new forms of practice which are managerial and/or preventative and community based will have to be developed' (p. 212). Sharatt, furthermore, pleads for more direct involvement by psychologists in issues of health and educational policy. Despite the political changes, education in the country continues to be in disarray. In keeping with my call for the revisioning of South African education (Holdstock, 1987a), Sharatt stresses the importance of re-thinking the basic principles on which it rests. Of primary importance is the promotion of the values, attitudes, and knowledge, as set forth by Deutsch (1993), in order that we can contribute to, and live in a peaceful world.

Like their colleagues in the United States, who have 'generally responded to the challenge of desegregation in a reactive rather than an innovative fashion' (Cook, 1985, p. 460), South African psychologists have, similarly, been reactively oriented. Two decades ago I accused South African psychology of arrogance reminiscent of colonial times in its exclusive Westrocentric focus (Holdstock, 1979; 1981b). Naidoo (1994), more recently, echoed similar sentiments. He challenged the 'hegemony of Eurocentric psychology' (p. 1) in South Africa.

As some American psychologists have indicated, 'The challenge is to encourage ourselves and our colleagues to become ethically engaged in a socially active community' (Hillerbrand, 1987, p. 118; also DeLeon *et al.*, 1995; Payton, 1984). On a par with the failure on the part of the white psychologists to do so, is their lack of consideration for the African worldview and the general disregard for African belief systems and customs. The same admonishment applies to the black psychologists in South Africa. With a few exceptions, they have also been amiss in celebrating the uniqueness of their Africanness. Bodibe (1994) is one of the few exceptions. In calling for a third voice in South African psychology, he has in mind the empowerment of black psychologists to speak out on their vision of the discipline.

However, despite the advances made by black psychologists in gaining a foothold in the professional body of psychology in the country, the orientation continues to be Westrocentric. This much is evident in a special issue of the *South African Journal of Psychology* (Duncan *et al.*, 1997). The special issue has been guest edited by the Forum for Black Research and Authorship Development that was established in 1995 in order to earn, in Manganyi's (1991) terms, some of the power associated with scholarship.

The empirical articles in this issue replicate some of the classic 'sins' for which mainstream psychology has been chastised (Letlaka-Renner, Luswazi, Helms, and Zea, 1997; May and Spangenberg, 1997; Mayekiso and Bhana, 1997; Moosa, Moonsamy, and Fridjhon, 1997). Exclusive use was made of an elite minority, students, as participants, while instruments of questionable validity provided the means of assessment. Simply substituting black for white experimenters in the pursuit of psychology as a universalist science is not going to bring about the paradigm shift that is needed in South African psychology. For a liberatory psychology to come about, the empowerment of black psychologists needs to be accompanied by the empowerment of an African psychology as well. A liberatory psychology has to endeavour to incorporate the broad base of African beliefs and behaviour patterns and apply methods in keeping with the African concept of the self. That this is uncharted territory certainly makes the challenge a formidable one. The aspirations of writers from various parts of central Africa can, hopefully, serve as a source of inspiration in this innovative venture.

In contrast to black South African authors who regarded writing and publishing in their mother tongue as an implicit validation of the Nationalist government's policy of apartheid, Wole Soyinka and Kole Omotoso from Nigeria, as well as James Ngugi from Kenya, called on their African colleagues to write and publish in their native languages and not in that of the former colonial powers.

> It is imperative that African languages should be developed, because they must move from the realm of the oral to the written. Kept at the level of incantation only, without the past and the present meaning of words being recorded in writing, no African language can truly transmit to its users the enormity of the changes Europe has introduced into Africa. Furthermore, if the continuing underdevelopment of the continent is to be reversed, Western knowledge will have to be made available in written form in the mother-tongue.
>
> (Omotoso, 1994, p. 36)

However, Omotoso also recognises that 'commitment to using indigenous African languages does not preclude taking the necessary advantage of European languages in Africa' (p. 36). He, therefore, advocates 'the use of the European language and the conscious cultivation of the indigenous African languages involved' (p. 32).

The bilingual or multilingual approach to language fits in well with the multicultural approach adopted in this text. Besides, pragmatic aspects, such as the fact that the linguistic expansionism of Anglo-Saxon culture has virtually ensured that English will prevail as the common international language, need to be taken into consideration. The internationally recognised South African author, André Brink, writes in Afrikaans, his mother tongue, and then rewrites and reworks his writing in English. Another prominent South African author and prisoner of the apartheid regime, Breyten Breytenbach, declared that 'You can only be part of the larger community if you are totally secure in the knowledge that you can fully "live out" and express yourself through your mother tongue' (Snyman, 1998).

Rock (1994) raised some interesting points with respect to the advocacy of psychology in the new South Africa. He warned that lobbying to secure a future for psychology in the new dispensation was likely to necessitate presentation of the discipline from a unified perspective. In so doing, the danger existed that 'a dialogic atmosphere in which the opportunity for richness evolving from mutual exchange would be lost' (p. 58). Only when a climate existed that allowed for the tension of opposing points of view to be expressed, could 'a prosperous, richly woven discipline which tolerates subtlety, contradiction and diversity' (p. 58) be developed. Rock's point of view is in harmony with the multicultural perspective that is suggested as a model for psychology in the twenty-first century.

It is in keeping with the view that dialogue between different points of view is essential that special attention is devoted to the position of the 'reactive mainstream' group. From a proactive perspective, there seems to be a double bind in the approach of this group. Their political focus directs attention to the psychological effects of apartheid. Yet, their professional focus remains firmly embedded within a psychological framework that is the result of the same colonial approach that created apartheid. South African psychology is criticised, quite justifiably, for not doing enough to combat apartheid. However, being critical of one aspect of psychology, while covertly supporting the ethnocentrism dominant in the discipline, unfortunately creates a double-bind that is apparent with respect to all aspects of psychology.

In the applied domain, the Organisation for Appropriate Social Services endeavoured to provide help to the victims of apartheid within the paradigms of established psychological principles (Flisher, Skinner, Lazarus, and Louw, 1993). In keeping with this approach, Nell (1993) and his colleagues investigated the structure of the primary health care system in the country and of the possible introduction of family therapy into the system. They endeavoured to do so by training nurses in the basic therapeutic skills (Mgoduso and Butchart, 1992; Seedat et al., 1991; Seedat and Nell, 1990, 1992). Needless to say, the integration of psychology into the public health infrastructure (Leviton, 1996) is of vital importance to the discipline and to the country, and the difficulties experienced by the South African professionals in achieving their objective is cause for concern. At the same time, however, the potential and the actual contribution of the thousands of indigenous African healers is not only neglected, but actually scorned. Yet, the practice of indigenous healing 'has kept millions of Africans alive for centuries before the advent of European history in Africa' (Gumede, 1974, p. 38), and continues to do so.

Apart from the inordinate difficulty of integrating indigenous approaches to mental health care, to which the mainstream groups are opposed anyway, with existing structures based on Western principles, there are more than enough problems with the latter approach alone. Concern has been expressed about the erosion of psychology's already limited contribution in the delivery of mental health care (Kriegler, 1993), counselling and guidance services (Euvrard, 1996), while Richter and her colleagues (1998) pointed out how few jobs are, in general, available for psychology graduates in South Africa. Perhaps it is in this light that the opposition to the inclusion of indigenous healers in the mental health system must be seen. Conceivably, the indigenous healers represent unwelcome competition? In terms of the needs of the country, the shortage of Western trained mental health personnel is all the more reason, however, for officially recognising indigenous healing practices (Holdstock, 1979). Moreover, Western styled psychotherapy is decidedly of questionable validity in addressing the needs of the diversity of the people in the country. Even in the United States psychologists have come to the realisation that cultural competence in most service settings is an unlikely dream. People 'question whether a provider of one

149

culture can really be helpful to a client of another culture' (Tomes, 1999, p. 31). The most that can realistically be expected in psychology is cultural sensitivity.

With respect to the South African situation, Seedat (1997), in following Bulhan and others, has stated that 'the extensive rendering of curative psychological services to groups, like ex-detainees, victims of police brutality and returnees traps progressive applied psychologists into reproducing the conventional roles of therapist, consultant and psychometrician' (p. 263). Seedat's statement is evidence of the growing awareness among 'progressive' psychologists involved in community action and practice that urgent revisioning of the function of psychologists is needed if the discipline is to play a role in the transformation of the new South Africa. Incorporation of psychologists in the Truth and Reconciliation Commission is a promising beginning (Gobodo-Madikizela, 1997). Despite its limitations, the healing that is accomplished by exposure of and to the truth in the proceedings of the TRC shows up the limited framework and restricted agenda of psychology.

The effects of apartheid warrant research, and important work has been done on racism and violence (Foster, 1993a,b; Manganyi and Du Toit, 1990), as well as on detention and torture in South Africa (Foster, Davis, and Sandler, 1987). Not only psychologists, but other disciplines have expressed concern about the extent of the violence in South Africa (e.g., Chidester, 1991; McKendrick and Hoffman, 1990). However, the 'role of poverty, meaningless work, unemployment, racism, and sexism in producing psychopathology' (Albee, 1982, p. 1043) is well documented. Does its investigation in the South African context have to constitute the principal aim of the country's psychology, as Dawes (1985) would like it to be? He regarded 'as the central concerns of a relevant South African psychology . . . the consequences of the policy of Apartheid itself' (p. 38). The main task of South African psychology was to focus on the effects and the treatment of the victims of apartheid (Foster, Nicholas, and Dawes, 1993). Important as such research is, it can prevent South African psychology from breaking out of its ethnocentric reactive bias.

As indicated in earlier chapters, a considerable number of psychologists have posited viewpoints contrary to Dawes' (1985) assumption 'that empirical research . . . is the 'currency' of our scientific *zeitgeist*' (p. 60) (e.g., Akbar, 1984a,b; Baldwin, 1989; Bronstein, 1986; Bulhan, 1985, 1993a,b; Gantous, 1994; Myers, 1991; White, 1991). Others who have been critical of an exclusively positivistic and reactive approach to psychology are those commenting from feminist (e.g., Bhavnani and Phoenix, 1994), humanistic, and transpersonal viewpoints.

In keeping with the awakening awareness of the dangers involved in restructuring the mental health services in South Africa on a curative basis alone, is the view of one of the doyens of psychologists in the United States. Albee (1992) stated that interventions that help groups of people that are already damaged – while humane and desirable – do nothing to affect incidence. The same has recently been restated with respect to the incidence of child abuse. 'Efforts that focus solely on abuse and neglect that has already occurred will never result in any meaningful reduction in the number of child abuse cases' (Rabasca, 1999, p. 30). Attempts to develop community mental health services and introduce lay mental health personnel in the structure of the primary health care system need, furthermore, to be evaluated in terms of the ideological perspective from which such attempts derive (e.g., Akbar, 1984a,b). Moreover, the imposition of ethnocentric approaches can be responsible for the iatrogenic causation of mental health problems (Gantous, 1994; Gergen *et al.*, 1996). I am also reminded of the words of Es'kia Mphahlele telling the white community that first they oppressed the blacks, then they researched them, and finally, they wanted to save them! Likewise, Omotoso (1994) has stated that 'The representation of the African as solely a victim has gone on for too long and needs to be challenged' (p. 15).

While the political importance of the organisation of psychology as a professional body is evident, several South African psychologists have taken stock of precisely what is involved in professionalisation. In documenting the organisation of psychology as a professional body, Louw (1988) has pointed out that professionalisation is not without drawbacks. He maintains:

> That the increased emphasis on application and professionalization of psychology, often in an unholy alliance with powerful social institutions, are at odds with the contribution psychology can and should make to a healthier way of life. Psychology's aim of 'prediction and control of behaviour', in an economic order where greater efficiency, productivity and profits are the most important considerations (cognitive-instrumental rationality), is much too close to social discipline and control for comfort.
>
> (Louw, 1988 p. 75)

Korber (1990) and Kottler (1988, 1990) have drawn specific attention to the implications of Western style professionalisation for the indigenous healing practices in the country.

The negation of culture in South African psychology

The ethnocentrism of the 'reactive' group is, furthermore, most apparent in their ambivalent attitude towards African culture. Some of their views have already been presented in Chapter 2. To recap, Nell (1990) states that although 'culture is as real as language or values, it has no pre-emptive claim to a place in all debates about the nature of psychology and the meaning of relevance' (p. 134)! Dawes and Davids (1983) described culture as a euphemism. Variables of class rather than of culture have been accentuated. According to Dawes (1996), 'What is conceived as the African mentality is rooted in the sorts of small-scale, underdeveloped, rural economic and societal arrangements, which are a feature of much life in Africa. It is the material character of these settings, and their ideological heritage, which in complex ways gives forth the social practice and psychological constructs, which are held to be common to Africa' (p. 10).

In keeping with his view of 'the African mentality', Dawes, in collaboration with Nsamenang (1998), constitutes that there is no 'African child', 'childhood is a social construct and not a natural phenomenon' (p. 79)! The African child is regarded as something mythical, yet the core concept in the eco-cultural approach of the cross-cultural psychologist, Berry, which the two authors entertain, 'is contextual "nicheness" – the fact that every developmental phenomenon or human action is embedded in a specific eco-cultural niche' (p. 80).

The paradox in the denial of Africanness, whether it is construed solely in geographic and materialistic terms, or in terms of contextual 'nicheness', is indeed difficult to comprehend. Several explanations suggest themselves. One explanation can be found in the concern about an 'overemphasis on culture' that may result in 'a love-affair with indigenous culture'. 'African cultural essentialism . . . can lead to problematic oversimplification' (Nsamenang and Dawes, 1998, pp. 82, 77). Another explanation regards the negation of culture as an exaggerated reaction to the system of political apartheid (Viljoen, 1995). In fact, it became politically inexpedient during the apartheid era to refer to differences between groups of people (Swartz, 1996). Culture operated as a synonym for race in apartheid discourse (Chidester, 1991) and served as a tool for domination rather than as a means of liberation.

The ambivalent attitude of the South African psychologists towards culture is mirrored by educationists (Patel, 1997), historians of religion (Chidester, 1991), and especially by anthropologists (Boonzaaier and Sharp, in Kottler, 1990). In fact, what has been termed the progressive South African anthropology of the 1980s (Swartz, 1996) has had considerable influence on shaping the approach to culture of the 'reactive' group of psychologists. Whereas Chidester warned against the reification of worldviews, the anthropologists simply ruled out terms like culture and ethnicity as social constructions serving political ends. '(D)ifferent races and ethnic groups, unique cultures and traditions, do not exist in any ultimate sense in South Africa, and are real only to the extent that they are the product of a particular world view' (Boonzaaier and Sharp, in Kottler, 1990, p. 28).

'Against the backdrop of the perceived political necessity of a universalist view of culture in the late 1980s and early 1990s' (Swartz, 1996, 121), no room was left for the discussion of differences. To use the term in a relativist sense implied being associated with the politics of apartheid (Kottler, 1988). Politically aware psychologists, it was implied, would avoid using the concept. In fact, the argument of the social construction of terms, which the universalists used with respect to culture, was cleverly employed by them to further their own approach. By aligning a cultural relativist framework with the apartheid regime, they effectively discredited any work related to African culture, which in itself is a political strategy with profound consequences. In the name of political correctness and scientific exactness, the 'reactive mainstream' psychologists, similar to the strategy of their colleagues in the United States (see Cushman, 1991), managed to entrench their ethnocentric view of the universalist search for psychological essentials, as the guiding principle for psychology in South Africa.

Following in the tradition of the sociology of knowledge, some 'progressive' South African social scientists have pointed out that terms are constructed in terms of the social reality of the time, often to serve political purposes. This is undoubtedly true, for it is precisely what the 'reactive' group has accomplished in politicising the concept of culture. The politicising of culture has been so thorough that the term has become a no-go terrain for psychological exploration. As Korber (1990) was brave enough to point out with respect to her discussion of indigenous healing, 'the universalist position is unsatisfactory because it seeks to impose the Western medical model on all societies and cultures, thus ignoring the important differences' (p. 50). She also stressed that 'while there exist certain universals, there exist simultaneously certain differences. Within the South African context these should be seen as enriching rather than as a motivation for separating and dividing facilities and people' (p. 50). Besides, as Staub (1996) has indicated, it is especially in difficult times, when personal identity is threatened, that people tend to turn to the group as a source of identity. 'This makes group self-concepts especially important' (p. 120). By considering only individual psychology, without the role of culture, social conditions, and group processes, Staub argues that we will be unable to understand and devise means to combat genocidal violence and contemporary youth violence.

In keeping with the sociology of knowledge, the concept of culture has been politicised to serve the purposes of an ethnocentric psychology. As one of the psychologists who has been most outspoken against culture, Dawes (1996) has nevertheless come to acknowledge the difficulty of comprehending the 'pre-modern' mind from a 'modern' perspective. Yet, he continues to maintain that the neo-positivistic approach provides the best means for the Africanisation of psychology. Following Hountondji (1983), Wiredu (1980), and Appiah (1993), who distinguish 'folk' from 'real' African philosophy, he argues that

> African psychology needs to be framed within the conventions of the discipline, if it is not to be confused with ethnopsychologies of particular communities. The project of psychology in the academy is different from that constructed by other communities in order to provide explanations of social and mental phenomena. The key difference lies in the ritual of theory construction, method and proof, which attend psychology.
>
> (Dawes, 1996, p. 9)

'Africanisation is a political psychological project. It seeks to give voice to the intellectual endeavours of African psychologists, and attempts to design an appropriate psychology which will better serve children in developing Africa' (Nsamenang and Dawes, 1998, p. 74). Despite the apparent double-bind with respect to African culture, Dawes has admittedly come a long way since the 1980s in acknowledging that 'the production of African psychology will founder if it does not take place in the dialogue between local and foreign perspectives' (Dawes, 1996, p. 11).

It is debatable, though, whether the paradigms of contemporary psychology to which the 'reactive mainstream' group of psychologists subscribe, can allow an effective dialogue between different cultural communities to occur. The critique of mainstream paradigms, which was discussed in previous chapters, is too damning for the *carte blanche* perpetuation of the ethnocentric status quo in contemporary psychology. To recap, Cushman (1991) states that 'Humans cannot be studied outside of their lived context. Any attempt to do that, and thereby to develop a set of universal laws of human nature, is bound to fail. It is not possible to develop universal, transhistorical laws because humans are not separable from their culture and history: they are fundamentally and inextricably intertwined' (p. 207).

Seedat (1997) is another South African psychologist who locates 'the quest for a liberatory psychology within the parameters of politics and economics' (p. 263), while remaining within the ethnocentric framework of contemporary psychology. In a scholarly article setting out the quest for a liberatory psychology, he follows the model of reactive identification, which Bulhan (1980) proposes in his theory of cultural in-betweenity. However, Seedat exhibits the same double-bind relationship with respect to culture, as does Dawes. He credits 'the study of supposedly uniquely African psychosocial phenomena that only indigenous African healers can remedy' (Seedat, 1997, p. 261), to have contributed to the liberatory discourse. Yet, he criticises the 'cultural determinist position' for depolitising the debate on the relevancy of psychology. However, drawing attention to the lack of respect for the cultural identity of groups seems to me an act loaded with political implications. In fact, it constitutes the most fundamental of political endeavours.

It has to be granted that it is when 'cultures are reified, portrayed as static and regarded as the primary force – above power and oppression – determining the psychosocial life of humankind', that Seedat (1997, p. 262) regards cultural sensitivity to be restricting. Yet, I cannot imagine that any social scientist today will be inclined to portray culture as a static concept. Neither can I imagine that it is possible to place culture, power, and oppression in a hierarchical order. The interactive effect of these three variables is so complex that it is not within the scope of any existing research methodology to unravel their relative importance on 'psychosocial life' in any rigorous empirical way. In his work on the cultural-societal roots of violence, Staub (1996) has elucidated some of the complexity of the interactive effects between ideologies and socio-economic conditions that were held to be at the root of genocide, mass killing, and youth violence.

With respect to the concern of Seedat (1997) and others about the reification of culture, it seems that it is especially the highlighting of African culture that is perceived as reification. For instance, in order to 'expand on the metaphysical, epistemological, ontological, ethical, psychological and legal principles of liberatory psychology' (p. 266) that will presumably be of relevance in the South African context, Seedat refers exclusively to Islamic sources. Without a doubt, the Islamic conception of human nature has a great deal to contribute to psychology. However, so do the African conceptions of human nature. In investigating the uniqueness of each of these great traditions, the emergence of their distinguishing features will not only reveal what they can contribute uniquely, but also what they have in common with each other and with contemporary psychology.

The question remains what the 11 or more official language groups in South Africa are to be called. 'If these groups are not national groups and they are not ethnic groups and not cultural groups, then what are they?' (Alexander and Smolicz, 1993, p. 4). As the Nigerian, Turaki (1991) pointed out, 'If agents of social change and development do not take into account cultural values and social structures, the result is socio-political conflict and social problems. It is for this reason that it is necessary for nation-state builders to carefully consider models, hypotheses, assumptions, methods and tools, on the one hand, and the cultural values and social structures on the other, in issues of development' (p. 142). As Kottler (1990) has pointed out, the universalist perspective, which she coined the 'similarities discourse', in its focus on material social factors, failed to consider intra-psychic structures and processes. Subjective psychological factors, such as identity, attitudes, beliefs, and personality, can be of central importance in determining cultural allegiance (Sue, 1998). In support of the relativist perspective, which Kottler referred to as the 'differences discourse', she quotes the medical anthropologist, Harriet Ngubane, as stating that 'concepts and values embodied in a culture, although usually implicit and open to change, nourishes a sense of identity and of possession of a heritage. This endows the people belonging to that culture with self-confidence and the kind of pride that makes for collective survival despite conquest and ensuing deprivation' (p. 31).

In response to the negation of cultural realities by the 'reactive mainstream' group, and in conjunction with the 'proactive' lobby, Gobodo (1990) states that the failure to recognise cultural diversity in South Africa is myopic and 'reflective of the cultural assumptions of the dominant minority culture' (p. 93). Whereas the neglect and negation of culture by 'progressive' white psychologists can be attributed to any one of many reasons, the same attitude on the part of black psychologists is not that easily explained. The most obvious explanation relates to the effectiveness with which contemporary psychology has colonised the discipline in the world. By the institutionalisation of psychology it has come to exert great influence and wield enormous power. Bodibe (in press) described the silent complicity of African psychologists in adopting a foreign psychological culture, as their Achilles heel.

With respect to the criticism of the 'reactive' group against the indigenous focus of the 'proactive' group is their failure to realise that the 'retraditional-isation' of African culture can take modernising forms. Retraditionalisation does not mean returning Africa to what the continent has been in times gone by. It involves 'a move towards renewed respect for indigenous ways and the conquest of cultural self-contempt' (Mazrui and Tidy, in Mudimbe, 1988, p. 169), which these authors consider necessary in order to achieve cultural decolonisation. Agyakwa (1976), similarly, considers the examination of the theoretical bases of Akan (Ghana) traditional ways of knowing important for accomplishing a smooth integration of indigenous and modern education. Since 'some of the pedagogical principles inherent in the Akan traditional educational methods are the ideals for which Western educators have been striving' (p. 237), for example the open classroom, it is important to 'retain the core of the indigenous education with respect to its methods and objectives while at the same time we borrow new elements from different cultures' (p. 241). Indeed, the confusion of the concepts of modernisation and transformation with Westernisation poses a major obstacle to the cultural decolonisation of psychology in South Africa and elsewhere in Africa.

Mphahlele (1987) has stated that the concept of the African personality is an ever-changing concept that needs constantly to be redefined by Africans themselves in order to prevent others from doing so. As is apparent from the previous paragraph, the emergent African personality does not need to exclude traditional cultural belief systems and behaviour patterns. Rather, the emergent has to be seen as superimposed on the traditional. It is not one or the other, but the blending of the old with the new that will provide the basis for the future. Many individuals have already exhibited the ability to function, not just adequately, but with distinction, in the contexts of traditional African and modern technological frameworks.

I am thinking of a family planning officer who exhibited sharply contrasting behaviour in her communication with gynaecologists in the city and tribal elders in the rural areas. It was evident that a deep respect for the reality of both groups, which differed culturally, socio-economically and politically, formed the basis of her effective communication with them. Perhaps even more indicative of the ability to alternate cognitive styles, is the example of an African Methodist minister with a Ph.D. in theology from a British university, who performs ritual sacrifices in honour of the ancestors on special occasions such as the visit of his children from overseas. Contrary to his white colleagues, who consider such practices as pagan, the African Methodist is comfortable in his polytheistic approach to God. Bohr's resolution of Einstein's particle and Thomas Young's wave theory of light springs to mind. According to Bohr, the particle and the wave explanations are two complementary and mutually exclusive descriptions of the same reality, both of which are necessary. The 'complementary view of the basic physical structure of the universe – particles vs. waves – are derived when different observations are made, different techniques are used, and different experiments are performed' (Pribram, 1982, p. 28).

Mamphele Ramphele, a physician-anthropologist and vice-chancellor of the University of Cape Town, has been active in the Black Consciousness movement of the 1970s that stressed the psychological importance of black identity and self-reliance. Harriet Ngubane, who has taught in Great Britain and has held the chair in anthropology at the University of Cape Town, took up a seat as a member of parliament for the Inkatha Freedom Party, which is based on Zulu ethnic identity. With respect to the Zulu people she wrote: 'They know who they are essentially, so at one level can indeed be Zulu, yet at a deeper level are Africans with a worldview or orientation common to Africans in general; while in a more external sense they are also South Africans' (in Kottler, 1990, p. 32).

Lovemore Mbigi, a management consultant and executive director of a big management company, stated that throughout his business career, he relied heavily on his tribal rather than his Western education. At the feet of his grandmother he was, through the use of folk stories, poetry, and proverbs, taught about tribal customs, history, religion, politics, morality, and leadership. His ability to integrate these teachings with modern business practices enabled him to turn non-profiting business companies into successful ones. He would use the format and the principles of indigenous open-air meetings on which to model the ceremonies for company cohesion and renewal. These communal meetings incorporated dancing, singing, drinking, and eating, punctuated by the moral instruction of the mediums and the elders. 'Parables and African proverbs, as well as traditional healers, folk singers, market women and traditional peasant farmers served as role models for inspiring and empowering leadership' (Mbigi and Maree, 1995, p. 43).

A final example will have to suffice. Bodibe (1993), a Ph.D. in psychology who has 'lived in the urban areas for more than 30 years and am married to a wife who holds an MA degree' (p. 53), professes to be puzzled by his participation in certain unique and pertinently African rituals which were carried out during the funeral preparations of his paternal grandfather. The rituals 'went against the very grain of logical positivism and my training in the "scientific method"' (p. 53). Although Bodibe could not come up with any answers to the specific question posed by the ritual performance, he was nevertheless certain that that would not prevent him from future participation in similar events and from imparting the custom to his children and their offspring. Apart from these selected examples, African people in general have exhibited great adeptness at the accommodation of multiple realities in their lives. The challenge awaiting psychologists in South Africa is to become equally adept in dealing with the multiple cultural realities existing within the country.

It is obvious that psychology cannot be revisioned in terms of only one of the interpretative models used by anthropologists to render intelligible the apparent diversity of human understandings. In keeping with the universalist perspective, the search for general laws underlying the behaviour of people needs to continue. Similarly, the laws underlying the psychological uniqueness of each group that experiences a cultural cohesion need to be investigated in terms of a relativist perspective. In terms of the arguments and statements by various influential psychologists in favour of the recognition of different cultural frameworks, mentioned earlier, a relativist perspective, superimposed on a universalist approach, offers the best option for a viable psychology for the twenty-first century. In fact, respect for differences can be considered to constitute the most fundamental universal law.

The trust of the cultural relativists in 'Different but equal' (Shweder and Bourne, 1991, p. 114) must be distinguished from the third interpretative model, evolutionism. While the evolutionists are also committed to diversity, they impose a hierarchy on the diversity. It is possible that those psychologists, who negate the reality of cultural differences, confuse the relativist with the evolutionist perspective. Since the evolutionists usually employ the criteria of their own culture, which they consider to be universally valid, in their evaluation of other cultures, such comparisons have strong negative overtones, are of questionable validity, and need to be avoided. In their use of ethnocentric criteria in investigating cultural differences, evolutionists exhibit commonality with the universalists, whose postulation of what constitutes the universal is all too often based on their own indigenous values or perspectives.

To what extent the ethnocentric approach to psychology can be modified remains an open question, for the power wielded by Western institutions and paradigms is undoubtedly very strong and difficult to resist. For those who adhere to it, the rewards can be appreciable. As Archbishop of the Anglican Church, Desmond Tutu serves as a prime example. By excelling in the hierarchy of the church, he established a platform from which he proved to be tremendously effective in combating the political system of apartheid and was justly awarded the Nobel Prize for Peace. Yet, the question remains whether he would have received the same recognition if, for instance, he had been the head of one of the independent African churches in South Africa. Does his position in the Anglican Church not convey the message that in order for Africans to achieve international recognition and be politically effective, it is necessary for them to function within the paradigms laid down by Western institutions? Yet, how can Africans be expected to be free when their soul is chained to 'alien churches', one T. Mphahlele (1988) wanted to know in a letter to a daily newspaper in Johannesburg.

Part II

WHAT AN AFRICAN PERSPECTIVE HAS TO OFFER

10

TOWARDS AN AFRICAN WORLDVIEW

Living holism

While the revisioning of the social structures that prevent the fulfilment of human needs undoubtedly poses a daunting task for the profession of psychology, the extent to which the structure of the discipline itself may thwart the actualisation of human potential ought, at least, to be more accessible to investigation. Whether psychology is capable of revisioning itself remains an open question. In order to work towards the application and transformation of contemporary psychology, not only on its home soil, but also on that of Africa, it is necessary, in addition to the critical assessment of the parent discipline, to provide possible alternatives, based on indigenous African perspectives. For this purpose, the psychological dimensions underlying the belief systems and behaviour of the African people need to be investigated.

The importance of belief, held individually and culturally, in determining behaviour, has been pointed out earlier in the text. Unfortunately, the lack of awareness of psychologists of the importance of their own beliefs in determining the nature of the discipline and their professional behaviour is complemented by a lack of knowledge of the belief systems underlying indigenous African psychology. The study of African perspectives has always been regarded as the domain of anthropology, not only by psychologists but, in my experience, especially by anthropologists themselves. Due to the compartmentalisation endemic within our professional endeavours, psychology and anthropology have remained virtual strangers to each other, and the limited integration which has occurred between the disciplines in the United States is still to take place on the African continent. Thus, whatever knowledge has been gained in anthropology about the African worldview has not been transferred to psychology.

In the chapter on African American perspectives the essential elements of African cosmology have already been highlighted. This chapter will build on the features that have been pointed out. At the outset it needs to be stated that the overview of the African worldview cannot be anything but of a very general nature. I have tried to integrate my experiences and observations in terms of already existing concepts and ideas, which provide a framework for incorporating them.

LIVING HOLISM

In contrast to the psychological principles to which contemporary psychology subscribes, which have been outlined in the previous chapters, the approach in sub-Saharan Africa is vastly different. Instead of standing aloof from others and from nature, of constantly teasing things apart and focusing on the isolated components, the underlying philosophy on the subcontinent is directed by a unitive consciousness, a holistic dimension that is much more pervasive than anything that can be conceptualised in the West. Even the concept of holism of those Western scientists who have come to regard the universe as an integrated web of relationships, dating back to the development of quantum physics and the early inspired work of Jan Christian Smuts (1926), is basically restricted to a rational and not a total organismic understanding.

Perhaps this fact is the reason why the grasp of holism and the realisation of the interrelated nature of human behaviour, at least in some circles, has not been able to prevent the fragmentation of psychology. In fact, the splintered character of Western epistemology suggests to Agyakwa (1976) 'that it is futile to attempt to make substantial borrowings from Western educational methods' (p. 237). Yet, the rediscovery of the holism of Smuts and others (see Ferguson, 1980), such as Whitehead's organic philosophy (in Agyakwa, 1976), holds the promise of bridging the gap between Western and African thought. It validates the understanding of African cosmology in terms which those Westerners and Africans who need such validation can understand. However, to think holistically if one has been educated in a fragmented way is difficult, if not impossible to achieve.

In Africa, holism is a lived experience. The belief that everything belongs together is directly translated into the actualities of daily living. There is infinite respect for the invisible thread that binds all things together. The African world is a coherent world where the different aspects of the divine interact, for the dynamics of African ontology is expressed in relationships (Uka, 1991a). In terms of classical Gestalt psychology, the part is always considered in the context to which it belongs, except that the context in African holism represents a spiritual as well as a physical reality. The most distinguishing feature of the spiritual context is undoubtedly the pervasive respect for the intricately woven pattern of the universe within which the individual, despite his or her relative insignificance, is nevertheless embraced.

Kruger (1974), in describing the worldview of southern Africa's indigenous healers, expresses Africa's holism well. He says that the indigenous healers live in an undivided world in which animals, plants, humans, dreams, and ancestors all form a part. Senghor (in Reed and Wake, 1979) expresses the same idea when he points out that the African does not distinguish him or herself from the object, the tree or stone, the person, animal or social event. The world outside one's skin is not kept at a distance, it is not analysed and objectified, but embraced trustingly and completely.

Senghor's belief that nothing exists in isolation finds expression in his verse. His animated landscape echoes the heartbeat of the universe. The pulsation of his poetry expresses the life force found in all natural phenomena, animate or inanimate, visible or invisible. His poetry sings, dances, breathes, it celebrates participation with the universal soul and identifies with the creative life force. He considered poetry to be the spiritual music, which was able to restore harmony to a discordant world. Through the rhythm of his words, Senghor enables the penetration of the essential features of the universe to respond to the tug of the life-tide.

While the themes of fragmentation and alienation reverberate in his early works, a reflection of his 'hybrid' status, being suspended between the cultures of Africa and Europe, Senghor is essentially a poet of reconciliation. Not only does he try to integrate the internal and external divisions of his life, but his poetry also dissolves the rigid dichotomies between the sacred and the material. Ever in search of confluence, he dreamt of integrating seemingly discordant elements, of finding a balance between divergent forces. His mission was to dissolve contradictions and to prepare the way for the creation of a universal fraternity.

By returning to his roots in the African soil, Senghor's search for 'the Kingdom of Childhood' has been derided as furthering the all too pervasive myth of Africa as a continent forever embraced in a veil of nativity and mysticism. These criticisms may be valid from an empirical and materialistic perspective. However, the ideas that nothing exists in isolation, that life is sacred, a communion of souls, cyclical, a constant renaissance, requiring an inner renewal of humankind to keep pace with the renewal of the cosmos, transcends the limitations of time and space, and cannot be evaluated from a linear perspective. Senghor's poetry exalts the essential vitality of the African, the organic bond between humankind and mother earth, the mystery of human existence, and the power of love as a necessity of human existence. It breaks down the boundaries between the conscious and the unconscious, as well as between dream and reality, life and death. The homage paid to Senghor on his 90th birthday in Joal, his home village in Senegal, and in the French town, Verson, where he resides with his wife, leaves no doubt about the esteem and the love of both the Sengalese and the French for this great son of Africa (Roberts, 1996).

Like Senghor, Césaire (1969) believed that black people were able to give themselves up to the essence of all things because they felt such an indivisible unity with everything in the world. It was due to their ability in this regard, Césaire contended, that black people could teach the white person of the north how to love, how to discover their essential being, and how to tame the instruments of technology to serve the needs of humankind.

Unitive consciousness can, sometimes, come to expression in rather dramatic fashion. How can an incident, which occurred at the Veterinary Research Institute at Onderstepoort in South Africa, otherwise be explained? Tests, which required the preparation of blood smears at regular intervals, were made on an antelope. Some difficulty was experienced in catching and holding the animal, until an African came along who said that he would calm the antelope. What transpired was witnessed by a number of level-headed scientists. The African went into the kraal and spoke to the antelope in a loud voice. The man then went into the adjoining stable followed by the animal. He made the antelope lie down and threw a thong over its body. It lay there, completely pacified while the blood smears were taken, until the thong was removed. This operation was repeated daily until the series of tests were completed (Mönnig, 1967).

I have been privileged to experience the unitive consciousness operative in Africa on numerous occasions in my association with the indigenous healers, artists, African students and colleagues. One of my earliest experiences dates back to the early 1970s. The occasion was the return of an indigenous healer to her place of birth in the Western Transvaal after she had graduated in Soweto. In walking with her brother through the veld in search of an ox which was to be sacrificed in honour of the ancestors of the healer, I was struck by the way he reacted to successive groups of cattle. Since the animal we were searching for had to answer to the specifications which the healer had dreamt about, we searched for a long time in the vast communal pasture to find the appropriate beast. And all the time, the cattle we encountered were 'greeted' with a 'Heia'. They in turn stopped grazing, turned their heads and looked at us in response to the sound or in acknowledgement of the greeting. At first I did not know what to make of the 'Heia's' directed at the cattle, until it dawned on me that here was the basic acknowledgement of one being by another. The animals were greeted and they in turn acknowledged the greeting. For my part, I felt no relatedness. The cattle were animals, and I did not even think of greeting them. I guess I regarded the lifting of their heads and the looking at us as nothing more than a response to the visual and auditory stimuli we provided. However, I have never forgotten the incident and the force with which the final realisation, about what was really transpiring in the veld on that autumn morning, dawned on me.

Many other examples can be cited which demonstrate the unitive consciousness operative in Africa. For instance, within the sphere of interpersonal relationships, mothers have been known to share the medicine for their sickness with their babies. They have also been known to ask for a prescription for their children when one has been written for them. Likewise, people consider themselves sick if someone close to them is ill. I know of incidents where persons who were reported to have been ill, when asked about their health, rather uncomprehendingly replied: 'She has died.' The sickness of the relative was also their sickness. To the uncomprehending despair of many white supervisors in the labour force, Africans request leave to attend the funeral of a father or a mother, after similar requests had already been submitted in the past. An African usually considers him or herself to have not just one father and mother, but several fathers and mothers. I was told that twins were not regarded as separate individuals but as one entity. A twin is not addressed in the singular and refers to him or herself in the plural, for he or she is also his or her twin brother or sister.

164

Upon the death of a twin the survivor symbolically descends into the grave during the burial ceremony.

An understanding of the importance of the belief in being in unity with others, and with an energy that is so pervasive that it is associated with the deity, can go a long way to clarify the misunderstanding people in the West have of the way of life in Africa. It can explain the strength of West and Central African art, which is not art, but sculptured pieces in obeisance of the deity. It explains why art as a discipline in its own right has not taken off on the continent. Even at present in South Africa, where many African artists produce gallery art, the call is toward art in the service of community.

In order to convey the nature of African holism in greater detail, it will be discussed under the headings of the cognitive, interpersonal, intrapersonal, and aesthetic dimensions. Each of these areas of major focus will again be subdivided, at times perhaps arbitrarily, for life does not lend itself that neatly to categorisation. In addition, the unitive consciousness operative in Africa comes to the fore in the concepts of sickness and health (e.g., Ngubane, 1977); the belief in the prophetic reality of dreams (e.g., Berglund, 1976); the practices of the indigenous healers (e.g., Holdstock, 1979) and the syncretistic churches (e.g., Schutte, 1972); as well as in the importance of symbols, such as the metaphysical significance of metallurgy in Africa (Richards, 1981). In these practices, ritual and ceremony serve to bring the living in contact with their spiritual essence. The performance of a ritual or ceremony requires special preparation and precautions, for it is an attempt to concretise the spiritual, to facilitate connectedness with the Vital Force or universal energy. It is spirit that gives being to matter. In fact spirit or energy achieves form in matter.

THE COGNITIVE DIMENSION

The cognitive dimension could also have been labelled the spiritual or the transpersonal dimension. Even the label religious would have sufficed. The choice of cognitive is a deliberate attempt to couch the discussion in terms with which mainstream psychology is most familiar. Besides, the cognitive dimension does not only incorporate rational thinking of a linear, but also of a non-linear, nature.

Religion and the concept of the deity

African people are highly religious, not necessarily in the sense of church participation or adherence to a specific religious dogma, but in the sense of honouring that which represents the ultimate concern of humankind. African religiosity portrays an awareness of a power or source that transcends the human condition, that participates in and shapes all living. It is as a result of this force at work that we become aware of it. Setiloane (1989) regards religion akin to an instinct, a sixth sense. Life, generally, is a religious encounter. Descartes' 'I think, therefore I am' can, according to Mbiti (1991a, b), be translated in African terms as 'I am religious, therefore I am.' The religion of Africa, quite uniform in concept before the advent of the missionaries (Awolalu, 1991; Ayisi, 1992; Dopamu, 1991; Gyekye, 1987; Mbiti, 1991a, b; Uka, 1991a, b), was not a formalised system which existed outside the mainstream of life. God was everywhere, to be communicated with at all times. Worship in the African context was not something that took place on special occasions or in special places. The missionaries failed to find visible signs of religious practice in the form of buildings and organised gatherings and therefore drew the conclusion that Africans were heathens. But, as Mbiti states, African religion is to be found in all aspects of life. African psychology, therefore, has to embrace African religion. Besides, the human organism does not have different sets of principles according to which it functions for the various disciplines (see Jahn, 1972; Uka, 1991b).

The concept of the deity in Africa reflects the difference in ontology between the continent and the West. In African context, according to Setiloane (1989), God was not considered as a personalised entity, separate from His creation, as was the case in the Christian concept. By setting the animate and the inanimate universe apart from the Creator, the Western world has lost its soul, what Nietzsche described as the death of God. 'Those who create a god that justifies for them the desire and will to shut other people out of their lives in order to establish an exclusive enclave for themselves must be utterly poor in spirit' (Mphahlele, 1984, p. 250).

In Africa, the deity was conceived as a 'power without beginning' (J.L. Stonier, 1996, p. 73), or as the ultimate Invisible (Campbell, 1983). Setiloane (1989) translates Akan, Yoruba, Sotho/Tswana, Zulu, and Shona terms of the deity along similar lines. The Batswana believe in Modimo (the creator and source of life, one who penetrates and permeates all being); the Xhosa refer to God as Umdali or Qamatha (the Creator); to the Zulu, God is Unkulunkulu (the unimaginably big) or Umvelinqanqi (one who appeared in time no one can remember); to the Bemba, God is Lesa (the Breath of all Life); to the Kono, God is Meketa (the Everlasting one). Mbiti (1991b) groups African ideas about God, as expressed in the thousands of names for God on the continent, in four general categories: what God does, images of God, the nature of God, and the relationship with God.

Nobel Laureate for Peace and president of South Africa, Nelson Mandela, once described traditional Xhosa religion as characterised by a cosmic wholeness, with little distinction between the sacred and the secular, between the natural and the supernatural. No aspect of life and living is too small to be imbued with significance and meaning in Africa. Sir Laurens van der Post (1975) expressed this aspect in the prosaic terms for which he became known. According to him,

The bushman makes gods out of all animals around him; the Hottentots kneel to an insect, the praying mantis; the Bantu listens to the spirits of his ancestors in the noise of his cattle stirring in their kraals of thorn at night; the negro appeases and invokes the gods in endless fetishes and images of wood and clay. But one and all they are humble parts of life and at one with knowing that, in order to get through their tiny, trembling day they are in constant need of support from a power greater than themselves.

(van der Post, 1975, p. 40)

How different is the way in which persons in the West trust their ability to master all problems, including each other, nature, and the universe. An understanding of the reality and strength of the belief in being part of the Vital Force, which is the deity in Africa, also casts a different perspective on what has rather degradingly been labelled, animism, personification and anthropomorphism. The tendency to imbue the natural world with power beyond that which can be understood by Western logic is a feature of life in Africa which is not at all understood by the scientific community, yet is amazingly in harmony with developments in quantum physics during the past century. By restricting itself to the observable and the rational, Western science lacks the ability and perspective to comprehend the African reality. However, as William James (1902/1985) observed, our rational consciousness is but a special type of consciousness. Ample evidence of an alternate consciousness exists in Africa. According to Senghor (in Reed and Wake, 1979), Europe has given the world a civilisation of analytical reasoning while Africa contributed a civilisation of intuitive reasoning.

The concept of vital force

In describing African psychology, Parrinder (1969) states that 'it is impossible to conceive of man existing in and by himself, without any close relationship to the forces all around him, both animate and inanimate. Man is not just an individual, or merely a social being; he is a vital force which is in close and continuing contact with other forces. He influences them, but they constantly influence him' (p. 123). The vital force is in all men and creatures and forms a bond between them. 'We are all flames of the same fire, which is God,' an African sage told me. Mphahlele (1984) cherishes 'the African's belief in the Supreme Being as a vital force, a dynamic presence in all organic matter and in the elements, in Man, where those of the western world feel uneasy with belief in the supernatural and dismiss African religion as magic' (p. 249).

In his description of the African conception of the human being as 'a vital force which is in close and continuing contact with other forces', Parrinder is undoubtedly following in the footsteps of Tempels (1959), who is generally credited with concretising the concept of vital force. While David Bohm, Nobel Laureate in physics, considers the universe to be the unfolding of the enfolded order, African cosmology considers it to be the unfolding of a vital force (Tempels, 1959). The analytical and the intuitive accounts of the universe seem to be amazingly similar.

167

The vital force is not only composed of other people but also of animals, plants, the ancestors, and even elements of the inanimate world. In its various manifestations the vital force is not time-bound, making the past as important as the present. Neither are all forces equal and it is important to discover one's relation to the other forces so that one can approach them with due respect, for it is in the nature of the relationship with other forces that one's essence is determined. In this aspect, African cosmology is very similar to the formal aspect of the Japanese self (Rosenberger, 1992). In the words of the sage, referred to above, we are all fingers of the same hand which is God. Each finger is different from the other, yet the strength of the hand is to be found in the co-ordinated action of its different components.

The human being is not just a vital force, but a vital force in participation. According to Mphahlele (1984), 'The basis of the African's traditional religion lies in the realm of social relationships . . . in the continued contact between us and the external nature through the spirits of the ancestors' (p. 249). More will be said in the section on interpersonal relationships about this vitally important aspect of African holism. Even though each individual is a refraction of the deity, one's humanness can be fully realised only by integration and participation in the community.

The belief in being part of a universal spiritual network of energies provides great sustenance for the African person. However, it also places great responsibility on the individual to discover and maintain the proper relationship with the multiple strands of the network of relationships. 'The person *alone* in his or her "isolated being" lacks power. It is only as part of the whole, that is, by being understood as representative *in his* or *her being* of the whole, that he or she gains force, takes on meaning, or becomes relevant' (Richards, 1981, p. 223). Clearly then, in Africa no person is considered to be an island.

The much-quoted account of African cosmology by Tempels (1959) has not been without its detractors, amongst whom Hountondji (1983) and Wiredu (1980) have been the most prominent. The critique of Hountondji, however, turns out to be directed principally towards the grounds upon which Tempels based his work, rather than the actual nature of what he described as African philosophy. According to Hountondji, Tempels based his ideas on a 'philosophy' that did not consist of texts documenting African philosophy, but consisted of a supposed inarticulate and collective wisdom with roots deep in Africa's past. Such a worldview, Hountondji argues, does not provide the basis for a genuine philosophical discourse. At best, it can be called an 'ethnophilosophy', which Hountondji does not regard as adequate for a philosophical practice worthy of the name. According to him, the discourse and the analytical process through which the African people try to define themselves do not constitute philosophy. It is clear that Hountondji defines philosophy strictly as a demarcated discipline along Western lines. As such, he has a point, in the same way that those who adhere to the paradigm of psychology as an empirical science are justified to regard this chapter not as psychology. Yet, I would like to think that it is equally, if not more,

168

meaningful than the brain and the sleep research that I was involved in during the initial phases of my career.

Hountondji (1983) also maintains that what is regarded as African philosophy arose, historically, from the work of European missionaries and anthropologists, rather than from African philosophers. Furthermore, the intention was to reach readers in the West and not in Africa. Mudimbe (1988) supports Hountondji's assumption about 'the European invention of Africa' (p. 69). In fact, he presents a scholarly account of the principles involved in this process and of the reaction by the African intellectual community. According to Mudimbe,

> Western interpreters as well as African analysts have been using categories and conceptual systems which depend on a Western episte-mological order. Even in the most explicitly 'Afrocentric' descriptions, models of analysis explicitly or implicitly, knowingly or unknowingly, refer to the same order.
>
> (1988, p. x)

> We might actually say that an anthropologist 'invents' the culture he believes himself to be studying, that the relation is more 'real' for being his particular acts and experiences than the things it relates.
>
> (1988, p. 27)

The question of knowing who can speak validly about Africa is one that has been debated heatedly in the appraisals of anthropological and missionary discourses. In psychology the debate has hardly started. The same issues are undoubtedly at stake, though. Perhaps the attempt to understand another culture presents primarily a means for comprehending oneself, as Mudimbe states. In my own career it has certainly been true. As has been stated earlier, contrast is not only of crucial importance in sharpening our perceptions, but also of our experiences generally. Exposure to alternative cultural perspectives facilitates clarification of the relative merits of what one values and what is valued by others.

Hountondji (1983) argues that the 'impressionistic sketches', which foreign scholars obtained on the basis of a hypothetical worldview of a given people, need to be replaced by a rigorous 'scientific' approach, such as Kagame's (in Hountondji) direct linguistic analysis. However, Hountondji even objects to the idea that oral literature can provide the basis for a philosophical discourse. To warrant consideration, oral literature needs to consist of 'the systematic trans-cription of everything that can be recorded of the discourses of our ancestors, sages and scholars who are still alive' (p. 25). Again, I have no argument with the validity of such an approach, except its exclusivity. It reminds me of a colleague in anthropology who argued that the account of African mythology, told to me by a sage, could not be true because it has not been documented in any textbook. In fact, he implied that anthropologists should have done the documentation!

The work of Tempels has also been criticised from a political perspective. Césaire (in Hountondji, 1983) considered the account of Tempels an attempt to divert attention from the fundamental political problems facing the then Belgian Congo. By emphasising the importance of ontological issues for the African people, attention could be deflected from the necessity of improving the material and economic conditions under which the people lived. Furthermore, as a missionary, the aim of Tempels was clearly to 'civilise' the people of Central Africa in terms of the worldview upheld by the missionaries.

A criticism more directly applicable to the essence of the 'philosophy' that Tempels encountered in Central Africa relates to the concept that not all vital forces are equal. Césaire asserted that Tempels invoked this concept to preserve imperialist domination and white superiority. The fact that the concept lends itself to abuse, does not, however, negate its validity. The animate and inanimate universe is replete with qualitative and quantitative differences in the levels of energy and consciousness within and between the levels.

The ancestors

Of the vital participations, none are more important than the relationship with the ancestors, for the ancestors are the intermediaries between the living and the dead (Ikenga-Metuh, 1991). Not surprisingly, the ancestors are often referred to as the living dead, an indication that the demarcation between life and death in Africa is not as definitive as it is in the West. I have been told on numerous occasions that once a person has died, he or she was of greater importance than when that person was alive. In fact, the ancestors are even of greater significance in the lives of the living than the deity. The main supernatural being is generally experienced as rather remote and unconcerned with the day-to-day affairs of humankind (e.g., de Jong, 1987; van Beek, 1994). 'Throughout Black Africa the "living dead," that is the remembered dead, are the principal intermediaries between the living of the tribe and the Invisibles. For, though themselves now invisible, they are still engaged in the world of the living' (Campbell, 1983, p. 14).

As with all generalisations there are exceptions to the rule, though. According to van Beek (1994), the ancestors in Dogon religion are of some importance as intermediaries between the living and *Ama*, the main deity, but they do not represent an important category in Dogon belief. Mishap does not stem from the ancestors, but from the gods or from living people.

Contrary to popular belief amongst Westerners, the ancestors are not experienced as deities, not even, according to Setiloane (1989), as spirits. They are experienced as persons, and there is a speaking relationship with them. They are the seniors of the lineage and their departure to realms closer to the 'ultimate Invisible', imbues them with the power to act on behalf of the living. The ancestors are tied up with every aspect of life in sub-Saharan Africa. J.L. Stonier (1996) points out the similarity between the concept of the ancestors in African ontology and the Christian saints. Mbigi draws a parallel between the spirit of the ancestor as hunter and the modern entrepreneur (Mbigi and Maree, 1995). Since the ancestors are considered to live in the shadow of the 'ultimate Invisible', they are often referred to as 'shades'.

The existence and the presence of the ancestors are not questioned. A world without them is not possible. This is equally true of people in the rural as well as the urban areas, where the traditional institutions are presumed to have broken down. Even Africans belonging to Christian churches have integrated their belief in the ancestors with the Christian notion of the Holy Spirit. 'God loves the ancestors. They are the angels of God. The Whites don't know what the ancestors mean. They call them angels instead' (Schutte, 1974, p. 118). Practices pertaining to the ancestors are considered to belong to the private, and Christianity to the public spheres of religion. Among the Christians who belonged to secret prayer groups, 'an hour is set aside during the night to allow each member to go outside to pray to his own ancestors' (Schutte, 1972, p. 256).

During his travels in South Africa, Mphahelele (1984) encountered a poet-farmer who told him that ever since he stopped going to the church and turned to his ancestors, he found that he could wake up in the morning without fear. To students Mphahlele explained that the ancestors constituted a vital part of African humanism. As a state of mind, it is imperative for those Africans who have lost their connectedness to their roots, to find their way back to the inclusiveness of African humanism.

There is no existence of the living separate from that of the ancestors, nor a realm of the ancestors separate from that of the living. The two are intimately tied together in kinship bonds that make the individual and the ancestors of a lineage interdependent on each other. The relation between the living and the ancestors is exceedingly vital and dynamic. J.L. Stonier (1996) described the relationship as a symbiotic one, 'with a mutual need to keep the other happy, content and healthy. It is therefore essential that communion and communication between those left on earth and those who have passed to the great beyond continues to take place' (p. 81). Lack of communication with the ancestors breaks down the harmonious relationship which is normally enjoyed with them. Without their constant intervention and nearness there can not be a happy future. As de Jong (1987) learned in Guinea-Bissau, not even the elders are exempted from the ritual obligations of 'courting' and being visited by the ancestors.

The spirits of the ancestors manifest themselves during waking in the form of visions and voices, or through the medium of a diviner. In sleep they manifest themselves through dreams. These manifestations are not experienced as abstract or far away, but as real encounters of great significance. Being experienced through their means of manifestation is regarded as sufficient evidence of their being obvious and real. Conceivably, the ancestor spirits are like Kirlian phantom leaves (Johnson, 1974, 1975; Moss, 1976) or phantom limbs even (Sherman, 1996), specific forms of energy which exist in relation to that which it has been a part of. As an indigenous healer told me, 'My father is departed, but he is.'

Because the ancestors are experienced as so real, encountering them can place heavy demands on a person, for the ancestors are jealous, they want to be remembered. Unless the customs are upheld and the proper rituals performed to honour and prepare the induction of the deceased's spirit into the ancestral realm, the ancestors pass into the unknown as dangerous spirits, from where they can exact a heavy toll on the living. Misery in this life is invariably considered to be due to ceremonial negligence in honour of the ancestors. 'A departed spirit for whom no feast of "accompanying" (*mahlohonolo*) has been performed will wander in limbo and return to haunt the living with the complaint, again transmitted in a dream, "Where is my blanket? I am cold"' (Murray, 1979, p. 352). It must be reiterated that remembering the ancestors is not just an empty custom, but one imbued with the greatest importance. In honouring the ancestors, the principles and values they represent are honoured.

Induction into the ancestral realm is a prerequisite for and a sanction of all future interactions between the living and the 'living dead'. When proper respect has been paid to the memory of the deceased by the performance of the appropriate ceremonies, the ancestors are, on the whole, experienced as benevolent guardians, capable of interceding on behalf of the living. It is for this reason that Africans are willing to make the heavy financial commitment that the proper obligations towards the dead requires, which, in the case of migrant workers, necessitates 'the transfer of resources on a massive scale from urban areas to rural areas' (Murray, 1979, p. 339).

The intimate relationship of the living with the realm of the ancestors in Africa can be understood in terms of the concept of the interdependent self. Stroebe, Gergen, Gergen, and Stroebe (1992) have pointed out that the loss of another, from an interdependent perspective, means a breaking of bonds that can destroy one's interdependent identity. Consequently, the bonds, even with the deceased, must be maintained or the self is threatened. Equally meaningful is an understanding of the ancestors in terms of Jungian or archetypal psychology. The concept of the 'shades', which is a popular reference to the ancestors, closely parallels the concepts of the shadow and of the daimonic (not demonic, although the daimonic can, just as the ancestors, be manifested demonically).

The ancestors present visitations or interferences from beyond ego-consciousness, what Jung regarded as complexes. They represent our personal and collective history, the personal and collective unconscious, and are, therefore, inextricably related to who we are. In order to know myself I need to be in touch with the realm of the ancestors, not primarily in a literal and personal sense, but as a means of getting in touch with a dimension of being which transcends my ego-consciousness. Hillman (1983) could very well have written about the concept of the ancestors in Africa when he discussed the various ways in which images have been conceptualised to work in us: 'they are legendary personages of history, showing culture at work in the channels of the soul. The land of the dead is the country of ancestors, and the images who walk in on us are our ancestors. If not literally the blood and genes from whom we descend, then they are the historical progenitors, or archetypes, of our particular spirit informing it with ancestral culture' (p. 60). Hillman quotes Nietzsche as stating that 'Immediate self-observation is not enough, by a long way, to enable us to learn how to know ourselves. We need history, for the past continues to flow through us in a hundred channels' (p. 60). As the psychic representations of our geographical, historical, and cultural contexts, the ancestors exert their claims on and power over us. According to Jung, 'The images . . . place a great responsibility upon a man' (in Hillman, 1983, p. 61). They represent powers with claims and we have a religious responsibility, an ethical obligation, to honour their moral claims. Hillman regards the question of morality to arise due to the encounter with the images themselves:

> As these imaginal figures bring a sense of internal fate, so they bring an awareness of internal necessity and its limitations. We feel responsible to them and for them. A mutual caring envelops the relationship, or, as the situation was put in antiquity, the daimones are also guardian spirits. Our images are our keepers, as we are theirs . . . they who call for ritualized devotions, who insist they be consulted before we act. Images are the compelling source of morality and religion as well as the conscientiousness of art.
>
> (Hillman, 1983, p. 61)

The spirits

Apart from being composed of the human spirits of the recently deceased and those who have died a long time ago, African cosmology also maintains that the universe is composed of nature spirits. All these spirits and deities have an explanatory function (de Jong, 1987). Horton (1967) considered this function to be the provision of a framework by means of which sense can be made of the diversity of everyday experiences in terms of the action of a relatively small number of different kinds of forces.

> Even where there is no biological life in an object, African peoples attribute (mystical) life to it, in order to establish a more direct relationship with the world around them. In this way the visible and invisible parts of the universe are at man's disposal through physical, mystical and religious means. Man is not the master in the universe; he is only the centre, the friend, the beneficiary, the user. For that reason he has to live in harmony with the universe, obeying the laws of natural, moral and mystical order. If these are unduly disturbed, it is man who suffers most.
>
> (Mbiti, 1991a, p. 44)

The nature spirits can belong to the realm of the heavens (e.g., the sun, the moon, the stars, the wind, thunder, and lightning), or the earth (e.g., mountains, rocks, boulders, trees, forests, water, lakes, the sea, rivers, metals). As with the sky, the earth elements are imbued with a presence that can be comprehended by human beings. The ancestors can also become associated with the elements of nature, by taking up residence in them (Thomson, 1994). For instance, there are the ancestors of the forest and those who live in the water.

Numerous examples abound that portray the oneness experienced with respect to the elements of nature. Massive 'fertility' stones dominate the landscape on one site in the Western Transvaal. Interestingly, 2 metre tall phallic symbols stand in line with *yoni* (the female organ of generation) stones, and I have been told that, by kneeling behind the *yoni* stone while one keeps one's eyes on the phallic stone, a symbolic mating of Mother Earth and Father Sky can be effected with good effects on the fertility of the surrounding fields. It was also suggested that these stones provided treatment for infertility and impotence. By touching the *yoni* or the phallic stone, the female or the male could be restored to fertility or potency.

Stones of various shapes and sizes have been used in healing practices, and although 'sympathetic magic' is no longer in widespread use, it is the oldest form of healing. The sick person was made to touch an object that looked like the part of the body that was diseased. Since sickness was believed to be a moving force, that of the stone could replace the spirit of the ailing organ. I have been shown stones shaped like kidneys that were to be held against the lower back to replace the ailing spirit of the kidneys. In essence, these practices predate the use of imagery in psychology and holistic healing today (e.g., Simonton, 1975).

Mbigi outlines the hierarchy of African spirits in the religion of his clan of the Shona people in the following order: the Rainmaker Spirit; the Hunter Spirit; the Divination Spirit; the War Spirit; the Family Spirit; the Wandering Spirit; the Avenging Spirit; and the Witch Spirit (Mbigi and Maree, 1995). From a Western perspective, the power of these various spirits, including that of witches and sorcerers, can, as has been indicated, most meaningfully be understood in terms of the paradigms of archetypal psychology.

THE INTERPERSONAL DIMENSION

Involvement with other people, near and extended family, as well as participation in the community at large, occurs to an extent that astonishes privacy-oriented Westerners. One only has to attend an African wedding, funeral, ritual ceremony, or simply spend a day or a weekend in an African home, to realise the importance of people to each other.

> Africans have always been more interested in human relations than in gadgets, even when they realize that they have to operate machines for a living. Africans have always gravitated towards people, not places and

things. Why they have not yet, to any significant degree, taken up the idea of a vacation at a holiday resort. People, and not places, give them real pleasure. They want a *social* climate where they can *make* music and fun and not just *listen* to music and *look* at a performance.

(Mphahlele, 1962, p. 91)

De Jong (1987) uses almost the same words as Mphahlele in stating that 'A Guinean is generally more concerned with persons than with things' (p. 28). As in other societies of the majority world, such as the Hindu, being separated from other people implies, for the African, a personal, cultural sense of hell.

Of the many concepts portraying the importance of relatedness, none is more expressive than *ubuntu* (Nguni), *vhuthu* (Venda), *unhu* (Shona) or *botho* (Sotho). Although it is difficult to translate *ubuntu* into English, the concept refers to that which ultimately distinguishes us from the animals – the quality of being human and ultimately of being humane. *Ubuntu* conveys the idea of strength based on the qualities of compassion, care, gentleness, respect, and empathy. Nobel Laureate, Archbishop Desmond Tutu (1981) described *ubuntu* as the attitude valued most highly by traditional and even present African society. In an article in *The Star*, a daily newspaper in Johannesburg, he wrote that the person who had *ubuntu* was known to be compassionate and gentle. The person with *ubuntu* used his or her strength on behalf of the weak, did not take advantage of others, in short, was someone who cared, who treated others for what they were, human beings. Having *ubuntu* meant more than anything else, for without it one lacked an indispensable ingredient of being human. A person without *ubuntu* is regarded as someone deserving pity or even contempt. Tutu's own life serves as a model of *ubuntu*.

Lebamang Sebidi (1988), co-ordinator of Adult Education at the Funda Centre in Soweto, describes *ubuntu* as African humanism and calls it *ubuntuism*. He differentiates *ubuntuism* from Western types of humanism due to the fact that it is inherently anti-individualism and pro-communalism. In addition, *ubuntu* is 'incurably religious. While the Western type of humanism is shut-in upon itself and is fundamentally centripetal, *ubuntuism* is expansive, transcendental and centrifugal' (p. 9). Western humanism places the human being at the apex of the evolutionary process with the resultant rejection of anything outside the human situation. 'Man is the sufficient and adequate reason of his own existence – he does not need the supernatural realm to explain anything: the WHAT, WHY and HOW of things' (p. 9). On the basis of the inclusivist and humane aspects of *ubuntu*, Aggrey Klaaste, editor of the *Sowetan*, has, in the late 1980s, in anticipation of the coming into political power of the African community in South Africa, in editorials and guest columns, linked the concept of *ubuntu* with the notion of nation building. If the future of the country could be based on *ubuntuism*, South Africa could be transformed into a country of *Abantu*, that is PEOPLE, freed from the disharmony, hatred, and disunity. President Mandela has endeavoured to do just that.

South African constitutional lawyers have seen fit to make explicit use of the concept of *ubuntu* in the epilogue of the constitution of the new South Africa. In fact, members of the constitutional court have described that document to be permeated in its entirety by *ubuntu* (in Gillmer, 1996). In the case of the State vs. Makwanyane and Mchunu in 1995, which effectively abolished the death penalty, the judge referred to *ubuntu* as a need that expresses

> the ethos of an *instinctive capacity for and enjoyment of love* towards our fellow men and women; the joy and fulfilment involved in recognizing their innate humanity – *the capacity this generates* in interaction within the collective community, the richness of *the creative emotions which it engenders* and the *moral energies which it releases* both in the givers and the society which they serve and are served by.
>
> (in Gillmer, 1996, pp. 95–96)

Gillmer cites another high court judge as defining *ubuntu* as follows: 'Generally *ubuntu* translates as humanness. In its most fundamental sense, it translates as personhood and morality. Metaphorically, it expressed itself in *umuntu ngumuntu ngabantu*, which roughly means that "a person is not a person without a community of other persons"' (p. 96).

Ubuntu has been suggested as a necessary principle on which to base the transformation of African management. According to Mbigi and Maree (1995), 'if Africans are going to undertake the challenge of development they need to discover their own collective self-identity. This has to be an inward journey, which should lead to a celebration of collective "personhood"' (p. 6). Mbigi and Maree consider respect, dignity, solidarity, compassion, and survival the five fingers of *ubuntu*. It is interesting that the two authors find a place for competitiveness in industrial relations when a spirit of *ubuntu* prevails. Could the same spirit of *ubuntuism* but touch the discipline of psychology!

Western concepts which provide the closest approximation to *ubuntu* are empathy, compassion, and unconditional positive regard (Holdstock, 1981b), as well as Buber's (1970) I–Thou relationship. Unfortunately, in psychology, empathy and positive regard have become more closely associated with effective professional therapeutic behaviour, where these attitudes are provided in exchange for financial reward, than with constituting the basic ingredients of everyday interpersonal relationships. In fact, the conditions, which Rogers (1951) described as necessary and sufficient for effective psychotherapy, are part and parcel of Africa's folk psychology. In contrast to the therapeutic approach, entering into an I–Thou relationship in Africa, is not done on the basis of any contractual exchange of money or services. Communication has no purpose other than to be enjoyed for its own sake. There is no ulterior motive for engaging the other. Westerners, who have had the opportunity to participate or observe African society, have often expressed surprise at the capacity Africans have for talking and being with each other, not with the aim of arriving at a particular conclusion but merely to enjoy being in each other's company.

Intimacy is not restricted to close friends only, but applies to a whole group of people who come together through work or residential requirement. Age and division of labour more or less naturally determine conversation groups. So, all boys whose job was to herd cattle would periodically gather at a popular spot to chat about their cattle, parents, heroes, and whatever was of importance to them. All commonly shared their secrets, joys, and woes; no one felt himself to be an intruder into someone else's business. On the contrary, manifest curiosity was welcomed and arose out of a desire to share. This pattern was common to all age groups. Among the elderly, visiting each other at home has always been a feature of their daily routine. No purpose, other than to be together, was needed for a visit. Organised encounter groups or other organised activities to allow people to be together, as is known in the West, have been unnecessary. This has been even truer of the San (Bushmen) who represent a community where encounter was part of the ongoing process of living.

Silberbauer (1965), who has lived with the San in the Kalahari Desert for almost 15 years, elaborated on their openness to interpersonal relationships. They resent someone who shies away from personal involvement and friendship and, within their kinship system, provide uninhibited feedback to each other. The daily battle against the environment is too serious to afford the disintegration of co-operative effort, which can result from unresolved conflicts. Friendship and good fellowship are essential for the unity of the band.

The approach of the people of Africa to interpersonal relationships contrasts vividly with the Western need for privacy and goal-oriented relationships. African consciousness tries to recapture some of the traditional sense of community where men and women are jointly involved in the quest for a composite answer to the varied problems of life. Living is about co-operation and not competition. While I run the risk of building a mystique round traditional African culture, as Mphahlele (1962) was afraid of doing, I do realise that tremendous changes have taken place in Africa and are still occurring. Yet, at some basic level, it is as if very little has changed. I am supported in my assumption by the countless instances of *ubuntu* and the many indications of Africa's holistic cosmology, which I have experienced and witnessed in a variety of urban and rural settings during the years of apartheid in South Africa. Black Consciousness leader, Steve Biko (1975; in Stubbs, 1979), also regarded the most important theme in African culture to be the importance attached to the other.

The other-centredness of African society finds expression in all aspects of the culture. Customary law accentuates the primacy of the community over the individual. Land was used and owned communally. Marriage is regarded as a union of two families and not just two people. While the majority of contemporary black South African art lacks the unitive consciousness with the spiritual dimension which is evident in the 'art' of West and Central Africa, its overriding theme is people. The inverted commas are used to convey that it is the view of the Western world, and not necessarily of West and Central Africa, that is reflected. Whereas the person has largely disappeared from the canvasses of Western artists, apart from the painting of portraits, people still represent the favourite subject of African artists in South Africa. People, in various forms of abstraction, are portrayed individually, in dyads, triads or larger groups – at work, making music, or at play. A well-known gallery owner in Brussels actually advised me to tell the African artists not to paint so many people!

It is also not surprising that African culture has been an oral one since the earliest of times. According to Senghor (in Reed and Wake, 1979), 'The permanency of the written word offers certain advantages, but advantages which are in some ways, dubious. Writing is synonymous with abstraction, and hence with impoverishment' (p. 50). Senghor attributed the oral nature of African culture to the spontaneity and responsiveness of Africans to the objects they were dealing with. Omotoso (1994) has, however, pointed out that the oral tradition is not without its shortcomings. According to him, African cultures need to strengthen the written aspect of their languages if they want to benefit from the advances in the international community. Mazrui (1990) is another who has pointed out the negative aspects of the oral culture. Besides keeping African societies relatively isolated, he writes that

> In the absence of the written word in most African cultures, many tentative innovations or experiments of a previous era were not transmitted to the next generation. The trouble with the oral tradition is that it transmits mainly what is accepted and respected . . . Oral tradition is a tradition of conformity, rather than heresy, a transmission of consensus rather than dissidence.
>
> (Mazrui, 1990, p. 140)

The importance of the community can also be traced to the mythology of creation amongst several African peoples. According to Setiloane (1989) there are two primary mythologies in Central and Southern Africa. The Nguni believe that the first people emerged from a bed of reeds, while the Sotho-Tswana believe the place to be a hole in the ground. In both instances, though, it is believed that our first parents emerged as a collective social unit, as a community – men with their wives and children and even their animals.

Perhaps the most dramatic example of Africa's relatedness is to be found in the reported instances of starving people in Sudan walking great distances in order to await death in the company of other starving people. Attributing such behaviour to the need for affiliation during times of stress fails to explain the essential nature of Africa's person-centredness. Africa's person-centredness is part of a philosophy, a way of life, a spiritual dimension which is, in all probability, as old as the continent itself. In fact, according to biblical mythology, Adam donated one of his ribs for the creation of Eve.

178

THE INTRAPERSONAL DIMENSION

Africa's other-centredness has important consequences for the way in which children are raised. It never ceased to amaze me, during weekends in Soweto or in some rural area, that crying or fighting occurred so infrequently among the large numbers of children who were invariably present. Despite the fact that children were allowed to participate in the social events, irrespective of the hour of the day or the night, they were seldom underfoot. While they went about their own business during the day, they gathered round the adults at night when stories were told and discussions held. In social gatherings, the smaller children were casually taken onto various laps, in the totally unselfconscious way of Africans where children are concerned.

Many is the occasion that I have witnessed a crying infant or small child being picked up and held by another child, not much older. Krige and Krige (1943) reported that Lovedu infants were never left to cry and were never left alone. Gelfand (1979) indicated that the same was true for Shona children, while Becker (1974) quotes a Xhosa informant as saying that 'an infant is part of a woman's own body' (p. 73). I can attest to babies sleeping peacefully on the mother's back during the most energetic of ceremonial dances or sitting on her lap as she beats the drums during some festival or ceremonial occasion.

Although bottle-feeding has made inroads into the African community, infants are usually breast-fed on demand. They sleep with their mothers immediately after birth and are carried on the backs of their mothers, other adults, brothers or sisters. This ensures close physical contact during the early years, in contrast to European babies who are placed in cots or transported in prams. Thus, the African baby experiences the environment as being supportive, without the need to manipulate it by crying to have its needs attended to. By being fed on demand, instead of at specified intervals, the foundation is laid for responding to an internal biological clock rather than to some external reference source. This experience extends into childhood. Even in the urban areas, African children are not made to keep to as structured a routine regarding play and going to bed as children in the Western world.

There is, undoubtedly, a great deal to be learned about the intimate bodily contact the infant has with the mother. We know that the brain can be entrained 'by repeated photic or auditory stimuli to produce peculiar subjective states' (e.g., Turner and Pöppel, 1988, p. 74). Other sensory modalities could, conceivably, exercise the same function. The fact that the transmission, via loudspeakers, of a 72 beats per minute heart rhythm has a greater calming influence on babies, than other rhythmic auditory stimuli, has been attributed to the possible conditioning to the auditory/tactile input of the mother's heartbeat during the last months of foetal life (Grüsser, Selke, and Zynda, 1988).

Grüsser and his co-workers also attach great importance to the fact that the mother–child holding pattern in different cultures, particularly during non-feeding interactions, exhibits a significant left-sided preference (also Saling,

179

Abrams, and Chester, 1983). This holding pattern serves to modify the functional left–right asymmetry of the brain even further. Since the baby's right side is in considerably closer contact with the mother than the left side, asymmetric acoustic and tactile stimulation of the infant's brain is the result. Interestingly, it is the right hemisphere that is credited with the ability to process spatially and holistically organised information. The left hemisphere excels primarily in linear functions (e.g., Joseph, 1988).

The asymmetric stimulation of the brain during the early years is, furthermore, likely to be influenced by the way babies are being carried on the backs of their mothers or caretakers. By being tightly wrapped against the mother's back, the exposure to her bodily rhythms is certainly intensified. Research into the baby's head position when strapped on the mother's back awaits exploration, though. Yet, the specificity of the way in which the baby is held, when being fed, suggests that the manner in which he or she is carried is likely to be equally or even more influential in the development of the infant's brain. Irrespective of possible lateralisation or bilateral hemispheric stimulation effects, the proximity of the infant with the mother's body will, most certainly, have a particularly affirmative effect on the development of trust in his or her organismic sensing.

Several brain researchers consider interhemispheric integration to be of central importance in aesthetic creativity (Grüsser et al., 1988; Levy, 1988; Regard and Landis, 1988). Levy states that the 'generation of the aesthetic experience or creation depends both on the cognitive and the affective processes of brains and a close intertwining between the two' (p. 220). 'According to scientific research, an optimally self-rewarding co-operation between right-hemispheric and left-hemispheric functions constitutes our experience of beauty' (Paul, 1988, p. 26). It is likely that the extended exposure to the bodily rhythms of the mother, while being carried on her back, facilitates hemispheric integration in a specific manner. It is likely that the infants will alternately rest both sides of their heads against the mother's back. Whatever the case may be, it is likely that the early childhood rearing patterns may very well be a factor responsible for the wealth of artistic talent evident in Africa.

The close and enduring physical contact between the African mother and her child, as well as the relatively freer way in which African children are allowed to structure their days, could, furthermore, lay the foundation, not only for artistic creativity, but also for the development of an implicit trust in the wisdom of the body. Carl Rogers called this bodily wisdom the 'ongoing psycho-physiological flow'. He considered it the primary referent to which the individual could refer when in doubt about the validity of his or her actions or experiences. During the height of the apartheid era I was constantly amazed at how centred the African people, with whom I had contact, remained throughout the degradation and the hardships they were submitted to under the political system. Contrary to popular belief, I seldom got the impression that the political system destroyed their sense of self. Undoubtedly, the early child-rearing patterns contributed to the establishment of a firm trust of the people in their own personhood. This trust of the individual African in him or herself has direct implications for mental health as well as for the ease in expressing oneself artistically. It is no small wonder that Miller (1976), in his research on African infants, ascribed their precocity to the child-rearing practices within which they were brought up. The relative lack of intervention in imaginary games which African children generally experience is another factor possibly contributing to the artistic proficiency on the continent. Undoubtedly, the child-rearing practices are also at the basis of the ease with which Africans reach out to others, and the greater kinship they feel with the animate and the inanimate universe.

The majority of Africans are still in relatively closer contact with nature than people living amidst the concrete of the industrialised parts of the world. According to Senghor (in Reed and Wake, 1979), the origin of the African psyche is to be found in the centuries of living close to the heat and the humidity of the tropics, the rhythms of the seasons, and the agricultural nature of African subsistence. It is, according to him, this physical closeness to nature that contributes so greatly to all aspects of life in Africa.

11

TOWARDS ROMANTICISM IN PSYCHOLOGY

AFRICA'S AESTHETIC DIMENSION

Although aesthetic preference and creativity constitute a complex aspect of cognition and conscious behaviour, it has not received much attention in psychology. According to Hillman (1996), this neglect can be attributed to the general lack of aesthetic sensitivity in psychology. 'Neither social psychology, experimental psychology, nor therapeutic psychology find a place for the aesthetic appreciation of a life story' (p. 35). Contemporary psychology 'tends to narrow understanding of complex phenomena to single-meaning definitions' (p. 10). The paradigms of the discipline simply do not account for the longing of the human heart for beauty, 'or engage with, and therefore ignore, the sense of calling, that essential mystery at the heart of human life' (p. 6).

Hillman (1996) pleads for a psychology that has 'its base in the imagination of people rather than in their statistics and their diagnostics' (p. 33). He wants the poetic and not the scientific mind applied to the study of case histories, so that they can be read for what they are, modern forms of fiction. Of all psychology's sins, Hillman regards the neglect of beauty to be the most mortal. 'A theory of life must have a base in beauty if it would explain the beauty that life seeks . . . Psychology must find its way back to beauty if only to keep itself alive' (p. 38), for 'Beauty is itself a cure for psychological malaise' (p. 38). Hillman attributes the 'exaggerated overreach toward cloudy glories' (p. 39) of the Romantics as their attempt 'to bring into this world forms of the invisible they knew were necessary for imagining what a life is' (p. 39). The splendour of the ceremonies and rituals accompanying various life events and with which mythologies are enacted in Africa can, apart from being an attempt to concretise the relationship with the mythological, be considered to belong to the same need to envisage the invisible essence of 'what a life is'.

Hillman's (1996) assertion that psychology needs to find its way back to beauty finds rather unexpected support from the work of neuroscientists in which they elucidate the survival and evolutionary importance of aesthetics (Eibl-Eibesfeldt, 1988; Epstein, 1988; Paul, 1988; Turner and Pöppel, 1988; Zollinger, 1988). In this regard, it is important that the traditional focus on the analysis of aesthetic objects and the ideas fixed in works of art be replaced by a more dynamic approach to art in which the focus is shifted towards the analysis of aesthetic behaviour (Siegfried, 1988). Although the study of aesthetic behaviour has been neglected in contemporary psychology, care has to be taken not to make the same mistake in the development of an Africentric psychology, especially since the aesthetic dimension constitutes such an important aspect of life in Africa.

Furthermore, as indicated in Chapter 2, glimmers of realisation of the importance of 'Romantic ways of knowing' are breaking through in mainstream psychology (Schneider, 1998). Schneider traces psychological romanticism to the eighteenth-century rebellion against seventeenth-century rationalism. He identifies two strains of psychological romanticism, the first of which derived from the literary and artistic legacy of eighteenth-century thinkers such as Lord Byron and Goethe. This strain stresses individual depth and experience. The second strain of romanticism emphasises collective depth and experience and 'focused on the "need for tradition and social order" in self-expression, over and above subjective individualism' (p. 280). Schneider discusses both the benefits of the romantic to psychology as well as the price of discarding the romantic. Africentric psychology, which can also be regarded as a revolt against the rationalism of the dominant branch of modern psychology, has a significant contribution to make in the revival of psychological romanticism. The purpose of this section is, therefore, to highlight some aspects of the psychological romanticism evident in an Africentric approach.

The views of Hillman (1996), with respect to beauty and the evolutionary importance of the aesthetic highlighted by the neurosciences, are captured by Senghor's description of art in Africa as 'an explanation and understanding of the world, *a sensitive participation in the reality which underlies the world*, that is, in a *surreality*, or rather, in the vital forces which animate the world' (Senghor, in Reed and Wake, 1979, p. 83). 'The realm of aesthetics is also the realm of values in which life and death, social issues, fertility, and wealth are all conjoined' (Strathern, 1988, p. 311). The meaning of the aesthetic element transcends the aesthetic itself. Art for art's sake, unrelated to social, cultural, and spiritual functions, is therefore, not common in Africa. The statement of Poincaré that 'the longing for the beautiful leads us to the same choice as the longing for the useful' (Levy, 1988, p. 238) expresses Africa's aesthetic pragmatism well.

During the past three decades art has also come to serve a decidedly more political purpose, at least in southern Africa. Due to the repressive socio-political climate of the time, African writers in South Africa have tried to liberate the spirit of the people. It has especially been the young writers who have become adamant about the need for art to deal with political realities (in Couzens and Patel, 1982). The turbulent 1970s in South Africa saw more poets being launched a year than most earlier decades (Gray, 1982). 'The battles of the day were being fought with the knives and lassos of words' (p. 18). Black playwrights in South Africa, who have 'tried humanism under the banner of multiracialism and found it wanting' (Sepamla, 1981, p. 15), came to realise that the whites 'wrote plays about us for us' (p. 15). The search for Africanness awakened the realisation that going back to one's roots meant more than just a digging into the past, that the past will be shaped for today by the demands of the future.

In Angola, aspects of culture have been playing a direct role in the civil war. In fact, the success of Savimba in his guerrilla warfare has been attributed to his respect for the beliefs and practices of traditional society. 'And so in the one-third or more of Angola controlled by Unita there is much dancing, singing and exchanging of stories and pleasantries with village elders' (Bridgland, 1984, p. 12). Spirit dancers, whose performances can be stunningly spectacular, perform with the villagers and the troops, and modern songs, in praise of Savimbi and the war effort, have been composed. The same has happened during the war of independence in Zimbabwe (Mbigi and Maree, 1995). The opposition guerrilla army of Mozambique, RENAMO, is also reported to have incorporated indigenous healers in regular army practices (in Sodi, 1998).

Art commits the person to the community. That is perhaps the reason why infants from the earliest age are exposed to the songs, the music, and the dances of the community (e.g., Burnett-van Tonder, 1987). Formal instruction in mastering any of these skills is seldom, if ever, given. 'The African mother sings to her child and introduces him to many aspects of his music right from the cradle. She trains the child to become aware of rhythm and movement by rocking him to music, by singing to him in nonsense syllables imitative of drum rhythms' (Nketia, 1974, p. 60). As mentioned earlier, mothers dance with babies on their backs and beat the drums with infants on their laps. Children acquire the artistic and dance skills in the same easy manner as they learn to walk and talk.

The necessity to shift the focus in aesthetics towards its dynamic aspect rather than the end product that has been pointed out by neuropsychologists is well demonstrated in Africa, for the key, the common denominator, to all artistic expression in Africa, is rhythm. 'We may postulate that there are basic rhythms, probably universal, which have a characteristic soothing or arousing influence on human behavior' (Eibl-Eibesfeldt, 1988, p. 55). 'There is a biological basis for pacing and tempo in the performance of music, which has psychological ramifications of the deepest sort' (Epstein, 1988, p. 93). Rhythm is how energy manifests itself in the body (Luce, 1973) and in the universe generally (Blair, 1976).

The importance of rhythm in the lives of the people of sub-Saharan Africa has been stated so often and by so many people that it has almost become a cliché. Rhythm is the architect of being, it is the purest expression of life force in Africa. Rhythm provides the internal dynamic, which structures African speech, music, dance, poetry, theatre, and athletic performance. Without rhythm, the African is said to be like a rudderless ship drifting on the sea of life. Rhythm brings purpose and meaning, enhances understanding and the sense of being. It unites the individual with the great cosmic force. It lifts the spirits and, in so doing, heals. It is at the basis of techniques used by indigenous healers to achieve altered states of consciousness, enabling them to divine and heal.

> When I am down in spirits
> Play for me those cowhide drums
> Beat them softly
> And produce African rhythms
> To soothe my dispirited soul
> And enliven my dull body
> With your beat
> Pump strength into my bleeding heart
> And let it carry me
> Above my sorrows
> (Tshume, 1980, p. 15)

The rhythm produced by the drum obviously symbolises a great deal more than can be expected from such an ordinary musical instrument. Apart from the recognition by neuropsychologists of the basic temporality inherent within our biological systems, recognition within the psychological community that rhythm provides the ground of being, is also becoming evident (e.g., Aldridge, 1989). In describing the importance of metered poetry, Turner and Pöppel (1988) stated:

> If we wish to develop the full powers of the minds of the young, early and continuous exposure to the best metered verse is essential, for the higher human values, the cognitive abilities of generalization and pattern recognition, the positive emotions, such as love and peacefulness and even a sophisticated sense of time and timing are all developed by poetry. Furthermore, our ethnocentric bias may be partly overcome by the study of poetry in other languages and the recognition of the underlying universal in poetic meter. (p. 87) . . . An education in verse will tend to produce citizens capable of using their full brain coherently – able to unite rational thought and calculation with values and commitment. (p. 90)

Obviously, the additional exposure to rhythm in various other modalities, as is the case on the African continent, can, therefore, be considered to be even more facilitative of the development of a fully holistic person. Being in touch with his or her 'ongoing psycho-physiological flow', in the broadest sense of the word, in all likelihood, shapes the African individual in ways yet to be explored by the psychological community.

Rhythm in poetry

The lateralisation model of brain functioning provides an interesting approach by means of which the nature of Africa's psychological dimension can be

185

understood. In contrast to the technologically oriented cultures favouring left hemisphere functioning, African cultures favour right hemisphere functioning. Admittedly, this is a broad and sweeping statement, that can, in the most general of terms, nevertheless, be of value in appreciating the nature of Africa's psychological dimension. The model provides a means of understanding what Schneider (1998) describes as the long, but relatively neglected, lineage of romanticism in psychology. In its revolt against the linear rationality, romanticism emphasised 'the interrelated wholeness of experience; access to such wholeness by means of tacit processes – affect, intuition, kinesthesia, and imagination; and qualitative or descriptive accounts of such processes' (p. 278).

The romantic ways of knowing have become associated with what we now know about right hemisphere functioning. The right hemisphere specialisation of romanticism parallels, as outlined earlier in the chapter, the type of knowing in which Africa excels. In this section attention will be devoted to its manifestation in the area of language, especially with respect to poetry. African languages are rich in images and symbolism. Words are distinguished according to tone and end on vowels or 'liquid' consonants, which are drawn out to lend a musical quality to the speech. Ideophones, that is gestures that must accompany a certain word, play a dominant role in most African languages. Much meaning is conveyed through sounds, not only the lowering of consonants or the use of softer consonants, nasals and sibilants, but grunts and similar utterances, have significance and elicit appropriate emotional responses.

> Zulu poetry being communal requires a special method of presentation. The poet does not just recite his poetry but acts it, uses variations of pitch, and aims at communicating his poem through the stimulation of all the senses. He produces at one level a symphonic chant, at another, a drama, and still another, a dance. The audience is thus held spellbound, not only by the meaning of words and their sounds but also by the performance. The audience demonstrates its approval or participation by either imitating the poet's movements or devising appropriate actions related to the meaning of the words.
>
> (Kunene, 1970, p. 12)

According to Senghor (in Reed and Wake, 1979), there is no fundamental difference between prose and poetry in African literature. For instance, in *Things Fall Apart*, Achebe (1988) captures the Ibo past not only through the use of Ibo proverbs and traditional folk stories, but also by recreating the speech patterns and the rhythms of Ibo metaphorical language. Prose is considered poetry with a less pronounced rhythm. For Senghor the poem is not complete unless it is sung or given a musical accompaniment. However, even without song, poetry is music. Senghor compares it to a jazz score and tells of the poets in his village who could not compose except when under the spell of the drums. He wrote, 'the power of the analogical image is only set free under the influence of rhythm. Only rhythm can set off the poetical short circuit and change copper into gold, words into the Word' (Reed and Wake, 1979, p. 93). Unless the image is rhythmical it is devoid of effect. The image is set free under the influence of rhythm. Senghor even speaks of the tyranny of rhythm. During the African night when the air throbbed with the invisible life and echoed with the pulsation of the drums, the poets lost themselves in the verbal dance, in the rhythm of the drum, and discovered their place in the cosmos. They allowed themselves to 'be carried away by the torrent a thousand feet under the earth' (p. 90).

Apart from its aesthetic function, poetry can also serve political purposes. Praise-poetry plays an important role in this respect and it is an art form of great importance, even in urbanised societies. Virtually anybody, in any number of contexts, can direct their poems at themselves and others, friends and enemies alike. They can praise objects and machines, domestic and wild animals. A father may praise one of his children, a wife a husband. A man can praise his beard, his phallus; he can praise his good suit, his liquor before swallowing it; cars, bicycles, and factory machinery. In the rural areas, herd boys praise their clay oxen, the live animals in their care, or their friends; a ploughman praises his lead ox and a hunter his dog. Even snakes can be objects of praise, while families and clans have sets of praises that can be used on ritual occasions to invoke the ancestors. Sports personalities also feature as favourite objects of praise.

Praise-poems serve as a valuable barometer for politicians and various other people in authority, for critical evaluation is allowed in praise-poetry. Thus, problems can be identified and dealt with before they become major issues. The praise-singer is able to concretise and verbalise public opinion. He is able to pull together in a phrase or two a variety of ill-defined emotions and sentiments felt by the public or the workers. The praise can be expressed verbally, in song, or in dance. A great array of poetic devices, including puns, metaphors, parallelism, various types of eulogies, linking, personification, and symbolism are utilised in order to enhance the effectiveness of the poem.

However, even when the praise-poet does criticise authority figures, the purpose is not to deride or depose that person, but to encourage more effective behaviour and to indicate socially acceptable ways in which it can be achieved. The function of the praise-poet is to mediate between the public and the authority figure, therefore, the criticism is often veiled in jocular talk or mimicry, thus making light of what is perhaps an important grievance, yet getting the message across. Considerable licence exists to use bawdy humour and obscene language, which is cause for much enjoyment by the audience, for entertainment is a decided function of praise-poetry. Mocking the ruler or the supervisor at work allows the people to vent their anger and grievances. In effect, the artistic event has therapeutic and political overtones; both aimed at maintaining social harmony (Mthethwa, 1988; Wainright, McAllister, and Wallace, 1978).

Rhythm in music

Common music concepts cut across all African peoples of the sub-Saharan regions. According to Nketia (1974) the musical cultures of African societies between the Islamic north and the European settled south, 'form a network of distinct yet related traditions which overlap in certain aspects of style, practice, or usage, and share common features of internal pattern, basic procedure, and contextual similarities. These related musical traditions constitute a family distinct from those of the West or the Orient' (p. 4). However, even in the south, the hostile attitude of the missionaries towards African music, especially towards drumming, which was associated with 'pagan' practices, and, later, the exclusion of traditional musicians and their music from educational institutions, unintentionally assured the continuity of traditional music in its unadulterated form (Nketia, 1974).

Just as in other forms of African art, music was originally not an end in itself. Music served as a means for people to be together, created a more meaningful sphere within which to work, and elevated ritual and ceremony to a spiritual plane. 'Nothing dramatises the eagerness of the African to communicate with each other more than their love for song and rhythm. Music in the African culture features in all emotional states' (Biko, in Stubbs, 1979, p. 42). Music does not only serve as a means of interpersonal communication, but also links the living with the ancestors and both with the deity. In African societies, music is the food of life in a literal sense (Mthethwa, 1988). It is generally understood as a human experience that incorporates poetry and dance. The three art forms belong to the same human experience. As was evident in the previous section, the purpose of music was less to please the ear than to reinforce speech and make it more effective. Poetry generates song, and song generates dance. It is generally believed that if a person can talk, he or she can sing, and if a person can walk, he or she can dance. African theatre without music and dance is, therefore, quite inconceivable.

Music co-ordinates the personal and social lives of Africans. Musical activities centre on leisure, recreation, the performance of ritual ceremonies connected to birth, initiation, puberty, marriage, death, and healing. In the urban areas children often provide the drumming in the afternoon and in the evening for the dancing which is such an important component of the training and the therapy of the aspirant healers. As a collective activity, music serves a multiple purpose. It binds the community, enabling the members to share in the expression of common aspirations, sentiments, beliefs, and values.

As is the case in poetry, rhythm is the dominant feature in African music. Rhythm is the signature to the purpose of the music. Rhythmic patterns distinguish secular from sacred music and one healing tradition from another. Rhythmic components are picked out of a melody and repeated over and over. Just as the cadence of words is aesthetically pleasing to the African ear, the rhythmic components of music are pleasing. According to Dargie (1988), the highly developed rhythms of Xhosa music make it very difficult to transcribe.

188

Almost every song, which he analysed, is built out of a combination of rhythms. It is this complexity of rhythms that cannot be readily expressed in conventional music notation. In the Xhosa songs, made popular by Miriam Makeba and Margaret Singana, the voice rhythm seems to be clear, but the body rhythms – dance, clapping and other body movements – seem to belong to another song.

Jones (1980) came to the same conclusion about the music of the Ewe people in Ghana. In some dances the movements of the dancers are so intimately linked with the drumming that it needs to be added on the score, but to include the choreography on the score is too complex. Since African drums do not give out a clearly defined note which the ear can easily recognise as being of definite pitch, the quality of the pitch varies. The score of African drumming should therefore, 'show not only the rhythm and the pitch of the notes but also *how* each note was made' (p. 11), which hand played it, what position on the drum-skin it was played, and whether or not the other hand was also employed simultaneously in producing the note. 'It is the combination or multiplication of rhythms, which brings the body to life in the song. The combination of different beat patterns triggers off the feelings of rapid pulse movement in the body – one rhythm moving in two's against another moving in three's tends to trigger off a pulse movement of $2 \times 3 = 6$' (Dargie, 1988, p. 8).

From a Western perspective, traditional African music is often perceived as monotonous and repetitive. As is the case with respect to the appreciation of the belief system of cultures other than one's own, Chernoff (1979) has pointed out, however, that musicians also have to let go of the categories and concepts they are accustomed to in order to achieve an understanding of musical perspectives they have not previously been familiar with. For instance, the concepts of up-beat and on-beat are of no great importance in African music, and a more appropriate description than repetitive would be that African music is cyclical, in contrast to Western music which is linear (Tracey, 1983). The cycle is a sequence of melodic/rhythmic ideas, which repeats itself continuously. 'Of the many cycle lengths used in Africa, 12 is the most frequent, followed by 16' (Tracey, 1983, p. 232).

Moreover, although African music may sound repetitive, it never returns to exactly the point of origin. The African ear has attained an infinitely subtle balance and approach to music, making every cycle, in fact, a spiral. It is a movement which most Western ears cannot hear. The African ear picks it up clearly. Clegg (1978) states that the cyclical or spiralling aspect of African music reflects the geographical aspects of the countryside and the routines of daily living. Every act, every journey has a beginning and an end, and contains, besides repetitiveness, which symbolises the infinite vastness of the landscape, also contrasting elements. The countryside is dotted with many hills and valleys, but every hill also differs from the other. These themes find expression in the music, mainly in the walking songs of the Zulu. As you walk through the countryside you come to terms, physically and spiritually, with the land you are walking in. There is a pace in the life of the flora and the fauna, as well as in the geological structures. You become the energy of the land, Clegg says.

According to Warren and Warren (1970), as well as Senghor (in Reed and Wake, 1979), repetition is the essence of African rhythm. Senghor maintains that repetition provides the necessary unifying force that permits the playing or hearing of complex polyrhythmic improvisations, without the basic form being disturbed. The Western ear is usually too unsophisticated to pick up the intricacies of the variations, due to dominance of the fundamental beat. Each of the variations has a unique value, which is guided by the basic rhythm to which it is subordinate. Together, the variations create a complexity of rhythms, though.

Tracey (1983), the director of the International Library of Music at Rhodes University, regards an additional function of the seemingly repetitive nature of African music to be the stating and restating of human and musical relationships. According to John Blacking (1976), the aim of the performance was concentrated on the process of making music rather than on producing a finished product. Making music provides people with a common purpose and provides them with the opportunity of being together. Thus, it not only establishes harmony in interpersonal relationships, but the beat of the music also entrains the biological rhythms. This entrainment could be responsible for the endurance displayed by indigenous healers in their marathon dance sessions and for the fact that I would be totally refreshed following a night listening to the sound of the drums.

In attempting to clarify the organising principles of African music, musicologists have come up with some intriguing notions, which relate to the unitive consciousness operative in Africa. According to these arguments, the musicians are so in touch with the playing of their instruments that an internal rhythm, complementing that which is being played on their instruments, is created within them. Because of their amazing musical sense, which is either innate or acquired, most likely both, African people are aware of certain beats that are not sounded, but which, nevertheless, are part of the rhythmic pattern. I guess what is intended here is something akin to the principle of the 'missing fundamental'. Complex tones consist of a low fundamental frequency and a series of higher frequencies called harmonics. If the human ear hears harmonics without their corresponding fundamental, the brain supplies the missing tone by itself.

According to Tracey (1983), the hidden beat can be explained by the notion of the pulse. The pulse is the smallest unit of time used in any particular piece of music. A stream of pulses is metronomically regular. Tracy describes it as the common rhythmic language of all the parts of a musical piece. When combined into beats, pulses provide the building blocks for the rhythm. Even when beats are omitted, the feeling of the pulse continues right through the musical piece. Western people, generally, do not have the same refined sense of pulse as Africans. Once one has witnessed the extent to which African people have been exposed to the kinaesthetic, auditory, and visual aspects of rhythm since early childhood, as described earlier, it becomes clear that their ability to experience music organismically, develops very differently from that of people who do not have the same background.

Related to the theme of unitive consciousness is the philosophy that conceives of primordial cosmic forces as binary. Internal rhythms resonate with external ones. Conceivably, this resonating capacity is more or less well developed in each of us. In Africa it is, in all likelihood, generally well developed. The dynamism engendered by each binary unit creates a tension that is felt as a third reality. This new reality in turn functions as a beat, leading to yet other binary units. One way of making this idea concrete is to think of the physical act of drumming to be as important as the sound that is produced. Though only one beat is heard, there are in reality two beats that create a third response, which is a gestalt of the original two. One can translate these in scientific terms by stating that the interaction between the physical, physiological, and psychological aspects of music needs much closer attention than it has received thus far (see Aldridge, 1989).

In the same way that a musician can be conceptualised as forming a binary unit with his or her instrument, creating a third reality, people generally can be conceived to be playing on the instrument of life, or vice-versa, and in the resonance a third reality is created and experienced. Just as some people have difficulty in producing an offbeat in music, or hearing a missing fundamental, there conceivably are those who experience difficulty in producing or hearing it in everyday life. Aldridge (1989), in fact, suggests that the identity of a person can be regarded 'as a musical form that is continually being composed in the world' (p. 91). He proposes a 'symphonic' rather than a 'mechanic' approach to the way we view people, based on the assumption that in every interaction the communication is based on the matching of the rhythms of the participants. This idea is not as far-fetched as it may seem. We know that the circadian entrainment of biological functions can occur between people (e.g., Luce, 1973). For instance, the menstrual cycles of women living together become synchronised (Stern and McClintock, 1998), and men appear to have a temperature cycle that is synchronous with the menstrual cycle of their cohabiting partner (Henderson, 1976).

Besides rhythm, harmony takes precedence over melody in African music (Mthethwa, 1986, 1988). In some African music, especially music with emotional overtones, harmony may override rhythm, so that it becomes the fundamental of the music. According to Mthethwa, harmony is generally regarded as an introspective element that tends to probe the inner feelings. Music with very intense harmonies is referred to as painful because of its ability to evoke such strong emotions. Africans generally, therefore, appreciate Western music of the baroque, classical, and romantic eras as music of the heart. In Zulu, harmony is metaphorically described by a word that depicts the horns of a beast, which converge to touch the skin of the animal. It conveys that this musical element emanates from the music makers but can, in turn, 'hit back', as it were, at both the performers and the listeners, thus provoking or 'stabbing' the inner feelings. Joy and sadness may also be vested in the rhythm of African music. The same conflict of joy and sadness, in Western music of more recent origin, may be conveyed by major and minor tonalities (Mthethwa, 1988).

Melody in Western music is understood as a pre-composed tune that must always be reproduced in its exact original notes in absolute or relative pitch. African melodic concepts define the tune as the 'path' for song, where song is the word, and the 'path' is subject to alteration. In other words, the notes of a tune may be altered in order to honour the rhythm or the tonal inflexions of some words. It is generally understood that melodies consist of diverse types conveying different moods. To be able to match the mood of a pre-existent tune with newly created words is considered to be a great musical challenge. Considering the contextual nature of African music, where people, like the praise singers, have to extemporise on the spur of the moment, it makes sense to memorise a substantial number of melodies that can be utilised to fit the occasion. Mthetwa (1988) describes the concept of melody in African music by means of the analogy of the different footprints being made by people walking the same path.

Classical music in the West has tended to accentuate the distinction in tone characteristics, to stress the separateness of instruments and the specialisation of their use. We thus have the notion of the virtuoso. African music, in contrast, does not attempt to specialise to the same extent. Rather, the qualities of different instruments and different rhythms fuse at metered intervals to create a different form of music, detached from the tone or qualities of the individual instrument. The music can, thus, be seen in terms of the notion of Gestalt psychology, where the whole is different from and vastly more than the sum of the parts.

An additional aspect of the uniquely interactive nature of African music pertains to the active participation of the audience. Finding and moving to beats and patterns that nobody may actually be playing, as such, is one of the techniques of African music that challenges and draws the listener into participating.

In answer to the question why there were no well-known African philo- sophers, posed during a conference on African culture and the business world in 1988, the speaker replied that African philosophy was to be found in the music of the continent. And indeed, as ought to be obvious from the preceding discussion, African music uses structures that express fundamental ideas about life. 'It puts people in harmony with each other, and emphasises the African belief that the most important thing is the *human being* – the importance of *people* and one's relationships with them. Life without other people is inconceivable' (Tracey, 1983, p. 227). 'The most fundamental aesthetic principle in Africa concerning music or anything else is that without participation there is no meaning. You can go so far as to consider African music as being a form of co-operation which happens also to produce sound. So *co-operation* is one of the first key words. Everything starts from the feeling of co-operation; the musical sounds come later' (Tracey, 1983, p. 227). About his experiences learning drumming in Ghana, Chernoff (1979) wrote that from the moment you begin to play, you have to relate to what others are doing. Co-operation comes first. In the Western approach, each musician in an orchestra masters his or her part before they begin to play their various parts in time with each other under the direction of the conductor. Once they have mastered their individual pieces, it is not unusual for the members of a section of the orchestra to practise together before the full orchestra begins to play together.

Some of the things Chernoff (1979) was taught related to the exact entry point in relation to the other drummers, and how his part co-ordinated with theirs. He had to learn to fill the gaps in the other rhythms, and similarly create a space in his own part to be filled by them. Thus, one can think of one rhythm defining another. Once he has become so totally at ease with his contribution to the musical piece that he could freely listen and respond to the other parts being played, the next phase was initiated. Now he was taught, usually by example, to express himself more forcefully. In so doing, he could give back some of the vitality which he had received from the others and, thus, enhance the overall quality of the musical performance.

Tracey (1983) points out that the inherent duality of co-operation/conflict, or interdependence/independence, is at the root of all African music. This encompassing of dualities puts a lie to the notion that the interdependence evident in Africa stifles creativity and breeds conformity. Using the *chimveka* dance of boys in Mozambique as an example, Tracey states that the various parts must be as different from each other as possible so that they can 'fight satisfactorily'. Tracey, whose father assembled the greatest collection of African music and musical instruments in the world, points out that each instrument is even designed to sound different enough so that it can be clearly heard against the others.

> There is more importance attached to difference than to blend, quite the opposite of the Western orchestra or choir . . . One part gains meaning in terms of the others; in fact one can say that a part only realises its full potential meaning *in relation to something else*. It can ruin some kinds of music if you join in by doubling what another part is playing . . . Two parts playing the same tune together is not music: there is nothing to refer to, no duality, no conflict.
>
> (Tracey, 1983, p. 230)

The spirit of independence within a larger sense of interdependence, of simultaneously performing individually and co-operatively, provides a figure-ground relationship, so well known in perception, that it is necessary to enhance the distinctiveness of the musical performance in order for our senses to achieve maximum acuity. It is no small wonder that Tracey (1983) wrote that the 'forms or structures of African music demand relationships that are a microcosm of national life, individual freedom and difference, joined together for the common good, basically democratic and socialist' (p. 230).

In the growing urbanisation of Africa, many of the young people come into increasing contact with a wide variety of musical expressions, which will undoubtedly lead to exciting new developments. In fact, it has already occurred. Fresh initiatives, drawing from the musical acumen of Africa as well as the West, have emerged. In Ghana, the Pan African orchestra has been founded; integrating African instruments not customarily played together, as well as African and Western elements of music. Paul Simon, likewise, has opened the eyes of the Western world about the possibilities of integrating the musical traditions of the two cultural orientations with his *Graceland* album.

On the basis of its sound philosophical and unique musical principles, traditional African music is bound not only to survive and grow, but also to provide the foundation upon which the new developments can find expression. Besides, the search for African identity in the politically independent continent has also awakened an awareness of the musical achievements of the past. The 'factors that shape and maintain musical practice in Africa operate in the direction of both change and continuity' (Nketia, 1974, p. 19). Selaelo Selota, who teaches guitar at the Faculty of Music at the University of Cape Town, strives to establish a uniquely new South African musical tradition by way of returning to his ancestral roots, for it is then when he feels most in balance. He has named his band *Taola*, in honour of the *diTaola*, the divination bones ('diTaola', 1998). In the words of Dizu Plaatjies, the leader of AmamPondo, 'We must never stop playing the music of our ancestors. We must carry on the culture and the tradition.' The emergence and popularity of bands like AmamPondo, verify the truth of the statement by Johnson and Magubane (1979) that urbanised Africans will never really completely lose their roots. 'Today's music in Soweto is more sophisticated, like everything else in Soweto. Today's musicians play with the same instruments used elsewhere, but the sound is pure Soweto. Soweto means Africa' (p. 164).

Rhythm in movement

Being wedded as Africa is to rhythm, it is no small wonder that movement provides an ideal means through which it can find expression. Like the South Americans, Africans are reputed to play soccer with a spontaneous joyfulness that contrasts starkly with the organised skill of European teams. 'In Africa you dance because you feel and you always dance someone or something. Dancing is discovery and *re-creating*. It is strengthening oneself with a life-force, living with a fuller life. It is being. It is the best mode of knowledge' (Senghor, in Reed and Wake, 1979, p. 32).

Dancing places the person in the centre of his or her world. It enables the individual to join forces with the energy of the rhythms in the immediate environment, it allows for the testing of the dancer's place in the world. It is saying yes to life in a dynamic way. The dancer goes out to meet life, to challenge life. To have felt and danced to the universal beat that thuds through African life is an experience that provides inner strength that can only be dimmed by time.

194

Muchato muchato muchato
my legs and feet
sunk in gumboots
ring of rattles
crackling in my ankles
I have outdanced men
of great magic

When I raised my foot
aloft and bombed
the hard rocky earth
men and women
beheld a spring
of sparkling water
Gone ancestors!
with merry frogs in it
while sexy ululations were tickling me

Muchato muchato muchato
women offered me
their pumpkin breasts
and promised their hips
for all my dance!
yet old and rigid
have grown those jests
knees are heavy
brittle as egg-shell
False lips! you all sneer
but that which grows
into the sky –
once shaken with
the elephant strength of time
bows down from high
like the old iron-wood tree
                    (Zimunya, 1981, p. 12)

In traditional African culture dance serves a multiplicity of functions. Clegg (1977) describes it as a lubricant, 'moving meanings quickly and subtly without confusing and distorting the overall ritual or field of communication' (p. 82). Dance is undeniably holistic. On the one hand, it unites all aspects of the individual: body, emotion, spirit, and reason into one transcendent whole, and on the other, it unites the dancer to both the world of the living and the deceased. Dancing serves an important function in socialising boys and girls in terms of the values of the group to which they belong and of maintaining those values among adults. It forms an integral part of the various initiation rituals of boys and girls and of providing them with the opportunity to get to know and express their preferences for each other during dances specifically designed for that purpose (Burnett-van Tonder, 1987).

In warrior dances there is a strong spiritual relationship between life and death. According to Zulu custom, the highest offer to *Umvelingqangi* is a ritual dance, and the end of the sacred dance is the end of a prayer that could have lasted a full day. The unitive function of dance is also evident in the fact that no diviner, chief, or priest can solemnise a Zulu wedding. It is only the dance that sacrilises the marriage (Mthethwa, 1986). Since the Bible also advocates worship with song and dance, the African Independent churches, which have integrated African and Western concepts and forms of religion, regard 'drumming' the earth with the feet as an integral part of religious practice.

Dance in Africa incorporates diffuse areas of social experience. It is intricately tied up with social conditions and generates meaning through action when other avenues, such as the political and trade unionism, have been blocked. Whereas Western society has divorced the dancer, the dance, and the community from each other, Africa considers them all one. Perhaps the clearest expression of this unity is in warrior dances in which the dancer explores his place within a wider social context. While the dancer explores himself in relation to others, his internal being manifests itself. Through words, body movements, and gestures the personal values and feelings of the dancer are explored and expressed. The physical body mirrors, and at the same time is constrained by, the social body (Clegg, 1977).

The holistic aspect of dance in Africa is further illustrated by the animal metaphors with which the dancers express important aspects of their culture. Zulu men associate themselves primarily with a bull, while San medicine men become the eland in their dance. Reminiscent of the kingbird of e.e. cummings, the male Zulu dancer, vested with the bull's characteristics, is brave, honest, and stands alone as an individual, yet recognises his duty to, and interrelatedness with, others and society. He knows his own potential and demands respect for it. The bull also embodies virility, which suggests natural productivity and growth, and at the same time is considered to be infinite, revealing the unity between the physical and the spiritual realms (Clegg, 1977, 1978).

The Zulu dancer becomes the bull. If your bull fights against another and wins, your spirit is stronger than that of the other person. You and the bull are one; therefore the bull's triumph is transferred to you in this metaphorical relationship. The Zulu dancer uses gestures and movements which represent the bull in order to explore his relationship to the bull. In this way he attains a conception of manhood. In addition, he is exploring society's perception of his role. A man who has not yet realised his full potential cannot be a bull, but only an ox. In Zulu culture a man strives to be a bull. If a man is a bull, he dances solo, yet he is still part of the dance team (Clegg, 1977, 1978).

Being human can be understood and interpreted best by living out the image of the bull. The use of metaphor in dance enables people to overcome their alienation from nature and other persons. The acting out of animals, for example, is a way of securing one's own subjectivity. As can be expected on the basis of their oneness with the desert region in which they live, the San are masters of portraying the ritual and characteristics attributed in their mythology to various animals. One of the most important and most frequently depicted animals is the eland. The eland is believed to possess a great deal of supernatural potency, and therefore features greatly in healing dances of medicine men. As the San medicine man approaches the threshold of his trance, the stages he experiences are very similar to the stages of death an eland goes through when it dies. In becoming the dying eland, the medicine man 'dies' and in 'dying' takes on the eland's supernatural potency. In this ambivalent state where the soul has left the body and the medicine man is in trance, he is in a position to protect the members of the band from whatever evil may be threatening them. The metaphorical relationship with the eland and the trance dances has also been featured extensively in rock paintings where the medicine men are depicted with antelope features. These therianthropes (figures combining animal and human features) represent the imaginative fusion 'of man and antelope to imply the exploitation of eland-power by trancing medicine men' (Lewis-Williams, 1983, p. 57).

A very distinctive characteristic of African dance is its relatedness to the soil. In Western dance forms the movements are light and fleeting. The dancers strive to float as lightly across the floor as possible. Only the forces of gravity prevent the release from the physical restraint that the dance aspires towards. Ballet provides perhaps the best example of the need in Western dance forms to break free of gravity. Even when still in touch with the ground, the ideal is to be 'sur-les-pointes'. African dance, on the contrary, stays low and close to the ground. If jumps are executed the purpose is always to return to and not to break contact with mother earth. Indigenous healers dance barefoot. To dance with shoes on is a sure sign that the healer has lost touch with the ancestors. In the words of the great English poet, Gerard Manley Hopkins, 'the soil/ Is bare now, nor can foot feel, being shod'. Though break dancing came into its own in the United States, its West African origins are considered to be responsible for the driving of the shoulders into the ground.

Rhythm in art and theatre

Rhythm is as much part of African theatre and art as it is of music, dance, and poetry. Just as most African musicians are self-trained, most artists and actors are self-trained as well. However, all these artists have in common that they follow Henry Thoreau's directive of stepping to the music which they hear, with the difference that the internal drummer is also tuned to the beat of the societal and cultural context. African theatre pulses with the rhythm of words, music, dance, and movement. Its vibrancy has spoiled me for the productions on the stages of the West End and of Broadway. African theatre answers the prediction of Kandinsky (1914/1977) made almost a century ago, that 'The composition for the new theatre will consist of these three elements: (1) Musical movement, (2) Pictorial movement, (3) Physical movement, and these three, properly combined, make up the spiritual' (p. 51).

Whereas the Western world is beginning to appreciate aspects of African music and theatre, it still does not afford African art the respect that it deserves – as has been indicated in Chapter 2. Yet, it is accepted that the greatest artists in the West, Picasso, Klee, Matisse, Brancusi, Ernst, Lipchitz, Modigliani, Léger, Dubuffet, Giacometti, and numerous others, drew major inspiration from African art. Even the Cubists, in their collecting, showed a marked preference for African art (see Rubin, 1984b). At times the art of the European masters approaches the African original so closely that one wonders about the thin dividing line between inspiration and plagiarism. Referring to the notion of an advanced consciousness in the West, Rubin states that 'insofar as art is a concrete index to the spiritual accomplishments of civilizations, the affinity of the tribal and the modern should give us pause' (p.73). There is even more reason for pause since the affinity, in so many instances, appears to be more than that.

While the aesthetic quality and religious significance of the sculptures of Central and West Africa have been recognised internationally, appreciation of the importance of prehistoric rock art, in the enactment of an extended network of ritual acts and beliefs, is of relatively recent origin (de Maret, 1994). It is especially in the rock art of southern Africa that the connection is most clearly documented (de Maret, 1994; Lewis-Williams, 1983). On the basis of existing ethnographic accounts of the metaphors and symbols of trance experiences, Lewis-Williams has elucidated the essentially shamanistic nature of San rock paintings. An interesting feature of his analysis relates to the supposition of universal features of trance, consisting of specific geometric forms. 'Because the nervous system is common to all people, certain hallucinations – neurological rather than cultural in form – are the same for all people' (de Maret, 1994, p. 187). The empirical foundation for the supposition of neurologically produced geometric forms in trance awaits exploration, however.

Mostly overlooked in the rock art of southern Africa are the rock engravings along the drier western parts of the subcontinent. From what I have seen of the paintings in the mountainous areas of South Africa and of the engravings on the rocks in the veld in the western regions, the nature of the rock engravings is distinctly different from that of the rock paintings. Like the overlooked rock art of Central Africa (de Maret, 1994), the engravings contain a high percentage of abstract geometric patterns: circles, circles within circles, lines, dots, and shapes of every conceivable form. This is not the case with the rock paintings. Animal engravings abound but are decidedly less shamanistic than those depicted in the paintings.

While this chapter has highlighted the holistic dimensions of the Africa belief system and way of life, the continent also has a responsibility towards developing those abilities that are traditionally associated with the left hemisphere.

Africa as a whole borrowed the wrong things from the West – even the wrong components of capitalism. We borrowed the profit motive but not the entrepreneurial spirit. We borrowed the acquisitive appetites of capitalism but not the creative risk-taking. We are at home with Western gadgets but are bewildered by Western workshops. We wear the wristwatch but refuse to watch it for the culture of punctuality. We have learnt to parade in display, but not to drill in discipline. The West's consumption patterns have arrived, but not necessarily the West's technique of production.

(Mazrui, 1990, p. 5)

12

CONCLUSION

The holistic dimension of the way of being in sub-Saharan Africa undoubtedly has a great deal to contribute to the manner in which we approach and conduct psychology generally and on the African continent specifically. It emphasises that the human being needs to be considered as a totality, with proper attention to the parts making up the whole. In African terms we are not just rational, but also affectively and somatically experiencing beings, existing fully in time and in contact with our bodies. As in Gestalt psychotherapy, a fluid alternation of attention is needed between the various components comprising each of us. We think, we feel, we move, we jump with joy. We need to work. We also need to imbue life with additional meaning. In addition, we are the other. Each one of us is embedded in an environment comprising, not only other people, but also the deceased and nature, as well as the larger societal, physical, and geographical structures. In its contextual embeddedness, the African approach shows great affinity with the thrust among some contemporary psychologists to approach the discipline from a humanistic, transpersonal and human contextual, dialogical, rather than a natural science perspective.

African psychology values the spiritual dimension as well as the mundane concerns of everyday living. In fact, the spiritual (the values transcending physical existence) comes to expression as much in the enactment of ritual as it does in the carrying out of daily chores. The extended interrelatedness, which is true of people everywhere, even though it is not often realised, is particularly evident in sub-Saharan Africa. In the West, the relationship with nature is the concern and the responsibility of the ecologists and the greens, societal issues the domain of sociology. The impact of physical structures on the human condition is the responsibility of architecture, town planners and others. Mental health, especially that of whites, is the province of psychology. African culture has been appropriated by anthropology, so has their mental health. Spiritual needs have become the property of religion; aesthetic needs the canvas of the artists, as if the human organism functions according to different principles for each discipline. We are connected with everywhere, yet our existence is increasingly fragmented. With all the diffusion of information, true knowledge remains rare and precious. Perhaps that is one reason for turning to the cradle of humankind.

In keeping with the worldview of the continent, development of an African psychology needs, therefore, to consider a more inclusive developmental framework. Various suggestions have already been made. Among these is the call for a closer integration of psychology with other disciplines. The Turkish psychologist, Kagitçibasi (1995) raises the prospect of thinking about human development in the way that the United Nations does. Nsamenang (1992) and other psychologists of the majority world, call for integrative approaches involving endogenous psychological knowledge and culture-sensitive theory development. While we are supposedly heralding a cognitive revolution in psychology, insufficient attention is paid to the belief systems of individuals and of larger collective entities. The unawareness in psychology of the belief system underlying its own approach is remarkable in a discipline credited with an introspective past. The emphasis in this text is on the here and the now. It is primarily a call for taking stock of the pros and the cons of the folk psychologies of the West and of Africa. The fact that the pros of African and the cons of Western indigenous perspectives are highlighted must be seen as an attempt to rectify existing imbalances.

Some aspects of Africa's interrelatedness, such as that of time and space (see Tiemersma and Oosterling, 1996), have not even been touched on in the text, yet deserve to be mentioned, if only in passing, for it resonates closely with the breakdown of the boundaries of time and space in the new information age (Ignatius, 1999). The challenge posed by a holistic approach for a discipline like psychology that has built its reputation on isolating and concentrating on a few variables at a time, and then, only on those that can be operationalised, is not to be underestimated, though. Little, if any cognisance is taken of the fact that humans are, in terms of chaos theory, open systems. The reason why psychology has not taken off on the African continent possibly relates to the fact that the ideologies and the methodologies of contemporary psychology do not fit into the inclusive value system of the African people.

Psychology, unfortunately, reflects our inability to appreciate and comprehend the inordinate complexity and interrelatedness of human existence. In the need to exercise control and operationalise that which is tangible and concrete, psychology fragments human existence to an extraordinary degree. In this process, the discipline has come to contribute to the estrangement from ourselves, from our emotions, from the physical-activity dimension as well as the spiritual nature of our being. It has also contributed to isolating us from each other and from nature. The focus on tangible bits of our material existence and on the rational order of things has erased the potential for wonder, and without that ability psychology has lost its potency to speak in a singularly unique way about and to the human condition. With its emphasis on daylight consciousness, the discipline not only neglects an important aspect of being, but also ignores the Romantic heritage of Western civilisation and bypasses the African continent.

In keeping with the prominence of the aesthetic dimension so evident in Africa, and with the Romantic tradition within Western civilisation, psychology needs to reclaim that aspect of humankind that is expressed in the yearning for beauty and wonder. In the language of archetypal psychology this component of being can be described as soul, in contrast to spirit that is rather cold, austere, and humourless, lacking the affective connotations of soul. However, the concepts of spirit and soul are interrelated. Attaining the lofty heights of spirit cannot be accomplished without first being grounded in soul. Soul, the poets contend, is the state of being that can be achieved through enhanced sensory awareness, something artists are particularly skilled at. Apart from enabling psychology to move away from its focus on debilitation, reclaiming the importance of the aesthetic can, conceivably, bring about a more meaningful role for psychology in sub-Saharan Africa than has hitherto been the case.

The greatest difficulty in reorienting our priorities undoubtedly lies in breaking away from the stereotyped and institutionalised way in which we have conducted ourselves thus far. Apart from a more integrated approach between the sub-disciplines of psychology, a holistic orientation will require the integration of various disciplines that have, traditionally, not been associated with one another. Edward O. Wilson, Harvard biologist and Pulitzer Prize winner, argues that most of the issues that vex humanity cannot be solved without integrating knowledge from the natural sciences with that of the social sciences and humanities (Azar, 1999). A major problem will be to overcome the power struggles that exist between disciplines and between the subdisciplines within psychology. In this respect we certainly mirror the global conflicts rampant throughout the world. In the final analysis, it is the very nature of our relationship and interaction with each other that has to be redefined.

With respect to the way we relate to each other in our daily activities, the concept of *ubuntu*, which runs like a continuous thread through sub-Saharan Africa's belief system and way of being, deserves special attention. In his Person-Centred approach, Carl Rogers endeavoured to propagate empathy, positive regard, and congruence as constituting the proper base for human relationships. An even more inclusive foundation can be laid on the basis of *ubuntu*. In my understanding and encounter of the way the concept of *ubuntu* comes to life in Africa, it incorporates the three conditions that Rogers considered to be necessary and sufficient for psychotherapy. In addition, *ubuntu* implies the active implementation of these considerations in one's everyday behaviour. *Ubuntu* is a function of being. Admittedly, the eventual goal of Rogers was similar, but the implementation became basically associated with and remained largely restricted to the professional sphere. The expression of *ubuntu* in daily behaviour is also apparent in a wider range of behaviour and attitudes than originally intended by Rogers. For instance, the San of the Kalahari Desert mistrust lack of intimacy and spontaneity in others and Africans visiting Europe generally express surprise at the apparent absence of these qualities among Europeans.

Steering psychology on a more holistic course will most certainly complicate the practice of the discipline even more than it already is. In the nomothetic search for universal lawfulness, many more variables will have to be considered in any one experimental design than has hitherto been the case. Whether such extensive control will actually be possible, considering the practical difficulties involved and our intellectual limitations in entertaining and controlling multiple variables, is an open question. Considering subjective elements compounds the problem even more. Similarly, in the ideographic approach, the complexity of, and the fluctuation in, the factors of significance in the life of the individual under consideration, need careful assessment.

Perhaps an integration of Africa's oral tradition with recent developments in contemporary psychology, based on a narrative approach, can indicate a meaningful way forward in psychological research. Stipulating a course of action for psychology in Africa in line with the natural science orientation to the discipline is difficult, and perhaps not the desired way to proceed. Senghor's statement that the West has given the world a civilisation of discursive reasoning, and that Africa contributed one of intuitive reasoning, springs to mind. In neuropsychological terms, Senghor's dictum can be rephrased in terms of the lateralisation of brain functioning. We know that the left and the right hemispheres are differentially specialised in their functions. To think of Africa as right hemisphere and the West as left hemisphere dominant offers an interesting model by means of which the psychological potential of the two parts of the world can be investigated. Additionally, in venturing forth it may be advisable to focus less on the behaviour of others, participants, clients, patients, and political victims, and concentrate more on who we are and what we do as psychologists. In becoming more introspective, our awareness of the manner in which we approach psychology will undoubtedly give rise to the emergence of alternative perspectives.

Not only does Africa's holism have far-reaching implications for psychology as a scientific discipline, but also as an applied profession. The movement towards an eclectic approach in psychotherapy can be broadened even more to provide room for the non-verbal dimensions of being. Even in its eclecticism Western psychotherapy concentrates primarily on the verbal, the behavioural, and the cognitive dimensions. Indigenous healing practices offer a great many perspectives from which psychotherapy can benefit. Apart from the integrated nature of indigenous healing, and besides its extensive involvement of movement (dance), music, and dreams in the healing process, it is centred in the community and taps into the archetypal. In addition, psychotherapy can learn about the importance of respecting the strangeness within ourselves, the relevance of the personal and the collective past, as well as the value of such mundane activities as the carrying out of daily chores. Even in its interpersonal orientation psychotherapy can benefit from the expanded humanness embodied in *ubuntu*.

The focus needs to shift more towards the actualisation of the potential of human beings and towards the prevention of mental illness. Ultimately, the societal structures responsible for causing problems in living need to be addressed. In this lies the greatest challenge for psychology. We certainly do not want to remain a purely reactive discipline, primarily skilled in the application of band-aids. Necessary as such applications are, they are not sufficient to alleviate the mental health crisis. On the contrary, they may, iatrogenically, actually be responsible for its escalation. The resources of the community in the prevention and the treatment of mental health problems need to be utilised more efficiently than has been done thus far.

An African worldview reinforces the notion expressed in cultural psychology that the individual cannot be studied in isolation from the context – historical, social, and geographical – in which the person lives. The implications of this seemingly self-evident fact for the discipline and the profession are vast. Undoubtedly, the challenge for psychology is not just to help individuals cope with the difficulties in living, but to revision the structure and the nature of the society within which we live so that it can be less harmful and more facilitative of the lives of its members. Belief systems play an important role in this regard. Just think of how attitudes towards sex prevent the fight against Aids in Africa and of the absolute misery that the belief in power has created in the world. For too long in our enlightened age have problems been solved by means of force rather than by consultation and mutual respect for each other.

At present one of the most daunting challenges facing humankind is how to allow maximum autonomy for various ethnic groups without infringing on the rights of other ethnic groups. We are facing a curious dilemma of homogenisation on the one hand and of cultural and ethnic diversification, on the other. While homogenisation is clearly the effect of globalisation, the enhanced juxtaposi-tioning of ethnicities and cultures probably also serve to sharpen awareness of and the need to preserve existing differences. In Africa, as elsewhere in the world, ethnic violence continues unabated at the cost of millions of lives. Psychology has only recently woken up to its responsibility in this regard. Since we are not educated to think in terms of molar issues, we really have to reinvent ourselves in order to come up with strategies to model and to alter the present competitive and combative approach to human relationships.

An aspect in the revisioning of ourselves will have to be consideration of the competitive individualism that has thus far been the hallmark of contemporary psychology. We cannot expect a new world order to come about if we continue to endorse a concept of the self as a closed and self-sufficient unit of the social system. If we, as a select group of professionals who specialise in human behaviour, mental health, and the actualisation of the potential of individuals, fail to endorse an alternative, interdependent concept of the self that is more facilitative of achieving the ideals we aspire towards, then we have little hope of bringing about any change in society. As it is, the chances are slim enough anyway.

With the exception of a few individuals, the challenge of redefining psychology in African terms has not yet been taken up by professionals on the continent and elsewhere. Endarkening psychology with the ancient psychological know-how existing in Africa can introduce an exciting new era in the discipline. In order to achieve this goal, the professional psychologists on the continent need to avoid making the mistakes of mainstream psychology that have been elaborated in

Part I. Apart from the sins of commission, the sins of omission need to be guarded against as well. Neglect or rejection of the Romanticism of the culture, the result of right hemisphere specialisation, will be particularly unfortunate. In Africa's mythology, poetry and literature, oral and written, in the various expressions of its great artistic acumen, the ritual enactment of its customs, and in the wisdom of its belief systems and holistic orientation, lie hidden buried psychological treasures. Even from those African politicians who have been poets and artists in their own right, and there have been a considerable number, a great deal can be learned about the integration of different dimensions of being. Thabo Mbeki, at the time of writing the President-Elect of South Africa, is the latest example. Generally perceived as a pragmatist, he has astonished political commentators with the poetic quality of his pre-election speeches. Naturally there are also those African politicians who provide food for psychological studies of the demonic.

The issue of Africanising psychology can no longer be skirted. Hopefully, the development of the discipline in Africa can avoid further colonisation. If this can be avoided, the benefits will not only be apparent in the coming about of a more meaningful psychology on the continent, but will also rub off on contemporary psychology in the Diaspora, and in the rest of the world, if ever so slightly. However, the difficulties in Africanising psychology on the continent must be realised. These are very real, for the power wielded by the institutionalisation of the discipline is enormous. Psychology in the politically new South Africa is an all too clear demonstration of such power and control. In terms of the sociology of knowledge, mainstream proponents have imbued the concept of science virtually with god-like qualities. Unquestioning obedience is required. Failure to do so dooms the heretic to the darkest pit of Erebus. Even experiential and intuitive knowing are discarded as unscientific and are, therefore, afforded no place in psychology! It does not matter that such greats as Einstein, William James, Michael Polanyi, and Carl Rogers, have not only given intuitive knowing their blessing but also considered it essential.

In aspiring towards a truly international psychology, the diversity or disunity, as so many concerned authors contend, will only become more enhanced by considering the folk psychologies of the African continent and other regions of the world. However, for the development of an international psychology, a synthesis, not of imposing uniformity on the disparate elements composing the discipline, but of allowing the elements to develop diversely in order to serve the unity of humankind, offers the best hope. In the way forward more tolerance of and respect for differences have to be evidenced. Conceivably, the threads that bind us all together will have the best chance of emerging if we do not have to fight so hard to be our individual and collective selves. There is no reason to expect that the principles, which provide the basis for the actualisation of the potential of the individual, do not apply with respect to groups of individuals as well.

The governments of the world are locked into behaviour patterns that only allow the resolution of conflict by using force. Billions of dollars are invested for military purposes. The economies of the United States and European countries thrive on selling arms to Africa. In being seduced by the tremendous destructive power of modern weaponry the danger exists that the traditional values of sub-Saharan Africa, epitomised by the concept of *ubuntu* and by a model of the self as an interdependent unit of the social system, can be totally eroded.

As Carl Rogers has so often pointed out in his career, for the price of one B-52 bomber the United States can dramatically improve its educational system. At present, we need only to think of the tremendous cost of a single 'smart' bomb or guided missile. In addition, there is the cost of the human element involved, as well as the cost of the material destruction and the psychological havoc that is created. Could not a fraction of the eventual cost of imposing a military and political solution to the conflict in Kosovo, for instance, have been invested towards reinventing Yugoslavia as a confederation allowing maximum autonomy for various ethnic groups?

We know that reinforcement is more effective in bringing about behaviour change than punishment. Why then, one wonders, is it so difficult for one of the established facts of our discipline to be implemented on a more global level? Has the psychological community perhaps neglected its duty in educating our policy makers about the factors involved in changing behaviour, especially where it matters most, the welfare of whole populations? The choice seems straightforward. We can either model our behaviour on power or on *ubuntu*. It is the challenge for psychology to bring home the futility of the one and the potential of the other.

Apart from initiating the revisioning of society by beginning with ourselves, psychology can endeavour to facilitate such restructuring through greater involvement in the educational system. The neglect of values in the educational process is accompanied by a neglect of feelings. In learning to deny these essential human attributes in ourselves, it is only natural that we will also fail to acknowledge them in others. One of Carl Rogers' most requested articles was, at the time, an unpublished paper, 'Current assumptions in graduate education: A passionate statement' (Rogers, 1969), that dealt with the neglect of the student as a proactive and affectively-experiencing person. The issue is compounded when African students are confronted by traditional Western educational systems. Seedat (1997) has expressed the emotional and intellectual estrangement, disorientation, and disempowerment, he and other black graduate students in South Africa experienced in being faced with 'the arsenal of psychological concepts that held the false promise of explaining familiar psychological experiences' (p. 261). In fact, it is a phenomenon that is common wherever psychology is taught.

Although the establishment of an empathic base for psychology seemingly constitutes a relatively minor or simple step, it will bring about a major shift in emphasis and orientation. Kenneth B. Clark (1980), whose early research contributed to the national policy on school segregation in the United States, argued for the teachability of empathy to a level necessary to counterbalance 'the more primitive animalistic determinants of behavior'. Clark considered empathy as a force counterbalancing egocentricity and power gratification. 'Empathy interferes with the sheer survival struggle and the functional efficiency of the power drive' (p. 188). He also believed that the capacity for empathy was 'a consequence of the evolution of the most recently developed portion of the human brain, the anterior frontal lobes' (p. 188). This raises questions about the structure and the functional development of the frontal cortex of the proponents of psychology as an exclusively logical positivistic and linear discipline.

A functional and structural retardation along the lines suggested by brain researcher, Paul MacLean (1967) seems to be the most likely outcome of an undeveloped empathic ability. Like Clark, MacLean proposed that there were different subdivisions of the brain concerned with self-preservation and the preservation of the species. He, too, localised the prefrontal cortex as the region of importance in facilitating insight into the feelings of others and suggested that there were critically receptive periods for such learning to occur. We know that failure to bring the neural circuits subserving the sensory modalities into play at certain critical times during development, result in the inability of the sensory system(s) to function adequately. Chimpanzees reared in darkness, for example, may be forever blind. Apparently, the retinal neurones atrophy and fail to function due to the lack of the necessary stimulation (Chow, Riesen, and Newell, 1957). Nobel Laureates, Hubel and Wiesel (1963), have shown that prolonged rearing without patterned light may lead not simply to a failure in forming neural connections in the cortex of kittens, but also disrupt connections that were there originally.

I want to believe that the neural circuits subserving *ubuntu* do not simply atrophy through disuse and that human insensitivity and destructiveness can be countered by educating people of all ages in *ubuntu*. In the 1960s, the President of Yale University, initiated a five-year BA programme to allow students to spend a year working in countries where the hardships of living were in evidence everywhere (in MacLean, 1967). If similar programmes could become part of the psychology curriculum, the nature of the discipline and the quality of the trainees might be altered dramatically. Fortunately, there appears to be the beginnings of an interest in psychology in the values embodied in *ubuntu*. As reports in the journals seem to indicate, empathy is no longer a concept solely of interest to the clinical field (Azar, 1997a). At the time of the hearings of the Truth and Reconciliation Commission in South Africa, it is significant that such topics as the 'human art of forgiveness' (Azar, 1997b) are finding their way into general psychology.

I have always found it paradoxical that statistics and methodology courses were compulsory for psychology students, irrespective of whether the students intended to enter an academic, a research, or a clinical career. Experientially oriented courses, designed to develop communication skills and the attitudes of empathy and *ubuntu*, on the other hand, are never incorporated into the core curriculum, or any part of the curriculum for that matter. My own attempts to introduce such courses have generally met with resistance from staff and even

from some students in The Netherlands, although those students who participated generally regarded the training to be valuable and directly relevant to the
careers they aspired towards.

The credo of 'scientific objectivity' has indeed permeated psychology to
such an extent that it dominates the training programmes in counselling and
clinical psychology. It is no small wonder that the scientist-practitioner model of
clinician training has, ever since its conception at the famous Boulder conference
more than four decades ago, been an enigma (Rice, 1997). Rice has suggested a
number of different scenarios for the future of contemporary psychology, and
it may well profit African psychology to develop the model further. In fact, the
debate about the pros and the cons of science-based practice is of crucial interest
to the future scenario of psychology on the continent. Is there room for the
notion that clinical work is applied science? If psychologists in the United States
debate the feasibility of 'two psychological professions, one scientific and academic and the other specializing in service provision.' (Rice, 1997, p. 1176), then
the question is certainly of relevance to African psychology as well. Furthermore,
in its service provision, account has to be taken of therapeutic approaches
indigenous to Africa.

Since the formal part of my training has been along the lines of the Boulder
model, I have been sufficiently indoctrinated to be partial to the preservation
of the Boulder model, if with considerable reservations, both on ideological and
applied grounds. For one thing, room has to be found in our view of science
for the incorporation of cognitive systems other than the linear-logical and
positivistic. Moreover, mental health approaches relevant to populations
belonging to different cultural orientations need to be respected and become
part of the armature of clinical psychology. It is important to keep in mind that
the theories and the principles assumed to be universal in psychology, derive
from research on white Americans, mostly males, who constitute but a small
percentage of the world's population (McGuire, 1999).

Questions regarding the discipline and the profession of psychology have
been elaborated throughout the book. Care has to be taken not to discard the
baby with the bath water, though. I have been sufficiently involved in empirical
laboratory research investigating the importance of the limbic system of the brain
in behaviour and on the significance of REM sleep in information processing, to
be intrigued by the scientific process. The shortcomings of the natural scientific
approach outside the laboratory cannot be overlooked, though. However, in the
appropriate context, the scientific approach has a great deal to offer. So has the
African approach. Unfortunately, this fact is not recognised in psychology. In
following Leopold Senghor, it is my belief that Africa can contribute to what he
called *La Civilisation de l'Universel*. Since psychology is so closely associated with
Senghor's aspirations, it can benefit more than most other disciplines from
registering the beat of the African pulse, even if it is but with a single finger.

REFERENCES

Abi-Hashem, N. (1997). Reflections on *International perspectives in psychology*. *American Psychologist*, *52*, 569–570.

Achebe, C. (1988). *The African trilogy: Things fall apart; No longer at ease; Arrow of God.* London: Picador.

Adair, J.G. (1996). The indigenous psychology bandwagon: Cautions and considerations. In J. Pandey, D. Sinha, & D.P.S. Bhawuk, (Eds.), *Asian contributions to cross-cultural psychology* (pp. 50–58). New Delhi: Sage.

Adamopoulus, J. (1988). Interpersonal behavior: Cross-cultural and historical perspectives. In M.H. Bond (Ed.), *The cross-cultural challenge to social psychology* (pp. 196–207). London: Sage.

Ager, A. (1993). Psychology and Africa. *The Psychologist: Bulletin of The British Psychological Society*, *6*, 490.

Agyakwa, K.O. (1976). *Akan epistemology and Western thought: A philosophical approach to the problem of educational modernization in Ghana.* Ann Arbor, MI: UMI Dissertation Services.

Akbar, N. (1984a). Africentric social sciences for human liberation. *Journal of Black Studies*, *14*, 395–414.

Akbar, N. (1984b). *Chains and images of psychological slavery.* Jersey City, NJ: New Mind Productions.

Akin-Ogundeji, O. (1991). Asserting psychology in Africa. *The Psychologist. Bulletin of the British Psychological Society*, *4*, 2–4.

Albee, G.W. (1982). Preventing psychopathology and human potential. *American Psychologist*, *37*, 1043–1050.

Albee, G.W. (1986). Toward a just society: Lessons from observations on the primary prevention of psychopathology. *American Psychologist*, *41*, 891–898.

Albee, G.W. (1990). The futility of psychotherapy. *The Journal of Mind and Behavior*, *11*, 369–384.

Albee, G.W. (1992). Powerlessness, politics and prevention: The community mental health approach. In S. Staub & P. Green (Eds.), *Psychology and social responsibility: Facing global challenges* (pp. 201–220). New York: New York University Press.

Albert, M.T. (1996). Eurocentrism: a worldwide phenomenon with regional peculiarities. *European Journal of Intercultural Studies*, *7*, 3–11.

Aldridge, D. (1989). A phenomenological comparison of the organization of music and the self. *The Arts in Psychotherapy*, *16*, 91–97.

Alexander, N., & Smolicz, J. (1993). The quest for core culture. *Bua!*, *8*, 4–7.

Al-Issa, I. (Ed.). (1982). *Culture and psychopathology*. Baltimore: University Park Press.

Allen, J. (1959). *"As a man thinketh"*. New York: Putnam.

Allik, J., & Realo, A. (1996). The hierarchical nature of individualism–collectivism: Comments on Matsumoto et al. *Culture & Psychology*, 2, 109–117.

Altizer, T.J.J. (1962). The religious meaning of myth and symbol. In T.J.J. Altizer, W.A. Beardslee, & J.H. Young (Eds.), *Truth, myth, and symbol* (pp. 87–108). Englewood Cliffs, NJ: Prentice-Hall.

Altman, I. (1987). Centripetal and centrifugal trends in psychology. *American Psychologist*, 42, 1058–1069.

Altman, I. (1996). Higher education and psychology in the millennium. *American Psychologist*, 51, 371–378.

American Psychiatric Association. (1994). *Diagnostic and statistical manual of mental disorders* (4th ed.). Washington, DC: Author.

Anastasi, A. (1990). *Are there unifying trends in the psychology of 1990?* Invited address at the 98th Annual Convention of the American Psychological Association, Boston.

Anderson, T. (1993). *Introduction to African American studies*. Dubuque, IA: Kendall/ Hunt.

Angier, N. (1996, 2 May). The importance of being social. *International Herald Tribune*, p. 10.

Angyal, A. (1965/1982). *Neurosis and treatment: A holistic theory*. New York: Da Capo Press.

Appiah, K. (1993). *In my father's house*. London: Methuen.

Armistead, N. (Ed.) (1974). *Reconstructing social psychology*. Harmondsworth, Middlesex: Penguin.

Asante, M.K. (1983). The ideological significance of Afrocentricity in intercultural communication. *Journal of Black Studies*, 14, 3–19.

Asante, M.K. (1992). *Afrocentricity*. Trenton, NJ: Africa World Press.

Atal, Y. (1981). Call for indogenization. *International Social Science Journal*, 33, 189–197.

Australië betuigt Aborigines spijt voor leed [Australia apologises to the Aborigines]. (1997, 28 May). *De Volkskrant*, p. 6.

Awolalu, J.O. (1991). African traditional religion as an academic discipline. In E.M. Uka (Ed.), *Readings in African traditional religion. Structure, meaning, relevance, future* (pp. 123–138). Bern: Peter Lang.

Ayisi, E.O. (1992). *An introduction to the study of African culture*. Nairobi: East African Educational Publishers.

Azar, B. (1997a, November). Defining the trait that makes us human. *APA Monitor*, 28, 1,15.

Azar, B. (1997b, November). Forgiveness helps keep relationships steadfast. *APA Monitor*, 28, 14.

Azar, B. (1999). E.O. Wilson to speak at APA's convention. *APA Monitor*, 30, 17.

Azibo, D.A. (1994). The kindred fields of black liberation theology and liberation psychology: A critical essay on their conceptual base and destiny. *The Journal of Black Psychology*, 20, 334–356.

Azuma, H. (1984a). Secondary control as a heterogeneous category. *American Psychologist*, 39, 970–971.

Azuma, H. (1984b). Psychology in a non-Western country. *International Journal of Psychology*, 19, 45–55.

Bakan, D. (1966). *The duality of human existence*. Chicago: Rand McNally.

Baldwin, J.M. (1968). The self-conscious person. In C. Gordon & K.J. Gergen (Eds.), *The self in social interaction* (pp. 161–169). New York: Wiley.

Baldwin, J.A. (1986). African (Black) psychology. Issues and synthesis. *Journal of Black Studies, 16,* 235–249. Reprinted in R.L. Jones (Ed.), *Black psychology.* Berkeley: Cobb & Henry.

Baldwin, J.A. (1989). The role of black psychologists in black liberation. *The Journal of Black Psychology, 16,* 67–76.

Barlow, D.H. (1991). Disorders of emotion: Clarification, elaboration, and future directions. *Psychological Inquiry, 2,* 97–105.

Barlow, D.H. (1996). Health care policy, psychotherapy research, and the future of psychotherapy. *American Psychologist, 51,* 1050–1058.

Bauserman, R. (1997). International representation in the psychological literature. *International Journal of Psychology, 32,* 107–112.

Becker, P. (1974). *Tribe to township.* New York: Panther.

Benson, C. (1993). *The absorbed self: Pragmatism, psychology and aesthetic experience.* Hassocks: Harvester Wheatsheaf.

Berglund, A. (1976). *Zulu thought patterns and symbolism.* Cape Town: David Philip.

Bergman, S.J. (1991). Men's psychological development: A relational perspective. *Work in Progress, # 48.* Wellesley, MA: Stone Center Working Paper Series.

Berkowitz, L., & Devine, P.G. (1989). Research traditions, analysis and synthesis in social psychological theory. *Personality and Social Psychology Bulletin, 15,* 493–507.

Betancourt, H., & López, S.R. (1993). The study of culture, ethnicity, and race in American psychology. *American Psychologist, 48,* 629–637.

Beutler, L.E., Williams, R.E., Wakefield, P.J., & Entwistle, S.R. (1995). Bridging scientist and practitioner perspectives in clinical psychology. *American Psychologist, 50,* 984–994.

Bevan, W. (1982). A sermon of sorts in three plus parts. *American Psychologist, 37,* 1303–1322.

Bevan, W. (1991). Contemporary psychology: A tour inside the onion. *American Psychologist, 46,* 475–483.

Bevan, W., & Kessel, F. (1994). Plain truths and home cooking: Thoughts on the making and remaking of psychology. *American Psychologist, 49,* 505–509.

Bhavnani, K-K., & Phoenix, A. (1994). *Shifting identities shifting racisms. A feminism & psychology reader.* London: Sage.

Biko, S. (1975). Zwart bewustzijn en het zoeken naar waarachtig menszijn (Black Consciousness and the search for being truly human). In B. Moore (Ed.), *Zwarte teologie in Zuid-Afrika* (Black theology / The African choice) (pp. 58–70). Baarn: Uitgeverij Ten Have.

Billig, M. (1991). *Ideology and opinions. Studies in rhetorical psychology.* London: Sage.

Blacking, J. (1976). *How musical is man.* London: Faber & Faber.

Blair, L. (1976). *Rhythms of vision.* St Albans, Herts: Paladin.

Blake, C. (1981). Understanding African national development. Some challenges to communication specialists. *Journal of Black Studies, 12,* 201–217.

Boahen, A.A. (1987). *African perspectives on colonialism.* Baltimore: Johns Hopkins University Press.

Boateng, F. (1983). African traditional education. A method of disseminating cultural values. *Journal of Black Studies, 13,* 321–336.

Bodibe, R.C. (1993). What is the truth? Being more than just a jesting Pilate in South African psychology. *South African Journal of Psychology, 23,* 53–58.

Bodibe, R.C. (1994, January). *The need for a third voice in South African psychology.* Paper presented at the Psychology and Societal Transformation Conference, University of the Western Cape, Bellville, South Africa.

Bodibe, R.C. (in press). Paradigms lost, paradigms to be regained: An African's view of counselling and psychotherapy. *International Journal for the Advancement of Counselling.*

Boorstein, S. (1997). *Clinical studies in transpersonal psychology.* New York: State University Press.

Brazier, D. (1996). *Zen therapy.* London: Constable.

Brent, J.E., & Callwood, G.B. (1993). Culturally relevant psychiatric care: The West Indian as a client. *Journal of Black Psychology, 19,* 290–302.

Bridgland, F. (1984, 19 September). Power from singing and dancing. *The Star,* 12.

Bronfenbrenner, U., Kessel, F., Kessen, W., & White, S. (1986). Toward a critical social history of developmental psychology. A propaedentic discussion. *American Psychologist, 41,* 1218–1230.

Bronstein, P. (1986). Self-disclosure, paranoia, and unaware racism: Another look at the black client and the white therapist. *American Psychologist, 41,* 225–226.

Brown, D.P., Engler, J., & Wilber, K. (Eds.) (1986). *Transformations of consciousness: Conventional and contemplative perspectives on development.* Boston: Shambala.

Brown, L.S. (1997). The private practice of subversion: Psychology as tikkun olam. *American Psychologist, 52,* 449–462.

Brown, P. (1987). Diagnostic conflict and contradiction in psychiatry. *Journal of Health and Social Behavior, 28,* 37–50.

Brown, P. (1990). The name game: Toward a sociology of diagnosis. *The Journal of Mind and Behavior, 11,* 385–406.

Buber, M. (1970). *I and thou.* New York: Scribners.

Bulhan, H.A. (1980). Dynamics of cultural in-betweenity: An empirical study. *International Journal of Psychology, 152,* 105–121.

Bulhan, H.A. (1985). *Frantz Fanon and the psychology of oppression.* New York: Plenum Press.

Bulhan, H.A. (1993a). Imperialism in studies of the psyche: A critique of African psychological research. In L.J. Nicholas (Ed.), *Psychology and oppression: Critiques and proposals* (pp. 1–34). Johannesburg: Skotaville.

Bulhan, H.A. (1993b). Family therapy and oppression: A critique and a proposal. In L.J. Nicholas (Ed.), *Psychology and oppression: Critiques and proposals* (pp. 167–189). Johannesburg: Skotaville.

Burlew, A.K.H., Banks, W.C., McAdoo, H.P., & Azibo, D.A. (Eds.) (1992). *African American psychology: Theory, research, and practice.* London: Sage.

Burnett-van Tonder, C. (1987). *Socio-etniese danse van die Venda-vrou* (Socio-ethnic dances of Venda women). Pretoria: HAUM.

Buros, O.K. (Ed.) (1975). *Personality tests and reviews, II.* Highland Park, NJ: The Guyphon Press.

Butchart, A., & Seedat, M. (1990). Within and without: Images of community and implications for South African psychology. *Social Science and Medicine, 31,* 1093–1102.

Butcher, J.N. (1987). Cultural factors in understanding and assessing psychopathology. Ethnic minorities (Special issue). *Journal of Consulting and Clinical Psychology, 55*(4).

Cahan, E.D., & White, S.H. (1992). Proposals for a second psychology. *American Psychologist, 47,* 224–235.

Cairns, E., & Darby, J. (1998). The conflict in Northern Ireland: Causes, consequences, and controls. *American Psychologist, 53,* 754–760.

Campbell, D.T. (1975). On the conflicts between biological and social evolution and between psychology and moral tradition. *American Psychologist, 30,* 1103–1126.

Campbell, J. (1973). *Myths to live by.* London: Souvenir Press.

Campbell, J. (1983). *The way of the animal powers. Vol. 1. Historical atlas of world mythology.* San Francisco: Harper & Row.

Candland, D.K. (1980). Speaking words and doing deeds. *American Psychologist, 35,* 191–198.

Cantor, N. (1990). From thought to behavior: "Having" and "doing" in the study of psychology and cognition. *American Psychologist, 45,* 735–750.

Capra, F. (1982). *The turning point.* New York: Simon & Schuster.

Carr, S., & MacLachlan, M. (1993). Asserting psychology in Malawi. *The Psychologist: Bulletin of The British Psychological Society, 6,* 408–413.

Cattell, R.B. (1993). What's wrong with psychology? *The Psychologist: Bulletin of the British Psychological Society, 6,* 22–23.

Cavalli-Sforza, L.L. (1998). The Chinese human genome diversity project. *Proceedings of the National Academy of Sciences, 95,* 11501–11503.

CERI/OECD. (1987). *Multicutural education.* Paris: CERI/OECD.

Césaire, A. (1969). *Return to my native land.* Harmondsworth, Middlesex: Penguin.

Cheetham, R.W.S. (1975). Conflicts in a rural African patient treated in an urban setting. *Medicine, 30,* 1563–1566.

Chernoff, J. M. (1979). *African rhythm and African sensibility: aesthetics and social action in African musical idioms.* Chicago: Chicago University Press.

Chidester, D. (1991). *Shots in the streets: Violence and religion in South Africa.* Cape Town: Oxford University Press.

Chidester, D., Mitchell, G., Omar, A.R., & Phiri, I.A. (1994). *Religion in public education: Options for a new South Africa.* Cape Town: UCT Press.

Chinweizu. (1987). *Decolonising the African mind.* Lagos: Pero Press.

Chow, K.L., Riesen, A.H., & Newell, F.W. (1957). Degeneration of retinal ganglion cells in infant chimpanzees reared in darkness. *Journal of Comparative Neurology, 107,* 27–42.

Chu, J.Y., Huang, W., Kuang, S.Q., Wang, J.M., Xu, J.J., Chu, Z.T., Yang, Z.Q., Liu, K.Q., Li, P., Wu, M., Geng, Z.C., Tan, C.C., Du., R.F., & Jin, L. (1998). Genetic relationships of populations in China. *Proceedings of the National Academy of Sciences, 95,* 11763–11768.

Clark, K.B. (1980). Empathy: A neglected potential in psychological research. *American Psychologist, 35,* 187–190.

Clegg, J. (1977). *Dance and society in Africa south of the Sahara.* Unpublished Honours dissertation, University of the Witwatersrand, Johannesburg.

Clegg, J. (1978, May). *Zulu dancing.* Paper presented at the conference on Indigenous Healing, Johannesburg, South Africa.

Cohen, D. (1977). *Dreams, visions, and drugs: A search for other realities.* New York: New Viewpoints.

Comas-Díaz, L., Lykes, M.B., & Alarcón, R.D. (1998). Ethnic conflict and the psychology of liberation in Gautemala, Peru, and Puerto Rico. *American Psychologist, 53,* 778–792.

Cook, S.W. (1985). Experimenting on social issues. The case of school segregation. *American Psychologist, 40,* 452–460.

Couzens, T., & Patel, E. (Eds.) (1982). *The return of the Amasi bird. Black South African poetry 1881–1981*. Johannesburg: Ravan Press.

Cox, J.L. (1986). *Transcultural psychiatry*. Beckenham, Kent: Croom Helm.

Craig, A.P. (1990). The project of social science and the activities of psychologists. *South African Journal of Psychology, 20*, 10–19.

Cushman, P. (1990). Why the self is empty: Toward a historically situated psychology. *American Psychologist, 45*, 599–611.

Cushman, P. (1991). Ideology obscured. Political uses of the self in Daniel Stern's infant. *American Psychologist, 46*, 206–219.

Daniels, E. (1986). Primary prevention: A challenge to the helping disciplines. *South African Black Social Workers Association Journal, 3*, 19–21.

Dargie, D. (1988). *Xhosa music: Its techniques and instruments, with a collection of songs*. Cape Town: David Philip.

Dawes, A. (1985). Politics and mental health: The position of clinical psychology in South Africa. *South African Journal of Psychology, 15*, 55–61.

Dawes, A. (1996, September). *Africanisation of psychology*. Paper presented at the 2nd Congress of the Psychological Society of South Africa, Johannesburg.

Dawes, A.R.L., & Davids, M.F. (1983). Is cross-cultural counselling possible? *Journal of Educational Guidance and Counselling Association, 7*, 5–8.

de Heusch, L. (1994). Myth and epic in central Africa. In T. D. Blakely, W.E.A. van Beek, & D.L. Thomson (Eds.), *Religion in Africa: Experience and expression* (pp. 229–238). Portsmouth, NH: Heinemann.

de Jong, H.L. (1992). *Naturalism and psychology: A theoretical study*. Kampen: Kok.

de Jong, J.T.V.M. (1987). *A descent into African psychiatry*. Amsterdam: Royal Tropical Institute.

de Klerk, F.W. (1995). *De rol van politiek leiderschap. Vertrouwen en geloof in de verandering van Zuid-Afrika* (The role of political leadership. Faith and belief in the transformation of South Africa). Amsterdam: Vrije Universiteit Press.

de Lange, F. (1989). *Individualisme: Een partijdig onderzoek naar een omstrede denkwijze* (Individualism: A partial study of a controversial topic). Kampen: Kok Angora.

DeLeon, P.H., Sammons, M.T., & Sexton, J.L. (1995). Focusing on society's needs: Responsibility and prescription privileges? *American Psychologist, 50*, 1022–1032.

de Maret, P. (1994). Archaeological and other prehistoric evidence of traditional African religious expression. In T.D. Blakely, W.E.A. van Beek, & D.L. Thomson (Eds.), *Religion in Africa: Experience and expression* (pp. 182–195). Portsmouth, NH: Heinemann.

den Hartog, D.N. (1997). *Inspirational leadership*. Published doctoral dissertation, Vrije Universiteit, Amsterdam.

Derrida, J. (1984). Guter Wille zur Macht (I). Drei Fragen an Hans-Georg Gadamer (With good intentions towards power (I). Three questions for Hans-Georg Gadamer). In Ph. Forget (Ed.), *Text und Interpretation* (pp. 56–58). München.

Deutsch, M. (1993). Educating for a peaceful world. *American Psychologist, 48*, 510–517.

DeVos, G., Marsella, A.J., & Hsu, F.L.K. (1985). Introduction: Approaches to culture and self. In G. DeVos, A.J. Marsella, & F.L.K. Hsu (Eds.), *Culture and self: Asian and Western perspectives* (pp. 2–23). London: Tavistock.

de Wit, H.F. (1991). *Contemplative psychology*. Pittsburgh: Duquesne University Press.

de Wit, H.F. (1995). *De verborgen bloei: Over de psychologische achtergronden van spiritualiteit* (The hidden flower: The psychological basis of spirituality). Kampen: Kok Angora.

"diTaola". (1998, 16 April). *Cape Argus*, p. 13.

Dokecki, P.R. (1990). On knowing the person as agent in caring relations. *Person-Centred Review*, 5, 155–169.

Doob, L.W. (1972). Biculturalism as a source of personality conflict in Africa. In S.H. Irvine & J.T. Sanders (Eds.), *Cultural adaptation within modern Africa*. New York: Teachers College Press.

Dooms, P. (1989, 24 February). Nation building idea not new. *Sowetan*.

Dopamu, P.A. (1991). Towards understanding African traditional religion. In E.M. Uka (Ed.), *Readings in African traditional religion: Structure, meaning, relevance, future* (pp. 19–37). Bern: Peter Lang.

Draguns, J.G. (1982). Methodology in cross-cultural psychology. In I. Al-Issa (Ed.), *Culture and psychopathology* (pp. 33–70). Baltimore: University Park Press.

Duncan, N., Seedat, M., van Niekerk, A., de la Rey, C., Gobodo-Madikizela, P., Simbayi, L.C., & Bhana, A. (1997). Black scholarship: doing something active and positive about academic racism. *South African Journal of Psychology*, 27, 201–205.

du Preez, P. (1991). *A science of mind. A quest for psychological reality*. London: Academic Press.

Durie, M., & Hermansson, G. (1990). Counselling Maori people in New Zealand (Aotearoa). *International Journal for the Advancement of Counselling*, 13, 107–118.

Durrheim, K. & Mokeki, S. (1997). Race and relevance: a content analysis of the *South African Journal of Psychology*. *South African Journal of Psychology*, 27, 206–213.

"Ebonics". (1997). Special section on Ebonics. *Journal of Black Psychology*, 23(3).

Eibl-Eibesfeldt, I. (1988). The biological foundation of aesthetics. In I. Rentschler, B. Herzberger, & D. Epstein (Eds.), *Beauty and the brain: Biological aspects of aesthetics* (pp. 15–68). Basel: Birkhäuser Verlag.

Eliade, M. (1964). *Myth and reality*. London: George Allen & Unwin.

Eliade, M. (1967). *From primitives to Zen*. London: Collins.

Enserink, M. (1999). Can the placebo be the cure? *Science*, 284, 238–240.

Epstein, D. (1988). Tempo relations in music: A universal? In I. Rentschler, B. Herzberger, & D. Epstein (Eds.), *Beauty and the brain: Biological aspects of aesthetics* (pp. 91–116). Basel: Birkhäuser Verlag.

Epstein, M. (1995). *Thoughts without a thinker: Psychotherapy from a Buddhist perspective*. New York: Basic Books.

Euvrard, G. (1996). Career needs of Eastern Cape pupils in South Africa. *British Journal of Guidance and Counselling*, 24, 113–128.

"Excuses aan Aboriginals, maar nog geen verzoening" [Apologies to Aborigines, but still no reconciliation]. (1997, 28 May). *NRC Handelsblad*, p. 6.

Fairchild, H.H. (1993a). The fires this time. Lessons from Los Angeles, 1992. In N.C. McKinney (Ed.), *No justice, no peace? Resolutions . . .* (pp. 13–19). Los Angeles: The California Afro-American Museum Foundation.

Fairchild, H.H. (1993b). Confronting white supremacy. *Psych Discourse*, 24, 11.

Fairchild, H.H. (1994). Whither liberation? A critique of a critique. *Journal of Black Psychology*, 20, 367–371.

Fairchild, H.H., & Fairchild, D.G. (1993). African Americans and Korean immigrants: Cultures in conflict. In E.R. Myers (Ed.), *Challenges of a changing America: Perspectives on immigration and multiculturalism in the United States* (pp. 167–174). San Francisco: Austin & Winfield.

Fanon, F.A. (1965). *Dying colonialism*. New York: Grove Press.

Fanon, F.A. (1970). *Black skin white masks.* London: Paladin.

Fanon, F.A. (1976). *The wretched of the earth.* Harmondsworth, Middlesex: Penguin.

Farber, S. (1990). Institutional mental health and social control: The ravages of epistemological hubris. *The Journal of Mind and Behavior, 11,* 285–299.

Farley, F. (1996). From the heart. *American Psychologist, 51,* 772–776.

Farson, R. (1974). Carl Rogers, quiet revolutionary. *Education, 95,* 197–203.

Farthing, G.W. (1992). *The psychology of consciousness.* Englewood Cliffs, NJ: Prentice Hall.

Ferguson, M. (1980). *The Aquarian conspiracy.* Los Angeles: J.P. Tarcher.

Firmage, G.J. (Ed.) (1965). *A miscellany revised.* New York: October House.

Fisher, I. (1999, 23 April). Rwanda turning to its traditional ways to do justice. *International Herald Tribune,* p. 2.

Flanagan, R., & Sommers, J. (1986). Ethical considerations for the peace activist psychotherapist. *American Psychologist, 4,* 723–724.

Fletcher, G.J.O. (1995). *The scientific credibility of folk psychology.* Hove: Lawrence Erlbaum Associates Ltd.

Flisher, A.J., Skinner, D., Lazarus, S., & Louw, J. (1993). Organising mental health workers on the basis of politics and service: The case of the Organisation for Appropriate Social Services in South Africa. In L.J. Nicholas (Ed.), *Psychology and oppression: Critiques and proposals* (pp. 236–245). Johannesburg: Skotaville.

Fogel, A. (1993). *Developing through relationships: Origins of communication, self and culture.* Hassocks: Harvester Wheatsheaf.

Foster, D. (1993a). On racism: Virulent mythologies and fragile threads. In L.J. Nicholas (Ed.), *Psychology and oppression: Critiques and proposals* (pp. 55–80). Johannesburg: Skotaville.

Foster, D. (1993b). The mark of oppression?: Racism and psychology reconsidered. In L.J. Nicholas (Ed.), *Psychology and oppression: Critiques and proposals* (pp. 128–141). Johannesburg: Skotaville.

Foster, D., Davis, D., & Sandler, D. (1987). *Detention and torture in South Africa: Psychological, legal and historical studies.* Cape Town: David Philip.

Foster, D., Nicholas, L., & Dawes, A. (1993). A reply to Raubenheimer. *The Psychologist: Bulletin of the British Psychological Society, 6,* 172–174.

Fowers, B.J., & Richardson, F.C. (1996). Why is multiculturalism good? *American Psychologist, 51,* 609–621.

Fowers, B.J., & Richardson, F.C. (1997). A second invitation to dialogue: Multiculturalism and psychology. *American Psychologist, 52,* 659–661.

Fowler, R.D. (1996). 1996 Editorial: 50th Anniversary issue of the *American Psychologist. American Psychologist, 51,* 5–7.

Fox, D.R. (1986). Beyond individualism and centralization. *American Psychologist, 41,* 231–232.

Fox, R.E. (1982). The need for a reorientation of clinical psychology. *American Psychologist, 37,* 1051–1057.

Fox, R.E. (1996). Charlatanism, scientism, and psychology's social contract. *American Psychologist, 51,* 777–784.

Frank, L.R. (1990). Electroshock: Death, brain damage, memory loss, and brain washing. *The Journal of Mind and Behavior, 11,* 489–512.

Freeman, M. (1991). Mental health for all – moving beyond rhetoric. *South African Journal of Psychology, 21,* 141–147.

Freire, P. (1970). *Pedagogy of the oppressed.* New York: Seabury.

Freire, P. (1971, No. 1). A few notions about the word 'concientization'. *Hard Cheese*, 23–28.

Furth, H.G. (1995). Self in which relation? *American Psychologist, 50*, 176.

Gabrenya, W.K. (1988). Social science and social psychology. The cross-cultural link. In M.H. Bond (Ed.), *The cross-cultural challenge in social psychology* (pp. 48–66). London: Sage.

Gantous, P. (1994). Stress drives high suicide rate among native Canadian Innu. *Psychology International, 5*, 3.

Gasquoine, P.G. (1997). American psychological imperialism in the fourth world. *American Psychologist, 52*, 570–571.

Gaubatz, M. (1997). Subtle ethnocentrisms in the hermeneutic circle. *American Psychologist, 52*, 657–658.

Geertz, C. (1971). *The interpretation of cultures*. New York: Basic Books.

Geertz, C. (1974). "From the nature's point of view": On the nature of anthropological understanding. In K. Basso & H. Selby (Eds.), *Meaning in anthropology* (pp. 221–237). Albuquerque: University of New Mexico Press.

Gelfand, M. (1979). *Growing up in Shona society*. Salisbury: Mambo Press.

Geller, L. (1982). The failure of self-actualization theory: A critique of Carl Rogers and Abraham Maslow. *Journal of Humanistic Psychology, 22*, 56–73.

Gerdes, L.C. (1992). Impressions and questions about psychology and psychologists. *South African Journal of Psychology, 22*, 39–43.

Gergen, K.J. (1985). The social constructionist movement in modern psychology. *American Psychologist, 40*, 266–275.

Gergen, K.J. (1990). Therapeutic professions and the diffusion of deficit. *Journal of Mind and Behavior, 11*, 353–368.

Gergen, K.J. (1991). *The communal creation of meaning*. Draft copy for the 1991 meetings of the Jean Piaget Society.

Gergen, K. (1994). Exploring the postmodern: Perils or potentials? *American Psychologist, 49*, 412–416.

Gergen, K. (1995). Postmodern psychology: Resonance and reflection. *American Psychologist, 50*, 394.

Gergen, K.J., & Gergen, M.M. (1988). Narrative and the self as relationship. In L. Berkowitz (Ed.), *Advances in experimental social psychology. Vol. 21* (pp. 17–56). New York: Academic Press.

Gergen, K.J, Gulerce, A., Lock, A., & Misra, G. (1996). Psychological science in cultural context. *American Psychologist, 51*, 496–503.

Gibbs, J.C., & Schnell, S.V. (1985). Moral development "versus" socialization. *American Psychologist, 40*, 1071–1080.

Gibran, K. (1954). *A tear and a smile*. London: William Heinemann.

Gilbert, A. (1989). Things fall apart? Psychological theory in the context of rapid social change. *South African Journal of Psychology, 19*, 91–100.

Gilbert, A., van Vlaanderen, H., & Nkwinti, G. (1995). Planting pumpkins: socialization and the role of local knowledge in rural South Africa. *South African Journal of Psychology, 25*, 229–235.

Gill, D., & Levidov, L. (Eds.) (1987). *Anti-racist science teaching*. London: Free Association Books.

Gilligan, C. (1982). *In a different voice: Psychological theory and women's development*. Cambridge, MA: Harvard University Press.

Gillmer, B. (1996). The good, the bad, and the mediocre (Review of book *Perspectives on personality*). *Psychology in Society, 21*, 95–98.

Gobodo, P. (1990). Notions about culture in understanding black psychopathology: Are we trying to raise the dead? *South African Journal of Psychology, 20*, 93–98.

Gobodo-Madikizela, P. (1997). Healing the racial divide? Personal reflection on the Truth and Reconciliation Commission. *South African Journal of Psychology, 27*, 271–272.

Goldfried, M.R., & Wolfe, B.E. (1996). Psychotherapy practice and research: Repairing a strained alliance. *American Psychologist, 51*, 1007–1016.

Goleman, D. (1972). The buddha on meditation and states of consciousness (Part II): A typology of meditation techniques. *Journal of Transpersonal Psychology, 4*, 151–210.

Gordon, C., & Gergen, K.J. (1968). The nature and dimensions of self: Introduction. In C. Gordon & K.J. Gergen (Eds.), *The self in social interaction* (pp.33–39). New York: Wiley.

Graham, S.R., & Fox, R.E. (1991). Postdoctoral education for professional practice. *American Psychologist, 46*, 1033–1035.

Gray, G.E., Baron, D., & Herman, J. (1985). Importance of medical anthropology in clinical psychiatry. *American Journal of Psychiatry, 142*, 275.

Gray, S. (1982, 30 October). What happened to the 70s? *The Star*, p.18.

Green, C.D. (1992). Is unified positivism the answer to psychology's disunity? *American Psychologist, 45*, 1057–1058.

Green, R.L. (1980). Psychology training programs: Implications for the nations's poor. *Journal of Black Studies, 10*, 335–344.

Greening, T. (Ed.) (1986). *Politics and innocence: A humanistic debate*. Dallas, TX: Saybrook.

Grugeon, E., & Woods, P. (1990). *Educating all: Multicultural perspectives in the primary school*. London: Routledge.

Grüsser, O-J., Selke, T., & Zynda, B. (1988). Cerebral lateralization and some implications for art, aesthetic perception, and artistic creativity. In I. Rentschler, B. Herzberger, & D. Epstein (Eds.), *Beauty and the brain: Biological aspects of aesthetics* (pp. 257–293). Basel: Birkhäuser Verlag.

Gudykunst, W.B. (1988). Culture and intergroup processes. In M.H. Bond (Ed.), *The cross-cultural challenge to social psychology* (pp. 165–181). London: Sage.

Gumede, M.V. (1974). Traditions and customs. *The Leech, 44*, 35–38.

Guthrie, R. (1970). *Even the rat was white*. New York: Harper & Row.

Guthrie, R.V. (1991). The psychology of African Americans: An historical perspective. In R.L. Jones (Ed.), *Black psychology* (pp. 33–45). Berkeley: Cobb & Henry.

Gyekye, K. (1987). *An essay on African philosophical thought: An Akan conceptual scheme*. New York: Cambridge University Press.

Haan, N. (1982a). Can research on morality be scientific. *American Psychologist, 37*, 1096–1104.

Haan, N. (1982b). Replies to Leary, Houts and Krasner, Waterman and Einhorn. *American Psychologist, 38*, 1256–1257.

Hall, C.C.I. (1997). Cultural malpractice: The growing obsolescence of psychology with the changing population. *American Psychologist, 52*, 642–651.

Hall, G.C.N., & Barongan, C. (1997). Prevention of sexual aggression: Sociocultural risk and protective factors. *American Psychologist, 52*, 5–14.

Hall, G.C.N., Barongan, C., Bernal, G., Comas-Díaz, L., Hall, C.C., Nagayama, G.C.,

LaDue, R.A., Parham, T.A., Pedersen, P.B., Porché-Burke, L.M., Rollock, D., & Root, M.P.P. (1997). Misunderstandings of multiculturalism: Shouting fire in crowded theaters. *American Psychologist, 52*, 654–655.

Hammond, O.W. (1988). Needs assessment and policy development: Native Hawaians as native Americans. *American Psychologist, 43*, 383–387.

Harding, T.W. (1975). Traditional healing methods for mental disorders. *WHO Chronicle, 31*, 436–440.

Harland, B. (1996, 3 May). America must learn to respect Asia's way of doing things. *International Herald Tribune*, p. 6.

Harper, R.A. (1959). *Psychoanalysis and psychotherapy: 36 systems*. Englewood Cliffs, NJ: Prentice-Hall.

Harper, R.A. (1975). *The new psychotherapies*. Englewood Cliffs, NJ: Prentice-Hall.

Harré, R. (1981). Psychological variety. In P. Heelas & A. Lock (Eds.), *Indigenous psychologies: The anthropology of the self* (pp. 79–103). London: Academic Press.

Harré, R. (1993). Reappraising social psychology. Rules, roles and rhetoric. *The Psychologist. Bulletin of the British Psychological Society, 6*, 24–28.

Harré, R. (1998). *The singular self: An introduction to the psychology of personhood*. London: Sage.

Hayashi, C. (1992). Belief systems and the Japanese way of thinking: Interchronological and international perspectives. In H. Motoaki, J. Misumi, & B. Wilpert (Eds.), *Social, educational and clinical psychology* (pp. 3–34). Hove: Lawrence Erlbaum Associates Ltd.

Hayes, G. (1984). The repression of the social. *Psychology in Society, 2*, 41–53.

Hayes, G. (1997). Editorial. *Psychology in Society, 22*, 1–3.

Hayes, W.A. (1991). Radical black behaviorism. In R.L. Jones (Ed.), *Black psychology* (pp. 65–78). Berkeley: Cobb & Henry.

Heelas, P., & Lock, A. (1981). *Indigenous psychologies. The anthropology of the self*. New York: Academic Press.

Heider, F. (1958). *The psychology of interpersonal relations*. New York: Wiley.

Helms, J.E., & Talleyrand, R.M. (1997). Race is not ethnicity. *American Psychologist, 52*, 1246–1247.

Henderson, M.E. (1976, February). *Evidence for a male menstrual temperature cycle and synchrony with the female menstrual cycle*. Paper presented at the Combined Meetings of the Endocrine Societies of Australia and New Zealand, Auckland, New Zealand.

Hergenhahn, B.R. (1994). Psychology's cognitive revolution. *American Psychologist, 49*, 816–817.

Hermans, H.J.M., & Kempen, H.J.G. (1998). Moving cultures: The perilous problems of cultural dichotomies in a globalizing society. *American Psychologist, 53*, 1111–1120.

Hermans, H.J.M., Kempen, H.J.G., & van Loon, R.J.P. (1992). The dialogical self. Beyond individualism and rationalism. *American Psychologist, 47*, 23–33.

Hillerbrand, E. (1987). Philosophical tensions influencing psychology and social action. *American Psychologist, 42*, 111–118.

Hillman, J. (1972). *The myth of analysis: Three essays in archetypal psychology*. New York: Harper & Row.

Hillman, J. (1975). *Revisioning psychology*. New York: Harper Colophon.

Hillman, J. (1979). Peaks and vales. The soul/spirit distinction as basis for the differences between psychotherapy and spiritual discipline. In J. Hillman, H.A. Murray, T. Moore, J. Baird, T. Cowan, & R. Severson (Eds.), *Puer papers* (pp. 54–74). Irving, Texas: Spring Publications.

Hillman, J. (1983). *Healing fiction*. Barrytown, New York: Station Hill.

Hillman, J. (1996). *The soul's code: In search of character and calling*. New York: Warner Books.

Hillman, J., & Ventura, M. (1993). *We've had a hundred years of psychotherapy and the world's getting worse*. San Francisco: Harper.

Ho, D.Y.F. (1985). Cultural values and professional issues in clinical psychology. Implications from the Hong Kong experience. *American Psychologist, 40*, 1212–1218.

Hofstede, G. (1980). *Cultures consequences: International differences in work-related values*. Beverly Hills: Sage.

Holdstock, T.L. (1979). Indigenous healing in South Africa: A neglected potential. *South African Journal of Psychology, 9*, 118–124.

Holdstock, T.L. (1981a). Recurring dreams of the black people of Southern Africa. *Odyssey, 5*, 26–31.

Holdstock, T.L. (1981b). Psychology belongs to the colonial era. Arrogance or ignorance? *South African Journal of Psychology, 11*, 123–129.

Holdstock, T.L. (1982). Psychology in South Africa is like an ostrich. *Psygram, 22*, 7–10.

Holdstock, T.L. (1985). Is psychology in South Africa lily-white? *Odyssey, 9*, 22–23.

Holdstock, T.L. (1987a). *Education for a new nation*. River Club, South Africa: Africa Transpersonal Association.

Holdstock, T.L. (1987b, 2 November). We must develop a truly South African culture. *The Star*.

Holdstock, T.L. (1990a). Can Client-Centred therapy transcend its monocultural roots? In G. Lietaer, J. Rombouts, & R. van Balen, (Eds.), *Client-Centred and experiential psychotherapy in the nineties* (pp. 109–121). Leuven: Leuven University Press.

Holdstock, T.L. (1990b, August). *The Africentric self: A holistic cosmology*. Paper presented at the 1990 Principles Congress, Amsterdam.

Holdstock, T.L. (1990c). Violence in schools: Discipline. In B. McKendrick & W. Hoffmann (Eds.), *People and violence in South Africa* (pp. 341–372). Cape Town: Oxford University Press.

Holdstock, T.L. (1991a). Het individuocentrisme in de klinische psychologie: Quo vadis? In J.A.M. Winnubst, P. Schnabel, J. van den Bout, & M.J.M. van Son (Eds.), *De metamorfose van de klinische psychologie* (pp. 199–207). Assen: Van Gorcum.

Holdstock, T.L. (1991b). *Can we afford not to revision the Person-Centred concept of self?* Paper presented at the 2nd International Conference on Client-Centred and Experiential Psychotherapy, Stirling, Scotland.

Holdstock, T.L. (1991c). Bodily awareness: A neglected dimension in Western education. In E.H. Katsenellenbogen & J.R. Potgieter (Eds.), *Sociological perspectives of human movement activity* (pp. 44–52). Stellenbosch: Stellenbosch University Press.

Holdstock, T.L. (1992–1993). Second phase education and training in clinical psychology: Quo vadis? *U&H. Tijdschrift voor Wetenschappelijk Onderwijs, 38*, 204–210.

Holdstock, T.L. (1993). Can we afford not to revision the Person-Centred concept of the self? In D. Brazier (Ed.), *Beyond Carl Rogers* (pp. 229–252). London: Constable.

Holdstock, T.L. (1994a). Is the cognitive revolution all it is made out to be? *American Psychologist, 49*, 819–820.

Holdstock, T.L. (1994b). The education and training of clinical psychologists in the Netherlands. *Professional Psychology: Research and Practice, 25*, 70–75.

Holdstock, T.L. (1996a). Dis-ease in psychology: The basis for a new beginning? In M.

Kwee & T.L. Holdstock (Eds.), *Western and Buddhist psychology: Clinical perspectives* (pp. 15–43). Delft: Eburon.

Holdstock, T.L. (1996b). Exploring our relatedness without. In M. Kwee & T.L. Holdstock (Eds.), *Western and Buddhist psychology: Clinical perspectives* (pp. 77–117). Delft: Eburon.

Holdstock, T.L. (1996c). Discrepancy between the Person-Centred theories of self and of therapy. In R. Hutterer, G. Pawlowsky, P.F. Schmid, & R. Stipsits (Eds.), *Client-Centred and experiential psychotherapy: A paradigm in motion* (pp. 395–403). Berlin: Peter Lang.

Holdstock, T.L. (1996d). Anger and congruence reconsidered from the perspective of an interdependent orientation to the self. In R. Hutterer, G. Pawlowsky, P.F. Schmid, & R. Stipsits (Eds.), *Client-Centred and experiential psychotherapy: A paradigm in motion* (pp. 47–52). Berlin: Peter Lang.

Holdstock, T.L. (1996e). Implications of developments regarding the concept of the self for Client-Centred theory and practice. In U. Esser, H. Pabst, G.-W. Speierer (Eds.), *The power of the Person-Centred approach: New Challenges – perspectives – answers* (pp. 83–90). Köln: GwG-Verlag.

Holdstock, T.L. (1999). The perilous problem of neglecting indigenous cultures. *American Psychologist, 54*, 838–839.

Holtzman, W.H. (1997). Community psychology and full-service schools in different cultures. *American Psychologist, 52*, 381–389.

Horton, R. (1967). African traditional thought and western science. Part I: From tradition to science. *Africa, 37*, 155–187.

Hountondji, P. (1983). On "African philosophy". *Radical Philosophy, 33*, 20–25.

Houts, A.C., & Krasner, L. (1983). Values in science: Comment on Haan. *American Psychologist, 38*, 1253–1254.

Howard, G.S. (1985). The role of values in the science of psychology. *American Psychologist, 40*, 255–265.

Howard, G.S. (1991). Culture tales: A narrative approach to thinking, cross-cultural psychology, and psychotherapy. *American Psychologist. 46*, 187–197.

Howitt, D., & Owusu-Bempah, J. (1990). Racism in a British journal. *The Psychologist: Bulletin of The British Psychological Society, 3*, 396–400.

Howitt, D., & Owusu-Bempah, J. (1994). *The racism of psychology: Time for change.* Hemel Hempstead: Harvester Wheatsheaf.

Hubel, D.H., & Wiesel, T.N. (1963). Receptive fields of cells in striate cortex of very young, visually inexperienced kittens. *Journal of Neurophysiology, 26*, 994–1002.

Idowu, E.B. (1975). *African traditional religion.* London: SCM Press.

Ignatius, D. (1999, 25 May). Look out, "the older social structures are cracking". *International Herald Tribune*, p. 8.

Ikenga-Metuh, E. (1991). The concept of man in African traditional religion: With particular reference to the Igbo of Nigeria. In E.M. Uka (Ed.), *Readings in African traditional religion: Structure, meaning, relevance, future* (pp. 53–68). Berlin: Peter Lang.

Illich, I. (1977). *Limits to medicine.* New York: Penguin.

Jackson, G.G. (1982). Black psychology. An avenue to the study of Afro-Americans. *Journal of Black Studies, 12*, 241–260.

Jackson, A.P., & Sears, S.J. (1992). Implications of an Africentric worldview in reducing stress for African American women. *Journal of Counseling and Development, 71*, 184–190.

Jacobson, N.S., & Christensen, A. (1996). Studying the effectiveness of psychotherapy: How well can clinical trials do the job? *American Psychologist, 51,* 1031–1039.

Jacoby, R. (1977). *Social amnesia: A critique of conformist psychology from Adler to Laing.* Hassocks: Harvester Press.

Jagers, R.J., & Mock, L.O. (1993). Culture and social outcome among inner-city African American children: An Afrographic exploration. *Journal of Black Psychology, 19,* 391–405.

Jahn, J. (1972). African systems of thought. In S.H. Irvine & J.T. Sanders (Eds.), *Cultural adaptation within modern Africa* (pp. 81–90). New York: Columbia University Press.

Jahoda, G.G. (1984). Do we need the concept of culture? *Journal of Cross-Cultural psychology, 15,* 139–151.

Jahoda, G. (1988). J'accuse. In M.H. Bond (Ed.), *The cross-cultural challenge to social psychology* (pp. 86–95). London: Sage.

James, W. (1902/1985). *The varieties of religious experience.* Cambridge, MA: Harvard University Press.

James, W. (1907). *Pragmatism: A new name for some old ways of thinking.* New York: Longmans.

Jansz, (1991). Sociale individualiteit (Social individualism). *De Psycholoog, 26,* 541–544.

Janzen, J.M. (1994). Drums of affliction: Real phenomenon or scholarly chimera? In T.D. Blakely, W.E.A. van Beek, & D.L. Thomson (Eds.), *Religion in Africa: Experience and expression* (pp. 160–181). Portsmouth, NH: Heinemann.

Jing, Q. (1994). Development of psychology in China. *International Journal of Psychology, 29,* 667–675.

Johnson, J., & Magubane, P. (1979). *Soweto speaks.* Johannesburg: Ad. Donker.

Johnson, K. (1974). *Photographing the non-material world.* New York: Hawthorn Books.

Johnson, K. (1975). *The living aura.* New York: Hawthorne Books.

Jones, A.M. (1980). *Studies in African music. Vol. 1.* Oxford: Oxford University Press.

Jones, R.A. (1986). Social psychological research and clinical practice: An academic paradox. *Professional Psychology: Research and Practice, 17,* 535–540.

Jones, R.L. (Ed.).(1991). *Black psychology.* Berkeley: Cobb & Henry.

Jones, S.L. (1994). A constructive relationship for religion with the science and profession of psychology: Perhaps the boldest model yet. *American Psychologist, 49,* 184–199.

Jordan, J.V. (1984). Empathy and self boundaries. *Work in Progress, # 16.* Wellesley, MA: Stone Center Working Papers Series.

Jordan, J.V. (1987). Clarity and connection: Empathic knowing, desire and sexuality. *Work in Progress, # 29.* Wellesley, MA: Stone Center Working Papers Series.

Joseph, R. (1988). The right cerebral hemisphere: Emotion, music, visual-spatial skills, body-image, dreams, and awareness. *Journal of Clinical Psychology, 44,* 630–673.

Josselson, R. (1987). *Finding herself. Pathways to identity development in women.* London: Jossey-Bass.

Josselson, R. (1990, September). *Identity and relatedness in the life cycle.* Paper presented at the symposium on Identity and Development, Amsterdam.

Jourard, S.M. (1971). *The transparent self.* New York: Van Nostrand.

Jovanovski, T. (1995). The cultural approach of ethnopsychiatry: A review and critique. *New Ideas in Psychology, 13,* 281–297.

Kagitçibasi, C. (1995). Is psychology relevant to global human development issues? Experience from Turkey. *American Psychologist, 50,* 293–300.

Kagitçibasi, C. (1996a). The autonomous-relational self: A new synthesis. *European Psychologist*, *1*, 180–186.

Kagitçibasi, C. (1996b). Cross-cultural psychology and development. In J. Pandey, D. Sinha, & D.P.S. Bhawuk (Eds.), *Asian contributions to cross-cultural psychology* (pp. 42–49). New Delhi: Sage.

Kambon, K.K.K., & Hopkins, R. (1993). An African-centred analysis of Penn et al.'s critique of the own-race preference assumption underlying Africentric models of personality. *Journal of Black Psychology*, *19*, 342–349.

Kandinsky, W. (1914/1977). *Concerning the spiritual in art*. New York: Dover.

Karasu, T.B. (1986). The psychotherapies: Benefits and limitations. *American Journal of Psychotherapy*, *3*, 324–342.

Katz, R. (1983/84). Empowerment and synergy: Expanding the community's healing resources. *Prevention in Human Services*, *3*, 201–226.

Kazdin, A.E. (1986). Comparative outcome studies of psychotherapy: Methodological issues and strategies. *Journal of Consulting and Clinical Psychology*, *54*, 95–105.

Kelly, G. (1955). *The psychology of personal constructs*. New York: Norton.

Kim, M.-S., Hunter, J.E., Miyahara, A., Horvath, A.-M., Bresnahan, M., & Yoon, H.-J. (1996). Individual- vs. culture-level dimensions of individualism and collectivism: Effects on preferred conversational styles. *Communication Monographs*, *63*, 29–49.

Kim, U. (1990). Indigenous psychology: Science and applications. In R.W. Brislin (Ed.), *Applied cross-cultural psychology* (pp. 142–160). London: Sage.

Kim, U. (1995). Psychology, science and culture: Cross-cultural analysis of national psychologies. *International Journal of Psychology*, *30*, 662–679.

Kim, U., & Berry, J.W. (1993). *Indigenous psychologies. Research and experience in cultural context*. London: Sage.

Kimble, G.A. (1984). Psychology's two cultures. *American Psychologist*, *39*, 833–839.

Kimble, G.A. (1994). A frame of reference for psychology. *American Psychologist*, *49*, 510–519.

Kimble, G.A. (1998, April). Letter. *APA Monitor*, *29*, 3.

Kimmerle, H. (1995a). *Mazungumzo. Dialogen tussen Afrikaanse en Westerse filosofieën* (*Mazungumzo. Dialogues between African and Western philosophies*). Amsterdam: Boom.

Kimmerle, H. (1995b). The multiversum of cultures: The mutual relations between the cultures and the end of modernity. *Hitotsubashi Journal of Social Studies*, *27*, 143–150.

Kimmerle, H. (1995c). Das multiversum der kulturen. Einstellungen der zeitgenössichen europäisch-westlichen Philosophie zu den Philosophien anderer Kulturen (The multiversum of cultures. The orientation of contemporary Euro-Western philsophy to the philosphies of other cultures). In R. Berlinger, E. Fink, T. Imamichi, & W. Schrader (Eds.), *Perspectieven der Philosophie. Neues Jahrbuch*, *Vol. 9*, 269–292.

Kipnis, D. (1997). Ghosts, taxonomies, and social psychology. *American Psychologist*, *52*, 205–211.

Kitayama, S., & Markus, H.R. (1994). Introduction to cultural psychology and emotion research. In S. Kitayama & H.R. Markus (Eds.), *Emotion and culture: Empirical studies of mutual influence*. Washington, DC: American Psychological Association.

Koch, S. (1981). The nature and limits of psychological knowledge. Lessons of a century qua 'science'. *American Psychologist*, *36*, 257–269.

Korber, I. (1990). Indigenous healers in a future mental health system: A case for cooperation. *Psychology in Society*, *14*, 47–62.

REFERENCES

Kottler, A. (1988). Professionalisation of African healers: Apparent problems and constraints. *Psychology in Society, 11*, 2–17.

Kottler, A. (1990). South Africa: Psychology's dilemma of multiple discourses. *Psychology in Society, 13*, 27–36.

Kraut, R., Patterson, M., Lundmark, V., Kiesler, S., Mukopadhyay, T., & Scherlis, W. (1998). Does use of the Internet on home computers affect social involvement and personal well-being? A groundbreaking study of families empirically examines the social effects on home Internet use. *American Psychologist, 53*, 1017–1031.

Kriegler, S. (1993). Options and directions for psychology within a framework for mental health services in South Africa. *South African Journal of Psychology, 23*, 64–70.

Krige, E.J., & Krige, J.D. (1943). *The realm of the Rain-Queen*. Cape Town: Juta.

Kruger, D. (1974). Xhosa divining and contemporary psychotherapy – a reciprocal perspective. *Fort Hare Papers, 6*, 37–47.

Kruger, D. (1988). In search of a human science of psychology. *South African Journal of Psychology, 18*, 1–9.

Kuhn, T. (1962). *The structure of scientific revolutions*. Chicago: University of Chicago Press.

Kukla, A. (1992). Unification as a goal for psychology. *American Psychologist, 45*, 1054–1055.

Kunene, M. (1970). *Zulu poems*. New York: Africana Publishing Company.

Kupfersmid, J. (1988). Improving what is published: A model in search of an editor. *American Psychologist, 43*, 635–642.

Kwee, M.G.T. (Ed) (1990). *Psychotherapy, meditation and health: A cognitive-behavioural perspective*. London: East-West Publications.

Kwee, M.G.T., & Holdstock, T.L. (Eds.) (1996). *Western and Buddhist psychology: Clinical perspectives*. Delft: Eburon.

LaFromboise, T.D. (1988). American Indian mental health policy. *American Psychologist, 43*, 388–397.

Laing, R.D. (1969). *The divided self: An existential study in sanity and madness*. New York: Penguin.

Laing, R.D. (1970). *The politics of experience and the bird of paradise*. Harmondsworth, Middlesex: Penguin.

Lambo, T.A. (1971, December). Interview with Dr. TA Lambo. *UNICEF News*, 9–14.

Landrine, H. (1992). Clinical implications of cultural differences: The referential versus the indexical self. *Clinical Psychology Review, 12*, 401–415.

Leary, D.E. (1983). On scientific morality. *American Psychologist, 38*, 1253.

Leary, D.E., Kessel, F., & Bevan, W. (1998). Sigmund Koch (1917–1996). *American Psychologist, 53*, 316–317.

Lee, G. (1998, April). Letter. *APA Monitor, 29*, 3.

Lee, Y-T. (1994). Why does American psychology have cultural limitations? *American Psychologist, 49*, 525.

Leicester, M. (1989). *Multicultural education: From theory to practice*. Windsor, Berks: Nfer-Nelson.

Leifer, R. (1990). Introduction: The medical model as the ideology of the therapeutic state. *Journal of Mind and Behavior, 11*, 247–258.

Lemmes, F., de Ridder, D., & Lieshout, P. van (1991). De fragmentatie van de psychotherapie. *Tijdschrift voor Psychotherapie, 17*, 281–296.

Letlaka-Rennert, K., Luswazi, P., Helms, J.E., & Zea, M.C. (1997). Does the womanist identity model predict aspects of psychological functioning in black South African women? *South African Journal of Psychology, 27*, 236–243.

Leung, K. (1995). Systemic consideration: Factors facilitating and impeding the development of psychology in developing countries. *International Journal of Psychology, 30*, 693–706.

Levenson, M.R. (1992). Rethinking psychopathy. *Theory & Psychology, 2*, 51–71.

Levine, R.A. (1970). Psycho-social studies in Africa.. *African Studies Review, 13*, 105–111.

Leviton, L.C. (1996). Integrating psychology and public health: Challenges and opportunities. *American psychologist, 51*, 42–51.

Levy, C.H. (1984). The metamorphosis of clinical psychology. Toward a new charter as human services psychology. *American Psychologist, 39*, 486–494.

Levy, D.A. (1992). A proposed category for the Diagnostic and Statistical Manual of Mental Disorders (DSM): Pervasive labeling disorder. *Journal of Humanistic Psychology, 32*, 121–125.

Levy, J. (1988). Cerebral asymmetry and aesthetic experience. In I. Rentschler, B. Herzberger, & D. Epstein (Eds.), *Beauty and the brain: Biological aspects of aesthetics* (pp. 219–242). Basel: Birkhaüser Verlag.

Lewin, K. (1951). *Field theory in social science.* Chicago: University of Chicago Press.

Lewis, C.D. (1965). *The poetic image.* London: Jonathan Cape.

Lewis-Williams, J.D. (1983). *The rock art of southern Africa.* Cambridge: Cambridge University Press.

Lindsey, D. (1977). Participation and influence in publication review proceedings: A reply. *American Psychologist, 30*, 486–494.

Lindzey, G., Hall, C., & Thompson, R.F. (1975). *Psychology.* New York: Worth Publishers.

Locke, D.C. (1992). *Increasing multicultural understanding: A comprehensive model.* London: Sage.

Locke, E.A. (1988). The virtue of selfishness. *American Psychologist, 43*, 481.

López, S.R., Grover, K.P., Holland, D., Johnson, M.J., Kain, C.D., Kanel, K., Melliins, C.A., & Rhyne, M.C. (1989). Development of culturally sensitive psychotherapists. *Professional Psychology: Research and Practice, 20*, 369–376.

Louw, J. (1988). Professionalisation as a moral concern. *Psychology in Society, 9*, 66–80.

Louw, J. (1992). South Africa. In V.S. Sexton & J.D. Hogan (Eds.), *International psychology: Views from around the world* (pp. 353–363). Lincoln: University of Nebraska Press.

Louw, J. (1997). Social context and psychological testing in South Africa, 1918–1939. *Theory & Psychology, 7*, 235–256.

Luce, G.G. (1973). *Body time: The natural rhythms of the body.* Frogmore, St. Albans, Herts: Paladin.

MacIntyre, A. (1988). *Whose justice? Which rationality?* Notre Dame: University of Notre Dame Press.

Mack, J.E. (1992). Toward a psychology of our time. In S.Staub & P. Green (Eds.), *Psychology and social responsibility. Facing global challenges* (pp. 399–413). New York: New York University Press.

MacLachlan, M., & Carr, S. (1997). Psychology in Malawi: Towards a constructive debate. *The Psychologist: Bulletin of The British Psychological Society, 10*, 77–79.

MacLean, P.D. (1967). The brain in relation to empathy and medical education. *The Journal of Nervous and Mental Disease, 144*, 374–382.

Maffesoli, M. (1995). *The time of the tribes: The decline of individualsim in mass societies*. London: Sage.

Magnusson, D., & Törestad, B. (1993). A holistic view of personality: A model revisited. *Annual Review of Psychology, 44*, 427–452.

Maher, B.A. (1985). Underpinnings of today's chaotic diversity. *International Newsletter of Paradigmatic Psychology, 1*, 17–19.

Malinowski, B. (1926). *Myth in primitive psychology*. London: Kegan Paul.

Manganyi, N.C. (1980). Emerging neurotic 'metaphors' and the possibilities of a therapeutic culture. In H.F. Swanepoel, J.W. Von Mollendorf, A.B. Fourie, A. Umlaw, & N.C. Manganyi, *Toegepaste psigologie en die swart Suid-Afrikaner* (Applied psychology and the black South African). Potchefstroom: Wetenskaplike bydrae van die PU vir CHO, Reeks A: Geesteswetenskappe, nr. 34.

Manganyi, N.C. (1991). *Treachery and innocence: Psychology and racial difference in South Africa*. Johannesburg: Ravan Press.

Manganyi, N.C., & du Toit, A. (Eds.) (1990). *Political violence and the struggle in South Africa*. London: Macmillan.

Manicas, P.T., & Secord, P.F. (1983). Implications for psychology of the new philosophy of science. *American Psychologist, 38*, 399–413.

Maquet, J. (1972). *Africanity. The cultural unity of black Africa*. New York: Oxford University Press.

Markus, H.R., & Kitayama, S. (1991). Culture and the self: Implications for cognition, emotion, and motivation. *Psychological Review, 98*, 224–253.

Markus, H.R., & Kitayama, S. (1994). The cultural construction of self and emotion: Implications for social behavior. In H.R. Markus & S. Kitayama (Eds.), *Emotion and culture: Empirical studies of mutual influence* (pp. 89–130). Washington, DC: American Psychological Association.

Marsella, A.J. (1998). Toward a "global-community psychology." *American Psychologist, 53*, 1282–1291.

Marsella, A.J., & White, G.M. (Eds.) (1989). *Cultural conceptions of mental health and therapy*. London: D. Reidel.

Masson, J. (1989). *Against therapy: Emotional tyranny and the myth of psychological healing*. New York: Atheneum.

Matarazzo, J.D. (1987). There is only one psychology, no specialities, but many applications. *American Psychologist, 42*, 893–903.

Matsumoto, D., Kudoh, T., & Takeuchi, S. (1996). Changing patterns of individualism and collectivism in the United States and Japan. *Culture & Psychology, 2*, 77–107.

May, R. (1982). The problem of evil: An open letter to Carl Rogers. *Journal of Humanistic Psychology, 22*, 10–21.

May, A., & Spangenberg, J.J. (1997). Androgyny and coping in men with a managerial orientation. *South African Journal of Psychology, 27*, 244–249.

Mayekiso, T.V., & Bhana, K. (1997). Sexual harassment: perceptions and experiences of students at the University of Transkei. *South African Journal of Psychology, 27*, 230–235.

Mays, V.M., Bullock, M., Rosenzweig, M.R., & Wessells, M. (1998). Ethnic conflict: Global challenges and psychological perspectives. *American Psychologist, 53*, 737–742.

Mays, V.M., Rubin, J., Sabourin, M., & Walker, L. (1996). Moving toward a global psychology: Changing theories and practice to meet the needs of a changing world. *American Psychologist, 51*, 485–487.

Mazrui, A.A. (1986). *The Africans. A triple heritage.* London: BBC Publications.

Mazrui, A.A. (1990). *Cultural forces in world politics.* London: James Currey.

Mbigi, L., & Maree, J. (1995). *Ubuntu: The spirit of African transformation management.* Randburg: Knowledge Resources.

Mbiti, J.S. (1975). *Concept of God in Africa.* London: SPCK Press.

Mbiti, J.S. (1991a). *Introduction to African religion.* London: Heinemann.

Mbiti, J.S. (1991b). Where African religion is found. In E.M. Uka (Ed.), *Readings in African tradition religion: Structure, meaning, relevance, future* (pp. 69–75). Bern: Peter Lang.

McCrae, R.R., & Costa, P.T. (1997). Personality trait structure as a human universal. *American Psychologist, 52,* 509–516.

McGovern, T.V., Furumoto, L., Halpern, D.F., Kimble, G.A., & McKeachie, W.J. (1991). Liberal education, study in depth, and the arts and sciences major – psychology. *American Psychologist, 46,* 598–605.

McGuire, P.A. (1998a). In Northern Ireland, stories of ethnic conflict from war-weary lands. *APA Monitor, 29,* 14–15.

McGuire, P.A. (1998b). Historic conference focuses on creating a new discipline. *APA Monitor, 29,* 1,15.

McGuire, P.A. (1999). Multicultural summit cheers packed house. *APA Monitor, 30,* 26.

McKendrick, B., & Hoffman, W. (1990). *People and violence in South Africa.* Cape Town: Oxford University Press.

McManus, F.E. (1993). Constructivists and creationists. *American Psychologist, 48,* 57–58.

McNally, R.J. (1992). Disunity in psychology: Chaos or speciation? *American Psychologist, 45,* 1054.

Mead, G.H. (1968). The genesis of the self. In C. Gordon & K.J. Gergen (Eds.), *The self in social interaction* (pp. 51–59). New York: Wiley.

Mgoduso, T., & Butchart, A. (1992). Authoritarianism and autonomy. 2. Power, politics and alienated nursing care in a South African primary health care system. *South African Journal of Psychology, 22,* 194–201.

Michael, S.O. (1997). Models of multiculturalism: implications for the twenty-first century leaders. *European Journal of International Studies, 8,* 231–245.

Miles, S. (1996). The cultural capital of consumption: Understanding 'postmodern' identities in a cultural context. *Culture & Psychology, 2,* 139–158.

Miller, J.B. (1976). *Toward a new psychology of women.* Harmondsworth, Middlesex: Penguin.

Miller, J.B. (1984). The development of women's sense of self. *Work in progress, No.12.* Wellesley, MA: Stone Center Working Papers Series.

Miller, J.G. (1988). Bridging the content–structure dichotomy: Culture and the self. In M.H. Bond (Ed.), *The cross-cultural challenge to social psychology* (pp. 266–281). London: Sage.

Miller, R. (1989). Critical psychology: A territorial imperative. *Psychology in Society, 12,* 3–18.

Milward, P., & Schoder, R. (1975). *Landscape and inscape.* London: Paul Elek.

Minoura, Y. (1996). A plea for a hypothesis-generating approach to link the individual's world of meaning and society's cultural orientation: A commentary on Oerter et al. (1996). *Culture & Psychology, 2,* 53–61.

Mirowski, J. (1990). Subjective boundaries and combinations in psychiatric diagnosis. *The Journal of Mind and Behavior, 11,* 407–423.

Mirowski, J., & Ross, C.E. (1989). Psychiatric diagnosis as reified measurement. *Journal of Health and Social Behavior, 30*, 11–25.

Misumi, J., & Peterson, M.F. (1990). Psychology in Japan. *Annual Review of Psychology, 41*, 213–241.

Mitchell, G., Mndende, N., Phiri, I.A., & Stonier, J. (1993). *The end of the tunnel. Religion education in South Africa.* Cape Town: ICRSA.

Moghaddam, F.M. (1987). Psychology in the three worlds: As reflected by the crisis in social psychology and the move toward indigenous third-world psychology. *American Psychologist, 42*, 912–920.

Moghaddam, F.M. (1990). Modulative and generative orientations in psychology: Implications for psychology in the three worlds. *Journal of Social Issues, 46*, 21–41.

Mönnig, H.O. (1967). *The Pedi.* Pretoria: J.L. van Schaik.

Moosa, F., Moonsamy, G., & Fridjhon, P. (1997). Identification patterns among black students at a predominantly white university. *South African Journal of Psychology, 27*, 256–260.

Moss, T. (1976). *The probability of the impossible.* London: Routledge & Kegan Paul.

Mphahlele, E. (1962). *The African image.* London: Faber & Faber.

Mphahlele, E. (1963). African culture trends. In Judd, P. (Ed.), *African independence* (pp. 109–139). New York: Dell.

Mphahlele, E. (1984). *Afrika my music. An autobiography 1957–1983.* Johannesburg: Ravan Press.

Mphahlele, E. (1987, November). *Images of the African personality.* Paper presented at the Conference on Black Culture and Business. Johannesburg.

Mphahlele, T. (1988, 5 December). Can only whites be liberals? *The Star.*

Mthethwa, B.N. (1986, July). *Shembe's religious dances: Can African Christianity survive without dance?* Paper presented at the NERMIC Conference, Johannesburg, South Africa.

Mthethwa, B.N. (1988, November). *The meaning of music and dance among African societies: Can the business world disregard culture?* Paper presented at the conference on Black Culture and Business, Johannesburg, South Africa.

Mudimbe, V.Y. (1988). *The invention of Africa: Gnosis, philosophy, and the order of knowledge.* Bloomington: Indiana University Press.

Murray, C. (1979). The work of men, women and the ancestors: Social reproduction in the periphery of Southern Africa. In S. Wallman (Ed.), *Social anthropology of work.* New York: Academic Press.

Myers, L.J. (1991). Expanding the psychology of knowledge optimally: The importance of world view revisited. In R.L. Jones (Ed.), *Black psychology.* Berkeley: Cobb & Henry.

Myers, L.J. (1993). *Understanding an Afrocentric world view: Introduction to an optimal psychology.* Dubuque, Iowa: Kendall/Hunt.

Naidoo, A.V. (1994, January). *Challenging the hegemony of Eurocentric psychology.* Paper presented at the Psychology and Societal Transformation Conference, University of the Western Cape, Bellville, South Africa.

Naranjo, C., & Ornstein, R. (1971). *On the psychology of meditation.* New York: Penguin.

Natsoulas, T. (1990). The pluralistic approach to the nature of feelings. *The Journal of Mind and Behavior, 11*, 173–218.

Nell, V. (1990). One world, one psychology: 'Relevance' and ethnopsychology. *South African Journal of Psychology, 20*, 129–140.

Nell, V. (1993). Structural blocks to a liberatory psychology in South Africa: Medical politics, guilt consciousness, and the clinical delusion. In L.J. Nicholas (Ed.), *Psychology and oppression: Critiques and proposals*. Johannesburg: Skotaville.

Nelson, A. (1985). Psychological equivalence. Awareness and response-ability in our nuclear age. *American Psychologist, 40*, 549–556.

Newman, F.L., & Tejeda, M.J. (1996). The need for research that is designed to support decisions in the delivery of mental health services. *American Psychologist, 51*, 1040–1049.

Ngubane, H. (1977). *Body and mind in Zulu medicine*. London: Academic Press.

NIMH (1995). *Basic behavioural science research for mental health: a national investment*. Washington, DC: National Institute of Mental Health.

Nisbett, R.E. (1978). A guide for reviewers: Editorial hardball in the '70s. *American Psychologist, 33*, 519–520.

Nketia, J.H.K. (1974). *The music of Africa*. London: W.W. Norton.

Nobles, W. (1972). African philosophy. Foundations for black psychology. In R. Jones (Ed.), *Black Psychology*. New York: Harper & Row.

Nsamenang, A.B. (1992). *Human development in cultural context: A Third World perspective*. Newbury Park, CA: Sage.

Nsamenang, A.B. (1993). Psychology in sub-Saharan Africa. *Psychology & Developing Societies, 5*, 171–184.

Nsamenang, A.B. (1995). Theories of developmental psychology for a cultural perspective: A view from Africa. *Psychology & Developing Societies, 7*, 1–19.

Nsamenang, A.B. (1996). Cultural organization of human development within the family context. In S.C. Carr, J.F. Schumaker et al. (Eds.), *Psychology and the developing world* (pp. 60–70). Westport, CT: Praeger.

Nsamenang, A.B. (1997). Towards an Afrocentric perspective in developmental psychology. *Ife Psychologia: An International Journal, 5*, 127–139.

Nsamenang, A.B., & Dawes, A. (1998). Developmental psychology as political psychology in sub-Saharan Africa: The challenge of Africanisation. *Applied Psychology: An International Review, 47*, 73–87.

Nürnberger, K. (1988). *Theological ethics. Study guide: Introduction to theological ethics*. Pretoria: Pretoria University Press.

O'Brien, M. (1989). *Reproducing the world*. Boulder: Westview Press.

O'Donohue, W. (1989). The (even) bolder model. The clinical psychologist as metaphysician-scientist-practitioner. *American Psychologist, 44*, 1460–1468.

Oduyoye, M. (1996). *Peace and justice, a theological hermeneutic through an African woman's eyes*. Amsterdam: Free University Press.

Ogbonnaya, A.O. (1994). Person as community: An African understanding of the person as an intrapsychic community. *Journal of Black Psychology, 20*, 75–87.

Omer, H., & London, P. (1988). Metamorphosis in psychotherapy: End of the systems era. *Psychotherapy, 25*, 171–180.

Omotoso, K. (1994). *Season of migration to the South: Africa's crises reconsidered*. Cape Town: Tafelberg.

Ornstein, R. (1972). *The psychology of consciousness*. San Francisco: W.H. Freeman.

Owusu-Bempah, J., & Howitt, D. (1994). Racism and the psychological textbook. *The Psychologist: Bulletin of The British Psychological Society, 7*, 163–166.

Owusu-Bempah, J., & Howitt, D. (1995). How Eurocentric psychology damages Africa. *The Psychologist: Bulletin of The British Psychological Society, 8*, 462–465.

Parker, I. (1989). *The crisis in modern social psychology – and how to end it*. London: Routledge.

229

Parrinder, E.G. (1969). God in African mythology. In J.M. Kitagawa & C.H. Long (Eds.), *Myths and symbols: Studies in honour of Mircea Eliade*. Chicago: University of Chicago Press.

Patel, F. (1997). Culture in science education. *European Journal of Intercultural Studies*, 8, 213–230.

Patterson, C.H. (1986). Culture and psychology in Hong Kong. *American Psychologist*, 41, 926.

Paul, G. (1988). Philosophical theories of beauty and scientific research on the brain. In I. Rentschler, B. Herzberger, & D. Epstein (Eds.), *Beauty and the brain: Biological aspects of aesthetics* (pp. 15–27). Basel: Birkhaüser Verlag.

Payton, C.R. (1984). Who must do the hard things? *American Psychologist*, 39, 391–397.

Pearce, J. (1996, 10–16 May). Academic search for an African identity. *Mail and Guardian*, p. 12.

Peavy, R.V. (1996). Counselling as a culture of healing. *British Journal of Guidance and Counselling*, 24, 141–150.

Peele, S. (1981). Reductionism in the psychology of the eighties. Can biochemistry eliminate addiction, mental illness, and pain? *American Psychologist*, 36, 807–818.

Peele, S. (1990). Behavior in a vacuum: Social-psychological theories of addiction that deny the social and psychological meanings of behavior. *The Journal of Mind and Behavior*, 11, 513–530.

Pelletier, K.R. (1978). *Toward a science of consciousness*. New York: Dell.

Peltzer, K., & Bless, C. (1989). History and present status of professional psychology in Zambia. *Psychology and Developing Societies*, 1, 53–64.

Penn, M.L., Gaines, S.O., & Phillips, L. (1993). On the desirability of own-group preference. *Journal of Black Psychology*, 19, 303–321.

Penn, M.L., & Kiesel, L. (1994). Toward a global world community: The role of black psychologists. *Journal of Black Psychology*, 20, 398–417.

Perloff, R. (1987). Self-interest and personal responsibility redux. *American Psychologist*, 42, 3–11.

Perry, J.W. (1974). *The far side of madness*. Englewood Cliffs, NJ: Prentice Hall.

Peterson, G.R. (1985). Twenty years of practitioner training in psychology. *American Psychologist*, 40, 441–451.

Petrinovitch, L. (1979). Probabilistic functionalism. A conception of research method. *American Psychologist*, 34, 373–390.

Phillips, L., Penn, M.L., & Gaines, S.O. (1993). A hermeneutic rejoinder to ourselves and our critics. *Journal of Black Psychology*, 19, 350–357.

Phinney, J.S. (1996). When we talk about American ethnic groups, what do we mean? *American Psychologist*, 51, 918–927.

Phinney, J.S., & Devich-Navarro, M. (in press). Variations in bicultural identification among African American and Mexican American adolescents. *Journal of Research on Adolescence*.

Pityana, N.B., Ramphele, M., Mpulwana, M., & Wilson, L. (Eds.) (1991). *Bounds of possibility: The legacy of Steve Biko and Black Consciousness*. Cape Town: David Philip.

Polanyi, M. (1960). *Personal knowledge*. Chicago: University of Chicago Press.

Prabhavananda, S., & Isherwood, C. (1953). (Trans.). *Bhagavad-Gita: The song of God*. London: Phoenix House.

Pribram, K.H. (1982). What the fuss is all about. In K. Wilber (Ed.), *The holographic paradigm and other paradoxes: Exploring the leading edge of science*. Boulder: Shambhala.

Prilleltensky, I. (1989). Psychology and the status quo. *American Psychologist, 44,* 795–802.

Prilleltensky, I. (1997). Values, assumptions, and practices: Assessing the moral implications of psychological discourse and action. *American Psychologist, 52,* 517–535.

Rabasca, L. (1999, April). Child-abuse prevention efforts still too few. *APA Monitor, 30,* 30.

Rao, K.R. (1997). Two faces of consciousness: A look at eastern and western perspectives. *Journal of Indian Psychology, 15,* 1–24.

Raspberry, W. (1997, 14 January). Sewing black Americans into the patchwork quilt. *International Herald Tribune.*

Reed, J., & Wake, C. (Eds.) (1979). *Senghor, prose and poetry.* London: Heinemann.

Regard, M., & Landis, T. (1988). Beauty may differ in each half of the eye of the beholder. In I. Rentschler, B. Herzberger, & D. Epstein (Eds.), *Beauty and the brain: Biological aspects of aesthetics* (pp. 243–256). Basel: Birkhaüser Verlag.

Reid, P.T. (1994). The real problem in the study of culture. *American Psychologist, 49,* 524–525.

Resler, H., & Walton, P. (1974). How social is it? In N. Armistead (Ed.), *Reconstructing social psychology.* Harmondsworth, Middlesex: Penguin.

Resolutions approved by the National Conference on Graduate Education in Psychology. (1987). *American Psychologist, 42,* 1070–1084.

Retief, A. (1989). The debate about the relevance of South African psychology – a metatheoretical imperative. *South African Journal of Psychology, 19,* 75–83.

Rhee, E., Uleman, J., & Lee, H. (1996). Variations in collectivism and individualism by in-group and culture: Confirmatory factor analyses. *Journal of Personality and Social Psychology, 71,* 1037–1054.

Rice, C.E. (1997). Scenarios: The scientist-practitioner split and the future of psychology. *American Psychologist, 52,* 1173–1181.

Richards, D. (1981). The Nyama of the blacksmith: The metaphysical significance of metallurgy in Africa. *Journal of Black Studies, 12,* 218–238.

Richter, L.M., Griesel, R.D., Durrheim, K., Wilson, M., Surendorff, N., & Asafo-Agyei, L. (1998). Employment opportunities for psychology graduates in South Africa: A contemporary analysis. *South African Journal of Psychology, 28,* 1–7.

Rijsdijk, F. (1997). *The genetics of neural speed: A genetic study on nerve conduction velocity, reation times and psychometric abilities.* Ph.D. dissertation, Vrije Universiteit, Amsterdam.

Rinder, W. (1973). *Spectrum of love.* Millbrae, CA: Celestial Arts Publishing.

Roberts, J. (1996, 14 October). African sage who won the hearts of the French. *The Independent,* p. 12.

Rock, B. (1994). A wolf in sheep's clothing?: Theoretical diversity and the drive toward sameness. *Psychology in Society, 18,* 56–59.

Rogers, C.R. (1942). *Counseling and psychotherapy.* Boston: Houghton Mifflin.

Rogers, C.R. (1951). *Client-centered therapy.* Boston: Houghton Mifflin.

Rogers, C.R. (1969). *Freedom to learn: A view of what education might become.* Columbus, OH: Charles E. Merrill.

Rogers, C.R. (1977). *Carl Rogers on personal power.* New York: Delacorte Press.

Rogers, C.R. (1979). Groups in two cultures. *Personnel & Guidance Journal, 38,* 11–13.

Rogers, C.R. (1980). *A way of being.* Boston: Houghton Mifflin.

Rogers, C.R. (1982). Notes on Rollo May. *Journal of Humanistic Psychology, 22,* 8–9.

Rogers, C.R. (1985). Toward a more human science of the person. *Journal of Humanistic Psychology, 23*, 7–24.

Rogers, J.D., Spencer, J., & Uyangoda, J. (1998). Sri Lanka: Political violence and ethnic conflict. *American Psychologist, 53*, 771–777.

Rogler, L.H., Malgady, R.G., Costantino, G., & Blumenthal, R. (1987). What do culturally sensitive mental health services mean? The case of Hispanics. *American Psychologist, 42*, 565–570.

Rogoff, B., & Chavajay, P. (1995). What's become of research on the cultural basis of cognitive development. *American Psychologist, 50*, 859–877.

Roland, A. (1992). *In search of self in India and Japan. Toward a cross-cultural psychology.* Delhi: Ajanta Publications.

Rosenberger, N.R. (1992). *Japanese sense of self.* Cambridge: Cambridge University Press.

Rosenthal, R. (1966). *Experimenter effects in behavioral research.* New York: Appleton-Century-Crofts.

Rosenzweig, M.R. (1984). U.S. psychology and world psychology. *American Psychologist, 39*, 877–884.

Rotter, J.B. (1954). *Social learning and clinical psychology.* Englewood Cliffs, NJ: Prentice-Hall.

Rotter, J.B. (1990). Internal versus external control of reinforcement: A case history of a variable. *American Psychologist, 45*, 489–493.

Rouhana, N.N., & Bar-Tal, D. (1998). Psychological dynamics of intractable ethno-national conflicts. *American Psychologist, 53*, 761–770.

Royce, J.R. (1970). *Toward unification in psychology. The first Banff conference on Theoretical Psychology.* Toronto: University of Toronto Press.

Royce, J.R. (1987). A strategy for developing unifying theory in psychology. In A.W. Staats & L.P. Mos (Eds.), *Annals of theoretical psychology (Vol. 2)* (pp. 275–284). New York: Plenum.

Rubin, W, (1984a). Modernist primitivism: An introduction. In W. Rubin (Ed.), *"Primitivism" in 20th century art. Affinity of the tribal and the modern (Vol. 1)* (pp. 1–81). New York: The Museum of Modern Art.

Rubin, W. (1984b). *"Primitivism" in 20th century art. Affinity of the tribal and the modern. Vols. 1 & 2.* New York: The Museum of Modern Art.

Rudin, S.A. (1997). Multiethnicity is divisive and basically a bankrupt idea. *American Psychologist, 52*, 1248.

Russell, R.W. (1984). Psychology in its world context. *American Psychologist, 39*, 1017–1025.

Rutter, M.J. (1997). Nature-nurture integration: The example of antisocial behavior. *American Psychologist, 52*, 390–398.

Ryan, W. (1971). *Blaming the victim.* New York: Pantheon.

Sahlins, M. (1996). The sadness of sweetness. The native anthropology of Western cosmology. *Current Anthropology, 37*, 395–428.

Saley, E. (1996). *The Truth and Reconciliation Commission: A prerequisite to nation building in the "new" South Africa.* Unpublished paper.

Saling, M., Abrams, R., & Chester, H. (1983). A photographic survey of lateral cradling preferences in black and white women. *South African Journal of Psychology, 13*, 135–136.

Samples, B., Charles, C., & Barnhart, D. (1977). *The wholeschool book.* Reading, MA: Addison-Wesley.

Sampson, E.E. (1981). Cognitive psychology as ideology. *American Psychologist, 36,* 730–743.

Sampson, E.E. (1985). The decentralization of identity: Toward a revised concept of personal and social order. *American Psychologist, 40,* 1203–1211.

Sampson, E.E. (1988). The debate on individualism: Indigenous psychologies of the individual and their role in personal and societal functioning. *American Psychologist, 43,* 15–22.

Sampson, E.E. (1989a). The challenge of social change for psychology: Globalization and psychology's theory of the person. *American Psychologist, 44,* 914–921.

Sampson, E.E. (1989b). The deconstruction of the self. In J. Shotter & K.J. Gergen (Eds.), *Texts of identity* (pp. 1–19). London: Sage.

Sampson, E.E. (1993). Identity politics: Challenges to psychology's understanding. *American Psychologist, 48,* 1219–1230.

Sampson, E.E. (1994). Sperry's cognitive revolution. *American Psychologist, 49,* 818–819.

Sarason, S.B. (1981). An asocial psychology and misdirected clinical psychology. *American Psychologist, 36,* 827–836.

Sarbin, T.R. (1990). Toward the obsolescence of the schizophrenia hypothesis. *The Journal of Mind and Behavior, 11,* 259–283.

Sawyer, H. (1970). *God, ancestor or creator?* London: Longman.

Scarr, S. (1985). Constructing psychology. Making facts and fables for our times. *American Psychologist, 40,* 499–512.

Schipper, M. (1998, 23 May). Een aangename orde is fundamenteel (Order that is pleasing is fundamental). *Vrij Nederland,* p. 66–67.

Schneider, K.J. (1998). Toward a science of the heart: Romanticism and the revival of psychology. *American Psychologist, 53,* 277–289.

Schneider, S.F. (1996). Random thoughts on leaving the fray. *American Psychologist, 51,* 715–721.

Schutte, A.G. (1972). Thapelo ya sephiri: A study of secret prayer groups in Soweto. *African Studies, 31,* 245–260.

Schutte, A.G. (1974). Dual religious orientation in an urban African church. *African Studies, 33,* 113–120.

Schutte, G. (1995). *What racists believe. Race relations in South Africa and the United States today.* London: Sage.

Schwartz, S.H. (1990). Individualism–collectivism: Critique and proposed refinements. *Journal of Cross-Cultural Psychology, 21,* 139–157.

Scott, T.R. (1991). A personal view of the future of psychology departments. *American Psychologist, 46,* 975–976.

Sebidi, L.J. (1988, 2 December). Towards a definition of '*ubuntu*' as African humanism. *Sowetan,* 9–10.

Seedat, M. (1997). The quest for a liberatory psychology. *South African Journal of Psychology, 27,* 261–270.

Seedat, M. (1998). A characterization of South African psychology (1948–1988): The impact of exclusionary ideology. *South African Journal of Psychology, 28,* 78–84.

Seedat, M., Butchart, A., & Nell, V. (1991). Family therapy in primary health care: Skills training and outcome evaluation. *Contemporary Family Therapy, 13,* 143–163.

Seedat, M., & Nell, V. (1990). Third world or one world: Mysticism, pragmatism, and pain in family therapy in South Africa. *South African Journal of Psychology, 20,* 141–149.

Seedat, M., & Nell, V. (1992). Authoritarianism and autonomy. 1. Conflicting value systems in the introduction of psychological seervices in a South African primary health care system. *South African Journal of Psychology, 22*, 185–193.

Segall, M.H. (1970). Comments on "Psycho-social studies in Africa". *African Studies Review, 13*, 113–114.

Segall, M.H., Lonner, W.J., & Berry, J.W. (1998). Cross-cultural psychology as a scholarly discipline: On the flowering of culture in behavioral research. *American Psychologist, 53*, 1101–1110.

Seligman, M.E.P. (1996). Science as an ally of practice. *American Psychologist, 51*, 1072–1079.

Seligman, M.E.P. (1998a, January). Building human strength: psychology's forgotten mission. *APA Monitor, 29*, 2.

Seligman, M.E.P. (1998b, April). Positive social science. *APA Monitor, 29*, 2,5.

Semmes, C.E. (1981). Foundations of an Afrocentric social science. Implications for curriculum-building, theory, and research in black studies. *Journal of Black Studies, 12*, 3–17.

Sepamla, S. (1981, 2 April). Towards an African theatre. *Rand Daily Mail*, p. 15.

Serote, W. (1978). *Yakhal'inkomo*. Johannesburg: Ravan Press.

Setiloane, G.M. (1989). *African theology: An introduction*. Johannesburg: Skotaville.

Sharatt, P. (1995). Is educational psychology alive and well in the new South Africa? *South African Journal of Psychology, 25*, 211–216.

Sherman, R.A. (1996). *Phantom pain*. New York: Plenum.

Shweder, R.A. (1994). *Thinking through cultures. Expeditions with cultural psychology*. Cambridge, MA: Harvard University Press.

Shweder, R.A., & Bourne, E.J. (1989). Does the concept of the person vary cross-culturally? In A.J. Marsella & G.M. White (Eds.), *Cultural conceptions of mental health and therapy* (pp. 97–137). London: D. Reidel.

Shweder, R.A., & Bourne, E.J. (1991). Does the concept of the person vary cross-culturally? In R.A. Sweder (Ed.), *Thinking through cultures: Expeditions with cultural psychology* (pp. 113–155). Cambridge, MA: Harvard University Press.

Shweder, R.A., & Sullivan, M.A. (1993). Cultural psychology: Who needs it? *Annual Review of Psychology, 44*, 497–523.

Siegfried, W. (1988). Dance, the fugitive form of art aesthetics as behavior. In I. Rentschler, B. Herzberger, & D. Epstein (Eds.), *Beauty and the brain: Biological aspects of aesthetics* (pp. 117–145). Basel: Birkhaüser Verlag.

Silberbauer, G.B. (1965). *Report to the Government of Bechuanaland on the Bushman survey*. Mafeking: Bechuanaland Press.

Simone, M. (1993). Western war machines: Contextualising psychology in Africa. In L.J. Nicholas (Ed.), *Psychology and oppression: Critiques and proposals* (pp. 81–127). Johannesburg: Skotaville.

Simonton, C. (1975). The role of the mind in cancer therapy. In S.R. Dean (Ed.), *Psychiatry and mysticism*. Chicago: Nelson-Hall.

Sinha, D. (1990). Applied cross-cultural psychology and the developing world. *International Journal of Psychology, 25*, 381–386.

Sinha, D. (1994a). Indigenisation of psychology in India. *Indian Psychological Abstracts and Reviews, 1*, 179–215.

Sinha, D. (1994b). Indigenous psychology: Need and potentiality. *Journal of Indian Psychology, 12*, 1–7.

Sinha, D. (1997). Indigenizing psychology. In J.W. Berry, Y.H. Poortinga, & J. Pandey

(Eds.), *Handbook of cross-cultural psychology, Vol. 1: Theory and method* (pp. 129–169). Boston: Allyn & Bacon.

Sleek, S. (1998, December). Psychology's cultural competence, once 'simplistic,' now broadening. *APA Monitor, 29*, 1,27.

Slife, B.D., & Williams, R.N. (1997). Toward a theoretical psychology: Should a subdiscipline be formally recognized? *American Psychologist, 52*, 117–129.

Sloan, T.S. (1990). Psychology for the third world. *Journal of Social Issues, 46*, 1–20.

Smart, N. (1983). *World views. Crosscultural explorations of human beliefs*. New York: Charles Scribner.

Smart, N. (1989). *The world religions. Old traditions and modern transformations*. New York: Cambridge University Press.

Smedslund, J. (1984). The invisible obvious: Culture in psychology. In K. Lagerspetz & P. Niemi (Eds.), *Psychology in the 1990s* (pp. 443–452). Amsterdam: North-Holland.

Smith, D.N. (1998). The psychocultural roots of genocide: Legitimacy and crisis in Rwanda. *American Psychologist, 53*, 743–753.

Smith, W.D., & Yates, A.C. (1980). Editorial in Black Studies. *Journal of Black Studies, 10*, 269–277.

Smuts, J.C. (1926). *Holism and evolution*. London: Macmillan.

Snow, C.P. (1963). *The two cultures: And a second look*. New York: Cambridge University Press.

Snyman, W. (1998, 7 April). Proud to be bastards. *Cape Times*, p. 11.

Sodi, T. (1998). *A phenomenological study of healing in a North Sotho community*. Unpublished doctoral dissertation, University of Cape Town, Cape Town.

Spence, J.T. (1985). Achievement American style. The rewards and costs of individualism. *American Psychologist, 40*, 1285–1295.

Spence, J.T. (1987). Centrifugal versus centripetal tendencies in psychology: Will the centre hold? *American Psychologist, 42*, 1052–1054.

Staats, A.W. (1981). Paradigmatic behaviourism, unified theory, unified theory construction methods, and the zeitgeist of separatism. *American Psychologist, 36*, 239–256.

Staats, A.W. (1983). *Psychology's crisis of disunity: Philosophy and method for a unified science*. New York: Praeger.

Staats, A.W. (1991). Unified positivism and unification psychology: Fad or new field? *American Psychologist, 46*, 899–912.

Staub, E. (1996). Cultural-societal roots of violence: The examples of genocidal violence and of contemporary youth violence in the United States. *American Psychologist, 51*, 117–132.

Steele, C.M. (1997). A threat in the air: How stereotypes shape intellectual identity and performance. *American Psychologist, 52*, 613–629.

Stephan, C.W., Stephan, W.G., & Pettigrew, T.F. (Eds.) (1991). *The future of social psychology*. New York: Springer-Verlag.

Stern, K., & McClintock, M.K. (1998). Regulation of ovulation by human pheromones. *Nature, 392*, 177–179.

Stevens, G., & Lockhat, R. (1997). 'Coca-Cola kids' – reflections on black adolescent identity development in post-apartheid South Africa. *South African Journal of Psychology, 27*, 250–255.

Stonier, J.E.T. (1996). *Oral into written: An experiment in creating a text for African religion*. Unpublished master's thesis. University of Cape Town, South Africa.

Stonier, J.E.T., & Derrick, T. (1997). *Sacred places: A new approach to religious education for South African primary schools*. Kenwyn: Juta.

Stonier, J.L. (1996). *Implications of "Africanness" for educational planning in the Republic of South Africa: A qualitative study of educational needs*. Unpublished doctoral dissertation, University of Stellenbosch, South Africa.

Strathern, A. (1988). The aesthetic significance of display. Some examples from Papua New Guinea. In I. Rentschler, B. Herzberger, & D. Epstein (Eds.), *Beauty and the brain: Biological aspects of aesthetics* (pp. 297–314). Basel: Birkhaüser Verlag.

Stricker, G. (1997). Are science and practice commensurable? *American Psychologist, 52*, 442–448.

Stricker, G., & Trierweiler, S.J. (1995). The local clinical scientist: A bridge between science and practice. *American Psychologist, 50*, 995–1002.

Strickland, B.R. (1989). Internal–external control expectancies: From contingency to creativity. *American Psychologist, 44*, 1–12.

Stroebe, M., Gergen, M.M., Gergen, K.J., & Stroebe, W. (1992). Broken hearts or broken bonds: Love and death in historical perspective. *American Psychologist, 47*, 1205–1212.

Strupp, H.H. (1996). The tripartite model and the *Consumer Reports* study. *American Psychologist, 51*, 1017–1024.

Stubbs, A. (Ed.) (1979). *Steve Biko. I write what I like*. London: Heineman.

Sue, S. (1988). Psychotherapeutic services for ethnic minorities: Two decades of research findings. *American Psychologist, 43*, 301–308.

Sue, S. (1998). In search of cultural competence in psychotherapy and counseling. *American Psychologist, 53*, 440–448.

Sue, S., & Zane, N. (1987). The role of culture and cultural techniques in psychotherapy. A critique and reformulation. *American Psychologist, 42*, 37–45.

Surrey, J.L., Kaplan, A.G., & Jordan, J.V. (1990). Empathy revisited. *Work in Progress # 40*. Wellesley, MA: Stone Center Working Papers Series.

Swartz, L. (1986). Transcultural psychiatry in South Africa. Part I. *Transcultural Psychiatric Research Review, 23*, 273–303.

Swartz, L. (1987). Transcultural psychiatry in South Africa. Part II. *Transcultural Psychiatric Research Review, 24*, 5–30.

Swartz, L. (1991). The reproduction of racism in South African mental health care. *South African Journal of Psychology, 21*, 240–246.

Swartz, L. (1996). Culture and mental health in the rainbow nation: Transcultural psychiatry in a changing South Africa. *Transcultural Psychiatric Research Review, 33*, 119–136.

Swartz, L., & Foster, D. (1984). Images of culture and mental illness: South African psychiatric approaches. *Social Dynamics, 10*, 17–25.

Szasz, T.S. (1961). *The myth of mental illness*. New York: Harper & Row.

Szasz, T.S. (1987). *Insanity: The idea and its consequence*. New York: Wiley.

Tart, C.T. (1975a). *Transpersonal psychologies*. New York: Harper & Row.

Tart, C.T. (1975b). *States of consciousness*. New York: E.P. Dutton.

Taylor, J.V. (1963). *Primal vision*. London: SCM Press.

Tedeschi, J.T. (1988). How does one describe a platypus? An outsider's questions for cross-cultural psychology. In M.H. Bond (Ed.), *The cross-cultural challenge to social psychology* (pp. 14–28). London: Sage.

Tempels, P. (1959). *Bantu philosophy*. Paris: Presence Africaine.

Teo, T., & Febbraro, A.R. (1997). Norm, factuality, and power in multiculturalism. *American Psychologist, 52*, 656–657.

Thomson, D.L. (1994). African religion & Mormon doctrine: Comparisons & commonalities. In T.D. Blakely, W.E.A. van Beek, & D.L. Thomson (Eds.), *Religion in Africa: Experience and expression* (pp. 89–99). Portsmouth, NH: Heinemann.

Tiemersma, D., & Oosterling, H.A.F. (Eds.) (1996). *Time and temporality in intercultural perspective*. Amsterdam: Rodopi.

Tiryakian, E.A. (1968). The existential self and the person. In C. Gordon & K.J. Gergen (Eds.), *The self in social interaction* (pp. 75–86). New York: Wiley.

Toffler, A. (1980). *The third wave*. London: Collins.

Tomasello, M. (1996). The child's contribution to culture: A commentary on Toomela. *Culture & Psychology, 2*, 307–318.

Tomes, H. (1999, April). The need for cultural competence. *APA Monitor, 30*, 31.

Toomela, A. (1996a). How culture transforms mind: A process of internalization. *Culture & Psychology, 2*, 285–305.

Toomela, A. (1996b). What characterizes language that can be internalized: A reply to Tomasello. *Culture and Psychology, 2*, 319–322.

Torrey, E.F. (1972). What Western psychotherapists can learn from witchdoctors. *American Journal of Orthopsychiatry, 42*, 69–76.

Tracey, A. (1983). Music in Mozambique: Structure and function. *Africa Insight, 13*, 227–233.

Triandis, H.C. (1988). Collectivism and individualism: A reconceptualization of a basic concept in cross-cultural psychology. In G.K. Verma & C. Bagley (Eds.), *Personality, attitudes and cognitions* (pp. 60–95). London: Macmillan.

Triandis, H.C. (1996). The psychological measurement of cultural syndromes. *American Psychologist, 51*, 407–415.

Trierweiler, S.J. (1987). Practitioner training: A model with rationale intact. *American Psychologist, 42*, 410–411.

Trimble, J.E. (1988). Putting the etic to work: Applying social psychological principles in cross-cultural settings. In M.H. Bond (Ed.), *The cross-cultural challenge to social psychology* (pp. 109–121). London: Sage.

Tseëlon, E. (1991). The method is the message. On the meaning of method as ideology. *Theory and Psychology, 1*, 299–316.

Tshume, F. (1980, June). For strength. *Staffrider*, p. 15.

Tuinier, A. (1979). Psychologie in Zuid-Afrika: een lelieblank geweten (Psychology in South Africa: A lily-white consciousness). *Psychologie en Maatschappij, 6*, 7–26.

Turaki, Y. (1991). Culture and modernization in Africa: A methodological approach. In B.J. van der Walt (Ed.), *Cultural diversity in Africa: Embarassment or opportunity* (pp. 123–144). Potchefstroom: Potchefstroom University Press.

Turner, F., & Pöppel, E. (1988). Metered poetry, the brain, and time. In I. Rentschler, B. Herzberger, & D. Epstein (Eds.), *Beauty and the brain: Biological aspects of aesthetics* (pp. 71–90). Basel: Birkhaüser Verlag.

Tutu, D. (1981, 13 August). My view. *The Star*, p. 22.

Uka, E.M. (1991a). The concept of God in African traditional religion. In E.M. Uka (Ed.), *Readings in African traditional religion: Structure, meaning, relevance, future* (pp. 39–52). Bern: Peter Lang.

Uka, E.M. (1991b). The impact of religion in a traditional African society. In E.M. Uka

(Ed.), *Readings in African traditional religion. Structure, meaning, relevance, future* (pp. 213–223). Bern: Peter Lang.

van Beek, W.E.A. (1994). The innocent sorcerer: Coping with evil in two African societies (Kapsiki & Dogon). In T.D. Blakely, W.E.A. van Beek, & D.L. Thomson (Eds.), *Religion in Africa: Experience and expression* (pp. 196–228). Portsmouth, NH: Heinemann.

van Beek, W.E.A., & Blakely, T.D. (1994). Introduction. In T.D. Blakely, W.E.A. van Beek, & D.L. Thomson (Eds.), *Religion in Africa: Experience and expression* (pp. 1–20). Portsmouth, NH: Heinemann.

Vandenberg, B. (1991). Is epistemology enough? An existential consideration of development. *American Psychologist, 46*, 1278–1286.

van den Berg, J.H. (1980). Phenomenology and psychotherapy. *Journal of Phenomenological Psychology, 10*, 21–49.

van der Heijden, H. (1990). *Tussen wetenschap en politiek (Between science and politics)*. Kampen: Mondiss.

van der Hooft, G.A. (1979). *De malopodans. Een trancultureel-psychiatrische studie* (The Malopo dance. A transcultural-psychiatric study). Published Ph.D. thesis, University of Leiden, Leiden, The Netherlands.

van der Post, L. (1975). *The dark eye of Africa*. London: Hogarth Press.

van der Veer, R. (1985). Similarities between the theories of G.H. Mead and L.S. Vygotsky: An explanation? In S. Bem, H. van Rappard, & W. van Hoorn (Eds.), *Studies in the history of psychology and social sciences* (Vol. 3). Leiden: Psychologisch Instituut.

van der Veer, R. (1996). The concept of culture in Vygotsky's thinking. *Culture and Psychology, 2*, 247–263.

van Eercke, W. (1975). The look, the body, the other. In D. Ihde (Ed.), *Dialogues in phenomenology* (pp. 224–246). The Hague: Nijhoff.

van Strien, P.J., & Hofstee, W.K.B. (1995). An interview with Adrian D. de Groot. *New Ideas in Psychology, 13*, 341–356.

Viljoen, H. (1995). Regverdiging vir 'n inheemse sielkunde (Justification of an indigenous psychology). *UNISA Psychologia, 22*, 18–24.

Visser, P.J. (1996). Reflecting on some unconscious and systematic elements of the old and new South Africa. *International Journal of Psychology, 31*, 32.

Voestermans, P. (1992a). Cultuurpsychologie: Van cultuur in de psychologie naar psychologie in "cultuur." (Cultural psychology: From culture in psychology to psychology in culture). *Nederlands Tijdschrift voor de Psychologie, 47*, 151–162.

Voestermans, P. (1992b). Psychological practice as a cultural phenomenon. *New Ideas in Psychology, 10*, 331–346.

Wachtel, L. A. (1996). With strength and struggle: A teacher's process of transforming science into multicultural science. Where is multicultural science in science education reform? *European Journal of Intercultural Studies, 7*, 33–41.

Wainwright, A., McAllister, P., & Wallace, P. (1978). *The Xhosa imbongi (praise poet) as a conveyor of social criticism and praise in the mining industry*. Research Report No. 39/78, Human Resources Laboratory, Chamber of Mines of South Africa, Johannesburg.

Walsh, R. (1977). Initial meditative experiences. Part I. *Journal of Transpersonal Psychology, 9*, 151–192.

Walsh, R. (1978). Initial meditative experiences. Part II. *Journal of Transpersonal Psychology, 10*, 1–29.

Walsh, R. (1984). *Staying alive: The psychology of human survival.* Boulder: Shambala.

Walsh, R. (1988). Two Asian psychologies and their implications for western psycho-therapists. *American Journal of Psychotherapy, 42,* 543–560.

Walsh, R., & Vaughan, F. (1993). *Paths beyond ego.* New York: Putnam Books.

Wang, Z.M. (1993). Psychology in China: A review dedicated to o Li Chen. *Annual Review of Psychology, 44,* 87–116.

Warren, F., & Warren, L. (1970). *The music of Africa.* Englewood Cliffs, NJ: Prentice Hall.

Waterman, A.S. (1981). Individualism and interdependence. *American Psychologist, 36,* 762–773.

Watts, A.W. (1957). *The way of Zen.* New York: Vintage Books.

Watts, F.N. (1992). Is psychology falling apart? *The Psychologist: Bulletin of the British Psychological Society, 5,* 489–494.

Weisse, W. (1995). Christianity and its neighbour religions: A question of tolerance? *Scriptura, 55,* 263–276.

Weisz, J.R., Rothbaum, F.M., & Blackburn, T.C. (1984a). Standing out and standing in. The psychology of control in America and Japan. *American Psychologist, 39,* 955–969.

Weisz, J.R., Rothbaum, F.M., & Blackburn, T.C. (1984b). Swapping recipes for control. *American Psychologist, 39,* 974–975.

Wesner, M.F. (1996). Assuaging the chaos of disunity and fragmentation of psychology. *International Journal of Psychology, 31,* 50.

West, M.A. (1987). *The psychology of meditation.* Oxford: Clarendon.

White, J.L. (1984). *The psychology of blacks: An Afro-American perspective.* Englewood Cliffs, NJ: Prentice-Hall.

White, J.L. (1991). Toward a black psychology. In R.L. Jones (Ed.), *Black psychology,* Berkeley: Cobb & Henry.

White, G.M., & Marsella, A.J. (1989). Introduction: Cultural conceptions in mental health research and practice. In A.J. Marsella & G.M. White (Eds.), *Cultural conceptions of mental health and therapy* (pp. 1–38). Dordrecht: D. Reidel.

Whitehead, A.N. (1927). *Symbolism, its meaning and effect.* New York: Capricorn Books.

Wilber, K. (1981). *No boundary: Eastern and Western approaches to personal growth.* Boulder: Shambhala.

Wilber, K. (1986). *Eye to eye: The quest for the new paradigm.* Boston: Shambala.

Wilber, K. (1995). *Sex, ecology, spirituality: The spirit of evolution.* Boston: Shambala.

Wilber, K. (1997). *The eye of spirit: An integral vision of a world gone slightly mad.* Boston: Shambala.

Williams, R.L. (1997). The Ebonics controversy. *Journal of Black Psychology, 23,* 208–214.

Wilmer, H.A. (1976). Origins of a Jungian-oriented therapeutic community for schizophrenic patients. *Hospital and Community Psychiatry, 27,* 338–342.

Wilpert, B. (1995, July). *The two-pronged challenge to psychology in the 21st century.* Paper presented at the IV European Congress of Psychology, Athens.

Wilson, M. (1969). The Nguni people. In M. Wilson & L. Thompson (Eds.), *The Oxford history of South Africa. Vol. 1: South Africa to 1870.* London: Oxford University Press.

Wineman, S. (1984). *The politics of human services.* Montreal: Black Rose.

Wiredu, K. (1980). *Philosophy in an African culture.* London: Cambridge University Press.

Wissing, M.P. (1990, August). *From unity vs. disunity, to differentiation and integration, and FHA as paradigm in the study of emotion.* Paper presented at the 1990 Principles Congress, Amsterdam.

Woods, D. (1978). *Biko*. New York: Vintage Books.

Yanchar, S.C., & Slife, B.D. (1997). Parallels between multiculturalism and disunity in psychology. *American Psychologist, 52*, 658–659.

Yu, A. (1994). The self and life-goals of traditional Chinese: A philosophical and psychological analysis. In A.M. Bouvy, F.J.R. van de Vijver, P. Boski, & P. Schmitz (Eds.), *Journeys into cross-cultural psychology* (pp. 50–67). Amsterdam: Swets & Zeitlinger.

Zimunya, M. (1981). The soliloquy of a traditional dancer. *Staffrider*, April/May, 12.

Zollinger, H. (1988). Biological aspects of color naming. In I. Rentschler, B. Herzberger, & D. Epstein (Eds.), *Beauty and the brain: Biological aspects of aesthetics* (pp. 149–164). Basel: Birkhaüser Verlag.

Zwier, S. (1998). *Patterns of language use in individualistic and collectivistic cultures*. Ph.D. dissertation, Vrije Universiteit, Amsterdam.

NAME INDEX

Uleman 90
Uyangoda 79

van Beek 21, 64, 75, 85, 170
van den Berg 43
van der Heijden 8
van der Hooft 39, 71, 83, 84
van der Post 17, 29, 66, 166
van der Veer 74, 98
van Strien 56
van Vlaanderen 6, 15
Vandenberg 61, 97
Vaughan 15
Ventura 3, 39
Viljoen 152
Visser 25
Voestermans 74–75
Vygotsky 98

Wachtel 87
Wainright 187
Wake 109, 135–136, 162, 167, 178, 181,
    183, 186, 189, 194
Wakefield 47, 55
Walker 14
Wallace 187
Walsh 15, 50
Walton 44, 46
Wang 14
Warren 189
Waterman 88
Watts, A.W. 73
Watts, F.N. 40
Weber 89

Weisse 87
Weisz 91
Wesner 42
Wessells 79
West 15
White, G.M. 6, 12
White, J.L. 13, 17–18, 27, 29, 35, 44, 50,
    53, 57, 82–83, 112–115, 121–123,
    125–128, 130, 134, 136, 141, 150
Whitehead 65, 162
Wiesel 207
Wilber 15, 63
Williams 40, 44, 47, 51, 55, 128
Wilmer 49
Wilpert 10, 12, 79
Wilson 21, 202
Wineman 93
Wiredu 153, 168
Wissing 43
Wittgenstein 82
Wolfe 47
Woods 87, 137–139
Wundt 11, 43–44, 53, 55

Yanchar 84, 86
Yates 35, 122
Yu 14

Zane 76, 95
Zea 147
Zimunya 195
Zollinger 182
Zwier 103
Zynda 179–180

SUBJECT INDEX

115–116, 152, 154, 157; power 4, 7, 8, 10, 12–13, 17–18, 20, 27, 31, 36–37, 46, 49, 57–58, 62, 64–67, 69–71, 73, 80, 83, 86, 94, 96–98, 100–101, 103, 105–106, 118, 121, 126, 130, 133, 139, 145–147, 154–155, 158, 163, 165–168, 170, 173–175, 186, 202, 204–207; psychological testing 34, 57; psychometric tools 113; racism 27, 31–35, 57, 88, 93, 113, 117, 119, 123, 128, 133, 141, 150; reductionism 45, 51, 54, 88, 115; remediation programmes 114; scientism 50, 88; sickness model 146; social amnesia 45; social control 8–9, 116–117; specialisation 42, 51, 186, 192, 205; theoretical psychology 44; too little attention to history 16, 18, 20, 31–32, 38, 46, 50, 54, 56, 59, 68, 70, 81, 86, 89, 94, 110, 114, 116–119, 121–125, 129, 132–133, 137–138, 144, 149, 154, 157, 172–173; too little attention to status 3–4, 6–7, 14,42, 50, 56, 73–75, 85, 94, 97, 111, 117, 126, 136, 140, 145, 154, 163; universalism 45, 88, 105; values 5, 7–8, 15, 17, 19, 21–22, 25, 32, 36, 40, 45, 53, 55–61, 74–75, 78–79, 88–90 112, 115, 119, 124, 127, 129, 133–135, 141, 147, 151, 155, 158, 169, 172, 183, 185, 188, 195–196, 200, 206–207; Western individualism 19

Critique of the concept of the independent self: challenge to liberal individualism 101; critical theory 101; cross-cultural 40, 94–95, 101–102, 117, 152; deconstructionism 83, 101; indigenous psychologies 12, 14–15, 23, 87, 101–102; transcultural disciplines 101

Cubists 198

Culture 5–7, 9, 12, 15–16, 18–21, 24, 26–27, 30, 32, 35–36, 41, 46, 48–49, 53, 59, 68, 70, 74–78, 80–87, 89, 92, 94, 97, 99, 100, 103–105, 107, 110, 112, 115–118, 120, 123, 129, 131–135, 137–138, 140–141, 145, 148, 150–155, 158, 169, 172–173, 177–178, 184, 188, 192, 194–196, 199–200, 205; collectivism 15; cultural dichotomies 20, 76; cultural pluralism 25, 83; Inuit 103–104; politicising of culture 153; Western individualism 19

Cultures in psychology: cognitive and an

affective science 56; cultures of science and practice 55; hard-headed and the soft-hearted 55; natural science psychology and a human science psychology 56; objectivist and subjectivist 56; oral and the writing traditions 56; rational and naturalistic psychology 55; science versus profession 55; scientist and humanist values 55; tough- and tender-minded 55

Daimonic 10–11, 107–108, 172
Darwinism 32
Despecialisation 73
Developing societies 28
Development 5–7, 14, 16, 20, 28, 30, 36–37, 42–47, 49, 54, 61, 64, 72–73, 76, 81, 85–86, 92, 97–98, 106, 113, 115–116, 120–122, 127–128, 130–131, 133–134, 137, 142, 145–146, 155, 162, 176, 180, 183, 185, 201, 205, 207; echo-cultural niche 152; environment 5, 21, 40, 45, 55, 91, 93, 97, 120, 127, 138, 177, 179, 194, 200; ontogenetic 97, 142; ontogeny 142; organismic sensing 180; phylogeny 142; sociogeny 142
Diagnosis 48, 49
Dialogue 35, 38, 78, 82–83, 120–121, 126, 149, 154
Discourse analysis 8, 33
Diversification 77–78, 80, 204
Divination bones: *diTaola* 194
DSM-IV 48

Education: educationists 152
Egoism: rational egoism 89
Empathy 69, 83–84, 175–176, 202, 206–207 (*see also* ubuntu); atrophy 207; forgiveness 18, 109, 207; prefrontal cortex 207; unconditional positive regard 176
Ethnic minority 15, 76
Ethnocentrism 11, 14, 22, 24–31, 45, 68, 77, 85, 88, 111–112, 120, 149, 151; ethnocentric blindspot 10
Ethnopolitical 79, 80
Ethnopsychology 22, 153
European: analytical thinking 37
Experiential 51, 63, 65, 106, 123, 132, 205, 207

Factor analysis 64